T0342352

The Root and the Branch

AMERICA IN THE NINETEENTH CENTURY

Series editors: Brian DeLay, Steven Hahn, Amy Dru Stanley
America in the Nineteenth Century proposes a
rigorous rethinking of this most formative period in
U.S. history. Books in the series will be wide-ranging
and eclectic, with an interest in politics at all levels,
culture and capitalism, race and slavery, law, gender,
and the environment, and regional and transnational
history. The series aims to expand the scope of
nineteenth-century historiography by bringing
classic questions into dialogue with innovative
perspectives, approaches, and methodologies.

The Root and the Branch

Working-Class Reform and Antislavery, 1790–1860

Sean Griffin

PENN

UNIVERSITY OF PENNSYLVANIA PRESS

PHILADELPHIA

Published by
University of Pennsylvania Press
Philadelphia, Pennsylvania 19104-4112
www.upenn.edu/pennpress

Printed in the United States of America on acid-free paper
10 9 8 7 6 5 4 3 2 1

Hardcover ISBN: 978-1-5128-2592-3
eBook ISBN: 978-1-5128-2593-0

A Cataloging-in-Publication record is
available from the Library of Congress

For my uncle, Michael F. Dwyer (1947–2019), who inspired me to become a historian and whose patience, gentleness, and humor continue to guide me.

CONTENTS

Introduction

In the single session of the ambitiously named International Industrial Assembly of North America, delegates strove mightily to create a labor organization that would bring together what its founders believed were some two hundred thousand workers already organized in trade and protective unions in the United States and Canada. After more than a year of planning, delegates arrived in Louisville from Buffalo, Boston, Cincinnati, Chicago, Detroit, St. Louis, and a host of other cities throughout the U.S. (the convention was, however, international in name only). In addition to urging "immediate action" toward organizing "all who labor for support," the body passed a series of measures and proposals. Among these were resolutions calling for the passage of laws recognizing eight hours as the standard day of work; proposing the creation of cooperative stores where workers could obtain goods at fair prices; demanding the abolition of the use of prison labor; calling for aid to striking printers in Chicago; and insisting that workers, not capitalists, should determine the compensation they derived from their labor. Before adjourning the delegates drafted a constitution that reiterated many of these same points but disappeared into history, like so many similar efforts in the period.

But the timing as well as the location of the International Industrial Assembly made this labor convention different. Although one would never know it from reading through the convention's records, which made no mention of the Civil War, slavery, or the possibility of organizing recently emancipated slaves, the group gathered in May 1865, less than a month after the surrender at Appomattox. Nor did the gathering acknowledge that it took place in what until recently had been a slave state, one that had never seceded from the Union but had been the site of an intense struggle between free labor and slavery. It neglected to mention that the Thirteenth Amendment, which secured the emancipation of some four million enslaved workers of

African descent, had been passed that January and was well on its way to ratification.[1]

Historians are frequently forced to confront evidence, or a lack thereof, that confounds what our training and inclinations lead us to believe *should* have happened. This was certainly the case as I began to explore the relationship between antislavery and workers' movements in early America. As one prominent historian of American labor recently put it, the search for a "working class speaking with a single voice on the issue" of slavery and antislavery has proven elusive.[2] Similarly equivocal has been the relatively scant recent historiography on the early labor movement and its relationship to antislavery, which at one extreme has depicted the two movements as so closely identified as to be practically indistinguishable, and at the other has described it as characterized by nearly relentless mutual hostility. If there is anything like a current consensus on this relationship among historians, it might look something like this: the two movements sprang from common origins and impulses, but they soon diverged and remained largely estranged before the Civil War, only to make a brief and incomplete reconciliation during the Reconstruction years and after.[3]

Much of what follows corroborates this picture of a relationship marked as much by conflict as by solidarity. The history of the early labor movement's relationship to antislavery can be better characterized as one of waxing and waning fortunes and contingencies than of linear progress toward the emancipation of all workers. Few antebellum labor organizations made opposition to chattel slavery a cardinal principle. Mentions of slavery, while not infrequent in the labor newspapers, speeches, articles of association, and other records left by labor reformers and organizations, seldom took center stage, and they often took the form of comparisons to so-called wages slavery or white slavery—terms labor reformers and others used to describe the status of nominally free workers forced into a state of dependence on employers for wages. Labor reformers and abolitionists frequently sparred in their respective newspapers, with the former accusing the latter of ignoring the plight of northern factory workers in favor of slaves on distant plantations, while abolitionists like William Lloyd Garrison reflexively consigned such "wage slavery" arguments to his "Refuge of Oppression" column in the *Liberator*, normally reserved for the most shameless proslavery propaganda. Like ships passing in the night, it would seem, the two most consequential social movements of the era alternately ignored each other, fought each other, and talked past one another, perhaps forever foreclosing an opportunity for an interracial alliance of workers and reformers to challenge the foundations of a system that, as the more perceptive members of both movements understood, undergirded both slavery and capitalist wage labor. One of the questions that runs throughout this book, then, is why a more robust and full-throated support for antislavery failed to emerge from the early labor movement, whose leaders frequently declared its purpose as being the emancipation of all labor. Why was it that what seems so obvious to us—as well as to contemporary observers like Karl Marx, who wrote that "labor with a white skin cannot emancipate itself where labor with a black skin is branded"—was only slowly and haltingly acknowledged by those who sought to represent the rights of labor, and even that then, labor leaders and reformers rarely spoke with one voice against slavery?[4]

In some ways, of course, these silences are not surprising. African Americans were generally excluded, whether formally or informally, from early trade unions and other white-dominated labor organizations, and white workers frequently responded with violence when African Americans attempted to move into skilled or semiskilled occupations, especially when employers used them as strikebreakers.[5] In the racially charged atmosphere of the antebellum North, white workers' perceptions of their self-interest often clashed with those of African Americans—a division that many employers were happy to exploit, in a pattern that repeats itself again and again in the history of American labor. Just as the contemporaneous Nativist movement pitted native-born workers against immigrants, defenders of the proslavery status quo stoked fears that if slavery were abolished, the formerly enslaved would flock north to take jobs away from white men. Meanwhile, as other historians have shown, the gradual abolition of slavery in the states north of Maryland, and its growth and spread in the states of the South and Old Southwest, took place in tandem with a rising ideology of race based on "scientific" conclusions about the alleged inferiority of people of color and a growing commitment to "whiteness" as a marker of American identity. Historians have long argued that the Early National and antebellum decades, particularly the so-called Jacksonian period, represented the high-water mark of a "white man's republic," in which racism permeated nearly every aspect of American life.[6]

It might be easy, then, to conclude that racism prevented a majority of men and women who made up the early labor movement from taking a strong stance in favor of abolition. Or that a growing sense of a shared identity based on "whiteness" prevented working-class northerners from including Black workers, whether enslaved or free, in their expressions of solidarity and sense of class consciousness. Another explanation, different but equally well established in the historiography, holds that abolitionists' economic liberalism and middle-class orientation alienated their potential allies in the labor movement, or that the intense "competition for reform" among the dizzying array of antebellum reform movements prevented the creation of an alliance between labor and antislavery.[7] While there is some truth to all of these interpretations, what follows complicates the assumptions on which they rest. The story of the relationship between labor and antislavery is one of conflict, racism, and missed opportunities on one hand, but there is another story to this relationship, one that historians have hinted at but rarely attempted to capture in full. A full decade before the meeting of the International Industrial Assembly in Louisville, a group of "free Germans" there, comprising mainly workers and veterans of the democratic 1848 revolutions, gathered at considerable risk to demand the prevention of the further extension of slavery and the repeal of the Fugitive Slave Act of 1850, along with guarantees to protect the equal rights of free Blacks.[8] Earlier, radical and largely working-class "corresponding societies" inspired by the democratic fervor of the late-eighteenth-century Age of Revolution were among the first on both sides of the Atlantic to call for the abolition of slavery; so closely was slave emancipation associated with democratic and plebeian radicalism in this era that early abolitionists in both Britain and the U.S. had to struggle to overcome the taint of "Jacobinism" with which their conservative opponents attempted to brand them. In the 1820s and '30s, labor leaders and working-class intellectuals associated with the Working Men's and Equal Rights ("Loco Foco") parties were among the earliest and most effective pioneers of the ideas about free labor, free soil, and an antislavery interpretation of the U.S. Constitution that would eventually pave the way for the flowering of a political variant of antislavery. In the 1840s, the Associationists—American followers of Charles Fourier, the French social thinker who conjured up one of the era's most influential blueprints for a more just and equitable society in response to emerging capitalism—not only drew many of their adherents from the abolitionist movement, but challenged abolitionists to think more seriously and deeply about economic inequality and the rights of labor. The organizers of the National Industrial Congress, an annual convention of reformers and labor leaders that constituted perhaps the most important pre–Civil War labor organization, praised abolitionists as "sincere, ardent, [and] heroic" and expressed the desire that Congress would function as a vehicle for uniting all the "Friends of Humanity."[9] Its annual meetings welcomed the participation not only of trade unionists and labor leaders but abolitionists, Fourierists, temperance reformers, peace activists, and—on multiple occasions—women and African Americans. In 1847, that same organization sent an emissary to a convention of political abolitionists known as the Liberty League. The result was a little-known and electorally unsuccessful political alliance that nonetheless prefigured and provided part of the inspiration for a later political coalition that did manage to mobilize large majorities of northern voters against the Slave Power.

This side of the relationship between labor reform and antislavery has faded from view in recent retellings for, I think, two related reasons. One is the emphasis on race and whiteness. Since the 1980s, historians of labor have rightfully reconsidered older histories that omitted or diminished the role of race and racism in early workers' movements, while shining a new and penetrating light on the role of whiteness in the development of working-class identities. As I hope I have made clear above and in much of what follows, there is no denying that racism and whiteness played a role in the failure of early workers' movements to more fully embrace abolitionism; far worse, racism all too frequently exploded into the episodes of anti-Black violence for which the period is notorious. But if racism can explain these incidents, and if the psychological "wages of whiteness" can help explain white workers' failure to forge a truly interracial working-class movement, it can't explain why so many white northern farmers, factory operatives, artisans, and "mechanics" signed petitions against slavery, joined antislavery societies, helped to build a political coalition dedicated to slavery's "ultimate extinction," and volunteered to fight in a war that—to again quote Lincoln—"all knew" was "somehow" caused by slavery.[10]

The second reason that a more complete assessment of the relationship between labor and antislavery has eluded historians is that, until quite recently, histories of American antislavery had largely forsaken the political abolitionists of the 1840s and '50s, as well as the gradual abolitionists of the late eighteenth and early nineteenth centuries, in favor of an emphasis on the immediate abolitionism of William Lloyd Garrison and the American Anti-Slavery Society. To the Garrisonians, a persecuted minority who generally shunned both voting and involvement with political parties and who ended the antebellum period by calling for disunion with the slaveholding South, a politics based on the self-interest of the mass of white northern voters was anathema to their uncompromising militancy and demands for "immediate" emancipation. At times, scholars of the antislavery movement have tended to take on something of the moralistic zeal of the abolitionists with whom they identify, and for whom anything less than the most idealistic standard was often viewed as tantamount to sinfulness or betrayal. And yet it was the

Figure 1. This carte de visite group portrait of abolitionist "Pioneers of Freedom," created in Boston immediately after the Civil War, includes political abolitionists Gerrit Smith, Henry Wilson, and Horace Greeley alongside the more familiar figures of William Lloyd Garrison, Henry Ward Beecher, and Wendell Phillips. Library of Congress, Prints and Photographs Division.

political variant of antislavery that garnered the most support from labor reformers, labor organizations, and ordinary voters—and eventually, a significant proportion of Black abolitionist leaders as well—and its success at the polls ultimately did the most to further the cause of emancipation, even if the course it took to do so was circuitous and made possible only by war.[11]

Labor reformers were prescient in other ways, too. Observing the condition of wage laborers struggling to pay rents in the cities of the Northeast, tenant farmers in thrall to semifeudal patroons in the Hudson River Valley of New York, and emancipated slaves in the British Caribbean, working-class reformers continually harried abolitionists with questions about what the lives of emancipated slaves would look like without access to land or other productive resources—questions that Garrisonian immediatists often seemed unprepared or unable to answer. The fact that pointed questions comparing enslaved people to "lacklanders" may at times have been intended to equivocate or prioritize the plight of white workers over Black ones does not detract from their salience in explaining why so many formerly enslaved people remained trapped in states of poverty and dependence after emancipation, as a generation or more of scholarship on Reconstruction has shown.[12]

Perhaps most importantly, antebellum labor reformers perceived that the problem of slavery transcended mere human capriciousness and that it was in fact deeply interconnected with a complex and still-evolving system of commerce, capital, property, and labor. Writing in the 1790s, the London Corresponding Society's John Thelwall warned of the rise of a new form of "Speculation-Commerce" that threatened to render "almost all the inhabitants of the universe . . . the saleable commodities of a few," while his comrade, the formerly enslaved Robert Wedderburn, charged both enslavers and large estate holders with "wickedly violat[ing] the sacred rights of man." Half a century later, Charles Hosmer, a shoemaker who joined the Brook Farm community, argued that "the whole system of labor for wages" was "wrong," since it compelled the laborer to sell himself "in the market-place, like a slave"; for his Fourier-influenced fellow reformer in Western Massachusetts, the Northampton Association's Erasmus Hudson, both slavery and wage labor were forms of "robbery," since profits went to "the sl[ave] holder and capitalist." Property in land, wrote the Industrial Congress organizer and *Working Man's Advocate* editor George Henry Evans, was "the *root* of the evil," responsible for the "vast inequality of condition now existing among us." Evans's ally, the militant abolitionist Gerrit Smith, agreed that "the Land-Monopoly" was, in the final analysis, "a far more abundant source of suffering and debasement" than slavery. Fortunately, from Smith's perspective, the two reforms were mutually reinforcing, since the system of slavery depended on a monopoly of the best lands and would not be able to withstand competition with free, non–slave-owning farmers. Land reform would not only "make Slavery impossible," agreed the anonymous author of an article published in *Frederick Douglass' Paper*—possibly Douglass himself—but would remove "the deep seated evil of poverty."[13]

Abolitionists and labor reformers alike often used the metaphor of a tree—or, more dramatically, the poisonous upas tree, an East Asian species alleged to be so toxic that it killed everything around it—to argue that their favored reform struck at the root of society's problems. "While we '*have* the axe,'" Evans demanded of his colleague across the Atlantic, the Chartist land reformer Feargus O'Connor, "shall we waste our time in fruitless sympathy [with the enslaved], or shall we *ply* the instrument to the *roots* of the *upas?*"

Figure 2. In this visual representation of the "root and branch" metaphor, two sturdy axemen chop down the tree of slavery. The semimythical, poisonous upas tree was often used as a particularly insidious illustration of the pernicious effects of slavery. I am grateful to Madeline Lafuse of the CUNY Graduate Center for bringing this image to my attention. New York Public Library, Schomburg Center for Research in Black Culture.

In contrast, the Wisconsin political abolitionist Sherman Booth agreed that the acknowledgment of a natural right to land would be "a blow . . . struck at the very root of all human slavery," but insisted that "if we can not kill the root . . . we should not in our indignation, refuse to lop off its branches."[14] Labor reformers and abolitionists tended to disagree about which reform should take priority. But within these disagreements lay not only a shared consensus about the immorality and injustice of slavery, but a constellation of ideas about slavery, freedom, and the nature of an emerging system of market-based capitalism that anyone who hopes to understand the period would do well to consider seriously.

As these botanical metaphors suggest, the land and its products were never very far from the minds of labor reformers in the first half of the nineteenth century. The emphasis on land, and to a lesser extent agriculture, is on one hand surprising, considering that most of the reformers and organizations this study describes lived in the crowded and fast-growing eastern metropolises of the Early Republic, especially New York, Philadelphia, and Boston, or in their smaller but booming newer rivals further west, places like Cincinnati; Rochester, New York; and Worcester, Massachusetts. And yet it stands to reason given the early nation's longstanding emphasis on western migration, landed independence, social as well as physical mobility, and the widespread availability of land that facilitated all of the above. From Paine's *Agrarian Justice* to the earliest declarations of the organized labor movement to the Fourierists and Free Soilers of the 1840s and '50s, demands for access to the land were central to working-class understandings of "free labor," which in the minds of antebellum labor reformers entailed access to productive property—land, workshop, tools, or labor power—that made one not just legally free, but free from dependence on banks, bosses, or other representatives of capital. Like Jefferson, whom many of these Democratic-leaning reformers idolized, or Lincoln, whom many of them ultimately supported, even the most radical and forward-looking labor reformers of the antebellum period hearkened back to an ideal of freedom that was rapidly receding into the past in the industrializing, market-oriented North: an ideal embodied by the independent, landowning yeoman farmer. A half century before Frederick Jackson Turner, one could have found no firmer believers in the "safety valve" theory than among the land reformers of the New York City–based National Reform Association.

And yet there was more to the "agrarianism" of these reformers than simply a reiteration of the yeoman ideal. In an ironic twist of language that has often gone unnoticed by historians interested in the "agrarian" ideology of Jefferson's Democratic-Republicans, the term had a far different resonance in the English-speaking world during the Age of Revolution. Associated in the minds of Enlightenment political thinkers with the ancient Roman brothers Gracchi, who launched an unsuccessful reform aimed at redistributing aristocratic landholdings to peasants and veterans in the second century BCE, by the early decades of the nineteenth century the term "agrarian" was often used synonymously with the emerging but still vaguely defined new ideology of socialism. Although socialistic ideas were occasionally tolerated by the respectable classes (Robert Owen, the Welsh "father of socialism," dedicated his first book to George IV, the prince regent, and was invited to deliver a speech in the House of Representatives during his trip to the United States in 1825), it was far more common throughout the period for "agrarianism" to be used as a scare word, often attributed to the democratic excesses of the French Revolution, and thus associated with "Jacobins" on both sides of the Atlantic. Thus, Thomas Paine cautioned readers of his *Agrarian Justice* (1797) that his plan for a modest system of government-funded social welfare based on taxing landholders differed in kind from an "Agrarian Law," which would presumably entail the confiscation and redistribution of landed property. Such disclaimers, however, failed to satisfy the period's conservative defenders of limited government and absolute property rights—least of all, southern slaveholders, who as the period's largest landowners and wealthiest men were doubly interested in securing their claims to property in both land and human beings. By the 1850s, slaveholding intellectuals like George Fitzhugh regularly equated abolitionism with agrarianism, even though Gerrit Smith was perhaps the only prominent abolitionist to identify himself with that label.[15]

In the decades between *Agrarian Justice* and Smith's conversion to agrarianism, a wide array of American workers, labor leaders, social thinkers, and reformers laid plans for alternatives to the liberal, capitalistic society that was rapidly taking shape in the North. Instead of a competitive race to the bottom for wage labor in the marketplace, labor would be reorganized based on principles of harmony, cooperation, and inclination (what Fourierists called "attraction"). The growing power of corporations would be tamed by legislation outlawing such "monopolies," and the wealth created by large landholdings or illicit concentrations of capital peacefully broken up and directly or indirectly redistributed to the producing classes. The poverty of burgeoning urban slums would be replaced by communal living arrangements in intentionally formed communities in the rural hinterlands, or by independent homesteads on 160-acre farms. What all of these approaches had in common was their dedication to what Daniel Mandell has recently labeled a "lost tradition of economic equality."[16] As Gerrit Smith put it, "I would, that no man be rich, and no man be poor." But for most of the so-called radicals that advocated greater economic equality throughout the period, this did not necessarily imply the abolition of class distinctions or the achievement of social leveling. Rather, antebellum labor reformers had in mind the kind of rough equality that had long been seen as indispensable to the maintenance of a republican system of government within the tradition of Anglo-American political thought. To this widely shared conviction, early labor leaders and working-class political economists added ideas derived from contemporary social theories emanating from revolutionary Europe, such as the labor theory of value, which in the hands of American labor reformers took the form of producerism—the idea that, as the producers of wealth, urban artisans and yeoman farmers had a right to demand an equal share of the fruits of labor. Radicals and labor reformers disagreed with the middle-class liberals who formed the Republican Party on many things, including basic definitions of what constituted "free labor," but few would have disagreed with Abraham

Lincoln when he argued that slavery robbed its victims of the basic right "to eat the bread . . . which his own hand earns."[17]

Ultimately, of course, it was Lincoln and the Republicans' more moderate vision of free labor and free soil that triumphed over the more expansive vision of free labor and the radical agrarian version of free soil championed by labor reformers. But only by understanding the latter can we arrive at a more complete picture of what was at stake for ordinary northerners in the conflict with slavery that brought about the Civil War. In what follows, I try to show that the reforms and ideals outlined above were not the mere abstractions of dreamers and utopians, but that they had real implications for the developing political economy of the early United States and its people. Perhaps the most obvious and direct outcome of the working class agitation for land reform was the passage of the Homestead Act in 1862, which eventually opened 246 million acres of territory for settlement at a nominal price and of which, one calculation has estimated, 46 million living Americans in 2000 were direct beneficiaries.[18] In other ways, of course, the Homestead Act had less sanguine, even disastrous consequences: workers and immigrants often lacked the skills and start-up capital necessary for homesteading; speculators and railroad companies gamed the system to gobble up much of the best land; the act and its follow-up, the 1866 Southern Homestead Act, disproportionately failed to benefit the formerly enslaved or other people of color; and its passage helped pave the way for the decimation and displacement of the Plains Indians and other Native groups and the extermination of their way of life. And yet, the Homestead Act was both characteristically American in the egalitarian impulse that lay behind it and anomalous in the way that it represented the largest redistribution of property (after a decades-long debate over whether that property was owned by the "people" or the individual states) in American history.

Such matters of property rights and their limitations may have ultimately been hashed out in the halls of Congress or other legal and political corridors of power, but they were not abstractions to the ordinary workers and reformers who had argued since the American Revolution that genuine freedom entailed a right to the means of subsistence. Nor were they an abstraction to the four million enslaved workers claimed as property, or to the abolitionists who identified "property in man" as an unacceptable violation of human rights—a conclusion that labor reformers also reached, even if they were sometimes frustratingly slow in drawing the connection between the capitalist's property in labor and the slaveholder's property in laborers. Nor, least of all, were they an abstraction for the slave owners for whom their enslaved labor force represented an estimated $2 billion in human property. Abolitionists and labor reformers largely agreed that the institution of "property in man" went against the very grain of the values of human freedom on which the country was purportedly founded. But labor reformers and the radical thinkers who sympathized with them went further, questioning the very legitimacy of property in land, natural resources, and human labor that was rapidly becoming the foundation of a new political economic order, one that the Civil War would finally establish as dominant and permanent. In doing so, labor reformers raised and engaged with some of the most pressing questions of the nineteenth century: what could, or could not, be legitimately commoditized and turned into private property in an evolving market economy? What was sufficient to guarantee human freedom in a liberal, democratic society— the legal ownership of oneself and protections of life, liberty, and property? Or did genuine freedom entail a right to the means of subsistence and security as well? How best to extend and fulfill the dream of human freedom that the American Revolution had brought closer to reality for millions of Euro-Americans, but still left millions of white and nonwhite workers trapped in various states of slavery, poverty, dependency, and inequality of wealth and power? Which was the root of these oppressions, which was the branch?

There are many reasons—historical, historiographical, and present-minded— why a better understanding of how labor reformers and abolitionists in antebellum America understood the intertwined relationship of slavery, freedom, and economic and racial injustice seems relevant in the United States of the early twenty-first century. I finished the dissertation on which this book is based on election night 2016. The subsequent election of Donald Trump brought about a torrent of editorializing and soul-searching, not least from historians and historically minded journalists. With few exceptions, post-election analyses and efforts to understand the Trump phenomenon by liberal pundits and news outlets focused on issues of race, racism, and the role of the "white working class" in bringing Trump to power. One side of the debate over the latter evinced sympathy with this apparently monolithic group, attributing their political choices to "economic anxiety" or struggling to understand why this demographic "voted against their own interests." Far more common, however, were analyses that pointed to anxieties over changing demographics, racism, white privilege, and white nationalism as lying at the root of both Trump's election and the seemingly undying loyalty he engendered among supporters. Some of the best of these relied heavily on the scholarship on whiteness undertaken by historians and others beginning in the 1990s. But ironically—especially given the whiteness scholarship's roots in labor history and Marxist-influenced scholars—sophisticated analyses of class dynamics and the role played by the seismic changes in American capitalism since the 1970s were generally absent.[19]

Turning from recent history to the historiography of the United States, perhaps the most important shift in the latter in the years since World War II concerns what historians view as the nineteenth century's essential "thing to be explained"—from the Progressive historians and their intellectual descendants in the early to mid-twentieth century, who viewed industrialization and urbanization as the century's key development, to the current consensus that sees slavery and its eradication during the Civil War as the defining feature of the period.[20] In important but seldom explicitly acknowledged ways, the recent body of literature on capitalism and slavery that was inaugurated in 2013 by Walter Johnson's *River of Dark Dreams* (but that can be traced to W. E. B. Du Bois in the 1930s and Eric Williams in the 1940s) has attempted to grapple with the implications of this profound shift, while responding to the demand for sharper and more critical historical interrogations of capitalism in the wake of the 2008 financial crash. Important contributions from Edward Baptist, Joshua Rothman, Caitlin Rosenthal, Sven Beckert, Seth Rockman, and others have revived studies of American capitalism, while shining a bright and revealing light on capitalist institutions' complicity with slavery.[21] But, while appreciative of this body of work's contributions and flaws—critics have pointed to problems in sources and methodology, a neglect of previous work by economic historians and historians of color, and a stubborn refusal to define capitalism—*The Root and the Branch* hopes to make two interventions into this important and still emerging field. One can be summed up by James Oakes's observation that the capitalism and slavery literature "pushes in [a] different direction" from well-established understandings of the economic origins of the Civil War. The new capitalism and slavery literature argues for the compatibility, indeed symbiosis, between capitalism and slavery, whereas the vast majority of work on the economic origins of the Civil War emphasizes "the fundamental difference and growing divergence between the free labor system of the North and the slave society of the South."[22] While accepting the capitalism and slavery literature's arguments that African slavery was critical to the development of American and global capitalism, this book nonetheless adheres to the view that the overwhelming economic trajectory of the antebellum North led it steadily in a direction away from any lingering dependence on slavery and toward an irreconcilable conflict with the South. Shifting the focus from enslaved to free labor—and considering how the latter served both as an ideology inscribed in laws and norms governing work and employment, and how it figured in the thinking and actions of free laborers themselves— offers one way to reconcile these seemingly incompatible interpretations. If the advent and spread of free wage labor was a defining feature of the kind of capitalism that was developing in the antebellum North, *and* if American slavery was identifiably capitalistic in important ways, what was the role played by free labor in bringing on the conflict between these two, at times compatible but increasingly antagonistic, forms of capitalism? By focusing on the ways in which the workers at the forefront of these changes understood and experienced the transformations that the shift to free labor capitalism entailed, this book hopes to shed light on the origins and evolution of these divergent forms of capitalist development and explain how they led to a conflict that could only be resolved by war.

In almost a mirror image of the debates on "capitalism and slavery," the historians of abolitionism have for many years debated the relationship between capitalism and *antislavery*—in particular, paying attention to abolitionists' attitudes toward the emerging market society of the eighteenth and nineteenth centuries. Why did the abolitionists focus so intently (and, to their critics, selectively) on the plight of enslaved Africans in the distant West Indies or the American South, while seemingly remaining complacent about the signs of growing urban poverty, child labor, low wages, and miserable working conditions in their own midst? This debate shares a common origin with the capitalism and slavery debates in the work of Caribbean scholar Eric Williams, who famously insinuated that the British abolitionists were hypocrites who only began to seriously challenge slavery after the advent of industrialization made Britain's once-powerful constituency of slave-owning Caribbean planters, the so-called West India interest, politically expendable. While departing from Williams's economic reductionism, the Yale historian David Brion Davis refined a version of his argument, lending it additional credence with his scholarship's many layers of intellectual, philosophical, and psychological complexity. In what has become known as the Davis thesis, the late dean of antislavery studies posited that the abolitionists, by reflecting and promoting ideals of moral uplift, self-ownership, free wage labor, and laissez-faire political economy, contributed both consciously and unconsciously to the development of a capitalist "hegemony." If Davis's interpretation holds— and there is significant evidence for it, from the elitism and antiradicalism of the English Clapham set to Garrison's curt dismissal of labor reform in the first issue of the *Liberator*—then it is easy to view the conflict between labor and antislavery as irreconcilable and the single-minded focus on the abolition of slavery as "foreclosing the possibility of more radical reforms," to use Eric Foner's phrase. But a number of important scholars, including Foner, Seymour Drescher, and most recently Manisha Sinha, have since chipped away at the Davis thesis, arguing that abolitionists were more sympathetic to labor reform and more antithetical to capitalist values than has been previously seen.[23] *The Root and the Branch* is sympathetic to this revision, highlighting new evidence of cooperation and overlap between abolitionists and labor reformers while attempting to retain Davis's central insights, as well as a sense of the very real conflicts and tensions that often divided the two movements.

At the same time, it seeks to answer Eric Foner's call in the revised edition to *Free Soil, Free Labor, Free Men*, his pathbreaking work on free labor ideology, to more fully explore "how different Americans might have infused [free labor] with different meanings."[24] Made more than twenty-five years ago, Foner's call has gone largely unanswered in the years since. One possible explanation for this is the state of the field of labor history. Despite some excellent recent work on working class Americans' relationship to slavery, antislavery, and free labor by scholars like Bruce Laurie, Mark Lause, and Keri Leigh Merritt, the once-robust field of early American labor history has gone into decline since the 1980s, a development that perhaps mirrors the fortunes of the American labor movement. As a result, most of the best recent work on the relationship between the early labor movement and slavery/antislavery has been done by historians of abolitionism, race, and/or whiteness. The whiteness scholarship, and particularly the work of David Roediger, has made an important intervention by placing race and racism at the center of working-class formation and identity. Roediger's *The Wages of Whiteness* contained the most thorough exploration yet undertaken of the meaning of "white slavery" and "wage slavery" rhetoric, spawning a debate that has since been taken up by a number of scholars, including John Ashworth, Mark Lause, and Gunther Peck.[25] But to some extent, the focus on wage slavery language—an admittedly confounding phenomenon that this book also engages with, if only because it is inescapable—has distracted historians from paying attention to the structural and ideological factors and material bases that shaped working-class Americans' attitudes and responses to slavery and abolitionism. In what follows, then, I have attempted to place wage slavery language in context, in order to better show how it evolved against the backdrop of debates with abolitionists over a range of issues related to free labor, poverty, and inequality, while showing how the spread of wage slavery language was tied to the shifting fortunes of economic and political developments. In short, by paying attention to what labor reformers *did* as well as what they *said*.

Much of what labor reformers and working-class radicals did, I argue, was political. This book is heavily influenced by recent accounts of abolitionism and emancipation that take political antislavery seriously. The men who founded and organized the Liberty, Free Soil, and Republican parties, this work has shown, cannot be reduced to an insignificant group of deluded dreamers, hapless at the polls (the Liberty Party) or caricatured as self-interested racists interested only in restricting slavery's further expansion westward (Free Soilers/Republicans). More often than not, they were principled men with solid roots in the abolitionist movement, who developed a coherent antislavery program and understood the importance of political power, coalition building, and appeals to the self-interest of ordinary Americans, including working-class Americans and African Americans. They recovered a strand of constitutional antislavery that had been submerged since the time of the Framers, but by the 1850s would become a powerful weapon in the hands of the new Republican Party, and they developed a concrete vision for slavery's destruction and the emancipation of enslaved people, much of which was later implemented during the Civil War. This book, then, not only heeds Bruce Laurie's call to better understand how workers responded to the rapidly shifting political developments around slavery in the antebellum decades, but argues that workers themselves contributed to these developments in ways that have been all but ignored.[26]

To better trace the ebb and flow of the first labor movement's relationship to slavery and antislavery and show how it was tied to political and ideological developments, I have adopted a longer time frame than is typical for most monographs on this subject, which have tended to focus on the 1830s and '40s. While *The Root and the Branch* views these decades as pivotal, it also makes the implicit case that the emphasis within the historiography of antislavery on "Garrisonian" abolitionism after 1831 has resulted in a distorted picture of the American antislavery movement and its relationship to capitalism and labor. Only recently have American historians of antislavery begun to emphasize the significance of both the pre-Garrisonian abolitionist movement (which stretches back at least to the Germantown Petition of 1688 and in which free Blacks were in the vanguard for much of the period 1780–1830) and of the political antislavery that finally came to fruition in the 1850s. Histories of

American labor, meanwhile, have long considered the early labor movement largely under the rubric of Jacksonian America, which ignores the movement's intellectual and cultural origins in a transatlantic and colonial context, while eliding the complexity and lack of consensus within working-class politics of the period. Similarly, this study has avoided the narrow focus on one city or geographic region that has characterized most of the studies of early American labor emerging from the social historians of the 1970s and '80s, arguing that (1) the early American labor movement and its relationship to slavery and antislavery can be understood only in terms of its British antecedents and the transatlantic flow of people and ideology, and (2) that a broader geographic framework is necessary for understanding the complexity and variety of this relationship in the antebellum North. The ways that northern workers and labor reformers positioned themselves in response to slavery and antislavery, and eventually the form of labor-abolitionism that developed as a result, looked different in Philadelphia than in Boston, and different in Boston than in Central or Western Massachusetts. While much of the following is based in the seaboard cities of the mid-Atlantic and New England (particularly Philadelphia, New York, and Boston), the narrative follows the trajectory of westward expansion during this period, the better to reflect the increasing conflict over the future of slavery in the young nation as well as the aspirations of urban workers themselves, who did not need the prolabor, antislavery editor Horace Greeley to urge them to "Go West, young man!"

The emphasis on working-class land reform and community formation raises several potential objections, which I attempt to address in what follows, but which are for the most part beyond the scope of this book. It is obvious in hindsight that the land reformers, together with the land speculators, railroad companies, and standing armies they viewed as their enemies, were engaged in a project of settler colonialism. Directly or indirectly, intentionally or not, the reform at the heart of their project—the settlement of public lands owned by the federal government, which the land reformers tended to imagine as a vast, unpopulated space ripe for cultivation but which in reality contained dozens of Native civilizations and a complex and challenging variety of terrains and ecosystems—ultimately led to appropriation, displacement, warfare, and genocide. The working-class land reform movement's relationship to Native Americans is, however, somewhat more complex. As explained further below, despite their Jacksonian roots and the name their most important newspaper shared with John L. O'Sullivan's Young America movement, the land reformers of the National Reform Association were not manifest destiny expansionists; rather, they defended Native American rights and argued that the system of land reform they envisioned would put an end to Indian wars and predation by speculators and settlers, while creating a homeland for Native people and the formerly enslaved.

Another potential criticism is just as difficult to answer. As reflected by the names of some of the early labor organizations, like the New England Association of Farmers, Mechanics, and Other Working Men, the United States was still overwhelmingly agricultural on the eve of the Civil War: only 20 percent of Americans lived in cities; perhaps a bare majority, even in the North, worked for wages.[27] As several important recent studies have emphasized, the strength of the antislavery movement, and the base of political antislavery's electoral support, lay among the small towns, farming communities, canal towns, and manufacturing villages of New England, Upstate and Western New York, Pennsylvania's Quaker towns and Iron District, Ohio's Western Reserve, and parts of the Middle and Greater West. So why focus on the statistically small numbers of urban mechanics, factory and wage workers, and "industrial" reformers based in eastern seaboard metropolises? To some extent, I hope this bias is compensated for by the emphasis on how urban workers, too, looked to agriculture and the land as the source of relief, as well as the book's overall trajectory, which moves from New York and Philadelphia to Ohio, Wisconsin, Kansas, and other parts west. The land and labor reformers of the mid-nineteenth century could not see what a later generation of Marxist historians discerned: that an agricultural "revolution in the countryside" had already rendered their brand of land reform obsolete, while precipitating momentous and, to these reformers, cataclysmic changes to the economy.[28] If there is a certain teleology in this focus on urban, industrial workers, however, I would argue that the significance of these groups does not lie entirely in hindsight. As evidenced by the endless labor jeremiads about the arrival of English-style "factory slavery" on America's shores, and by the name of the most important Fourierist periodical, the *Harbinger*, antebellum workers and labor reformers were aware that vast changes to the nature of labor and capital were afoot, and that they probably spelled the demise of both the hated system of chattel slavery and the Jeffersonian ideal of artisan-yeoman independence that many still cherished.

The Root and the Branch employs a fairly straightforward chronological framework, beginning in the years after the ratification of the U.S. Constitution and the outbreak of revolution in France, but paying particular attention to the pivotal periods of 1790–1800 (an era of radical, revolutionary, and antislavery ferment in both Britain and the United States), 1827–1831 (the rise and fall of the Working Men's movement and the emergence of the Garrisonian abolitionists), 1845–1850 (the Mexican-American War and the rise and decline of the Free Soil coalition), and 1854–1860 (the rise of the Republican Party and the outbreak of the Civil War). Chapter 1 explores the common origins of both antislavery thought and working-class activism in the radical republican tradition that grew out of the Age of Enlightenment and the revolutions in the United States, France, and Haiti. The more radical variant of the republican tradition embraced not only ideas about natural rights and universal humanity, embodied in the language of *Rights of Man*, but also a deep concern with inequalities of property and a willingness to scrutinize the very legitimacy of claims to property rights in land, labor, and human beings. From republican writers in the era of the English Civil War to Paine's *Agrarian Justice* to the radical working-class agrarianism of Thomas Spence, radical thinkers challenged the legitimacy of large concentrations of wealth and called for the redistribution of landed property or its equivalent. Others, like John Thelwall of the London Corresponding Society and the formerly enslaved Jamaican Spencean Robert Wedderburn, attacked the emerging systems of global commerce and metropolitan finance by explicitly linking them to the slave trade and slavery. Very quickly, however, these critiques became conflated with the latest iteration of "white slavery" rhetoric—one that made an explicit comparison between African slaves and impoverished British tenant farmers and factory workers. Originating with West India slave owners, this version of white slavery language became part of the vocabulary of British radicals, who frequently found themselves at odds with the elitist and religious antislavery of the abolitionist "saints." White slavery comparisons between enslaved Africans and white workers soon made their way across the Atlantic, where they became embroiled in the partisan political debates and controversies over slavery in the early United States.

In the years after the Missouri Crisis of 1819–1820, the advent of a Jacksonian coalition that brought together northern artisans and yeomen and southern slave owners, together with the explosive growth in the productivity and profitability of cotton, served to make slavery yet more deeply entrenched in America's political economy. The appearance of Garrison's American Anti-Slavery Society in 1831 pointed the way toward new and more radical approaches to abolitionism, but also prompted a backlash that not infrequently spilled over into antiabolitionist and anti-Black violence. Against this dark backdrop, however, a group of radical figures associated with the Working

Men's movement and the radical wing of the Democratic Party—the subjects of chapter 2—helped to pioneer a powerful brand of antislavery, one based on economic arguments about slavery's inferiority to free labor, demands for access to the land in territories kept free from bondage, and an antislavery interpretation of the U.S. Constitution. By articulating and advancing a more expansive vision of free labor—one that included a right to "the fruits of" if not "the whole product of" labor—working-class reformers prompted many Americans, including some abolitionists, to reconsider an emerging free labor consensus based on wage labor, self-ownership, and freedom of contract.

Chapter 3 continues to trace these developments by reconsidering the Associationists, the name adopted by American followers of French social theorist Charles Fourier in the 1840s. Not only did the Associationist movement win the participation and support of a number of abolitionists, but this chapter shows that Associationist thinkers and Fourierist labor leaders thought deeply about the connections between capitalism, slavery, and property, declaring themselves opposed to "all slavery" and in favor of "integral emancipation." While the language of "all slavery" could sometimes be used to elide direct confrontation with chattel slavery, antislavery Associationists forged connections with workingmen's organizations in the North and in Great Britain, developed communitarian schemes aimed at eradicating slavery, and, in at least one well-documented instance, welcomed African Americans as community members. In chapter 4, the focus shifts to the land reform movement, organized by New York City Working Men's Party veteran George Henry Evans in 1844. Evans's National Reform Association, which quickly gained national attention as a result of its involvement in the Dorr Rebellion in Rhode Island and the Anti-Rent movement in Upstate New York, not only called for federal government intervention to create free, inalienable homesteads on the public lands, but challenged the very idea of a right to property in the soil. Such stances earned the National Reformers widespread support from northern wage workers while putting them on a collision course with slaveholding expansionists, even as Evans's enthusiastic embrace of "white slavery" language undermined his earlier abolitionism. Despite this paradox, Evans won a powerful convert to land reform in the person of abolitionist Gerrit Smith, whose land-grant scheme for free Blacks was partially inspired by land reform ideology.

Chapter 5 chronicles a moment of cohesion and coalition, when land reformers, Associationists, Ten Hours Act supporters, abolitionists, and others joined forces under the aegis of the National Industrial Congress, described above. During these same years, the Mexican-American War (1846–1848) and the Wilmot Proviso (1846) thrust the issue of slavery's expansion back onto the national center stage. The subsequent emergence of the Free Soil Party was anticipated in some ways by the National Reformers, who continued to use the term "free soil" to describe their program, even as they argued for more radical forms of land redistribution and insisted that land reform would pave the way for the elimination of chattel slavery. Although the "union of reformers" imagined by the founders of the National Industrial Congress would, like the Free Soil coalition, prove short-lived, the National Industrial Congress and affiliated workers' organizations took a strong stance against the Mexican war and slavery's expansion, and they forged a political alliance with a faction of the abolitionist Liberty Party.

Chapter 6 depicts a period of transition, in the aftermath of the collapse of the Free Soil Party, the defeat of the 1848 revolutions in Europe, and the passage of the 1850 Compromise. But although Evans's National Reform Association began to go into decline during these years, the land reform movement attracted significant support in the West, where it was often combined with antislavery, and homestead measures began to win mainstream acceptance in state legislatures and in Congress. Workingmen's groups adopted strong stances against the 1850 Compromise and the Fugitive Act, while the arrival of vast numbers of immigrants, including veterans of the 1848 revolutions, helped to revitalize the labor movement even as it complicated its antislavery stances. A number of free Black abolitionists and workers, meanwhile, increasingly voiced support for both political abolitionism and land reform, and implemented their own visions of "free labor" in Colored Conventions, refugee communities, and artisan workshops, while the participation of Black delegates to the National Industrial Congress tested the limits of racial egalitarianism in the pre–Civil War labor movement.

Chapter 7 charts the culmination of these developments, detailing how the passage of the Kansas-Nebraska Act in 1854 helped tip the scales against slavery's further expansion and future survival by directly threatening the land reform project and prompting a vocal backlash from northern workers and their organizations. The new antislavery political party that emerged from the anti-Kansas opposition—the Republican Party—benefitted from the absorption of a number of radical and progressive figures, including those with direct ties to the land reform and Associationist movements, while rebranding and mainstreaming ideas about free labor, free soil, homestead reform, and tariffs in an effort to attract support from northern workingmen. Although limited evidence suggests that these efforts were only partially successful, the Republicans' formula of combining free soil antislavery with an appeal to the self-interest of ordinary northerners at last made antislavery, in William H. Seward's words, "a respectable element in politics," guaranteeing the party's electoral success and hastening the arrival of an armed conflict with the slaveholding South. Less propitiously, the Republicans' endorsement of more narrow understandings of free labor and land reform and the party's role in guiding the country's transition to a new form of industrial and financial capitalism virtually guaranteed the prevalence of labor strife in the post–Civil War period and helped ensure that millions of freedmen and freedwomen would remain trapped in a state of landlessness and economic dependence. A brief epilogue spells out some of the postwar implications of these momentous developments.

Like any work of historical interpretation, the current one can only be of limited utility in shedding light on present-day questions. But by taking seriously race and class, politics and economics, material interests and ideology, *The Root and the Branch* does aspire to illuminate the historical origins and ongoing implications of a debate that was never fully resolved and that continues to reverberate in the twenty-first century. If it points inescapably to the conclusion that the quest for greater economic and social equality must be accompanied by the struggle for racial justice, it also aims to show that what has sometimes been portrayed as a conflict between the proponents of economic equality on one hand and racial equality on the other was neither inherent nor inevitable. Out of the clash of ideas, ideologies, outlooks, and interests represented by these two reform movements emerged, if not a consensus, a set of broadly shared values and ideas as well as a fragile yet transformative coalition—one that, while not revolutionary or even particularly radical in and of itself, nonetheless launched a political, economic, and social revolution that culminated in the destruction of slavery and the transformation of American, indeed global, capitalism. The long-overlooked examples of cooperation and collaboration across reform movements and racial barriers that *The Root and the Branch* brings to light—what antebellum labor activists termed the Union of Reformers—may yet hold lessons for those interested in organizing political coalitions and translating social movement activism into political power and lasting progressive achievements in the twenty-first century.

CHAPTER 1

Tom Paine's Progeny: Slavery, Labor, and Democracy in the Radical Atlantic

One of Thomas Paine's few public statements on slavery came in April 1776 in a letter to the *Pennsylvania Journal* that appeared a few months after the publication of his epoch-making pamphlet *Common Sense.* Already looking forward to victory in the war for the colonies' independence, Paine proposed that, in fashioning a new government for themselves, Americans should "forget not the hapless African." The plea on behalf of enslaved people appeared in a footnote at the bottom of the letter, beneath a passage that described the "slavery" of white Americans forced to live under British rule. The message seems clear: however genuine Paine's concern for the plight of enslaved Africans, it was relegated to a footnote, subordinated to the symbolic slavery of white men.[1]

One might be tempted to end the story there. Recent scholarship has cast serious doubt on Paine's once vaunted antislavery credentials. It now appears unlikely that he wrote the two antislavery essays published in 1775 and long attributed to him, "African Slavery in America" and "A Serious Thought." Nor is it likely that Paine wrote the preamble to Pennsylvania's 1780 Act for the Gradual Emancipation of Slavery, as scholars once believed. Although he did join the first antislavery society in the American colonies, the Pennsylvania Society for Promoting the Abolition of Slavery and the Relief of Free Negroes Unlawfully Held in Bondage (better known as the Pennsylvania Abolition Society), he did so only belatedly, attending a few meetings in 1787 before departing for Britain. In his letters to his former revolutionary compatriots in the United States, Paine anguished over the persistence of slavery in the newly independent nation and urged that steps to be taken toward its eradication, and while in Britain he coauthored with Joseph Priestley an anonymous tract calling for the abolition of the slave trade. For the most part, however, Paine confined his antislavery sentiments to private correspondence and generalized abstractions, rather than proclaiming them publicly or taking an active role in abolitionist organizations.[2]

Toward the end of his life, when he had been forced to flee from revolutionary France and forsaken by friends in postrevolutionary New York, one of Paine's strongest admirers and sharpest critics took him to task for this failure to match principle with deed. The famous ex-revolutionary, the critic complained, had failed to utter "a syllable against Negro slavery," despite his current residence "in the State of New York, surrounded by Negro slaves."[3] Edward Rushton knew of what he spoke. A former sailor turned radical editor and bookseller in Liverpool, which for most of the eighteenth century served as the center of the British slave trade, Rushton had encountered slavery firsthand during a slaving trip to Dominica. His attempts to alleviate the suffering of enslaved captives during an outbreak of ophthalmia on board led to Rushton's own subsequent blindness; on reaching shore, he found himself charged with mutiny as a result of his challenges to the ship's captain over the treatment of its human cargo. Rushton overcame the charges, his blindness, and even an assassination attempt to become a determined abolitionist and spokesman "in favor of the rights of man." An admirer of the American Revolution and of Paine, Rushton was deeply disturbed by the new nation's failure to eradicate slavery, as well as the failure of revolutionary patriots to sufficiently speak out against it. Sometime during the 1790s, he took pen to paper to write letters to both Paine and former president George Washington, chastising them for failing to condemn the "tyranny" of the "republican planter" and "democratic slave holder."[4]

Washington, still one of the country's largest slave owners, failed to reply, but Rushton might have expected more from the author of *Rights of Man*. Unlike the ex-president, Paine acknowledged receipt of Rushton's letter and sent his "verbal respects," but he did not offer any further explanation for his failure to condemn slavery more forcefully. When the abolitionist Thomas Walker had posed a similar question, Paine had claimed that the very intensity of his feelings against slavery made him unsuited for the task. "An unfitter person for such work could hardly be found," Paine insisted. "The cause would have suffered in my hands. I could not have treated it with any chance of success; for I could never think of [enslaved peoples'] condition but with feelings of indignation."[5] Although such a strictly rational approach to abolition may have made sense to the author of *The Age of Reason*, it is doubt-ful Paine's self-exculpation would have satisfied Edward Rushton.

And yet, Paine's antislavery significance looms larger than the few state-ments he made about the subject during his lifetime. More than any other figure in Anglo-American political culture during the Age of Revolution, Thomas Paine embodied the challenge to the inequalities rooted in rela-tionships of property, power, and tradition, of which slavery represented the era's most extreme expression. Throughout the English-speaking world, both during his life and for generations after his death in 1809, Paine was the idol of democratic revolutionaries and reformers, and—as a former staymaker and cobbler who experienced poverty at various times in his life—the embodi-ment of the common man's challenge to wealth and power. For many—not least the slaveholders who associated antislavery with social leveling and Jacobinism—such a stance also represented an implicit challenge to slavery. Among the constituent elements of the Paineite brand of antislavery that resulted were an Enlightenment universalism that posited a common origin for all human beings and argued that everyone was entitled to basic natural rights; a sense of cosmopolitan identity as "citizens of the world" who sought solidarity with other oppressed peoples; and a questioning of the political, legal, and moral foundations of the claims to certain kinds of property. Such ideas made Paine a byword for radicalism in his lifetime and beyond—a dan-gerously democratic demagogue, leveler, and infidel to his enemies, and the scourge of tyrants, kings, and slaveholders to his followers.

Particularly conspicuous among those who looked to Paine for inspiration were the democratic radicals who organized "corresponding societies" and working-class political movements in Britain between 1790 and 1820, and the artisans and laborers in cities like New York and Philadelphia, who organized America's first labor movement in the 1820s. Toward the end of this period, a new generation of immediate abolitionists also found inspiration in Tom Paine, and many embraced him as one of their own, thus contributing to the confusion about the extent of Paine's actual antislavery activism that persists to this day.[6] That Paine himself does not qualify as an abolitionist thus raises a twofold question: what accounts for the conflicts that began to emerge between abolitionists and working-class radicals, beginning in the 1790s? And how did Paine and the radicals he inspired—those who might be termed "Tom Paine's progeny"—nonetheless form an important part of the ideological foundation for both the antislavery and labor movements on both sides of the Atlantic?

Paine's *Rights of Man* and the Challenge
to Slavery and Inequality

By some accounts the most widely read political tract in the Atlantic World during the 1790s, Paine's *Rights of Man*, was the key text for radicals of all stripes in both Britain and America. Published beginning in 1791, its timing was critical. In the years since the publication of *Common Sense* in 1776, the events in the thirteen colonies of British North America that Paine had described as "not the concern of a day, a year, or an age" had metastasized into a global Age of Revolution, with revolutionary conflicts raging in France and Haiti and soon to make their way into nearly every corner of Europe and the Americas. At the same time, a revolution in technology was underway in places like London, Manchester, and Birmingham (and to a lesser extent in Philadelphia, Boston, and New York), one that would transform the political economy of the Atlantic World as well as the everyday lives of millions of working people around the globe. The same fifteen-year period had witnessed the beginnings of the first organized movement against slavery, with the founding of the British Society for Effecting the Abolition of the Slave Trade, the French *Société des Amis des Noirs*, and the abolition societies of Pennsylvania and New York, as well as some of the first trade unions, workingmen's societies, and organized democratic political movements on either side of the Atlantic. Paine himself made explicit the connection between popular revolution and antislavery, framing the revolution in France as a contest between "freedom or slavery." Perhaps more importantly, the peripatetic Paine—who had first abandoned Britain for America and would soon be forced to flee France—inspired readers by insisting that natural rights were not the sole purview of any one nation or race of people, and by urging solidarity with oppressed peoples around the world, a sentiment captured in *Rights of Man*'s famous phrase, "my country is the world; my religion is to do good."[7]

Written as a direct outgrowth of Paine's encounter with the French Revolution, and intended in part as a rebuttal to Edmund Burke's antirevolutionary *Reflections on the Revolution in France*, *Rights of Man* proved highly influential, and also highly controversial. Having encountered extreme poverty and the first signs of a permanent class of "labouring poor" in the streets of London and Paris (and perhaps recalling his own experience as an impoverished staymaker who had barely escaped indentured servitude), Paine had been moved to think deeply about the root causes of poverty and economic inequality. In *Rights of Man, Part the Second*, published in 1792, Paine offered

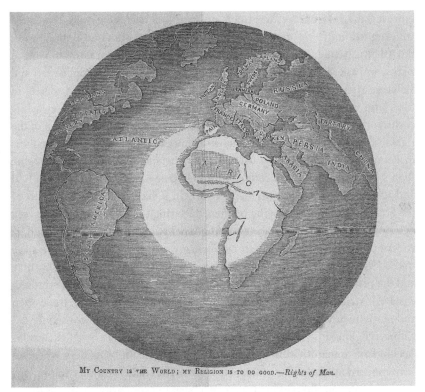

My Country is the World; my Religion is to do good.—*Rights of Man.*

Figure 3. This illustration from an 1847 compendium of abolitionist writings juxtaposes Paine's quote from *Rights of Man* with an image of an illuminated Africa at the center of the globe. Yale Beinecke Library.

his first detailed consideration of economic inequality and its implications for republican politics. Purposefully blurring the lines between representative government and direct democracy, Paine proposed that governments controlled by the people could provide a peaceful and democratic solution to the problem of such "unnatural" distinctions of wealth and property. By proposing a variety of social measures, including progressive taxation, funding for public education, a government-funded pension system, unemployment relief, and public works programs, Paine redefined the purpose and scope of republican government, anticipating the social welfare states that emerged in the twentieth century.[8]

Like Paine's other works, *Rights of Man* had little to say directly about the widespread and glaringly unequal practice of enslavement. By the early 1790s, however, the very phrase "the rights of man" had become closely associated with opposition to slavery. Democratic writers and editors on both sides of the Atlantic frequently couched their opposition to slavery in terms of natural rights, and asked readers to imagine themselves in the place of oppressed and suffering Africans.[9] A 1792 petition to Congress from an abolition society in Maryland used the phrase no less than three times in as many pages, while correspondents calling for an end to the slave trade and the recognition of the rights of African-descended peoples in Democratic-Republican newspapers in Pennsylvania and Massachusetts signed their letters as "A Friend to the Rights of Man."[10] The same connections held true across the Atlantic. In 1791 and again in 1792, an Irish militia company in Belfast marched in support of the French Revolution carrying banners declaring their opposition to slavery as a violation of "the rights of men" and offered public toasts, accompanied by volleys of gunfire, to Paine, Irish nationalism, and the abolition of the slave trade. A native of Stamford, England, lamenting the failure of the local gentry and the respectable middle classes to take a strong stance against the trade in enslaved Africans, rejoiced that there was a "third class of us, viz. tradesmen and mechanics, who make up in number what we may want in consequence." Citing religious-inspired ideals of universal brotherhood as well as secular "feelings of humanity," the Stamfordian challenged those readers who had "any concern for the rights of man" to oppose the traffic. Another transatlantic correspondent thought he discerned a "striking similarity" between *Rights of Man* and the work of antislavery poet William Cowper, connecting both to denunciations of the *"Trade in human Misery."* By the same token, conservatives frequently showed their hand by linking their opposition to slave trade legislation and abolitionism to a stance against radicalism and Jacobinism. In the House of Lords in 1794, Lord Abingdon (Willoughby Bertie, the Fourth Earl of Abingdon) objected to a bill to abolish the slave trade, not only because it would "deprive individuals of 7,000,000 [pounds] of property," but because he viewed such measures as "founded on French principles—Equality—and what was erroneously called, the Rights of Man."[11]

Abingdon was not mistaken in drawing a connection between slavery's sanctioning of property in man and the threat to that property posed by revolutionary and Paineite ideology. Although John Locke's famous formulation of "life, liberty, and property" formed a major part of the ideological foundation of the American Revolution as well as the basis of slaveholders' defense of their right to hold property in human beings, ideas about the *limitations* of property rights were in many ways equally well-established in republican political thought. In this alternative tradition, which stretched back at least to the period of the English Civil War, republican thinkers distinguished between legitimate and illegitimate forms of private property, attacking large concentrations of wealth and calling for interventions into the property rights of large landholders and others in the name of promoting the *res publica*, the good of the people. From the Diggers and Levellers who hoped that the English Civil War would bring about a "Jubilee," in which landholdings and other property would be equalized, to the English political essayist James Harrington, whose *The Commonwealth of Oceana* (1656) speculated that a truly republican society would be one in which wealth would be more or less evenly distributed, to religious mystics like Johannes Kelpius, who tried to create an egalitarian utopia in seventeenth-century Pennsylvania, political thinkers and theorists dreamed of a society free of the drastic inequalities of wealth and property that characterized Early Modern Europe.[12]

Long before the emergence of Marxian socialism, or even the protosocialism of Robert Owen or Henri de Saint-Simon, the term "agrarian" was used by advocates and critics alike to describe various forms of wealth redistribution, particularly in regard to land or its equivalent.[13] In the early eighteenth century, the authors of the influential *Cato's Letters* argued that "Liberty can never subsist without Equality, nor Equality be long preserved without an Agrarian Law," and, somewhat later, even more mainstream figures like Thomas Jefferson and the New England Federalist Noah Webster agreed that, in Jefferson's words, "the earth is given as a common stock for man to labour and live in." In the 1790s, the radically egalitarian ideas popularized by the French Revolution, the emergence of Democratic-Republican societies and "Jacobin clubs," and the publication of works like Paine's *Rights of Man* and *Agrarian Justice*, William Godwin's *Political Justice*, and Volney's *The Ruins* (the last three were all published in the United States within a year, between 1796 and 1797) conspired to facilitate the circulation of radically democratic ideas throughout the revolutionary Atlantic, inspiring a host of radical critiques of the existing political-economic order. In time, a small but significant handful of political thinkers would link such democratic and "agrarian" ideas to the critique of property in human beings.[14]

Sailors and other maritime workers were instrumental in carrying these ideas across the Atlantic Ocean and to the far corners of the world, where they were picked up and adapted for local use. But it was in Britain, where the rise of new forms of industrial and financial capitalism, the collision of long-standing democratic traditions with an entrenched system of class privilege, and the paradoxes inherent in an empire where slavery was tolerated in the colonies but banned in the metropole, that political radicals first drew connections between the exploitation of wage labor and the political economy of slavery. By attacking economic inequality, the exploitation and commodification of labor, and the illicit accumulation of wealth and property, these transatlantic democrats lay the groundwork for an expansive vision for the emancipation of oppressed laborers, both enslaved and free. At the same time, however, their resort to "white slavery" comparisons between British workers and enslaved Africans in the Caribbean inaugurated a less auspicious tradition, one that would contribute to developing tensions between abolitionists and political radicals on both sides of the Atlantic.[15]

English Jacobins, Antislavery, and "White Slavery" in Great Britain

Inspired by Paine, *Rights of Man*, and the revolutions in America and France, radicals in Great Britain began forming democratic clubs and associations in the early 1790s, building on a rich tradition of plebeian and middling class political organizing that stretched back to the Glorious Revolution and encompassed everything from tavern debating societies and coffeehouse political clubs to the Country Party of the mid-eighteenth century to the Wilkesite movement of the 1770s. In 1780, John Cartwright's Society for Constitutional Information (SCI) was established to advocate for parliamentary reform and the expansion of the suffrage under the existing British constitution; its mostly middle-class membership had included Paine as well as a number of prominent British abolitionists, including Granville Sharp and Josiah Wedgwood.[16] But between 1790 and 1792, a number of so-called corresponding societies began to spring up across Britain. Comprising mainly "small shopkeepers, artisans, mechanics, and labourers," groups like the London Corresponding Society (LCS) advocated such radical measures as the institution of universal suffrage, an annually elected Parliament, and the abolition of the slave trade. While officially republican and reformist, many of the corresponding societies' members harbored revolutionary aspirations, leading to their widespread denunciation as Jacobins, after the radically democratic political club in Revolutionary France.[17]

The LCS remains the best known of these organizations, but the corresponding societies also established a strong presence in rapidly industrializing manufacturing towns like Manchester, Sheffield, Birmingham, and Norwich, whose growing populations continued to be unrepresented in Parliament. These new industrial centers, with growing numbers of factory operatives and wage workers, were also hotbeds of anti–slave trade activity and petitioning: Manchester alone garnered more than ten thousand anti–slave trade petition signatures in 1788, a figure that doubled to twenty thousand (a third of the city's population) four years later.[18] Thomas Hardy, the Piccadilly shoemaker generally considered to be the founder of the LCS, claimed direct inspiration from abolitionists within the SCI; among the latter's freely distributed tracts, "some excellent pamphlets by Granville Sharp" had originally inspired Hardy's antislavery. Paine was another major influence; after reading *Rights of Man*, Hardy proclaimed, there could be no doubt that "natural rights" applied to "the whole human race black or white, high or low, rich or poor." John Thelwall, the LCS's leading theorist and intellectual, had been influenced by abolitionist Thomas Clarkson's use of mass lectures, while Thelwall's fellow traveler, the poet Samuel Coleridge, proved adept at translating the antislavery arguments of Clarkson, Anthony Benezet, and other abolitionists into a radical popular vernacular.[19]

The involvement of two of the best-known Black abolitionists in Britain, Olaudah Equiano and Ottobah Cugoano, further highlights the early ties between radicalism and abolitionism in 1790s London. Both were members of the LCS, and they both helped to foster connections between the radical societies, abolitionists, and London's growing African diaspora community, using their adopted status as English "gentlemen" to cultivate these connections across lines of both race and class. The Sons of Africa, a corresponding society Equiano and Cugoano formed in 1787, enlisted the aid of prominent Britons like William Pitt and Charles James Fox against the slave trade and on behalf of London's "Black Poor," a group that included waves of formerly enslaved refugees evacuated by the British during the American Revolution. At the same time, Cugoano drew on radical rhetoric in his increasingly incendiary publications, and other members of the Sons of Africa were involved in rioting and other street actions to support favored political candidates, or to prevent Black Londoners from being kidnapped into slavery.[20]

After the publication of his autobiographical *The Interesting Narrative of Olaudah Equiano, or Gustavus Vassa, the African* (1789), sometimes considered the first slave narrative, Equiano became something of an antislavery celebrity. His lectures and publications were sponsored by Selina Hastings, the Countess of Huntingdon, and he had close ties to Sharp, Thomas Clarkson, and other abolitionists associated with SEAST (the Society for Effecting the Abolition of the Slave Trade). During his 1791–1792 tour of Britain to promote *Narrative*, Equiano acted as a go-between among the LCS, abolitionists, and other radical groups. In Belfast, he was hosted by Samuel Neilson, publisher of the Paineite *Northern Star* newspaper and founder of the United Irishmen, a soon-to-be-outlawed Irish independence group inspired by the French Revolution. Back in London, he lodged with Hardy, and after Hardy and other members of the LCS were put on trial for treason in 1794, he helped to raise money for their defense. The symbiosis between radicalism and abolitionism is underscored by a letter from Hardy to Sheffield abolitionist Thomas Bryant in 1792, in which Hardy credited Equiano for having recommended Sheffield as a fertile ground for radical activity and Bryant as a likely ally. Since (as Hardy put it), Bryant was known to be "a zealous friend to the abolition of that cursed traffic, the Slave Trade," Hardy could safely assume that "*you are a zealous friend to freedom on the broad basis of the RIGHTS OF MAN.*" "I am fully persuaded," Hardy continued, "that there is no man, who is, from principle, an advocate for the liberty of the black man, but will zealously support the rights of the white man, and *vice versa.*" William Hodgson, another LCS member, provided a visual representation of Hardy's point in the engraving on the frontispiece for his *The Commonwealth of Reason* (1795), which showed a Black man and a white man facing each other while clutching a liberty pole, with an inscription reminding readers that "all by Nature are equal and free, and no one can without the utmost injustice become the Slave of his like."[21]

If the ties between abolitionism and radicalism were readily apparent in 1790s Britain, however, fissures between the two movements nonetheless began to appear. At the abortive British Convention in Edinburgh in 1793, which brought together members of the SCI, the LCS, and other radical societies from across England and Scotland, resolutions in favor of abolishing the slave trade passed overwhelmingly. But in their writings and speeches, convention organizers Joseph Gerrald and Maurice Margarot were more likely to apply the terms "slaves" and "slavery" to oppressed British or French subjects than to enslaved Africans in the West Indies. Gerrald, the son of a West India planter on Saint Kitts who never disavowed his inheritance of property that included enslaved men and women, apparently saw no irony in comparing "British freemen" to "slaves" at his subsequent trial for sedition in 1794.[22]

Such "white slavery" comparisons had a long genealogy that probably stretched back to the origins of the West African slave trade in the fifteenth century.[23] As numerous scholars have pointed out, white slavery tropes (later

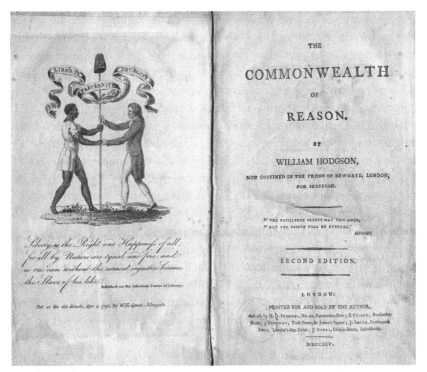

Figure 4. The frontispiece to William Hodgson's *The Commonwealth of Reason* (1795) depicts a Black man and a white facing each other as equals, gripping a liberty pole topped by a Phrygian cap and emblazoned with the slogan of the French Revolution. Modern Records Centre, University Library, University of Warwick.

sometimes rendered as "wage slavery" or "wages slavery") were common, even ubiquitous, in an era in which slavery functioned as "the gold standard of oppression." The comparisons appeared in political rhetoric, in the language of song and poetry (including the lyrics to "Rule Britannia"), in satirical prints, and in the reformist vernacular of those who championed such diverse causes as women's rights, temperance, and the abolition of corporal punishment. Paine had written of the "slavery" of those suffering under hereditary monarchies in *Rights of Man*, and earlier, supporters of the Patriot cause in America had compared American colonists to slaves so frequently that they prompted the English author Samuel Johnson to question why "we hear the loudest yelps for liberty among the drivers of negroes."[24]

Arguably, however, the language of white slavery took on a new and more insidious meaning after the rise of an organized abolitionist movement and the emergence of an industrial working class, beginning around the 1780s. During these years, the language of white slavery ceased to function as a mere rhetorical device or metaphor for oppression and took on a more specific meaning in the sense of direct comparisons between impoverished English laborers and enslaved people of African descent. It seems probable that such comparisons originated with West Indian slaveholders, like William Beckford, a Jamaica plantation owner and Lord Mayor of London, whose *Remarks Upon the Situation of Negroes in Jamaica* (1788) claimed that the former were better off than the London poor.[25] In 1792, however, a further innovation was added to the growing genre of white slavery literature, perhaps in an effort to conceal the class interests of efforts like Beckford's. The anonymous author of London publisher John Bell's *The True State of the Question* presented himself as "A Plain Man" who had been hoodwinked into signing an anti-slave trade petition, but now expressed regret after being informed that Jamaican slaves lived in comfortable houses and regularly dined on "fine fowls, very good beef, English bottled porter, and wine." Variants of these arguments that became commonplace tropes in white slavery discourse in the period not only compared the conditions experienced by free and enslaved workers, but argued that the freedom of the English wage worker was nominal, if not illusory. Enslaved people, these authors were fond of pointing out, not only received free food, clothing, and shelter, but could look forward to some kind of care and shelter on reaching old age, unlike the English worker, who must work or starve. Another favorite tactic was to emphasize the alleged hypocrisy of British abolitionists, who were supposedly fixated on the distant West Indies while ignoring abuses at home. For those who could not read, satirical prints by the likes of James Gillray and Richard Newton drove the message home.[26]

As disingenuous and transparent as these early white slavery tropes were, elite abolitionists' own political and cultural biases and attitudes left them susceptible to charges of hypocrisy. William Wilberforce, the best-known abolitionist in Britain and the leader of the antislavery forces in Parliament, was the scion of a wealthy merchant who was closely associated with the Clapham Sect, a group of wealthy and conservative members of the Anglican Church. In 1787 Wilberforce, then a recent convert to evangelical Christianity, encouraged King George III to issue a proclamation against immorality and vice, which paved the way for Wilberforce's own, lesser-known role as one of the leaders of the Proclamation Society (later the Society for the Suppression of Vice), which attempted to enforce observance of the Sabbath and prosecute the publication of blasphemous and licentious books and other printed material. "Free thinking" radicals inspired by Paine's religious skepticism, like Richard Carlile, became frequent targets, often sentenced to harsh jail terms on charges of sedition and blasphemy.[27]

International and local political developments soon conspired to drive a further wedge between abolitionists and democratic radicals. Alarmed by the prospect of Jacobinism and revolution in Britain, William Pitt's government moved swiftly to charge leaders of the LCS and other societies with sedition after the outbreak of war with France in 1793, infiltrating their organizations with spies and sentencing several to transportation. Abolitionists like Wilberforce and Clarkson were forced to distance themselves from so-called Jacobinism and any association with working-class or radical causes—and, in a strategic shift, to identify abolitionism with a pro-British and anti-French foreign policy and national identity.[28] Wilberforce supported Pitt's suspension of habeas corpus in 1795 and worked with him to draft the repressive Two Acts, which banned large meetings and other forms of political expression. The Proclamation Society prosecuted the publisher of Paine's *The Age of Reason*, and its membership overlapped with John Reeve's reactionary Association for the Protection of Property Against Republicans and Levellers. Wilberforce frequently visited imprisoned radicals in jail in an effort to convert them—and, when that failed, sometimes personally oversaw their prosecution for seditious libel and other offences. Whether fairly or unfairly, such stances helped to cement the image of abolitionists as sanctimonious, hypocritical elites in the popular imagination.[29]

As the wars with France dragged on, with accompanying high prices, privation, mandatory military service, and government repression, complaints about abolitionist hypocrisy grew louder. In 1797, the LCS's John Thelwall, a principled opponent of slavery, chastised Wilberforce for seeking "so wide for objects of thy benevolence" when the "seed, the root of oppression is here and here the cure must begin." In what would become an oft-repeated refrain, Thelwall challenged Wilberforce to prove his sincerity as a champion of human rights by committing himself to the causes of poor relief and parliamentary reform at home. "If we would dispense justice to our distant colonies," Thelwall intoned, "we must begin by rooting out from the centre the corruption by which that cruelty and injustice is countenanced and defended." Elsewhere, he wondered aloud whether "the condition of the negro, in our West India Islands," was not "preferable that of many of our own peasantry." Unlike some of his radical contemporaries, however, Thelwall never abandoned his commitment to internationalism and racial egalitarianism, defending the Haitian Revolution against the conservative author Edmund Burke and calling on fellow Englishmen to reject "national feelings" and "national distinctions" in favor of solidarity with fellow "citizens of the world" in France, the West Indies, Africa, and beyond. As Thelwall explained, "the light of reason" had awakened English people to the fact that African-descended people were "our brother[s]."[30]

British radicals who fled to the United States to avoid charges of sedition or treason, however, sometimes appeared more reticent to take strong antislavery positions once arrived in the new environment of the slaveholding republic. Transplanted to the New World, in closer proximity to actually existing chattel slavery, issues of slavery and antislavery inevitably took on a more charged significance. In 1794, a group of self-styled "Republican Natives of Great-Britain and Ireland" in New York published an address to Joseph Priestley, the famed scientist, political theorist, and religious dissenter then living in exile in Pennsylvania. The expatriate republicans expressed their dismay that their adopted government should be "tarnished" by slavery and looked forward to a "yet more perfect state of society" in which the *Equal Rights of Man* were extended "to every human being, be his complexion what it may." But Priestley's reply declined to make any mention of slavery, despite the scientist-philosopher's well-known opposition to the institution. Others, like the erstwhile antislavery polemicist Thomas Branagan or the Democratic-Republican editor (and former member of both the LCS and United Irishmen) John Binns, found their early antislavery principles overwhelmed by a growing commitment to racial separation and whiteness.[31]

Ironically, closer proximity to slavery often seemed to enhance, rather than diminish, its malleability as a metaphor for various kinds of oppression. Democratic radicals in the early United States seized on and in some ways expanded on the language of white slavery, adapting it to the fiercely contested partisan political climate of the 1790s in ways that were often divorced from the realities of chattel slavery and gradual emancipation that surrounded them. In 1798, Thomas Yarrow, a former LCS secretary, began a Fourth of July oration in Westchester County, New York, by denouncing the celebration of kings and tyrants in "countries debased by slavery"—a category in which he did not include his newly adopted homeland. Around the same time, "Citizen" Richard Lee, a radical publisher associated with the LCS who had taken refuge in Philadelphia, offered a detailed and penetrating analysis of the emerging conditions of capitalist wage labor in industrializing Britain. Perhaps responding to the Federalist push to promote domestic manufacturing, Lee's "Remarks on

Industry" concluded with a chilling warning to his new countrymen about the ways in which British factory labor had reduced freemen to slaves. "The only difference," Lee claimed, "is, that while the latter has only one master . . . whose interest dictates clemency, the former is subject to the oppression of ten thousand masters, every one of whom has some appropriate instrument of oppression."[32]

In 1805, when Philadelphia's Federal Society of Journeyman Cordwainers went out on strike for higher wages in what was perhaps the first significant labor action in the Early National period, another transatlantic radical, the Democratic-Republican printer William Duane, came to their aid. Duane's *Aurora* was the only Philadelphia paper to support the strikers—in vain, as it turned out. *Commonwealth v. Pullis*, the landmark early labor case that ensued, declared the strikers guilty of an illegal conspiracy, a decision that cast doubt on the legality of strikes and labor unions for at least the next thirty years. As several historians have pointed out, Duane utilized white slave metaphors to defend the strikers in the *Aurora*. But fewer have noted that counsels for both the prosecution and the defense in the cordwainers' subsequent trial also referred to white workers as slaves, a reflection of the term's malleability as a metaphor. Of the several references to white slavery during the trial, surely the most elaborate was made by the prosecution. Citing the landmark 1772 antislavery *Somerset* case, which declared the freedom of enslaved people once they set foot on British soil, prosecuting attorney Jared Ingersol asked jurors to consider whether "the pavement of Philadelphia" had the opposite effect, transforming the freeman into a slave by forcing him to "resign his independence of opinion" (in other words, force him to join a trade union in violation of his freedom to contract for wages).[33]

If their use by both sides in the Journeyman Cordwainers' trial suggests the ubiquity of white or wage slavery metaphors in the period, the case of Robert Wedderburn suggests the difficulties in assuming they aligned with proslavery or racist ideology. Wedderburn was the mixed-race son of a white planter and an enslaved mother in Jamaica; after gaining his freedom, he settled in London, where he eked out a living as a tailor and minister and became part of the same radical Black London milieu that included Equiano and Cugoano. Wedderburn is best known for his 1824 antislavery pamphlet, *The Horrors of Slavery*, and he cultivated a close relationship with William Wilberforce. But he denounced the abolitionist tactic of petitioning Parliament as "degrading," and, in an "Address to the Planters and Negroes of the Island of Jamaica," he counseled his enslaved brethren that, without landed

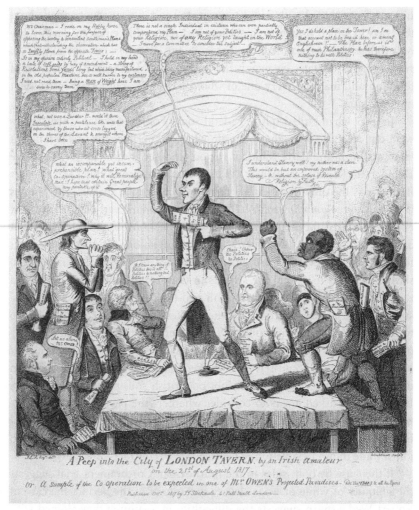

Figure 5. British political caricaturist George Cruikshank's satirical image purports to take the viewer inside the City of London tavern, known as a meeting place for British radicals. In Cruikshank's rendering, Robert Owen stands atop a table clutching a copy of his *New View of Society*, debating with a Quaker abolitionist (wearing a large-brimmed hat, at left), the Republican reformer Major John Cartwright (seated, in a wig), radical publisher Thomas Wooler (seated, to the right of the abolitionist), and a Black man whom Cruikshank may have intended to depict Robert Wedderburn. ©*The Trustees of the* British Museum.

property to cultivate food and secure independence, freedom was "not worth possessing." Elsewhere, he connected the traffic of African women in the slave trade to the "slavery" of white Englishwomen in cotton factories, blaming both "slaveries" on "Parliament men." More shockingly still, in a pamphlet addressed to abolitionist M.P. Henry Brougham, Wedderburn announced that he had "always considered, [that] the condition of slaves was far superior to that of European labourers."[34]

Whether his comment reflected a belief that enslaved West Indians were better off than English workers, or merely functioned as a rhetorical flourish, it would seem to imply that comparisons between white workers and enslaved people did not always preclude a genuine concern for the latter. In Wedderburn's case, they stemmed from his close ties to radicalized artisans, his personal encounters with poverty among both Black and white Londoners, and his desire to establish solidarity among these variously oppressed groups. This is not to say that white slavery metaphors could not also be used to undermine or blunt the impact of abolitionists' attacks on the institution of holding human beings in property, a tendency we will see numerous examples of in what follows. But it does suggest that the pro- or antislavery valence of white slavery metaphors depended heavily on context, including who was wielding them and for what ends. Rather than constituting a rejection of abolitionism, Wedderburn's use of such a metaphor in his letter to Brougham may have reflected his growing awareness of the interconnectedness of global systems of capital, labor, and property that relied on the domination and exploitation of workers, whether enslaved or free.[35]

Early Radical Ideology and the Reconsideration of Property Rights

A deeper look into early radical ideology further reveals how even some of those who criticized abolitionists and resorted to white slavery metaphors developed an analysis that convincingly situated slavery and the slave trade in a global matrix of empire, finance, and economic self-interest. John Thelwall was perhaps the foremost intellectual in the LCS; the son of a merchant family fallen on hard times, he had apprenticed as a tailor but also had received training in medicine and law. In a 1795 treatise published in his periodical, the *Tribune*, Thelwall blamed both the ongoing wars with France and the perpetuation of the slave trade on a "compact" between the West India interest, government contractors, and politicians who maintained their seats in Parliament through the antidemocratic system of "borough-mongering" (winning seats in gerrymandered districts with few if any eligible voters). Singling out Prime Minister William Pitt, he blamed parliamentary leaders for giving lip service to abolishing the slave trade while failing to pass legislation against it, despite the "almost unanimous wish" of the British people. Elsewhere, perhaps influenced by a 1787 pamphlet authored by Cugoano, he connected the persistence of the slave trade to a specific critique of commercial relations under the emerging conditions of financial capitalism. Like other radical thinkers in the republican tradition, Thelwall praised free trade when it was conducted in a "fair and liberal spirit." But he distinguished between that commercial activity which constituted a "fair and equitable exchange" and that which constituted a "monopoly," or what Thelwall labeled "Speculation-Commerce." A new commercial-financial class, Thelwall feared, based on the circulation of currency and credit rather than commodities, was "now riveting the equally intolerable chains of corruption and influence." Under the latter, "almost all the inhabitants of the universe are rendered, as it were, the saleable commodities of a few," even if the "open barter" of human beings appeared only in the "infamous African slave-trade."[36]

Thelwall's main criticism of the emerging system of financial-mercantile capitalism, that it turned people into "commodities," thus anticipated one of the most powerful arguments later adopted by abolitionists, that slavery's institution of owning property in human being was a violation of the natural and moral order. But it also points to another powerful strain of radical thought within the Anglo-American tradition: the critique of economic inequality based on spurious or excessive accumulations of wealth and property. Although John Locke is better known for his robust defense of individual property rights, which he saw as one of the fundamental "natural rights" along with the right to life and liberty, he also argued that the only legitimate property was that created by an individual's own labor, a concept known as the labor theory of property. While economic liberals, including slaveholders, utilized Lockeian ideas in defense of an absolute right to property, working-class radicals and sympathetic political economists interpreted Locke quite differently, extrapolating some vastly different conclusions. First was the labor theory of *value*, the idea that since labor was what imparted value to a finished product, the worker was entitled to a proportionate share of the value. Second, that the worker's labor itself was a form of property, one which could not be alienated from the laborer without his consent. And third, that claims to ownership of certain kinds of property were illegitimate, and could be rejected outright.[37]

Thomas Paine articulated the first and third ideas in what is perhaps his least-known work, *Agrarian Justice*. In *Rights of Man, Part the Second*, Paine had first raised his criticisms of excessive accumulations of property and considered the possibility of government assistance to the poor. But in *Agrarian Justice*, he connected the two ideas in way that he believed comported with republican ideas of both economic equality and respect for property rights, in contrast to an "Agrarian Law," i.e., a forcible redivision and redistribution of landed property. Published in 1795–1796 after his narrow escape from revolutionary France, the scheme was presented by Paine as a moderate alternative to the more radically socialistic ideas like those of François-Nöel Babeuf (known as Gracchus after the ancient Roman progenitors of agrarianism), who attempted a failed "Conspiracy of Equals" in Paris in the year that *Agrarian Justice* was published.[38]

In the late eighteenth century, land was arguably the most important form of wealth in both Europe and the early United States. The key to the wealth and privilege of Europe's hereditary aristocracy, in the United States the widespread availability of cheap land was thought to be a major driver of the economic mobility and "rough equality" that characterized the young nation. At the same time, the right to vote was still dependent on the ownership of land or other property in all of the states of the early U.S. except Vermont, New Hampshire, Georgia, and Kentucky. The accumulation of headrights, land grants, and other landholdings from the colonial period ensured that a handful of families dominated affairs in places like Tidewater Virginia and the Hudson Valley of New York, and rampant speculation in western lands (often seized from Native Americans through deception and/or warfare) kept them out of the reach of those of lesser means. In *Agrarian Justice*, Paine identified the appropriation of land by the powerful as the original source of the "unnatural" distinctions of wealth that led to the creation of a powerful aristocracy and a permanently impoverished underclass. In mankind's "natural state," land had once been "the common property of the human race," but the advent of civilization had resulted in the dispossession of lands held in common "without indemnification" to the original owners. Here, Paine drew a distinction between "natural property," the land, the air, and the water, and "artificial, or acquired property," those improvements that were the product of added labor. Over time, the right to the latter had become "confounded with" the right to the former, resulting in an illegitimate accumulation of

landholdings which led to the creation of a titled nobility and robbed everyone else of their "natural" right to the soil. Large landowners thus owed "on
every principle of justice ... a part of that accumulation back to society."
Since the "improvements" to landed property were inseparable from the land
itself—and since Paine was unwilling to go so far as to advocate the actual
seizure and division of landholdings—he instead proposed the creation of a
"National Fund," in which each citizen would receive a small cash payment
drawn from a tax paid by landowners. Subsequent annual payments after
reaching the age of fifty would provide for security in old age. This would
compensate the landless poor for the historic loss of their original right to the
soil and bring about an "equality of natural property."[39]

The impact of *Agrarian Justice* in the United States was muted; although
several newspapers published excerpts, Paine's scheme likely went too far for
most Americans, and by the 1790s his name had been tarnished by dint of
his association with the French Revolution and his reputation as an atheist.
But many Americans did call for measures promoting social and economic
equality, and some, like Revolutionary veterans Robert Coram of Delaware
and Joel Barlow of Connecticut, invoked the idea of a "social debt" to argue
that some form of compensation, whether land, free public education, or
some other equivalent, was owed to postrevolutionary generations to offset
the unjust appropriations of former times. Some of Barlow's contemporaries, like the Philadelphia physician and revolutionary Benjamin Rush and
the Virginia lawyer St. George Tucker, were among the first to draw connections between the accumulation of large landholdings and the institution of
holding property in human beings. Rush argued that the abolition of slavery would "promote that equal distribution of property, which appears best
calculated to promote the welfare of a Society," while Tucker—a slaveholder
himself and an unlikely but ardent proponent of gradual emancipation—
blamed slavery and the concentration of landholdings in the hands of slave-
owning planters and speculators for sowing "the seeds of an aristocracy."
Neither Tucker's plan for gradual emancipation nor his proposal to limit land
sales to "actual settlers" on "agrarian principles" made much headway, but
Tucker's fellow Virginian, Thomas Jefferson—a much more ambiguous advocate of gradual emancipation—succeeded in passing laws abolishing primo-
geniture and entail in Virginia and banning slavery north of the Ohio River
in the Northwest Ordinance.[40]

Such developments, of course, contained multiple ironies in a nation
where white settlement depended on Native dispossession, and slaveholders

like Jefferson were among the biggest landowners. But in England, where land was still highly concentrated in the hands of a feudal aristocracy, Paine's work was influential enough to serve as the subject of a public debate staged by the LCS. For one British reader, Thomas Spence, *Agrarian Justice* did not go far enough. Spence and his followers, known as the Spencean Philanthropists, called for the outright abolition of private property in land and its substitution by public ownership in "democratic parishes," along with universal suffrage (including for women) and a social guarantee for the unemployed. Spence's call to abolish private landholding was based on his belief that the land's value, and hence the landowner's wealth, had been created by "slaves," who had been "exlude[d] from a share in the soil, [so] that want may compel them to sell their labour for daily bread."[41] But, assuming that Spence was referring to English peasants and wage workers rather than enslaved Africans, the first figure to combine calls for the redistribution of land with a demand to end the enslavement of Africans in the Americas was one of Spence's followers. By 1813, Robert Wedderburn had become a convert to Spence's radical agrarianism. In the six issues of a periodical he edited, *The Axe Laid to Root*, Wedderburn laid out a vision of a slave uprising in Jamaica based on Spencean ideas about land reform and inspired by slave revolts in Haiti and elsewhere. Addressing enslaved Jamaicans directly, Wedderburn counseled them to "above all, mind and keep possession of the land," and recommended that they embark on a coordinated work stoppage by sleeping in an hour late on an appointed day, a tactic similar to that employed by London artisans (and, within a few years, by enslaved workers in the Demerara Rebellion). Elsewhere, Wedderburn charged "landholders" and other "despots" with "wickedly violat[ing] the sacred rights of man," and envisioned a revolt led by West Indian slaves and maroons armed with Spence's pamphlets, who would ultimately bring about a landholding utopia. Wedderburn's background as a Spencean land reformer, then, makes his later comparison (quoted above) between enslaved Africans and European laborers more intelligible, as it anticipated another criticism frequently made by working-class radicals in the period: that without access to land or other productive property, the formerly enslaved would fare little better than they had under slavery.[42]

By the early nineteenth century, then, transatlantic radicals, including some who had been enslaved, had developed a concept of freedom that went far beyond the emerging liberal consensus based on free labor and contract freedom, and the rights to life, liberty, and property envisioned by the more moderate exponents of natural rights theory. For these thinkers, the mere freedom of self-ownership, together with the right to contract with employers for wages, meant little without the corresponding rights to access to the land or other productive property; basic protections in case of accidents, sickness, or old age; and a say in the decisions of government, regardless of wealth or status. In time, radical calls for the recognition of these rights would only grow louder, setting up a conflict with those who focused their reforms more narrowly on slave emancipation, while at the same time challenging the latter to adopt more expansive conceptions of slavery and freedom.

Philadelphia: Slavery, Antislavery, and Radicalism in the Politics of the Early American Republic

As the city at the heart of America's independence movement and a hotbed of early labor activism, Philadelphia was an obvious destination for plebeian radicals, including English democrats, Irish nationalists, and others who fled the crackdown on radicalism in Britain during its wars with France. Strikes had been recorded in Philadelphia as early as the 1760s and continued with some regularity through the Revolution and in the immediate post-Revolutionary years. At the same time, the Quaker City's geographic proximity to southern slave states, its large free Black population, and Pennsylvania's comparatively strong antislavery tradition made Philadelphia a primary site for contestation and conflict over slavery. During the colonial period, nearly half of Philadelphia's artisans had owned slaves, a figure that had, however, dropped precipitously during the immediate pre-Revolutionary years, as enslaved Africans were replaced by the white indentured servants and "redemptioners" who flooded into the city in the 1760s and '70s. In the 1770s, Anthony Benezet and other Philadelphia Quakers organized the country's first formal abolitionist society, the Society for the Relief of Free Negroes Unlawfully Held in Bondage. Known as the Pennsylvania Abolition Society after its reorganization in 1787, the group initially comprised mainly artisans (particularly tailors and shoemakers), shopkeepers, and manufacturers, only later becoming dominated by wealthy merchants, lawyers, and elite politicians. In the meantime, Pennsylvania had become a trailblazer of slave emancipation, passing the nation's first gradual abolition act in 1780.[43]

Before the triumph of the Jeffersonians in 1800, national politics in the new nation were dominated by Washington and Hamilton's Federalists, who coalesced around ideas of a stronger central government with a centralized system of banking and credit, support for manufacturing, economic diversification and protectionism, and a shared consensus that elite men were best fit to rule. Given these antidemocratic tendencies, not to mention the Federalists' hostility toward immigrants in general and Jacobins in particular, it was natural that most of the English and Irish expatriate radicals in the United States would gravitate to the opposition, then coalescing in the form of "democratic-republican" associations and clubs. In Philadelphia, the *Aurora and General Advertiser*, edited by Benjamin Franklin's grandson, Benjamin Franklin Bache, served as the mouthpiece for this opposition. Having been swept up by the revolutionary ferment emanating from France, Bache turned his back on the Philadelphia elite of his birth, and his paper's increasingly radical editorial line earned him the scorn of conservatives and the admiration of Democratic-Republicans in Philadelphia and nationally. The *Aurora* carried the latest news of the revolution in France, published Paine's *Rights of Man* in serial, and attacked slavery, asking readers to consider "the rights of man, without regard to . . . colour or complexion." Citing an understanding of natural rights that included a right to revolution, Bache even went so far as to defend the right of enslaved people to kill their white oppressors in order to gain their freedom.[44]

Bache's successor as editor of the *Aurora* was William Duane, an American-born, Irish-reared transplant to Philadelphia who had joined the LCS while in London and spent time in various parts of the British Empire. Duane's career as a radical editor demonstrates both continuity with the strain of antislavery editorializing begun by his predecessor and the tendency of many northern Democratic-Republicans to temper their antislavery leanings in order to accommodate their southern allies in the Jeffersonian coalition. The Democratic-Republicans' leadership by a succession of southern slave owners and its voting base in a coalition of southern planters with northern artisans and small and "middling" farmers combined to ensure that many northern democrats, Duane included, would sometimes sacrifice their antislavery convictions to the expediencies of national and party unity. As a partisan weapon, however, antislavery could cut both ways; one of Duane's earliest diatribes refocused the antislavery spotlight on Federalist president George Washington. Duane accused Washington of being a "slaveholding tyrant" responsible for holding "FIVE HUNDRED of the HUMAN SPECIES IN SLAVERY" while continuing to enjoy "the FRUITS OF THEIR LABOUR WITHOUT REMUNERATION." Over the next two decades, the *Aurora* took an editorial line that, while it ebbed and flowed with the imperatives of partisan politics, maintained a relatively consistent stance on slavery. Duane defended the abortive slave rebellion in Virginia led by Gabriel Prosser, hailed the abolition of the slave trade in 1807, and argued for the inclusion of African American men as soldiers during the War of 1812. Like most democratic radicals, Duane believed that slavery and democracy were fundamentally incompatible, and yet his comments betray another common trait of early antislavery democrats: a naive faith, often predicated on an underestimation of slaveholders' commitment to maintaining the institution and an overestimation of their goodwill, that slavery would inevitably disappear. It was simply "absurd," he wrote, to imagine that "FREEDOM and SLAVERY can exist long in the same country." While such comments may speak to the sincerity of Duane's antislavery convictions, they also suggest a blithe refusal to recognize the need for concerted and sustained action against the institution.[45]

The *Aurora* also emerged as a champion of Philadelphia's nascent labor movement, and Duane, like other early labor advocates, based his condemnation of slavery largely on its denial of enslaved workers' right to "the fruits of their labour." Throughout his long tenure as editor, the *Aurora* repeatedly insisted that laboring "producers" were menaced not only by Hamiltonian economic policies—particularly innovations like paper currency, a central banking system, and chartered corporations—but by the advent of British-style industrialization, pernicious signs of which were already becoming visible in the Philadelphia of the early nineteenth century. Duane's wing of the Democratic-Republican Party in Philadelphia drew its strength from the working-class Irish and German wards of emerging industrial slums like Northern Liberties and Southwark, and the *Aurora* argued that since "those who acquire support from labor" made up the "greatest number," the policies that ensured the happiness of the laboring majority should prevail.[46] Like other "labor republicans," however, Duane was suspicious of what was already being touted as "free labor." His skepticism stemmed in part from his experience as an administrator in colonial India, where the British East India Company and other colonial authorities utilized the labor of cheap indentured servants and contract laborers from around the subcontinent and elsewhere in South Asia. To Duane, the British government's importation of Malaysian foremen to oversee so-called free workers in Ceylon was little different from its use of Scottish troops to suppress rebellions in Ireland, and its importation of South Asian indentured servants to offset the shortage of West African slaves in the Caribbean amounted to little more than an illicit "*trade in free labourers*!!!" Although Duane's descriptions of British East Asia trafficked in racial and ethnic stereotypes—contrasting the "meek" and "inoffensive" inhabitants of the Indian subcontinent with the "hardy, robust, and unsusceptible African"—undergirding them all was the suspicion that what British authorities labeled "free labor" was anything but free.[47]

Duane's long and well-documented career as a partisan editor makes him particularly susceptible to charges of inconsistency and hypocrisy on slavery, and his antislavery convictions sometimes seemed to ebb and flow with the exigencies of democratic politics. Unlike Edward Rushton, who criticized Washington and Jefferson alike, Duane exaggerated the extent of Jefferson's commitment to antislavery and ignored the founding father's racism. His advocacy in favor of enlisting Black troops to fight against the British in the War of 1812 was predicated on deeply engrained ideas of white superiority, and following Jefferson's lead, he evinced a naive conviction that the "diffusion" of enslaved people across America's vast territories would hasten the demise of the institution. At the same time, however, conflicts over slavery, race, and emancipation in the Early Republic were often highly localized, and they rarely fell neatly along party lines. In New York, Federalists led the push for gradual emancipation and won the votes of most eligible free Black voters. But slaveholding Federalists in the South were at least as determined in their defense of human bondage, while many Democratic-Republicans in Pennsylvania and other northern states continued to be outspoken in their attacks on the institution. Moreover, both parties frequently resorted to racist appeals, sometimes even while simultaneously courting the votes of eligible free Blacks.[48]

Duane's willingness to sacrifice principle for politics, however, was not unbounded. Perhaps his strongest statements against slavery came toward the end of his long career, in response to the most aggressive act of slaveholder expansionism to the point: the effort to introduce slavery in the new state of Missouri. In the aftermath of the Missouri Compromise of 1820, which legalized slavery in Missouri while prohibiting it north of the 36°30' line, Duane and his protégé Stephen Simpson turned decisively against the Virginia slaveholder president James Monroe, whom they derided as a "*slave president,*" and urged the election of DeWitt Clinton, "a foe to slavery." Framing the election as an opportunity to "*record your vote against the curse of slavery,*" the *Aurora* failed to prevent Monroe's reelection, but helped to unseat Pennsylvania's incumbent governor and replace him with Joseph Heister, who had voted against the Compromise while in Congress.[49]

Democratic-Republican and radical opposition to slavery in Missouri could be, indeed often has been, portrayed as primarily an expression of a commitment to whiteness and *herrenvolk* democracy—keeping the territories free of enslaved people, as well as slavery. But a deeper understanding of how radicals in the Age of Revolution conceived of access to land as an essential precondition for achieving a democratic, egalitarian society, together with their status as the inheritors of an antislavery tradition that reached across the Atlantic and stretched back at least to Paine, suggests that there was more at stake for these plebeian political thinkers than whiteness or mere self-interest. Moreover, by linking these antislavery and egalitarian traditions to the self-interest of large majorities of northern voters, radicals like Duane hit on what eventually became a winning formula for attacking slavery as a political issue, despite the serious obstacles to abolition posed by the Constitution, the profitability of slavery, and the racism of white Americans. Another generation would elapse before an incident like the Missouri Crisis, which Jefferson famously referred to as a "firebell in the night," would bring ordinary northerners' interest in free soil and free labor into direct conflict with the institution of slavery. But in the interim, the rise of a new brand of immediate abolitionism would challenge the inheritors of the Paineite tradition, forcing them to confront their ambiguities and shortcomings over the institution. At the same time, an explicitly political movement dedicated to the uplift of those who labored would continue to develop and refine ideas about labor, land, and property.

CHAPTER 2

"A Very Intimate Connexion": The Working Men's Parties, Equal Rights Democrats, and Antislavery Immediatism

In the early days of January 1831, "W" was inspired to take pen to paper and send a letter to the editors of the *Liberator*, the new abolitionist newspaper published by William Lloyd Garrison and Isaac Knapp. Abolitionists had not yet "perceived it," W believed, but there was "a very intimate connexion between the interests of the working men's party and your own." "*You* are striving to excite the attention of your countrymen to the injustice of holding their fellow men in bondage, and depriving them of the fruits of their toil," he wrote. "*We* are aiming at a similar object, only in application to another portion of our fellow men." According to W, the similarities did not end there. Both the chattel slavery of people of African descent and the oppression of free white workers were rooted in the same historic foundations, now lost to the mists of time, that enabled "a fortunate *few* among our ancestors" to claim "the right to command the labor and services of the mass of their fellow countrymen" as villains, vassals, serfs, slaves, and other unfree laborers. The passage of time had degraded the intelligence and morality of those who worked with their hands, while hardening the associations between manual labor and dependence—just as abolitionists believed that the experience of enslavement had left most African Americans impoverished and ignorant, thereby feeding unfounded assumptions about Black inferiority. Both the abolitionist and Working Men's movements, "W" concluded, sought to "enlighten" their fellow countrymen by means of education and appeals to morality—and failing that, they could resort to the ballot box.[1]

"W" was Samuel Whitcomb, a New England–born education reformer who served as the corresponding secretary of the Working Men's Party of

Dorchester, an industrializing suburb outside of Boston. Garrison's response, which came in the form of a lengthy article on the "Working Classes," was cool, even dismissive. Although Garrison found "nothing to which we object" in Whitcomb's letter, he demurred that "it remains to be seen how far we shall agree in the mode of redress." The abolitionist appeared to blame laborers themselves for their predicament, suggesting that their present discontent was caused by their envy of the wealthy, and warning that those who spread the "pernicious doctrine" of class conflict were "the worst enemies of the people." The article prompted an angry reply from Whitcomb, who objected above all to Garrison's suggestion that inequality was an inescapable feature of republican society. Garrison's second response, published in the *Liberator*'s fifth issue, was scarcely more conciliatory than his previous one; he claimed that Whitcomb had "misrepresented his views," and he quoted Edmund Burke to the effect that those who advocated the "levelling" of society only "pervert[ed] the natural order of things."[2]

The correspondence between Garrison and Whitcomb, along with similar snippets of the ongoing dialogue between abolitionists and labor reformers, has been used to paint a picture of the relationship between the two movements as essentially antagonistic: abolitionists, it has been argued, helped to validate an emerging capitalist hegemony based on liberal understandings of self-ownership, an aversion to class politics, and a narrow vision of free labor, while labor reformers prioritized the abolition of "white slavery" to the exclusion of any genuine concern for the enslaved laborers of the South.[3] Although there are important truths at the heart of these interpretations, a more detailed look at the critical decade between 1827 and 1837—which witnessed both the rise of Garrisonian immediatism and the first efforts by workers to organize politically—shows that the conversation did not end with Garrison's curt dismissal in 1831.

While the exchange between Garrison and Whitcomb in some ways captures how ideological misalignments and individual personalities combined to estrange labor reformers and abolitionists from one another, other factors posed far more serious obstacles to the development of labor abolitionism in the 1820s and '30s. As numerous studies on the relationship between slavery and capitalism have shown, both industrialization in Great Britain and New England and America's rise to economic superpower status during these years were fueled by cotton grown by enslaved labor. By 1831, the year of the Nat Turner Rebellion and the first issue of the *Liberator*, the U.S. was producing some 354 million bales of cotton annually, or 43 percent of the world market share.[4] Although it is possible to exaggerate the degree of symbiosis that existed between the emerging industrial capitalism of the North and the slave–cotton plantation economy of the South in this period—and while only a tiny minority of northern workers toiled as factory operatives in massive new textile mills like those financed by the Boston Associates at Lowell, Massachusetts—it is clear that slave-grown cotton was a key driver of the economic changes that transformed America's economy, along with the lives of thousands of northern workers, during this period. Less clear is what these men and women (women made up the majority of employees in the new textile manufactories that sprang up in New England) thought about their connection to slavery. Female mill workers at Lowell sang songs that included the lyric "Oh! I cannot be a slave / I will not be a slave" during the famous strikes there, but other studies have shown that the "mill girls" were among the most likely northern workers to sign antislavery petitions and join antislavery societies.[5]

Cotton's preeminence also provided the rationale for the Democratic Party's successful and long-running coalition, one based on an alliance between northern artisans and yeomen and southern slave-owning "producers." Although the election of Andrew Jackson in 1828 was initially opposed by many labor radicals, as well as by more moderate labor leaders with roots in the National Republican and Federalist parties, most eventually followed their constituents into the Jacksonian Democratic coalition, often tempering or subordinating their antislavery convictions in the process. During these same years, the proliferation of pseudoscientific ideas about race and the spread of political participation and so-called universal suffrage gave rise to a growing sense of class and national identity based on white supremacy.[6] This confluence of developments had dramatic and sometimes catastrophic consequences for both enslaved people in the South and free Blacks in the antebellum North. Rather than the gradual dying out of slavery and the dispersion, assimilation, or removal that many in the founding generation had envisioned, the enslaved population swelled to more than 2 million by 1830, and between 1815 and 1860 some 1 million enslaved people were forcibly displaced from the upper South to South Carolina, Georgia, and the newer states of the Cotton Kingdom via a revitalized internal slave trade. Northern states passed, often by popular majorities, exclusionary laws such as Ohio's 1804 and 1807 Black Laws and New York's racist 1821 state constitution, which all but barred Black men from voting. Anti-Black and antiabolitionist "riots" were another inescapable feature of the period, and while historians have demonstrated that many of these were led and organized by "gentlemen of property and standing," others, such as the Cincinnati riots of 1829, were fueled by working-class racism in tandem with fears about competition over working-class jobs.[7]

Nonetheless, working-class and labor voices also provided some of the loudest—sometimes the only—opposition to the frequent anti-Black pogroms of the period. While some pro-labor voices deployed the ubiquitous wage slavery language to ridicule or forestall abolitionism, others used it to highlight how both slavery and exploitative wage relationships robbed the worker of the "right to the fruits of their labor." A labor newspaper, the *Working Man's Advocate*, offered one of the very few public defenses of the period's most significant slave revolt, the Nat Turner Rebellion in Virginia, privileging solidarity based on oppression rather than on skin color. More important, and more frequently overlooked, is the fact that working-class reformers in this period—sometimes simultaneously or working in tandem with abolitionists—helped develop a set of ideas that would eventually form the foundation of political antislavery. Among these were ideas about the superiority of free over slave labor, the desirability of access to land free from the deleterious effects of slaveholding, the threat to free speech and democracy posed by an aristocratic Slave Power, and the latent antislavery powers that lay hidden in the Constitution. While none of these ideas were new in the 1830s, more radically inclined labor reformers, together with a small group of heterodox abolitionists, sometimes paired them with demands for wealth redistribution, government intervention, and/or the abolition of certain forms of property altogether, especially property in land and human beings. Together, these strains formed the basis of a labor abolitionist ideology—one that, while it contained numerous contradictions and ebbed and flowed with political developments as well as reformers' varying degrees of commitment, eventually led many labor reformers and working-class northerners into the antislavery political coalition of the 1850s.

Abolitionists, Labor Reformers, and the Many Uses of "Wage Slavery"

The period after 1815—the end of the Napoleonic Wars in Europe and the War of 1812 in North America—witnessed sweeping changes in the nature of the economies and societies of both the United States and Britain. In the latter, industrialization was already well underway, fueled in part by imports of slave-grown cotton from the southern United States, which provided the raw material for Britain's textile mills, the first major industry to employ steam power on a wide scale, along with new machines like the power loom and the spinning jenny. While propelling the explosive growth of industrial cities like Manchester, such technologies displaced traditional handloom weaving and other trades, and many workers found themselves reduced to dependence on employers and replaced by unskilled factory operatives, often children. Whether despite or because of their transatlantic ties to cotton slavery, and whether out of emulation of or bitterness toward the British abolitionist movement, which was then heading toward its ultimate triumph in the Slavery Abolition Act in 1833, British factory workers and those who took up their cause commonly referred to such workers as "slaves."[8] Perhaps following the lead of Britain's best-known radical, William Cobbett (who rebranded himself as "the Poor Man's Friend" after returning to Britain from America, where he had distinguished himself as a conservative thorn in the side of radicals like Thomas Paine and William Duane), many British labor reformers attacked the abolitionists as hypocrites who cared more for enslaved Blacks in the distant West Indies than for suffering workers at home. Although, as in America, abolitionism continued to garner strong support from working-class petitioners and spokesmen, British reformers across the spectrum, from the free thought firebrand Richard Carlile to middle-class parliamentarians Richard Oastler and Michael Sadler to Chartists like Bronterre O'Brien and Feargus O'Connor, relied heavily on wage or white slavery metaphors.[9]

Parliamentary testimony on British "factory slaves" that led to the passage of reforms between 1829 and 1833 provided riveting details about the abuses of the new economic regime, as well as fodder for working-class reformers in the U.S., who were alarmed by the arrival of the "factory system" in places like Waltham and Lowell in Massachusetts and Pawtucket in Rhode Island. Already buffeted by the revival of trade with Britain in 1815 and the Panic of 1819 (caused in part by speculation in cotton and western lands), even those apart from the small minority of American workers who toiled in manufactories felt threatened by the advent of British-style industrialization. The increasing reliance on mechanization and the division of labor, the decline of paternalistic labor relationships like those between master and apprentice, and the growing numbers of skilled workers who remained trapped in the status of journeyman or wage worker all threatened the livelihoods of those who worked with their hands as well as the ideal of republican independence that was central to male artisans' sense of themselves as citizens and men. In response to these changes, workers organized a series of Working Men's parties between 1827 and 1830. The most prominent were in Philadelphia, New York, and Boston, but dozens of organizations calling themselves Working Men's parties, "mechanics and farmers associations," and similar appellations emerged in such far-flung places as Woodstock, Vermont, and Zanesville, Ohio. They held meetings and rallies, published accounts of their proceedings, elected leaders and officers, and nominated their own candidates for office—sometimes sharing a ticket with, but just as often challenging, the reigning Jacksonian Democrats. More than fifty newspapers in fifteen states supported their cause, with many serving as the parties' official organs. Although they differed on issues like the desirability of protective tariffs, and although they never coalesced into a national movement, their demands were similar everywhere: opposition to banks and other forms of special privilege and monopoly; support for mechanics' lien laws and the expansion of the suffrage; opposition to convict labor and imprisonment for debt; and demands for free public education and access to land.[10]

In the minds of these "artisan republicans," the over-competitive, race-to-the-bottom market for cheap wage labor reduced artisans and other "freemen" to a slave-like state of dependence on employers. In a series of influential lectures and pamphlets, the Providence, Rhode Island, carpenter and labor agitator Seth Luther seized on British factory testimony to warn his fellow laborers that the slave-like conditions of industrializing Britain were menacing American workers, often adding details from New England mill towns as evidence that "factory slavery" had already arrived on American shores. In 1836, in one of the period's several "coffin handbills," striking tailors in New York declared, in response to a court decision that robbed them of their right to organize, that the "Freemen of the North are now on a level with the slaves of the South!"[11]

Indeed, reformers in the 1820s and '30s spoke of an entire range of "slaveries" that threatened to ensnare their fellow Americans, including the "slavery" of imprisonment for debt, the "slavery of poverty," or the prospect of being worked "like a slave." One might be enslaved to ignorance, or a slave to the temptations of drink. Even Maria W. Stewart, the pioneering African American abolitionist and feminist, complained that the economic position and work conditions of free Blacks in the North were "but little better" than those faced by the enslaved.[12] Those who labored for a living tended to view slavery in the terms expressed by Langton Byllesby, a Philadelphia-born printer and inventor who argued in his influential *Observations on the*

Sources of Unequal Wealth (1826) that "The very essence of slavery is in being compelled to labour, while the proceeds of that labour is taken and enjoyed by another . . . therefore, in proportion as any one is compelled to relinquish those proceeds without compensation, he approximates that condition, however specious the form or process by which it is done, or the appearance of option whether to labour or not."[13]

Other working-class reformers, however, rejected wage slavery comparisons. Some simply refused to countenance the view that white workers were as "degraded" as enslaved people of African descent, but others, like "Truth Teller," "an intelligent workingman" and correspondent to the *Liberator*, discerned the substantive differences that gave the lie to wage slavery comparisons. Truth Teller saw "a wide, and irreconcilable difference" between the free worker "in the worst possible circumstances, and the most highly favored slave ever written down as property." The latter distinction in particular, Truth Teller believed, placed the free worker "almost infinitely above the slave, in everything which relates to humanity." Other labor reformers took a different tack. Defending the *Liberator*'s exposé of the "evil of slavery," members of the Working Men's Party assembled in New York's Military Hall argued that it should prompt reformers to action "on behalf of the oppressed white man, [as well] as in aid of the enslaved negro."[14]

In the future, such claims to be in favor of the abolition of "all slavery"—both wage and chattel—would grow more common among American labor reformers. Such proclamations, as we will see, were made with varying degrees of sincerity or disingenuousness, but they also suggest that wage slavery rhetoric could be repurposed for legitimately antislavery ends. One abolitionist who did so quite effectively was William Goodell. An evangelical convert to abolitionism who grew up poor in Connecticut and suffered from financial difficulties throughout his life, Goodell had been an early supporter of labor reform, printing a letter protesting the hours of labor for Rhode Island mill workers. There was "a natural sympathy between the Southern Slave-master and the northern Aristocrat," Goodell believed, since both shared in the belief that "the working-men of the North are on a level with the slaves of the South." By contrast, what Goodell called "the industrious middle classes—the hardy yeomanry and mechanics" would prove to be the country's salvation, since "the laboring people of the North *alone*" comprised "the only *real* democracy in our republic." Goodell rejected the idea that wage workers were more oppressed than enslaved Blacks, but he acknowledged that factory conditions warranted "investigation," and he expressed sympathy for the

idea that, since slavery was synonymous with "human degradation and suffering," it was natural that labor reformers would turn to such comparisons
"as a figure of rhetoric." More dramatically, he emphasized how the rhetorical
could become literal, seizing on comments by slave-owning politicians like
John Calhoun and George McDuffie to suggest that it made little difference
to slaveholding aristocrats whether their workforces were Black or white. In
a series of articles addressed to working-class readers, Goodell warned "the
laboring classes, especially the operatives in the manufactories . . . to *beware*
how they sanction the doctrine of unrequited labor," for "the aristocracy that
grinds the colored man will soon break over the distinction of color." If the
"aristocrats" of the North and South had their way, northern workingmen
might one day be literally enslaved.[15]

While such views may have been outside the abolitionist mainstream, they
were not unique to Goodell. At the American Anti-Slavery Society (AASS)
convention in 1836, Gerrit Smith, who would soon join Goodell in organizing
the antislavery Liberty Party, warned white workers that they should not "flat-
ter themselves" that racial distinctions "will long continue to be the ground
of enslavement." Elsewhere, "An Operative" denounced the "sad spectacle"
of southern slaveholders who claimed to be republicans but were in practice
"nothing but aristocrats," while "A Democrat of the Old School" warned that
"slavery in its strictest sense, is not confined to any particular color of the skin,
nation or people; it exists wherever there is 'tribute paid to Ceasar [*sic*].'" A
group of Rhode Island abolitionists went so far as to warn that if slaveholders
had their way, "uneducated laboring people and operatives" might be "shot
down as dogs in the streets." In Cincinnati, James G. Birney devoted an entire
front page of his newspaper, the *Philanthropist*, to broadcasting McDuffie's
unflattering comparison of free workers to slaves, agreeing with Goodell that
"the hope of the republic" lay with the "working class," who would never agree
to the idea that the "*employer* ought to *own* the employed." The *Philanthropist* supported striking tailors and seamstresses and proclaimed sympathy
with labor, even as it prioritized "the heavier oppressions of slavery" over "the
lighter burdens that press on the free."[16]

Meanwhile, William Lloyd Garrison was reconsidering his earlier rejection of labor reform. As early as 1832, he announced his support for ten-hour
laws and other prolabor measures, although the *Liberator* would continue to
butt heads regularly with labor reformers over the next few decades. But while
abolitionists often clashed with labor activists and with one another, one thing
that immediatists like Garrison, political abolitionists like Goodell and Birney,

and labor abolitionists like Truth Teller could agree on was the centrality of the chattel principle—the claim to hold property in other human beings. In the evolving capitalist society of America in the 1830s, with its unregulated markets, a high level of speculative economic activity, and the acquisitive, "go ahead" spirit so often commented on by foreign visitors, the question of what could and not be commoditized, bought, and sold in the marketplace was an issue of increasing concern.[17] Were the abstract instruments of finance, banking, and credit, traded in New York, London, and Amsterdam, a form of property? Were distant parcels of land on the public domain, purchased sight unseen by speculators and sold at a profit? Were human beings forcibly imported from Africa property, along with their descendants?

For most abolitionists, including Garrison, the answer to the latter was an emphatic "no," but their emphasis on "property in man" lent itself to an understanding of "self-ownership," rather than economic independence, as the defining condition of freedom. A minority, however, began to discern connections between their own assault on slaveholders' claims to property and the conflict between the propertied and the propertyless emphasized by reformers like Whitcomb and Goodell. Similarly, although most labor reformers continued to understand slavery in the terms expressed by Byllesby—as a system of oppressed and unrequited labor, rather than of property in man—many also understood that slavery exacerbated what Byllesby critiqued as the concentration of "unequal wealth" in the hands of a few. Where property was too unevenly distributed, Whitcomb wrote, a few could control "the labors and earnings of the multitude," a state of affairs made possible by the "perpetuation of the institution of slavery."[18] Conversely, defenses of slavery were frequently made in terms of a defense of absolute property rights, with similarly unequivocal implications for the relationship between capital and labor. As Charles Follen, an abolitionist and liberal German émigré, put it, "Those who hold property in men, would persuade all those who hold property in things, that all attacks upon slavery are virtually assaults upon property; and that instead of trying to convert the slaves of the South to free laborers, the men of property should combine to convert all laborers into slaves." Even more conservative abolitionists, like Edmund Quincy, recognized that "it is the idea that the abolitionists are attacking property, that arouses every thing that is sordid and selfish in human nature to oppose our efforts."[19]

Although the divergence of interests between workers who owned little or no property and slaveholders who claimed to own property in their workers would only widen as time went on, the notion of class conflict between northern workers and slave owners would most often be merely hinted at, rather than fully exploited, in antislavery literature. But during the 1830s, antislavery labor reformers along with a small but influential group of heterodox abolitionists, including Goodell, would begin to lay the groundwork for a political movement based on identifying the interests of the masses of ordinary northerners with those of the enslaved. Ideas about property—in land, labor, and human beings—would be central to the appeals of both groups.

The Philadelphia Working Men: Republican Free
Soil and the Political Economy of Free Labor

It was no accident that the first self-consciously working-class political movement in the United States originated in Philadelphia. There, a robust tradition of strike activity, a strong sense of class identity based on ideals of republicanism, artisan independence, and "producerism," and an injection of radical democratic and labor ideology from English-speaking immigrants set the stage for a fusion of trade union activism with political organizing. After the failure of a carpenters' strike for a ten-hour working day in 1827, painters, glaziers, shoemakers, and other tradesmen joined forces to found the Mechanics' Union of Trade Associations (MUTA), the nation's first multitrade union. In May 1828, MUTA began to pass resolutions to nominate candidates "to represent the interests of the working classes" in the upcoming November elections, and the nation's first labor party, the Working Men's Party of Philadelphia, was born.[20]

No figure embodies the radicalism of Philadelphia's early labor movement better than William Heighton, an English immigrant shoemaker who helped establish the Working Men's Party and who edited and published the *Mechanic's Free Press*, the nation's first labor newspaper. Strongly influenced by the political philosopher John Gray and other early English socialists, Heighton injected a new language of class consciousness into the city's artisan milieu, casting stark distinctions between "producers" and "non-producers"—terms he used interchangeably with "working classes" and "capitalists." Heighton articulated an unequivocal and potentially radical articulation of the labor theory of value, the idea that all wealth was "the *sole* and *exclusive* product of LABOUR." Although he was a leading figure in both the Working Men's political party and MUTA, Heighton believed that neither political solutions nor trade unionism could supply the answer to workingmen's woes "so long

as the present wretched system of commerce is suffered to continue." A radical restructuring of society, with the substitution of cooperation for competition and the redistribution of wealth in the form of both higher wages and
access to landed property, were the keys to maintaining America's republican
traditions against the encroachments of a new aristocracy.[21]

Although nearly the entirety of its run appeared before Garrison's *Liberator* signaled the arrival of antislavery immediatism, Heighton's antipa-
thy toward slavery and sympathy for abolition ran throughout the pages of
the *Mechanic's Free Press*. Quoting a proponent of gradual emancipation in
North Carolina, the paper expressed its approval of the idea that the "slave
system" was a "radical evil . . . founded in injustice and cruelty" and editori-
alized that "every true laborer in the cause of philanthropy" should sympa-
thize with the cause of abolition.[22] Heighton reprinted antislavery poems and
parables from abolitionist Benjamin Lundy and antislavery reformer Robert
Dale Owen (son of the famous English socialist) and reserved some of his
harshest criticism for the trade in enslaved human beings and those who participated in it.[23] The *Mechanic's Free Press* also maintained an amicable, and
at times supportive, relationship with abolitionists. The paper ran a glowing
biography of Lundy, as well as a notice lauding a recent speech by a relatively
unknown William Lloyd Garrison, then working as an assistant on Lundy's
newspaper *Genius of Universal Emancipation*. In May 1830, after Garrison
was imprisoned in Baltimore for his abolitionist activities, the *Press* protested
the young abolitionist's arrest and jailing, arguing that his only crime had
been to attack "the *inhuman traffic of dealing in human flesh.*"[24] A correspondent urged Heighton not to let the matter drop, adding that since "your paper
is professedly designed to break down those distinctions that have arisen in
our country so inimical to republicanism," there was a "peculiar propriety"
in its objection to slavery. In a postscript, the letter writer urged the paper to
use its influence to "enlist the working men of Baltimore in the cause of the
oppressed" slaves; after all, he pointed out, hadn't northern workers "known
enough of oppression themselves to properly feel for others?"[25]

Although the answer to that question remained unclear, the correspondence and editorial line of the *Mechanic's Free Press* seemed to answer in the
affirmative. Anticipating later critiques the linked the Money Power to the
Slave Power, one of the *Press*'s correspondents accused those who advocated
only modest reforms to the nation's banking system of "reasoning like the
slaveholders of the south," who "admit that slavery is an evil, but yet decline
to make an effort to rid themselves of it." Citing the efforts of abolitionists

as an example that workingmen might follow, "Vertical" reflected that "the men who first engaged in the cause of the helpless Blacks" had once been "as obscure and destitute of influence in the community, as the generality of the working people now are," but concluded optimistically that they had "succeeded in obtaining their object in so far that none but slaveholders doubt of their final success." If "Vertical" was somewhat premature in reaching this conclusion, he nonetheless indicated a possible path of solidarity and cooperation with, rather than mutual exclusion from, the abolitionist movement.[26] At times, the *Press* seemed to endorse wage slavery comparisons, but it seldom did so in a way that undermined abolitionists' efforts to eradicate chattel slavery. One article, reprinted from the Boston *Working Man's Advocate*, revisited John Adams's comment describing the difference between free laborers and slaves as "a custom of speech," and concluded that the former president had been correct: so-called free labor was really a form of "fraud," since the choice between accepting an employer's wages or dying from starvation lacked the voluntary nature of true freedom. But directly below this, Heighton placed another article that attacked the domestic slave trade, depicting slave traders as "inhuman monsters" and demanding that Congress pass a law against "this wholesale traffic in human flesh." Whether its placement was deliberate or not, the article offered a quiet rebuke to wage slavery arguments; after all, no northern mechanic, its author pointed out, had to live in fear of being preyed on by "vampyres" who schemed to kidnap them and sell them into slavery.[27]

These antislavery positions were sometimes informed by Heighton's freethinking religious bent, which stood in stark contrast to the evangelical fervor of the so-called Second Great Awakening that informed many of the reformers of the period, including most abolitionists and many workingmen.[28] The *Mechanic's Free Press* risked further identifying the Working Men's movement with religious "infidelity" by devoting column space to the views of Frances Wright and Robert Owen, as well as those of an unknown contributor who went so far as to suggest that "European theologians" deserved opprobrium for using Christianity to keep enslaved Blacks "meekly obedient and satisfied with their wretchedness." Another article favorably contrasted Islamic laws regarding slavery with the slave codes of the South and concluded that "professed Christians may here learn a striking lesson of *justice*" from Muslim countries.[29] Occasionally, the *Mechanic's Free Press* resorted to the kind of stereotypical depictions of African Americans that were ubiquitous in the period's print culture. But in more than one instance, it did so in a way that upended white assumptions about Blacks' alleged inferiority: in one example, a "New York Negro" got the best of a Kentucky slaveholder, thereby demonstrating the "republican principle" that "gives a Black man as much liberty as a white one," while an anecdote about "Tom," an enslaved man accused of receiving stolen goods, was turned into an object lesson on the theft inherent in owning human beings.[30]

Opposition to slavery also dovetailed with one of antebellum workers' main concerns: access to land. As we have seen, prolabor radicals like William Duane and Stephen Simpson were vocal in their opposition to slavery's extension in the Missouri Crisis of 1819–1820, even to the point of abandoning political loyalties. In the same issue of the *Liberator* where Garrison had published Samuel Whitcomb's letter to the editor, the abolitionist had included an unattributed reprint of a letter Whitcomb had written to the *Boston Yankee* in 1819, railing against the prospect of slavery's further expansion.[31] Like political antislavery in general, labor reformers' opposition to slavery's territorial expansion was a mixture of principle and self-interest. While most Euro-Americans cherished the idea of abundant land for settlement in the West, artisans and laborers in Eastern cities were perhaps more invested than most in the idea of the West as a "safety-valve," with freely available land ripe for settlement and farming (at the expense, however, of Native Americans, a reality eastern labor reformers seem to have given little thought to). Regardless of how many actually settled there, the idea of readily available western land held a powerful allure for eastern wage workers—not only could they escape the competition, low wages, and cramped quarters of crowded cities, they could recover their independence by becoming self-sufficient tillers of the soil, beholden to no one. Consequently, although practical bread-and-butter demands for wages and conditions ranked highest among the priorities of the Working Men's parties and trade union organizations of the 1820s and '30s, calls for access to land followed close behind. In October 1828, the *Mechanic's Free Press* published a petition drawn up by the Philadelphia Working Men's Party urging Congress to place "all the Public Lands, without the delay of sales, within the reach of the people at large, by the right of a title to occupancy only." All men, the petitioners held, had "naturally, a birth-right in the soil"; if this was not recognized, "they may be deprived of life, liberty, and the pursuit of happiness." Such a measure to secure the public lands of the West from the grasping hands of speculators and slaveholders, the Working Men's Party declared, was "the only effectual prevention of future monopoly."[32] In 1830, the *Mechanic's Free Press* inaugurated a regular series of articles urging "industrious mechanics with small available capitals" to pool their resources and leave the city to become proprietors of the soil in small, self-sustaining communities, organized on a "semi-co-operative principle." Such colonies, the articles' anonymous author explained, would allow the wage worker to escape from the tyranny of banks and place him "beyond the reach of fluctuating markets, and above the fear of 'want of employment,'" thus enabling him to live "under the shadow of his vine and fig tree, in the enjoyment of *all* the fruits of his own Labour." And in 1834, the National Trades' Union, one of the first efforts to form a national or "general" association of trade unions, included among the resolutions made at its first national convention that "every citizen" had a "just claim to an equitable portion" of the public lands, and called for their distribution to "actual settlers."[33]

To these radical early iterations of free soil, Philadelphia's Working Men's Party added a radical vision of free labor, one that combined the classical political economy of Adam Smith and David Ricardo, the homegrown free labor economics of Mathew and Henry Carey, ideas drawn from English socialists like John Gray and Robert Owen, and Heighton's emphasis on producerism and class conflict.[34] Stephen Simpson was the son of a Bank of the United States official and an ardent anti-Jacksonian who nevertheless became William Duane's protégé and the Working Men's Party candidate for Congress in 1830. Simpson was labeled "the American Cobbett" by those who admired his fiery eloquence, but his antislavery stance and sophisticated, historically grounded critique of inequality put him more in line with John Thelwall or the Paine of *Agrarian Justice*. Simpson made clear his distaste for slavery in an early poem entitled simply "Slavery Denounced," which depicted the institution as a "brutal" form of "torture" as well as a "stain" and a "curse" on the young nation.[35] Like the earlier generation of radicals, Simpson associated economic inequality with land monopoly and slavery, and he blamed longstanding associations between manual labor and servile status for labor's current degradation. "To labour for another, even among us of the 19th century, is held as disreputable," Simpson observed in his 1831 treatise on political economy, *The Working Man's Manual*. From ancient Egypt, Greece, and Rome, to the feudal barons of Europe in the Middle Ages, to the present-day rule of slave owners in the South and of "Capital, Banks, and Monopoly" in the North, laboring for someone else had always been associated with servility and dependence. What all these forms had in common was a relationship marked by "power, instead of justice." Wage labor was no different in this respect, since the power relations that determined and regulated wages stemmed not from the invisible hand of the market but from "masters, not less absolute than a South Carolina slave-holder." Since, as Locke had argued, "labor was the parent of all wealth," it was "self-evident" that the "industry" of the individual ought to determine its distribution, rather than "laws that have their origin in despotism, and customs founded upon the antiquated relations of master and slave."[36]

In a detailed analysis of the economics of a Louisiana sugar plantation published in the *Mechanic's Free Press*, Simpson pushed this comparison between slavery and wage labor still further. Reminding readers that the planter's "slaves are his working men," he argued that it was the labor of enslaved workers that added value to "the inert and passive mass of capital" and created the slave owner's profits. But Simpson rejected the wage slavery comparisons that had become central to radical labor discourse. While such direct comparisons between manufacturing workers and slaves or serfs may have made sense in Britain, whose factory workers made up "a *serf* class," they did not apply to the United States, where "our operatives are *freemen*." Like Whitcomb, who recognized "the connexion, and sympathy of interest that exists, and ought to be felt, between the labouring and producing classes of mankind, in all countries, and throughout the world," Simpson realized that "the spirit which operated to the vassalage and depression of our Working People" was "the same spirit that introduced the SLAVE trade, and peopled our southern plantations with a human race, doomed to *eternal toil*." Perhaps most significantly, Simpson insisted that the abolition of "every vestige of bondage and servitude" was "an indispensable prerequisite" to the emancipation of labor.[37]

This, however, was about as close as Simpson came to unequivocal support for abolitionism. Neither Simpson, Heighton, nor any other figure associated with the Philadelphia Working Men took an activist stance on the immediate abolition of chattel slavery, nor, despite many references to the ideal of "all men are created equal," did they demand the integration of trade unions or otherwise make common cause with the African American Philadelphians who made up the largest free Black population in the urban North. As the 1830s wore on, Simpson and others among Philadelphia's "Old School" Democrats were eclipsed by probusiness "New Schoolers" and the Working Men's movement faded. Heighton retreated to obscurity in rural New Jersey, only to briefly reemerge in the public eye near the end of the Civil War. It would fall to others to develop the connections between antislavery and radical egalitarianism that Heighton and Simpson had begun to trace in the 1820s and '30s.

The New York Working Men: Antislavery and "Agrarianism"

In October 1829, in the aftermath of a strike in support of a maximum ten-hour workday the previous spring, the Working Men's Party of New York issued a stunningly radical document. Presented at a public meeting held at Military Hall on Wooster Street, the report of the Committee of Fifty began with the proposition that "human society, our own as well as every other, is constructed radically wrong." The error, the committee believed, had derived from "the first foundation of government in this state [in which] the division of the soil should have been equal." The report proceeded to lay out the standard demands of the Working Men's parties then coalescing around the country, but only after calling for a political revolution that would leave "no trace of that government which has denied to every human being AN EQUAL AMOUNT OF PROPERTY." Rejecting definitions of free labor that viewed wages and work as being governed by freedom of contract, the workingmen argued that there was little practical difference whether one was enslaved by brute force "or whether the sword of want extort our consent . . . to a voluntary slavery."[38]

The author of the report was Thomas Skidmore. Born in Connecticut, Skidmore had traveled up and down the Eastern Seaboard working as a machinist and inventor before settling in New York City, where he became involved in politics—not as a Jacksonian, but as a pro–Adams National Republican. Skidmore had already developed some of the ideas laid out in the report in *The Rights of Man to Property!*, published in 1829. *The Rights of Man to Property!* held that all private property was essentially illegitimate, since the basis of its ownership was constructed on the foundation of the unequal and forceful distributions that had preceded the formation of governments. From this radical proposition, Skidmore proposed a solution that went a step further than Paine's *Agrarian Justice*: a "General Division" in which landed property would be redistributed, inheritance abolished, and all citizens, on reaching the age of maturity, would receive an equivalent in return for the land that been usurped back during the dawn of civilization.[39]

Radical as it was, *The Rights of Man to Property!* had many antecedents within Anglo-American political culture. Neither Paine's *Agrarian Justice* nor the works of Thomas Spence were well known in the U.S., but Robert Owen, the Welsh industrialist and factory reformer who envisioned a "new moral world" based on cooperative labor and communal living, became a modest media sensation in the mid-1820s. William Duane's *Aurora* had reprinted

Owen's *A New View of Society* in serial beginning in 1817, and when Owen arrived in the U.S. in 1825, he was invited to speak before the House of Representatives, where he denounced the emerging economic system that created a "surplus of wealth and power to the few," while imposing "poverty and subjection on the many." Among those who welcomed Owen on his arrival in New York was Cornelius Blatchly, whose *An Essay on Common Wealths* argued that property in land had been given by God for "*general* use and benefit and not for *individual* aggrandizement" and called for the abolition of inheritance. Within the year Owen had founded New Harmony, a cooperative labor community on land purchased from a German religious community in Indiana and was attacking what he called the "threefold horrid monster" of private property, religion, and marriage. Both Heighton and Langton Byllesby, the Philadelphia printer who penned *Observations on the Sources and Effects of Unequal Wealth*, were influenced by the English socialist John Gray, and the American edition of Gray's *A Lecture on Human Happiness* had appended a constitution for a cooperative community to be established in Valley Forge, Pennsylvania, patterned after a similar plan for a "Co-operative Society" in London. Earlier, homegrown works like James Reynolds's *Equality: A Political Romance* (1802) had helped prepare the ground for the reception of Owenite ideas in America by imagining a workers' utopia in which both money and wage labor had been abolished, land was held in common, and workers enjoyed a four-hour workday.[40]

Unlike these earlier works, however, *The Rights of Man to Property!* also attacked the institution of slavery directly. Scrutinizing the origins of private property, Skidmore drew a direct correlation between the origins of property in land and that of property in human beings. Like his idol Jefferson, Skidmore blamed slavery on British colonizers rather than American slaveholders, and his work was liberally sprinkled with white slavery comparisons.[41] It was self-evident, Skidmore believed, that if slavery had somehow taken root on U.S. soil after the American Revolution, "all our governments, both State and National, would have directed their efforts to destroy it immediately, and to prevent its further introduction among us." Much like slavery, the vast landed estates of the wealthy were the tainted legacy of aristocratic Europe, not republican America. Both derived their titles from "grants made by our proprietary governors" and "the governments of Europe," but "the people of this country in forming a government for themselves, would never have sanctioned" either. But unlike many democratically inclined radicals, Skidmore did not stop at white slavery metaphors or Jeffersonian attempts to shift the blame for slavery. Rather, he continued in this line of reasoning to argue for the emancipation of enslaved people in the South and the enfranchisement of free Blacks in the North. Anticipating the usual objection that emancipated Blacks would be unable to fend for themselves, Skidmore had a ready answer: on gaining their freedom, the formerly enslaved should be "presented with lands, and other property also, wherewith to obtain substance." While he acknowledged the reality of white racism, Skidmore did not believe it posed an insurmountable obstacle to emancipation, for it was "possible" that the poor southern white could "renounce his prejudices against the slaves and to admit that it is no more consistent with *right*, that the slaves should be subservient to him, than it is for the poor white man, to be subservient to the rich one." That effected, the formerly enslaved "might at once be admitted to an equal participation" in politics and society. Thus enabled to become self-sufficient, nothing short of outright prejudice could circumvent "this easy and natural method of extinguishing slavery, and its ten thousand attendant evils."[42]

Skidmore's passage on slave emancipation occupied only a few pages of his nearly 400-page treatise, and he admitted that his emancipation scheme might be impossible "under the present circumstances." But closer to home, Skidmore recognized that property ownership and political rights for the formerly enslaved were explicitly connected. In New York, the 1821 state constitution had eliminated property requirements for white male voters while raising them for Black men. Skidmore objected to this development on racially egalitarian principles. "The former existence of slavery among us," he wrote, was no reason to deny African Americans the vote, for "the black man's right to suffrage is as perfect as the white man's." Just as emancipation made little sense if not accompanied by the right to access land, the redistribution of land would be an absurdity under New York's existing white-supremacist constitution, for without the franchise, there was "no power, but unlawful force" by which Black men could defend and maintain their property holdings. A political revolution, one that included the right of suffrage for women as well as African Americans, was thus a necessary complement to the "general division" of landed property that Skidmore called for.[43]

But although Skidmore had been elected to head the Committee of Fifty, he had difficulty getting traction for his ideas within the Working Men's Party. Ironically, his main challengers for the leadership of the New York Working Men were Frances Wright and Robert Dale Owen, two figures also closely associated with abolitionism and agrarianism. Owen, the son of the

New Harmony founder who had briefly overseen the community after his father's departure and before New Harmony's collapse in 1827, had recently embarked on a new communitarian venture with Wright, a tall, striking Scotswoman whose penchant for public speaking and support for women's rights made her the scourge of the nation's respectable classes. Wright's Nashoba community had aimed to demonstrate the feasibility of emancipation by preparing a small group of enslaved people for freedom utilizing a system of cooperative labor. The "Nashoba plan," however, had ended in abject failure, culminating in the enslaved peoples' resettlement in Haiti, the experiment as well as Wright's reputation tarnished by rumors of interracial sex and physical abuse. Together Owen and Wright attempted to launch a political career in New York from the headquarters of their Hall of Science, a lecture hall the two opened on Broome Street in a former Baptist church.[44] The centerpiece of their appeal was what they called the "state guardianship plan," a program of free, compulsory education that appealed to workers' demands for publicly sponsored education. Alarmed by Skidmore's success, Owen enlisted the help of the *Working Man's Advocate*, a new labor journal edited by George Henry Evans, to push the plan. Meanwhile, a third faction of Working Men emerged, comprising more cautious master artisans, manufacturers, and shopkeepers who supported Noah Cook, a merchant and entrepreneur, and Henry Guyon, a master carpenter.[45]

For the moment, these new factions united to denounce the "wild Agrarian scheme" of the Skidmorites. One group of Owen supporters circulated a handbill signed by a "Real Working Man" who renounced the "deluded" efforts of the "Agrarian Minority," while pro-Tammany journals and conservative dailies alike expressed their horror at the rise of a "party founded on the most alarming principles."[46] At a subsequent party meeting at Military Hall in December 1829, supporters of Cook and Owen overwhelmed the Skidmore faction and stripped them of power; several months later, Cook's faction turned on the Owenites at a party convention upstate and declared their allegiance to National Republican standard-bearer Henry Clay. In the state elections of 1830, pro-Jackson Tammany candidates gleefully filled the resulting void, reversing the Working Men's gains in the city wards that had voted for them the previous year.[47]

Finished as a viable political movement, most of the remaining Working Men followed leaders like Evans and Commerford into the Jacksonian fold. Skidmore died a premature death during the cholera epidemic that struck New York in 1832, and, for a time, his brand of labor abolitionism and understanding of the relationship between slavery, inequality, and property seemed to die with him. But in subsequent decades, some of Skidmore's contemporaries would come around to his ideas, and a new generation of "Workies" would prove more receptive to his combination of agrarianism and antislavery.

Rioting, Politics, and the Rise of Antislavery Constitutionalism

On the evening of Thursday, May 17, 1838, Philadelphia's Pennsylvania Hall was burned to the ground. One of the largest and most architecturally distinguished buildings in the city, built at a cost of more than $40,000, the hall had been open only a few days when it was destroyed in an arson attack by an antiabolitionist mob. Intended to serve as "a Temple to Free Discussion," the building instead became a symbol of the violent attempts to silence free speech by antiabolitionist forces. Six months earlier, Elijah P. Lovejoy had been murdered by a mob in Alton, Illinois, his printing press thrown into the Mississippi River. A few years before in the summer of 1834, a series of antiabolitionist riots had torn through New York and other northern cities, leaving a trail of destruction that targeted Black communities, churches and meeting halls, and the homes of abolitionists. In October, 1835, William Lloyd Garrison was dragged through the streets of Boston by an angry mob—on the same day that Gerrit Smith witnessed another mob, this time in Utica, New York, forcibly break up an antislavery convention there. Other groups of white northerners petitioned to make disseminating abolitionist materials a criminal offense; vandalized and forced the closure of Prudence Crandall's integrated boarding school in Canterbury, Connecticut; and rioted to prevent the founding of a "manual labor school" for free Blacks in New Haven.[48]

The role of working men and women in this orgy of anti-Black and antiabolitionist violence has long been disputed. Wage workers, journeymen, and skilled artisans were surely among the crowd that hurled rocks to smash the windows of Pennsylvania Hall while Angelina Grimké was speaking inside, before torching the building on the following day. But as a contemporary account noted, of those who subscribed to pay for the cost of erecting the building, a "majority" were also "mechanics, or working men." On the afternoon before its destruction, Pennsylvania Hall had been the site of the Requited Labor Convention organized by Lewis C. Gunn and other abolitionists associated with Philadelphia's free produce movement. The movement, which sought to develop producers' and consumers' cooperatives for the exchange of non–slave produced goods, was dominated by local Quakers from the radical Hicksite sect. But Gunn and others worked hard, with some success, to attract support from artisans and wage workers, asserting that "ARTICLES PRODUCED BY SLAVE-LABOR ARE STOLEN GOODS, because every man has an inalienable right to the fruits of his own toil."[49]

Research into the composition of antiabolitionist mobs in the 1830s, meanwhile, has shown that "gentlemen of property and standing" were more likely to have been both the organizers of antiabolition mobs and the largest occupational grouping within them. Contemporaries like William Goodell echoed this point. Goodell believed that antiabolitionist mobs were led and directed by an "aristocracy," who "love to trample upon the laboring classes" and "grind the faces of the poor." The hidden hand behind such outbursts was the "thousands of northern merchants, manufacturers, and others" who shared an economic interest with southern masters in the "unjust gains of slavery."[50] Thomas Brothers, the editor of the Philadelphia *Radical Reformer and Working Man's Advocate*, described the "prime movers" behind the antiabolitionist agitation as "a few sordid mercantile souls who feared that their business with the South would be injured." Perhaps Philadelphia lawyer David Paul Brown, who witnessed the burning of Pennsylvania Hall, came closest to the truth when he claimed that "the last and lowest class" was responsible: "I do not mean the mechanical or laboring classes . . . but the *mob*, made up of the refuse of *all* the other classes, and preying upon *all*."[51] Just as importantly, the evidence points to the conclusion that in many parts of the North, artisans, wage workers, and men of little or modest wealth made up the bulk of the antislavery rank-and-file. One study has found that the "overwhelming majority" (60–70 percent) of petition signers in half a dozen industrializing cities in New York and Massachusetts in the 1830s owned little or no taxable property. The propertyless also made up the majority of the abolitionist society members in Boston, while those who owned only modest property formed the majority in Providence, Rhode Island, and Lynn, Massachusetts.[52]

Whatever the actual class composition of those took part in antiabolition violence, workingmen also took the lead in denouncing it. In 1834, two working printer-editors, George Henry Evans, editor of the labor newspapers the *Working Man's Advocate* and *The Man*, and William Leggett, of the radically Democratic *Evening Post*, were nearly alone among New York newspaper editors of either party affiliation in condemning the rioters that summer.

To be sure, such denunciations did not necessarily translate into support for immediate abolitionism. Evans complained that the Garrisonian immediatists were "actuated by a *fanatical* enthusiasm," and he blamed the riots on "Bank wigs [*sic*]," the conservative press, and the influence of "*Southern money*," among other factors. But he nonetheless believed that abolitionists were "*honest* in their principles and the measures they propose are *just*," contrasting the immediatists favorably to the colonizationists of the American Colonization Society, whose measures "tend to *perpetuate*" slavery while distracting attention from more "*practicable* ways of *abolishing* it." A few days later, *The Man* gave column space to members of the executive committee of the AASS (which at that time included Arthur and Lewis Tappan, William Goodell, Elizur Wright, and Samuel Cornish), and published a lengthy explication of the abolitionists' views.[53]

Evans had launched his weekly, the *Working Man's Advocate*, at the height of the Working Men's movement in 1829. After the Working Men's electoral defeat, he helped steer the remainder of the party toward support for Jackson and the Democrats. Unlike many northern Democrats, however, Evans never reconciled himself to the Jacksonian alliance between northern workingmen and southern slave owners. Rather, he was conspicuous for the striking if somewhat inconsistent arguments he made against chattel slavery and in favor of Black equality. Throughout the 1830s, in the columns of the *Working Man's Advocate* and *The Man*, Evans railed against the internal slave trade, defended abolitionists' right to free speech, printed notices of antislavery meetings, and stood up for the rights of oppressed people of color, whether enslaved or free. "We believe it is our duty to take the part of the oppressed, against the oppressor, whatever may be the kindred or country of the oppressor and the oppressed," the *Working Man's Advocate* declared. "In relation to the question of slavery our kindred are mankind—our color is the color of freedom."[54]

Perhaps the most striking indication of Evans's willingness to offer support on behalf of the oppressed, regardless of race, came in August 1831. That month, Nat Turner, an enslaved preacher who claimed to be guided by religious visions, led a group of perhaps one hundred fellow slaves in a bloody massacre of local whites in the area around Southampton, Virginia. The incident, which resulted in the deaths of some sixty whites and caused widespread panic throughout the South, became known as the Nat Turner Rebellion. Astonishingly, the *Working Man's Advocate*, almost alone among the country's newspapers, defended the enslaved insurrectionaries. "However absurd or

cruel" the Turner rebels had been, Evans wrote, "if their *object* was to obtain
their freedom ... their cause was *just*." Like Garrison's *Liberator*, Evans laid
the blame for the massacre squarely at the feet of southern slaveholders (who,
he alleged, had failed to take the necessary steps to abolish slavery), compared
the Turner rebels to freedom fighters, and heaped scorn on northern editors,
like the *Courier and Enquirer's* James Watson Webb, who reserved their outrage for white victims while doubling down on defenses of slavery. To Evans,
the events in Southampton proved that slavery operated to the detriment of
both Blacks and whites, although he emphasized that, while some fifty-eight
whites had been killed, "ONE HUNDRED or more with dark skins" were put
to death in the rebellion's aftermath, "for crimes of which most of them were
entirely innocent."[55] His defense of the rebellion earned Evans the enmity of
Jacksonian editor Duff Green, who referred to him in the *Washington Tele-
graph* as a "miscreant ... dangerous to society, [who] deserves to be treated as
an incendiary or an outlaw." But Evans remained defiant, refusing to retract
a word of his original statement and turning the charge of "fanatic" against
proslavery Democrats like Green. In a moment of self-criticism, Evans also
castigated the labor reform movement as having been "negligent" in advancing the cause of enslaved Blacks. Labor reformers, Evans admitted, "might ...
have done more for the cause of emancipation" than they had done so far.
"Our only excuse is, that the class to which we belong, and whose rights we
endeavor to advocate, are threatened with evils *only inferior* [italics added] to
those of slavery, which evils it has been our principal object and endeavor to
eradicate ... [but] we are now convinced that our interest demands that we
should do more, for EQUAL RIGHTS can never be enjoyed, even by those
who are free, in a nation which contains slaveites enough to hold in bondage
two millions of human beings."[56]

Such statements aside, what may have been Evans's most important contribution to the antislavery tradition is less obvious. The Turner Rebellion
and the claim put forth by James Watson Webb (whose *Courier and Enquirer*
would fan the flames of the 1834 antiabolition riots a few years later) that
"*property in slaves is guaranteed to their masters by the Constitution*" had
prompted Evans to rethink this conventional wisdom. The Founders had pur-
posely omitted the word "slave" from the Constitution, Evans pointed out in
the *Advocate*. Although the three-fifths and fugitive slave clauses recognized
the existence of slavery, nowhere did the Constitution offer specific protections for slave property or define a "right" to property in human beings. The
federal government might be obligated to prevent slave insurrections, like

the one that had just occurred in Virginia, but it could best do that by providing funds to emancipate slaves, not by contributing to the development of
a permanent "standing army." "The idea is too absurd for belief," Evans concluded, "that the framers intended even to *recognize* the right of the minority
of the people of any state to hold the majority as *property*," and it was "monstrously absurd" to imagine that they intended to guarantee the right to such
"property." Slavery could be abolished within a decade, Evans suggested; the
primary obstacles were the "pecuniary interest" of slaveholders and their
claims that the Constitution guaranteed their right to hold human beings as
property, a doctrine that should be "exploded, and slaves should be emancipated as soon as they can be with safety to themselves and to those who hold
them in bondage." Although he believed, in keeping with the dominant interpretation of the Constitution, that the federal government could not abolish
slavery in the states without a constitutional amendment, Evans was alarmed
by what he labeled the "new and abominable Tory-Whig doctrine" that even
the states could not constitutionally abolish slavery within their own borders.
Moreover, if slavery could not be abolished by the federal government outright, it *could* be abolished "by means of the general government, or by the
general government withholding the means of perpetuating it." Here, Evans
anticipated the idea that the federal government could "divorce" itself from
slavery, thereby depriving it of any means of support—an idea that would
later become central to the Republican Party.[57]

As the Working Men's parties faded and the 1830s wore on, the Equal
Rights Party emerged as a radical alternative to the Tammany Hall–controlled faction of the Democratic Party in New York. Organized by veterans
of the Working Men's movement, the Equal Rights faction—dubbed Loco
Focos by political enemies and the press, after the brand of matches members
supposedly used to illuminate an early meeting after the gaslights were shut
off—were known for their "ultra democratic" principles, including opposition to any form of monopoly or special privilege and a strict dedication to
ideals of free trade and laissez-faire. Their chief spokesman was William Leggett, a former navy midshipman turned journalist. Leggett assumed editorial
control of William Cullen Bryant's Democratic newspaper, the *Evening Post*,
only weeks before the antiabolitionist riots in July 1834. Beginning with an
editorial denouncing the "Riot at the Chatham-Street Chapel," Leggett slowly
gravitated toward defense of the abolitionists and support for antislavery,
gradually making good on his newspaper's promise to "convince me that a
principle is right in the abstract, and I will reduce it to practice, if I can." In

1835, the specter of antislavery mob violence, this time in Haverhill, Massa-chusetts, again prompted Leggett to reconsider his earlier denunciation of abolitionism. Having railed against the "money power" in the form of banks and paper currency, he now turned decisively against the "monster slavery" and endorsed the platform of the AASS.[58]

In the meantime, a storm was brewing in Congress over the issue of slav-ery in Washington, D.C., and the drive to eliminate it—a strategic and decid-edly political approach not only aimed at the symbolism of slavery's presence in the nation's capital, but predicated on the notion that the Constitution gave Congress the power to regulate slavery there, because of Washington's status as a nonstate. Benjamin Lundy had been the first to focus attention on abol-ishing slavery in the District of Columbia in the 1820s, an approach followed by Garrison, who echoed Lundy's call for a petition drive aimed at abolishing slavery in the District in the first issue of the *Liberator*. A major effort did not get underway until 1835, but within a year, Congress was being flooded with hundreds of thousands of petitions, prompting southerners to secure passage of the infamous "gag rule," which mandated that antislavery petitions be automatically tabled. The gag rule set the stage for a showdown that would last the better part of a decade and see the two sides—the proslavery faction, led by John Calhoun in the Senate and John H. Hammond and Henry A. Wise in the House, and the antislavery side, led by former president John Quincy Adams and Jacksonian Democrats Thomas A. Morris and William Slade in the House—rehearse a set of arguments about the Constitution's relationship to the idea of property in man that would go on to form the foundations of both pro- and antislavery politics up to the Civil War.[59]

Equal Rights Democrats such as Leggett embraced a political philosophy predicated on free trade, opposition to centralized banks and monopolies, and devotion to principles of limited government and a strict construction of the Constitution. But just as Leggett's and his fellow Loco Focos' commitment to laissez-faire did not preclude support for labor unions and striking workers, Leggett's reading of the Constitution did not prohibit the federal government from interfering with slavery, as it did for John Calhoun and other southern proponents of the "compact theory." Leggett recoiled from Calhoun's "mon-strous" doctrine that slavery was a "positive good" as well as his "very insulting allusions to the free labourers of the northern states" and his emerging under-standing of the Constitution as intrinsically antislavery dovetailed with ideas being developed simultaneously by antislavery politicians like Slade and abo-litionists like Theodore Dwight Weld. Weld, the famous "Lane rebel" who had led seminary students in a walkout protesting a ban on discussion of abolition at Lane Theological Seminary in Ohio, first laid out his ideas in a series of articles in Leggett's own *Evening Post* beginning in 1837 before publishing them as *The Power of Congress over the District of Columbia* the following year. By that time, Leggett had already reached the conclusion that the Constitution gave Congress the power to abolish slavery in the District. Combining now-familiar free labor arguments with a sophisticated refutation of Calhoun's compact theory, Leggett asserted that "nowhere" did the Constitution "countenance the idea that slaves are considered *property*," nor did the freeing of slaves violate the "takings clause" of the Fifth Amendment, as Calhoun insisted. In a new weekly, the *Plaindealer*, Leggett reiterated Weld's arguments and advocated the restoration of the suffrage and other rights for free Blacks, viewing them as the logical extension of "the fundamental article of the creed of democracy, which acknowledges the political equality, and undeniable right of freedom, of all mankind." In perhaps his most radical statement on slavery, Leggett shamefully admitted that "the banner of our country is the emblem, not of freedom and justice, but of oppression," since it stood for an "outrageous contradiction of the great principle of liberty, "the right of one man to hold another as property." Endorsing, as Evans had, the right of enslaved people to violent insurrection, he concluded that "every American who, in any way, authorizes or countenances slavery, is derelict in his duty as a christian, a patriot, and a man."[60]

For his embrace of antislavery, Leggett was effectively read out of the Democratic Party, and thereby deprived of the patronage on which the *Evening Post* depended. Commenting on Leggett's expulsion, the *Washington Globe*, the Democratic Party's semiofficial organ, noted that while Leggett's "spirit of Agrarianism" may have been excusable, "he has at last . . . taken a stand *which must forever separate him from the Democratic Party.* His journal now openly and systematically encourages the Abolitionists." Despite this official excommunication, Leggett remained a hero to the radical and prolabor element of the Democratic Party, which had found a new if temporary home with the formation of the Equal Rights Party, or Loco Focos. Although the Loco Focos as a whole were far from abolitionists, the *Globe* was far from the only paper to equate Loco Foco radicalism with antislavery and "agrarianism." The conservative *New York Times* lumped together "Agrarians . . . Working Men's faction . . . Fanny Wright Men . . . [and] Infidels," while the *Sunday Morning News* assured its readers that "every one knows that [abolitionism] was one of the original doctrines of the Fanny Wright, no-monopoly, no-property, and no-marriage party."[61]

Fitzwilliam Byrdsall, author of a history of the Loco Focos, later opined that Leggett's "agrarianism" had been more dangerous and threatening to the party establishment than his abolitionism. But by the early 1840s, as Byrdsall noted with approval, Leggett's "agrarian spirit of anti-monopoly" had become Democratic Party doctrine. The same could not be said for the party's stance on antislavery. In 1838 after the popular stage actor Edwin Forrest declined the Democratic nomination for a seat in Congress, former Loco Focos submitted Leggett's name instead. Despite evidence of widespread support, party officials forced Leggett to answer a questionnaire on his views on abolition in the District of Columbia. Leggett restated his belief that Congress had "full constitutional power" to abolish slavery in the District, and his nomination was promptly shuttered.[62]

Leggett would continue to proclaim his abolitionism until his premature death that same year. He would not live to see the resurrection of his anti-slavery constitutionalism by Liberty Party founders William Goodell and James G. Birney, who made D.C. abolition a central focus of their brand of political antislavery, nor by Salmon P. Chase and others who readily acknowledged Leggett's influence when crafting the Free Soil Party platform in 1848.[63] As yet, the analysis of antislavery labor radicals like Leggett and Evans did not lead most northern labor reformers into a full-throated assault on slavery; as Thomas Skidmore had put it, "the day of inquiry into rights" was "yet in its morning."[64] But attacks on abolitionists and other violations of free speech, and the slaveholders' increasingly shrill insistence that slavery be defended and expanded, would soon cause even some of the most recalcitrant northern labor radicals to question their assumptions about the relationship between free and slave labor, and between northern "producers" and slave-owning southern ones. As the antislavery Democrat Thomas Morris of Ohio put it in his final speech in the Senate in 1839, the two gravest threats "now uniting to rule this country"—"the slave power of the South, and the banking power of the North"—were both predicated on "the unrequited labor of others."[65] Before the "Slave Power" could displace the Money Power as the leading threat to equal rights in the minds of labor radicals, however, a devastating economic depression would derail the efforts of reformers like Evans, Heighton, Simpson, and Leggett. In the following decade, fallout from the Panic of 1837 would cast a long shadow over the remnants of a decimated and divided workingmen's movement.

CHAPTER 3

"The Genius of Integral Emancipation": Antislavery and Association

The year 1840 witnessed the publication of two milestones of antebellum radical thought: Orestes Brownson's essay "The Laboring Classes," published in the *Boston Quarterly Review,* and Albert Brisbane's *The Social Destiny of Man,* an exposition of the ideas of French social theorist Charles Fourier. Both were written partly in response to the Panic of 1837, the country's most serious financial crisis to date. Rippling out from financial centers in London and New York beginning in May of that year, the Panic's deeper underlying causes included rampant speculation in land and enslaved human beings, fueled by the easy availability of credit and the oversupply of paper currency. Americans of many stripes, including intellectuals like Brownson, middle-class reformers like Brisbane, and the artisans and laborers thrown out of work by the Panic's aftermath or left behind by rapid economic change, began to question the still-evolving system of capitalist wage labor.[1]

While Brownson's scorching essay on "wage slavery" was the more incisive and penetrating of the two works, Brisbane's was arguably the more influential. Within a few years, Brisbane was publishing a regular column on Fourierism (or Association, as American followers of Fourier called their movement) in one of the United States' most widely read newspapers, the *New-York Tribune.* The movement's official periodical, the *Phalanx* (which in 1845 merged with and was superseded by the *Harbinger*), drew on some of the country's finest literary talents, including many, like future *Tribune* coeditors George Ripley and Charles A. Dana, associated with the burgeoning Transcendentalist movement. Brisbane converted the *Tribune*'s influential founder, Horace Greeley, to the cause of Association, and eventually inspired followers to organize the cooperative communities that Fourierists called

Figure 6. The editorial staff of the *New-York Tribune*, as photographed by Matthew Brady in the 1850s, included Horace Greeley (seated, second from right), Charles A. Dana (standing, center), and George Ripley (seated at right), all of whom promoted Association in and outside of the pages of the *Tribune*. Library of Congress, Prints and Photographs Division.

phalanxes in places like Brook Farm, Massachusetts; Monmouth, New Jersey; and Ceresco, Wisconsin. Although only a few thousand Americans actually joined the phalanxes, at the height of its popularity in the mid-1840s perhaps one hundred thousand men and women could be considered followers of Fourierism, with thousands joining Fourierist clubs, societies, and affiliates of the American Union of Associationists, subscribing to the *Harbinger* or to dozens of other Fourierist newspapers and periodicals, or participating in Fourierist-dominated labor organizations like the New England Labor Reform League.[2]

Nonetheless, Fourierism and the related communitarian movements of the 1840s have gone relatively unexamined by historians of both antislavery and antebellum labor.[3] To some extent, this neglect is understandable. Unflattering contemporary accounts as well as those of later observers like Marx's collaborator Friedrich Engels dismissed the communitarianism of the 1840s as "utopian," a term that seems fitting when one considers its combination of religious perfectionism and its radically transformative vision of society, not to mention Fourier's more eccentric flights of mental fancy. The latter famously included science fiction–like speculations about the changes to the natural world that would take place after mankind had attained a state of cooperative perfection, as well as Fourier's fervid imaginings about the sexual freedom that would be permitted inside the phalanxes once traditional ideas of marriage and sexuality had been abandoned. American Fourierists, however, largely suppressed these more outlandish aspects of Fourier's system, emphasizing instead its most pragmatic features, as well as its compatibility with both capitalism and Christianity. Under the imagined roof of the phalanstery, the grandiose community building at the heart of Fourier's utopian plan, American Associationists wedded strains of millenarian religious perfectionism emanating from the Second Great Awakening, the desire for social cohesion and the spirit of improvement derived from the National Republicans and Whigs, and the passion for democracy and equality that drove the Loco Focos and antebellum labor radicals. And they thrust themselves into the debates then raging over the nature of the relationship between labor and capital and the place of slavery in a nation ostensibly dedicated to freedom, offering an expansive if incomplete vision of what a nation shorn of the chains of slavery might look like.[4]

As the above description implies, Association differed from the largely secular, Enlightenment-inspired communitarianism of Robert Owen and Frances Wright. But, apart from the fact that followers of both movements described their system as a form of "socialism," the two shared considerable overlap in terms of their promise to offer a refuge from the harshest features of early American capitalism and their ability to attract middle-class intellectuals and working-class adherents alike. For a few years at least, American Associationists enjoyed an influence that far surpassed that of the earlier Owenites, whose impact in the United States was decidedly on the wane by 1840. Part of the attraction was the promise to bring about what Associationists called "the Harmony of Capital and Labor," the idea that workers and employers were not mutually antagonistic, but that their interests could be reconciled if brought together in a unified corporate body. The phalanxes were to be created by the pooling of capital in a joint-stock company; wages would be replaced or augmented by profit sharing and a system of "mutual guarantees" in case of sickness or accident and in old age; and men and women would live and work cooperatively, their labor organized on the basis of Fourier's theory of "attraction," the idea that people would inevitably be

drawn to the type of labor for which they were best suited. Middle-class intellectuals, sympathetic capitalists, and the religiously inclined were drawn in
by Association's promise to bring the harsher aspects of market competition
more in line with Christian ideals, while working-class members were likely
attracted by the movement's emphasis on the dignity of labor, its proposals
for profit sharing and provisions for a social safety net, and its promise to
ultimately abolish the wage system entirely.[5]

Given the growing salience of slavery in the mid-1840s and the myriad
ways that it intersected with related issues of labor, capital, and property, the
Associationists could hardly ignore the slavery question. Fourier himself,
although he frequently used the term "slavery" as a metaphor for all kinds of
societal injustices, had published a plan for gradual emancipation in 1836.[6]
The year that Brisbane and Brownson published their opening salvos was also
the year that the Garrisonian abolitionist organization, the American Anti-
Slavery Society (AASS), split apart over internal disputes concerning a number of issues, including Garrison's religious unorthodoxy and opposition to
government and politics; disagreement over the desirability of pacifism (or
"non-resistance") versus armed resistance to slavery; and debates over the
proper role of women in the movement. The resulting schism and departure
of more conservative members may have made some remaining Garrisonians
more receptive to reform approaches that transcended the "one idea," as more
orthodox abolitionists called their approach to antislavery. As the abolitionist
editor and founder of the antislavery Liberty Party, Gamaliel Bailey, no friend
to Fourierism himself, was forced to concede, many of Association's "most
efficient advocates . . . have sprung from the ranks of Abolitionists." The Associationists' approach to antislavery—what one group of Fourierists called the
"genius of integral emancipation"—was at the heart of a sweeping program of
reform aimed at correcting the abuses of North and South alike, and bringing
them into line with an egalitarian vision based on industrial cooperation and
Christian social harmony.[7] Among those who took leading roles in Associationist organizations, who organized phalanxes or other intentional communities, or who espoused related ideas of communitarianism and socialism in
the 1840s and early '50s were Garrisonians John A. Collins, Elizur Wright, Jr.,
Adin Ballou, George W. Benson, and Bronson Alcott; the Unitarian minister
and theologian William Henry Channing; the abolitionist author and leader
of the Lane Seminary rebels, Theodore Dwight Weld; and Weld's wife, the pioneering feminist and abolitionist Angelina Grimké. Abolitionists James Birney
and Gerrit Smith sent their children to the school where Weld and Grimké

taught at Raritan Bay Union, the Fourierist phalanx founded by abolitionists Marcus Spring and his wife Rebecca (the latter was the daughter of Arnold Buffum, a founding member of the AASS). Wright, who promoted Associa- tion in the pages of his *Daily Chronotype* newspaper, had been corresponding secretary of the AASS before breaking with Garrison, while Collins was the general agent of its most important branch, the Massachusetts Anti-Slavery Society (MASS).[8] As one correspondent to the *Liberator* put it, involvement in Association was a natural outgrowth of "the deep and sympathetic spirit fostered by the antislavery movement, which . . . has been the entering wedge to the *radical* reformatory movements of the day."[9]

The sometimes heated debates in the pages of abolitionist and Associa- tionist journals, however, as well as retrospective recollections by both former abolitionists and historians (some of whom sought to distance the antislavery movement from the perceived excesses of antebellum reform), have tended to obscure the degree of overlap and convergence between abolitionism and communitarianism. As John Humphrey Noyes, the founder of the utopian socialist Oneida Community, later recalled, reformers' receptivity to Associ- ation had to some extent been primed by abolitionism, which by the early 1840s had been "gathering into itself all minor reforms and firing the northern heart for revolution" for more than a decade. Frederick Douglass, who visited the Fourierst-influenced Northampton community sometime in the middle of the decade, would later recall his own youthful attraction to "communism," recollecting that many of "the men and women who were interested in the work of revolutionizing the whole system of civilization were also deeply inter- ested in the emancipation of the slaves." Others who combined abolitionism with communitarianism never explicitly identified themselves as Association- ists but became fellow travelers in the movement and incorporated elements of Fourierism in the various communities they helped to found.[10]

Nor should their middle-class leadership or emphasis on the "harmony of interests" between labor capital mean that the Associationists can be reduced to a set of utopian dreamers or dilettantes hoping to jump on the bandwagon of labor reform, as an earlier generation of labor historians viewed them.[11] As we will see, American Associationists were unstinting in their criticisms of wage labor, and they advocated a sweeping transformation in the relationship between employer and employee, among the many human institutions they wished to revolutionize. Although Association's class composition is difficult to parse, evidence suggests that the phalanxes attracted large numbers of arti- sans and mechanics in addition to the middle-class intellectuals, reformers, and literary types that often comprised its leadership and gained an out-sized share of attention, in part due to the latter's association with Transcendentalism and their role in creating memoirs and other written accounts. Regardless, the leading Associationists made common cause with labor organizations like the New England Workingmen's Association (NEWA; later the New England Labor Reform League) and the land reform movement, and important labor leaders like NEWA spokesmen and *Voice of Industry* editors John Allen and John Orvis, land reformers John Ryckman and H. H. Van Amringe, and Lowell Female Labor Reform Association founders Sarah Bagley and Huldah Stone either endorsed Fourierism outright or cooperated closely with Associationists in editing labor newspapers, organizing ten-hours campaigns, and appearing together as speakers and lecturers. Such figures undoubtedly played a conspicuous role in exposing their working-class audiences to Fourierism, imparting a disproportionately Associationist cast to the labor publications and pronouncements of the decade.[12]

The connections briefly outlined above might in themselves be enough to dispel the prevailing view of communitarian movements in the 1840s as an ephemeral phenomenon that lent a certain novelty to the reformist fervor of the period, but left little lasting impact after the short-lived phalanxes dissolved. While the abolitionist movement as a whole remained skeptical of Fourierism and labor reform in general, the overlap of ideas and personnel between abolitionism and Association helped to shape abolitionists' evolving ideas about capitalism and labor—challenging deeply held ideals about the morality of competitive wage labor, highlighting capitalism's connections to slavery, and forcing abolitionists to sharpen their attack on the institution of human property. In the 1840s, as the abolitionist movement was rocked by internal dissention and with its options limited by the political stalemate over slavery, the debates between abolitionists, Associationists, and other radical labor advocates formed a crucible out of which antebellum ideas about slavery, property, and free labor would emerge transformed. Far from dissolving into consensus, the debates over the meanings of slave and free labor would continue to rage in the period after 1848, when a renewed crisis over slavery would thrust many abolitionists and former Fourierists into the realm of electoral politics. In the meantime, the encounter between abolitionism and Association—an encounter perhaps better described as a process of dialectic, rather than discord—would transform both movements, forcing each side to hone its arguments and develop a genuine if sometimes grudging respect for the other.[13]

A "Broad Platform on Which We Can All Meet":
Communitarianism and Abolitionism in the 1840s

Perhaps unsurprisingly, given the region's status as the stronghold of abolitionism and a primary site of early industrialization and labor organization,
the ties between labor reform, communitarianism, and abolition were especially strong in New England. The correspondence of Isaiah Coffin Ray, a
New Bedford, Massachusetts, boot and shoe merchant and AASS organizer,
provides evidence of how existing abolitionist connections helped to foster
the creation of a network of Associationist labor activists in the Bay State
and beyond. Ray exchanged letters not only with Garrison and MASS general agent John A. Collins, but with Associationists Albert Brisbane and William H. Channing, New England labor leaders John Allen and John Orvis,
and the Chartist émigré John C. Cluer. As Ray's neighbor and correspondent,
the Quaker abolitionist Rebecca T. Pool, observed, many of those who had
left New Bedford to join an Associationist phalanx were "the same whose
names I have seen on Anti Slavery records." To Pool, this was only logical,
since she doubted whether "a person can be a good Associationist who is not
an Abolitionist. If one cannot see that the Slavery system is a violation of the
social order & therefore wrong I do not think they could see any real wrong
anywhere in Society."[14]

For some abolitionists, the Panic of 1837, increasing contact with British labor reformers and familiarity with labor conditions in Britain, and the
abolitionist schisms of the early 1840s all contributed to a greater receptivity
to Association and related reforms. Abolitionists such as Henry C. Wright,
the political abolitionists Joshua Leavitt and Alvan Stewart, and Garrison
himself all pointed to what they described as a corrupt alliance between
northern capital and southern slavery as being to blame for the Panic and
its attendant miseries. The *Liberator*'s internationalist motto, "Our Country
is the World—Our Countrymen are Mankind," bore a striking similarity to
the idea expressed by Paine in *Rights of Man*, and by the late 1830s Garrison,
like Paine, found himself accused by conservative clerics of religious "infidelity" for his condemnation of established churches and rejection of the
Sabbath. Garrison defended himself with the reply that he was but a "poor,
self educated mechanic," and his travel to Great Britain to attend the World
Anti-Slavery Convention in 1840 aroused his sympathy for the suffering of
industrial workers, an experience replicated by other Garrisonians, including John A. Collins, Frederick Douglass, and James N. Buffum. Garrison

published letters and held respectful debates in the *Liberator* with labor reformers like Brownson, William West, and Charles M'Ewan, and his stance of nonresistance (civil disobedience) was inspired by Noyes as well as Adin Ballou, founder of the Hopedale Community.[15]

The links between Association and abolition were cemented at the Fourierist-inflected Convention of the Friends of Social Reform in Boston in late 1843. Despite its lingering reputation for Puritanism and its powerful Brahmin ruling class, Boston's status as the intellectual "Athens of America," as well as a hotbed of abolitionism, religious unorthodoxy, and labor reform, made it a natural site as the seeding ground of Association. The convention, advertised in the *Liberator* as well as in Brisbane's *Phalanx* and Parke Godwin's *Present*, declared itself opposed to "Repugnant Industry, Tyranny of Capital, Chattel Slavery and all forms of bondage and oppression of the Human Race" and in favor of women's rights. Meeting at the Tremont Temple, a former theater recently purchased by Free Church Baptists that would become the site of many antislavery meetings, the convention elected Lynn abolitionist William Bassett as president, while the four vice presidents were abolitionists Adin Ballou, George W. Benson, and James N. Buffum, as well as George Ripley, the Transcendentalist author and guiding spirit at the Brook Farm community. Ballou, a Unitarian minister and a Garrisonian, had gotten a jump start on the communitarian movement, establishing the Fraternal Community Number One, better known as Hopedale, the previous year. Garrison himself not only attended the convention but also appeared as one of the featured speakers, while Frederick Douglass was appointed to a committee in charge of preparing resolutions. Other speakers were William H. Channing, John A. Collins, Albert Brisbane, and Orestes Brownson. As might be expected with such a divergent group, the *Tribune* reported that "wildly different opinions in respect to the best mode of Social Reorganization" were expressed, but it insisted that a "spirit of Love and Harmony" prevailed. Association, the *Tribune* proclaimed, was "the broad platform on which all can meet, and extend the right hand of fellowship."[16]

The reality, of course, was not quite so harmonious. Both Garrison and Douglass had become more sympathetic to labor reform over time, but in the years after the Social Reform Convention, they remained personally aloof from Fourierism. Garrison frequently sparred with advocates of Association in the pages of the *Liberator*, consigning their wage slavery arguments to the "Refuge of Oppression" column he reserved for proslavery sentiments, and Douglass took a similar position, although he retained an abiding interest in reforms aimed at achieving economic equality.[17] But this general reticence and occasional rancor masks intimate individual and institutional connections between the two reforms. The career of John Anderson Collins represents one important example. A Vermonter by birth and graduate of Andover Theological Seminary, Collins had become a key figure in the Massachusetts branch of the Garrisonian AASS. As general agent of MASS, Collins bore the considerable responsibilities of organizing and fundraising, a duty he discharged with what the MASS board of directors described as great "energy and rare ability." In the summer of 1841, Collins had been the one to recruit Douglass as a lecturer for the movement after he and Garrison encountered the fugitive from slavery at an antislavery meeting—Douglass's first—on Nantucket. The previous year, suffering from ill health and mourning the sudden death of his wife and child, the thirty-year-old Collins had been sent by the AASS as its representative on a fundraising trip to Great Britain.[18] There, Collins was shocked by the levels of poverty and degradation he found among factory workers and other laborers, as well as by the cold reception he received from British abolitionists hostile to what was now being called "the old organization" of Garrisonian abolitionists, to distinguish them from the Tappans and others who had split to form the American and Foreign Anti-Slavery Society. "Too much, vastly too much has been made of English anti Slavery feeling + sympathy," Collins reported in a letter to Garrison. The English found it easy to condemn the American "prejudice against color," yet in Collins's eyes, they were guilty of exhibiting a similar prejudice toward their own poor. A closer analysis of British society revealed that it was founded on "a vast and complicated system of slavery," with "the poor + laboring classes" in "precisely in the same condition with the slaves of our country," although the former perhaps suffered less "physical cruelty." True, Collins concluded, British political and economic slavery was a "milder system of Slavery than that of Am. Slavery," but that made it all the more "dangerous" in its tendency to give the worker "the ostensible appearance of freedom" while "grind[ing] him to powder."[19]

Dismayed by the slander and rumormongering that accompanied abolitionist schisms over women's rights and issues of religious orthodoxy, and denouncing those American abolitionists who refused to condemn the British class system, Collins sought solidarity with a group of workingmen in Glasgow, who returned the favor by defending Collins's character and lamenting the "present rupture" within the antislavery movement. Turning their appeal to the workingmen of the United States, the Glaswegians expressed their "deep regret" on hearing rumors that "our working brethren across the

Atlantic, form a powerful obstruction to the abolition cause." Linking the plight of the enslaved to their own cause for "liberty," the Glasgow working-men urged their American counterparts to take a stronger position against slavery, a stance they described as "a sacred duty which we owe to ourselves, to society, and our fellow-bondsmen."[20]

Douglass later recalled that Collins returned from Great Britain "full of communistic ideas," while Garrison wrote that he had become "entirely absorbed in his 'community project.'" Yet the indefatigable Collins played a key role in the antislavery movement after his return, organizing dozens of abolitionist meetings during the One Hundred Conventions of 1843, a flurry of abolitionist activity that attempted to recruit new members outside of New England and repair the damage done by the schism of 1840. Whether out of sympathy for labor reform or as a favor to his longtime comrade, Garrison more than indulged Collins's newfound passion for the rights of labor in the *Liberator*, dedicating an entire page of the February 17, 1843, issue to the discussion of "Social Reform." In the weeks and months that followed, the *Liberator* published numerous notices from Collins, including the proceedings of a "Property Meeting at Lynn" that featured discussion by Douglass and Charles L. Remond, and a social reform convention in Ohio that nominated Lucretia Mott (albeit without her knowledge) as one of its vice presidents.[21]

While helping to organize the 1843 conventions, Collins also seized the opportunity to promote his new cause. As Noyes later recalled, Collins's method was "to get up a rousing Anti-slavery Convention, and conclude it by calling a socialistic Convention, to be held on the spot immediately after it." Douglass remembered that at one antislavery meeting in Syracuse, New York, in the summer of 1843, Collins, along with Associationist John Orvis and communitarian John O. Wattles, had proposed "to adjourn our anti-slavery discussions and take up the subject of communism." Douglass strongly objected to what he perceived as an attempt to undermine the anti-slavery purpose of the convention, even threatening to resign from the AASS in protest. Interestingly, however, his objections did not prevent him from attending and speaking at the Social Reform Convention held in Boston that December. In the event, Collins was the one to resign from his position in the MASS, his enthusiasm for social reform seemingly overshadowing his long-term commitment to abolition. But the terms of his departure were more than amicable, with a MASS resolution thanking him for his "zeal" and "rare ability" during his four years of service as general agent. That October, Collins had purchased some 350 acres of land in Upstate New York, located near the abolitionist hotbed of Syracuse. There, his Skaneateles Community would attempt to push communitarianism and religious heterodoxy beyond that espoused by American Fourierists or even the followers of Owen and Wright, practicing community of property, denying the authority of all government, and advocating a religious skepticism that verged on atheism. This radical agenda, however, did not prevent the well-known and respected abolitionists Nathaniel P. Rogers and Arnold Buffum from speaking at a gathering marking the community's founding, held in a barn on the property's farm.[22]

The Skaneateles Community's dissolution was rapid even by the standards of other communitarian experiments of the period, and Collins's subsequent career, which saw the erstwhile abolitionist pursuing politics and business ventures in California, is shrouded in mystery and hearsay.[23] Of longer duration, and perhaps more representative of the overlap between abolitionism and Associationist reform—despite the fact that it never formally adopted Fourierism—was the Northampton community. Officially known as the Northampton Association of Education and Industry, the Western Massachusetts community was founded by a group of reform-minded manufacturers and abolitionists as part of an effort to revive New England's flagging silk industry. At first utilizing a joint-stock approach and a modified system of wages, the Northampton Association soon moved toward a more democratic model and, after internal debate spurred by an influx of working-class members and reformers, ended up scrapping the wage system altogether. At the time of the community's establishment in 1842, seven of its eleven founding members had been abolitionists, and more than half of the Northampton Association's eventual residents had identifiable abolitionist connections or sympathies.[24] Although not officially Fourierist, Northampton's founding precepts were strongly influenced by the writings of Brisbane and the well-publicized example of Brook Farm, and it received an injection of Associationist ideas from members like George W. Benson and David Mack, as well as the New England labor leader John Allen, who lived in the community briefly in 1844. While Northampton's founders were largely derived from men and women of modestly middle-class and professional backgrounds, a majority of the community's members (64 percent) were artisans and laborers, and all presumably shared the belief expressed by the community's articles of association that workers were entitled to "the exclusive right of enjoying and disposing of the fruits of their labors."[25]

Although other Associationist communities, like Ohio's Prairie Home Community, occasionally sheltered refugees from slavery, the Northampton

Association also seems to have been unique among the communitarian experiments of the time by inviting Black men and women to live permanently among them.[26] Among the more prominent African Americans who took up this offer were the itinerant preacher and lecturer Sojourner Truth, the New York Vigilance Committee secretary David Ruggles, and the fugitive slave Stephen Rush. Little is known about the day-to-day lives of African Americans at Northampton, but their presence there and their own recollections about their experiences testify to the community's dedication to principles of racial and social equality, which it practiced to an extent almost unheard of for the period. Frederick Douglass, who visited the community sometime in the mid-1840s, wrote that Truth was "much respected" there as "one of the most useful members of the Community," and she and Ruggles remained there for several years, the former until Northampton's disbanding in 1846. Both were active within the Association and in the wider community of Northampton, with Ruggles chairing antislavery meetings convened by the local African American community and Truth delivering what may have been her first public address, on "the practical workings of slavery in the North." Northampton's interracialism reflects not only the influence of abolitionists like Ruggles and Truth, but was derived from an apparently sincere effort to put the community's socialist and Fourierist principles into practice; its founding articles declared the Association's intention to reject all "distinction[s] of rights and rewards . . . between the strong and the weak, the skilful [sic] and unskillful, the man and the woman, the rich and the poor." To cite but two examples of the latter, Abner S. Meade, a shoe cutter from Danvers, Massachusetts, toiled on an equal footing with Joseph S. Wall, a Worcester shoe dealer who might have been Meade's employer under different circumstances, while James A. Stetson, a mechanic who had been forced to sell his workshop after the Panic of 1837, became a sales agent for the Association's silk manufacturing business.[27] Douglass, writing with the benefit of hindsight, recalled of his visit there that "the place and the people struck me as the most democratic I had ever met. . . . There was no high, no low, no masters, no servants, no white, no black." In the rougher grammar of someone whose experience was more recently rooted in slavery, the fugitive Stephen C. Rush wrote after leaving the community that "I don't find a place like the association yet for I believe that they live out a principle that the world no [sic] nothing about."[28]

If the world as yet knew little about what transpired inside the phalanxes, outside realities were nonetheless about to catch up with them. Even as the communities succumbed to the pressures created by internal tension and

dissent, inadequate planning and financing, and the gap between American individualism and Fourierism's communitarian vision, the country was
forced to confront the realities of slavery in new and inescapable ways as a
result of Texas annexation and the Mexican War, the unflagging agitation of
abolitionists, and the growing numbers of fugitives like Rush. Meanwhile,
as northern workers found themselves increasingly subject to competition,
mechanization, and wages that were inadequate to support a family or attain
the property necessary for social mobility, Fourierist reformers proved themselves to be among the most insightful critics of the new economic regime.
Although most stubbornly clung to the language of "wage slavery," they added
a new and more sophisticated layer of analysis to the social conditions they
sought to capture with this phrase—an intervention that would challenge
some abolitionists as well as many labor reformers to reconsider the relationship between capital, labor, property, and slavery.

"Should We Not Confront Capital?": Labor, Property, and Slavery in Associationist Thought

In an 1845 letter to an antislavery convention in Cincinnati, Horace Greeley,
then at the height of his zeal for Association, expressed an understanding of
slavery that diverged sharply from that of most abolitionists. Slavery, Greeley
wrote, was simply "that condition in which one human being exists mainly as
a convenience for other human beings." As Greeley went on to explain, "slavery" encompassed various kinds of forced obedience or servility, including
the subjugation of one class by another, the appropriation of land by landowners, and the tendency to squeeze workers' wages to the point of starvation. In a statement that must have infuriated abolitionists, Greeley added a
homegrown spin to the arguments made by British apologists for the West
Indian slave interest a half century earlier: "if I am less troubled concerning
the Slavery prevalent in Charleston or New-Orleans, it is because I see so
much Slavery in New-York, which appears to claim my first efforts."[29]

Today Greeley is mainly remembered for his problematic postwar turn as
the leader of the Liberal Republicans during Reconstruction, but in the 1840s
and '50s both he and his *New-York Tribune* were regarded as bulwarks of
northern antislavery opinion.[30] If Greeley's capacious definition of "slavery"
strained the limits of credulity for more orthodox abolitionists, however, it
did not necessarily stray far from the way that labor reformers understood

it. The same year that Greeley's letter was published, the Associationist periodical, the *Harbinger*, devised a typology of nine separate species of "slavery,"
which included "Slavery of the soil" and "Slavery of Capital, [or] hired labor,"
as well as "the Sale and seclusion of women in seraglios," "Military Con-
scriptions and Impressments," and—perhaps most perplexing—"Perpetual
Monastic Vows." Although "chattel Slavery" ranked at the top of the list, the
author (probably Brisbane) made his reform agenda clear a few lines further
down. In response to objections that such an approach to antislavery was
"too vast" and rendered "vague by its excessive universality," Brisbane clarified how he envisioned the emancipation of human labor unfolding: the elevation of "the white laboring classes" should come first, after which "means
will be revealed ... to enfranchise all other classes of the enslaved," since
"the science of society teaches that it is the wisest policy, and the quickest
in results, to elevate the most advanced classes of the oppressed to complete
liberty." Greeley later claimed that his "leading idea" had been that "slavery
is to be abolished, or at least its abolition rendered feasible, by *improving and
elevating the condition of the Free Laborer*, white or black, male or female."
But even granted Greeley's more racially egalitarian language and his long-
standing antislavery commitments, it is not difficult to see how such claims
to stand for the abolition of "all slavery" could serve as a mask for their prioritization of white workers over the enslaved.[31]

It might be easy, therefore, to dismiss such claims by Associationists as
disingenuous and evasive, as well as racist. In that sense, they were in keeping with much of the labor movement rhetoric about slavery throughout the
period. During the 1840s, prolabor newspapers and other publications continued and even amplified the by then well-established tradition of comparing
white workers to slaves. The *Northampton Democrat*, a Democratic newspaper notorious for its antagonistic exchanges with the *Liberator*, defined
slavery as the "deprivation of freedom" that occurred when man's "right to
all that he produces" is infringed, while the *Awl*, a labor newspaper from the
shoemaking town of Lynn, defined it as "subjection to the will of another,"
regardless of whether the "other" was an individual slaveholder or a class
of capital-owning employers. Mike Walsh, the flamboyant Irish American
spokesperson for the laboring poor of New York City's lower wards, chose
to illustrate a similar distinction with an evocative, if dehumanizing, image
that might have resonated with his rural Irish–born constituents. The "poor
negro," he explained, was a "farm horse" whose master would continue to
care for it in sickness and old age, while the "poor white man" was a livery

horse hired out to many masters, only to be sent to the knacker's yard after it had outlived its usefulness.[32]

The Associationists were certainly susceptible to the racism that permeated American society, including the early labor movement; as Rebecca Pool observed during her visit to the North American Phalanx in New Jersey, despite the "good deal of Anti Slavery thinking" that predominated there, there was also a "considerable prejudice against color."[33] But the movement's official mouthpiece, the *Harbinger*, denied that Associationists were opposed to Black equality. Like the Owenites, Associationists believed that human character was the product of education and circumstance, not of an innately sinful nature that made the poor more inclined toward wickedness. And like the first wave of Enlightenment-influenced abolitionists, they believed that the poverty, ignorance, and vice that whites often attributed to African-descended peoples in America were the products of environment—in this case, the "degradation" associated with slavery—rather than the intrinsic characteristics of "race." Associationists not only shared abolitionists' assumptions about an "environmentalist" understanding of the effects of condition on human character and behavior, they expanded on them to the point where they were frequently accused of undermining individualistic ideals of self-reliance and moral responsibility.[34]

Associationist understandings of slavery were, moreover, grounded in elaborate theories of history and human nature. Influenced by European social thinkers, including Owen, Lassalle, and the antimonarchist revolutionaries associated with the 1848 revolutions, Associationists viewed both slavery and wage labor as vestiges of feudalism, the overthrow of which they viewed as part of a world-historical struggle that would inevitably lead to the replacement of barbarism by a more perfected civilization. Their understanding of slavery as a historical phenomenon was therefore one based in class conflict rather than race. While this historical vision theoretically united white workers in solidarity with the enslaved, however, it was also predicated on a reading of history through a specifically European lens, one that arguably left little room for analysis of the racially specific conditions of American slavery. In its reply to the *Anti-Slavery Standard*, for example, the *Harbinger* expressed its vague approval of the *Standard*'s colorblind racial egalitarianism, but implausibly claimed that northern whites were "unanimous" in viewing African Americans as "men" entitled to equal rights.[35]

The presence of more committed abolitionists in the Associationist movement further complicates the distinction between what was genuinely

Figure 7. An undated portrait of William Henry Channing. Collection of the Massachusetts Historical Society.

antislavery and what was merely ostensibly so within the broader labor reform movement. One figure who articulated a more convincingly antislavery version of wage slavery arguments was William Henry Channing, the scion of a famous abolitionist family who was also the founder of the Religious Union of Associationists, a Boston-based group that combined Fourierism with Christianity. At an "Anti-Slavery Celebration" in Waltham, Massachusetts, in July 1847, Channing sought to distinguish his use of "wage slavery" to describe the conditions of oppressed workers from that of "reformers of the Mike Walsh and Northampton Democrat stamp." Unlike them, Channing clarified, he was not disposed "to lose sight of the far worse evils of the South." Although he knew it might "complicate the question," Channing insisted that the issue of slavery inherently "touche[d] upon the question of capital and labor." Abolitionists, he argued, must seriously consider how emerging forms of financial domination and the exploitation of labor impacted their movement: "Should we not confront capital, and say, it shall not rule us?"[36]

While Channing's comment points to divisions within the abolitionist movement over issues surrounding capitalism and wage labor, it also suggests that Associationists were instrumental in prompting abolitionists to debate and, in some cases, reconsider their stances on these issues. For abolitionists, the problem with such arguments against "all slavery" lay less in their radical overtones than in the fact that they lay outside the abolitionist consensus that saw property in human beings as the defining characteristic of slavery and "self-ownership" as the essential precondition of freedom. Abolitionists had been developing and refining the "property in man" argument since at least the early 1830s, when antislavery thinkers like Theodore Dwight Weld helped to revive liberal ideas of self-ownership, a tradition that may have originated with radical Puritans in the 1640s and that was refined by Enlightenment thinkers like John Locke.[37] In part, abolitionists were responding to southern slaveholders, who argued that African slavery was no more oppressive than other forms of exploited labor, including northern factory labor, and that the whippings, sexual assaults, and brutal physical punishments that abolitionists often highlighted in antislavery literature were the exception, not the rule, in the slave South. While the "chattel principle"—the idea that property in other human beings is slavery's defining characteristic—continues to serve for most historians as the *sine qua non* of slavery, by the 1840s it had become practically an article of faith among abolitionists. As Henry Highland Garnet explained to a British audience in 1850, "an American slave is an article of property—a chattel personal . . . [the English wage laborer] may be compelled to toil hard for a livelihood; but he toils for himself. He may not own an inch of soil; but he owns himself." "The being of slavery, its soul and body, lives and moves in the chattel principle, the property principle, the bill of sale principle," agreed James W. C. Pennington, who like Garnet had been formerly enslaved. Similarly, the *National Anti-Slavery Standard* responded to Associationist wage slavery arguments by insisting that "the assertion of the first right of man—the right to himself . . . underlies all other reforms." In the *Standard*'s opinion, the slave's status as human chattel meant that there was "all the difference in the world" between an enslaved person and even the most impoverished or oppressed free laborer; as the *Standard* concluded, "poverty is not Slavery."[38]

Associationists insisted that they, too, "absolutely den[ied] the right of any man to claim property in another man." But they disagreed that mere self-ownership, together with the freedom to make contracts with employers, constituted genuine freedom. Writing in the *Harbinger*, Charles Dana disputed the idea that the kind of labor performed by women and children in factories like the Lowell mills was "voluntary." Rather, "the whip which brings laborers to Lowell is NECESSITY," brought on by such factors as poverty, indebtedness, and the lack of a social safety net. In the summer of 1847, several labor reform papers, including the *Harbinger*, reprinted an excerpt from a speech given by Wendell Phillips at a gathering of the AASS in Boston, in which the famed abolitionist was quoted as saying that suffering Irish famine victims and northern factory operatives would "not be lost sight of in sympathy for the Southern slave." Phillips quickly wrote a letter to the *Liberator*, hoping to correct the "erroneous impression" that "I placed the laborer of the North and the slave on the same level, and talked perhaps of 'white slavery,' or 'wages slavery,' &c." Phillips made it plain that he rejected such comparisons, and he argued that the conditions faced by American workers were not even remotely analogous to those prevailing in Europe. "Except in a few crowded cities and a few manufacturing towns," Phillips declared, "I believe the terms 'wage slavery' and 'white slavery' would be utterly unintelligible to an audience of laboring people, as applied to themselves." He went on to explain that "there are two prominent points which distinguish the laborers of this country from the slaves. First, the laborers, as a class, are neither wronged nor oppressed: and secondly, if they were, they possess ample power to defend themselves, by the exercise of their own acknowledged rights . . . Does capital wrong them? Economy will make them capitalists. Does the crowded competition of cities reduce their wages? They have only to stay at home, devoted to other pursuits, and soon diminished supply will bring the remedy."[39]

The *Harbinger*'s response underscores how labor reformers' tendency to view oppression in class, rather than individual, terms contributed to the ideological distance between them and abolitionists. "We are sorry that Mr. Phillips has no better method to propose of elevating the laborer in this country," the editors replied, "than the preaching of 'economy, self-denial, temperance, education, and moral and religious character.' It is a poor consolation to tell the haggard operative in our factories . . . that he can escape the wrongs of capital by becoming a capitalist himself." Although a few individuals with sufficient "craft and skill" might achieve this goal, the "system of Labor for Wages" ensured that a permanent class of low-wage, hireling workers would remain. In contrast to Phillips's optimistic faith in free-market competition, the *Harbinger* believed that "wasteful" competition in the market for wages created a race to the bottom, thus tending "to sink all classes of worker to an equilibrium."[40]

Indeed, for many of those who toiled in early factories, where workers were heavily supervised and surveilled, paid paltry wages for monotonous and often dangerous tasks, and subjected to twelve- or fourteen-hour workdays (and sometimes to physical punishment), the distinction between the employer's claim to ownership in the worker's labor and the slave owner's claim to ownership of the laborer must have seemed largely academic. Labor reformers, journalists, political economists, and others in the period frequently conflated these terms, referring to "labor" to mean both the work performed by laborers and the laborer him- or herself, or to workers collectively. Perhaps because they viewed their labor power as intrinsic and inalienable, many labor reformers claimed to see little difference between the selling of one's labor and the selling of oneself. As Charles Hosmer, a shoemaker who joined the Brook Farm community during its Associationist phase, put it, God had "created all *equal*: not a part to sell themselves, whether more or less completely, any more than to be sold, to the rest, at whatever price their necessities may compel them to take." Thus "the whole system of labor for wages" was "wrong, an accursed system," since it entailed that the laborer "stands in the market-place like a slave, and is bought by the highest bidder, like any other commodity."[41]

Hosmer's comment suggests the ways that working-class reformers in the 1840s anticipated Marxian arguments about the exploitation inherent in depriving the worker of "the whole product of labor" in exchange for wages. Such understandings provided another point of potential congruence between those who opposed the unremunerated labor of slavery and those who viewed any labor arrangement in which nonproducers appropriated profits from the surplus value of a worker's labor as illegitimate. For men like Erasmus Hudson, one of the founding members of the Northampton Association, both slavery and wage labor were forms of "robbery"—slaveholders might "claim other men as chattels, and forcibly take from them their honest earnings," but in both cases, the profits of labor went "not into the pockets of the laborer—but [to] the sl[ave] holder and capitalist."[42]

A few communitarians in the 1840s went even further, denying not only the right of the employer to appropriate profits from wage labor, but the notion of an individual right to property at all. Associationist leaders like Brisbane, Greeley, and Godwin emphatically disavowed any such intention, but Collins's Skaneateles community called for the holding of all goods in common, while the heterodox abolitionist Nathaniel P. Rogers urged his readers to give up the idea of owning property in "the land and its products," declaring that the idea of property in land was as absurd as the claim to hold property in water, air, sunshine, or human beings. Nor were the well-established legal precedents for land ownership a sound defense, for slaveholders similarly used the law to uphold their claims to property rights in slaves, and a legal regime based on notions of an absolute right to property could just as easily be used to "enslave . . . any other class of mankind."[43]

Rogers, who elsewhere used "wage slavery" arguments to promote what he hoped would become an alliance between enslaved and free workers, was atypical. But an exchange between the *Harbinger* and the *National Anti-Slavery Standard*—the official organ of the AASS—suggests that the two movements tending toward greater convergence, rather than estrangement, as time went on. The *Standard* declared that it was "not blind to the other evils" that affected workers and reiterated its "deep interest in" Association, as well as its approval of all "wise efforts for the re-organization of society." But it insisted that all such reforms depended on the recognition and realization of a deeper, more fundamental principle: "the *right of man to himself*." In reply, the *Harbinger* expressed its approval of the abolitionists' "theory of man and human rights" and agreed that chattel slavery represented "the extremest [*sic*] and most perfect summing up" of "fraud, oppression, and injustice." But it argued that slavery, along with myriad other social ills, sprang from a deeper "root": the "system of universal competition and antagonism of interests" that led each individual to become "an unnatural tyrant" with nothing but disregard for the rights of others. The "rule of Might makes Right," the *Harbinger* suggested, made possible not only slavery but "the extortions of commerce . . . the cruel formalities of soul-less corporations, [and] the oppressions of the wages system." It also explained why the northern wage worker had failed to fully embrace antislavery, since ruthless competition in the market for wages had the effect of "putting down of the best instincts of humanity within him." Abolitionists were thus mistaken to think that they could eradicate slavery by focusing solely on the chattel enslavement of southern Blacks, for when such a spirit of competitiveness was "every where, there must be Slavery somewhere."[44]

By the end of the 1840s, then, Associationists and abolitionists remained divided over which reform should take precedence, but they shared much in common when it came to their understanding of how systems of economic oppression and chattel slavery mutually reinforced and sustained one another. "There can be scarcely a social or political problem raised," the *Harbinger* concluded, "which does not assail slavery in its solution, and which does not involve also, the solution of that other problem, greatest of

all, the Organization of Labor." Most Associationists agreed, moreover, that
chattel slavery was a grave injustice that had no legitimate place in American society.[45]

However, this broadly antislavery consensus concealed divisions within
Association itself. The annexation of Texas as a slave state in 1845 and the
war with Mexico from 1846 to 1848 convinced abolitionist-leaning Fourierists like William H. Channing that "Northern capitalists were combined
with Southern slaveholders to manage and control labor." By 1846, Channing could discern two Associationist positions on slavery: one condemning slavery in principle but holding that the implementation of Fourierism
would pave the way for its extinction and another holding that slavery must
be abolished before a more thoroughgoing reorganization of society could
take place. Channing believed that the group holding the latter position was
"rapidly increasing," and in June 1846, he persuaded the convention of the
American Union of Associationists in Boston to accept a strongly worded
resolution condemning the Mexican War and pledging nonviolent resistance
to it. At the group's next gathering in 1847, he issued a demand that the organization refuse to accept any money from slaveholders or the products of slave
labor. Although the resolution narrowly failed, a significant number joined
Channing in resolving that "the Anti-Slavery victory must be won, before our
day of triumph for Association can come." That same year, at a convention
of the New England Labor Reform League in Boston, carriage maker and
former Brook Farmer Henry P. Trask likewise submitted a resolution stating
that "American slavery is an evil of such gigantic magnitude that it must be
uprooted and overthrown, before the elevation sought for by the laboring
classes, can be effected."[46] Democratic-leaning Fourierists like Parke Godwin continued to support the war, prioritizing Western expansion, which
they believed would lead to the creation of available homesteads for workers, over antislavery. But even Manifest Destiny expansionists like Godwin
would soon come to see how their cherished dream of expanding the frontier
for settlement by free laborers was threatened by the simultaneous expansion of slavery. In 1850, one of the final meetings of the American Union of
Associationists reiterated its opposition to "all and every kind of Slavery," but
identified southern chattel slavery as the most inimical to the freedom of the
public lands, a major demand of working-class land reformers. Seemingly,
a growing cohort of northern workers and reformers were becoming more
cognizant of the connections between the "elevation of the Laboring Classes"
and the emancipation of enslaved laborers.[47]

"The Question Has Never Been Answered":
Association and Plans for Emancipation in the 1840s

Associationists were far from alone among reformers of the period in seeking solutions to the problems stemming from urbanization, population growth, and the spread of market capitalism in intentionally organized communities. In addition to the followers of Robert Owen in the 1810s and '20s and of Fourier in the 1840s, Shakers, Harmonites, Mormons, and a host of other groups actuated by reformist or religious impulses organized dozens of intentional communities in the decades between 1815 and 1860—approximately one hundred in all.[48] Most lasted only a few months or years, while others became the basis of permanent or long-term settlements. Only a few, however, considered enslaved people when drawing up their plans to implement ideals of cooperative labor or communitarian living. After spending time in Owen's New Harmony community in 1825, Frances Wright was struck by the potential of applying Owen's cooperative principles to the emancipation of enslaved people. If "the effects of united labor" were as superior to "individual labor" as Owen's efforts at New Harmony and in his textile factories in Scotland seemed to suggest, it occurred to Wright "that if individual labor c[oul]d not stand in competition with united labor in a free state how much less c[oul]d it do so within the regions of slavery."[49] Unfortunately, the experiment at Nashoba, described briefly in chapter 2, turned out to be a disaster. Some twenty years later, Owen himself published a plan in the Washington National Era that combined gradual emancipation, apprenticeship, state-funded education, and colonization, although it seems to have attracted little attention. Owen's son, Robert Dale Owen, who had played an important role in both New Harmony and Nashoba, had somewhat more success; although he gave up on communitarianism, he went on to a successful political career in the Republican Party, becoming a strong advocate of emancipation during the Civil War and serving on the Freedmen's Commission in the years immediately after.[50]

Given these precedents as well as the overlap between Association and abolitionism detailed above, one might ask why more Associationist thinkers did not apply Fourierist or communitarian principles to plans for slave emancipation. Although Fourier himself viewed slavery as only one of many "servitudes" stemming from the misguided social arrangements of "Civilization," and many Associationists followed suit under the assumption that chattel slavery would simply disappear once society was reorganized, in 1836

Fourier's Guadeloupe–born disciple Charles Dain had published a plan for gradual emancipation that was routinely advertised in the *Harbinger* and other Associationist publications.[51] Parke Godwin seems to have been the first American to consider applying the principles of Fourierism to emancipation, publishing a plan in his short-lived weekly the *Pathfinder* in 1843. The idea stuck with him; encountering a newspaper article about the plans to resettle some four hundred former slaves recently emancipated by John Randolph in Virginia, Parke Godwin wrote excitedly to Charles Dana in 1845 to inquire "whether there be not some of our people, who would be willing and able to take these poor fellows, and organize their labour." If by such a "grand experiment," emancipated slaves could be made into "freemen and productive loving Christians" under the system of Association, Godwin speculated, "what becomes of your slavery question and slavery too?"[52]

Ironically, the first fully elaborated Associationist plans for emancipation originated with two southern-born Fourierists: Osborne Macdaniel (part of the New York group of Fourierists but born in Georgetown in the District of Columbia) and Marx Edgeworth Lazarus, the scion of a slave-owning Jewish family in North Carolina who was active in a host of antebellum reform movements and lived at the North American Phalanx in New Jersey. To some extent, these plans emerged in response to the increased pressure for a concrete Associationist stance on antislavery stemming from the new urgency created by the Mexican-American War and the drift of many Fourierists toward abolitionism as the phalanxes began to collapse. In 1847, Albert Brisbane wrote to Thomas Durant, one of a handful of southern Fourierists based in New Orleans, inquiring whether northern Associationists should "attack slavery openly and strongly as one of the evils of Civilization" or continue to "conciliate the South." Durant's response—that Associationist should attack slavery, but should do so by appealing to reason, not emotion—helped give rise to Macdaniel's and Lazarus's plans.[53]

Like other Associationists, Macdaniel believed that slavery was wrong, but also that abolitionism was a "narrow" and "partial" reform that would only "produce a state of things in which the slaves are worse off than before." Macdaniel chose Louisiana as the site of his planned experiment, both because it was the home of Durant's small but influential circle of New Orleans–based Fourierists and because the natural resources of the Attakapas region in the southwest part of the state convinced him that it was an ideal site for a Fourierist phalanx. At a lecture on Association in Franklin, Louisiana, Macdaniel outlined a plan in which enslaved Blacks, purchased from philanthropic owners at market prices, would "earn" their freedom by working to construct phalanxes until they had accumulated enough earnings to compensate their former masters. Rotating tasks and organizing work in small teams that Fourierists called "serials," the promise of emancipation would make work more "attractive" for the enslaved, with the added benefit (for true believers like Macdaniel) of spreading Associationist phalanxes throughout the South. Macdaniel's enslaved workers would thereby "establish Association with the Whites," although the latter would gradually replace the former as the newly emancipated were replaced by fresh supplies of enslaved as well as free white laborers. The emancipated might be colonized somewhere outside the United States, or they might remain "for their own good in the career of improvement and training," but only as "subordinates" to whites. Lazarus's plan was similar—the enslaved would work extra hours for wages in order to purchase their freedom, thus inculcating in them the values of industry and time discipline—but in his scheme, newly emancipated Blacks would remain in the South, although on what terms is unclear.[54]

Much like Wright's Nashoba scheme, then, Macdaniel's and Lazarus's plans for slave emancipation were confounding mixtures of antislavery intentions, interracial cooperation, and a racist prioritization of the needs of white laborers and slaveholders over those of the enslaved.[55] That such proposals—which lagged far behind the immediate abolitionist vanguard in their endorsement of gradual, compensated emancipation and implicit racism—represent the fruits of many years of Associationist thought on slavery seems a disappointing denouement indeed. But in one important way, the Associationist schemes for emancipation, like similar plans devised by labor reformers in the period, pointed to an important critique of immediate abolitionism: abolitionists, the Associationists charged, lacked a concrete vision for the fates of formerly enslaved people after emancipation, offering only vague paeans to values of hard work, self-help, and other virtues associated with the liberal version of free labor. Pointing to the generally landless, impoverished condition of former slaves in the British Caribbean more than a decade after the Emancipation Act there, Associationists warned that a similar fate awaited emancipated Blacks in the United States if measures were not taken to provide them with land and other means of independence and subsistence.[56]

Just as importantly, the response to Macdaniel's and Lazarus's schemes from their fellow Associationists suggests that much had changed since Frances Wright's ill-fated experiment two decades earlier. When Lazarus's plan was published in the *Harbinger* in 1847, its editors attached a note disavowing any responsibility for his views. In the *Daily Chronotype*, Elizur Wright, Jr., was more directly critical, comparing Lazarus's plan for compensated emancipation to the paying of ransom to kidnappers. Then, after Macdaniel's lecture was reprinted in the *Planters' Banner*, a Louisiana paper geared toward slaveholding sugar planters, northern readers inundated the *Harbinger* with angry letters to the editor. J. L. Clarke, a Rhode Island Fourierist, wrote that he "exceedingly regretted" that Macdaniel's plan might be taken as representative of the Associationist position on slavery, since "the claim of right of property" in human beings was so "monstrously unjust and unnatural, that for persons who propose to reform society, to give this claim any acknowledgment" was "most absurdly inconsistent." A Cincinnati paper, while praising other Associationist measures, similarly blasted Macdaniel's lecture as "pandering" to slaveholders by "admitting their claim of property . . . and apologizing for Slavery in true Calhoun style, by deprecating liberty." A slave owner truly acting in accordance with the principles of Association, the author implied, would "emancipate his slaves, and compensate them for the past injustice he has inflicted upon them." Macdaniel, responding to Clarke's letter, tried to backpedal, claiming to "heartily unite with Abolitionists in condemning Slavery as a gross violation of human rights," but insisting that a more "practical solution" than abolitionist moral suasion must be undertaken. The question of how to go about abolishing slavery, Macdaniel pleaded, "has never been answered—*what is the remedy?*"[57]

Victims of their own failures to bridge the gap between idealism and pragmatism, the Associationist phalanxes had mostly dissolved or been abandoned by the early 1850s. And yet, in some ways, the Associationists remain among the most astute observers and critics of the era's most glaring disjuncture between principle and practice—the continued toleration of slavery, along with other forms of labor exploitation, in a land dedicated to freedom. Granted the insightfulness of these criticisms, as well as the ways that Associationists were deeply enmeshed in the broader coalition of antebellum reform movements, it should not be surprising that the many of the leading Associationists would coalesce around antislavery as the period wore on. "Logically," as William H. Channing put it, "I have never been able to separate the anti-slavery movement from all those which are directed to raise *Labor* universally."[58] Nor were such conclusions limited to those Associationists who prioritized the abolition of chattel slavery over wage slavery, a group that included Channing, Elizur Wright, Jr., Henry P. Trask, and others, mainly based in New England. After a series of explosive events beginning with the annexation of Texas in 1845 and reaching their peak with the Kansas-Nebraska Act of 1854, many of those who had previously subordinated their antislavery to other reform priorities—most importantly Parke Godwin, Charles A. Dana, and Horace Greeley—would go on to become leading figures in a new antislavery coalition, the Republican Party. In the meantime, what remained of Fourierist labor reform would increasingly converge with another working-class inspired movement, one prefigured by the challenge that Associationists and other early socialists had posed to the idea that property rights could exist in resources like land, labor, and human beings. Like the Associationists with whom they frequently made common cause, the land reformers of the 1840s and '50s would soon find themselves inextricably entangled with questions of slavery and abolition.

CHAPTER 4

_____

"The Greatest of All Anti-Slavery Measures":
Working-Class Land Reform and
Antislavery's Common Ground

On a winter day in early 1844, a small group of workingmen met in the back room of John Windt's printing shop on Thompson Street in New York City. The meeting had been convened by George Henry Evans, editor of the long-running *Working Man's Advocate* and veteran of the Working Men's movement of the 1820s and '30s, who had recently returned to New York City from an extended hiatus in rural New Jersey. After the defeat of the Working Men's Party in 1830, Evans had tended his small farm near Granville, in Essex County, mulling over ideas about land and labor while sporadically continuing to publish the *Advocate*. Like Evans, all of the men who gathered in Windt's office that winter day in 1844 were skilled tradesmen (several of them printers) with substantial backgrounds in the radical working-class movements of the previous decade and a half, including the Working Men's and Loco Foco parties, Owenite communitarianism, and the Chartist movement. Evans, Windt, Thomas A. Devyr, Lewis Masquerier, William V. Barr, and James Pyne formed the nucleus of an organization they at first referred to as the National Reform Union or the Agrarian League but soon rechristened as the National Reform Association. Although the group's formation went little noticed at the time, for much of the next decade the National Reformers would be at the forefront of a working-class movement for one of the most popular and consequential reforms of the Civil War Era: free homesteads on the public domain.[1]

Within a few weeks after this initial meeting, the National Reform Association held more than twenty public meetings in New York City; launched a newspaper, the *People's Rights*; and began to hold weekly meetings on

Thursday nights in their headquarters in Evans's office at Chatham and Mulberry Streets. Over the next decade, in the pamphlets and circulars issuing from the offices of the *Working Man's Advocate*—in street corner stump speeches and street cart processions, in rallies in city parks and public buildings, and in labor newspapers, labor reform conventions, and auxiliary organizations that spread from New York City to the Nebraska Territory—the brand of working-class land reform developed by Evans and the National Reformers would be debated and discussed, challenged and refined, before slowly making its way into the popular consciousness, and eventually into political party platforms and legislation. As it did so, the seemingly unrelated issue of land reform would intersect inescapably with what was becoming the political and social issue overshadowing all others: the question of slavery and abolition.[2]

Over the next few months, the National Reform Association spelled out a three-point program to address the issues identified in its report. First, the public lands must be divided into 160-acre plots that would be given away free of charge by the government to "actual settlers," rather than speculators. Second, the right to these landholdings must be inalienable. The seizure of homesteads for debts would be abolished; settlers might sell any "improvements" to the land, like farm buildings, homes, or fences, but the land itself could not be sold or rented. And third, the quantity of land that any one individual might occupy would be limited by law.[3]

In looking to the land for salvation, the National Reformers were promoting a panacea, the roots of which stretched back to the very origins of colonial British North America, with more recent and direct precedents that included Paine's *Agrarian Justice*, Skidmore's *Right to Property!* and the Working Men's movement's demand for access to the public lands. Even as Evans was issuing the National Reformers' first manifestos in the mid-1840s, similar schemes were being hatched across the Atlantic by groups like the Chartist Land Company, an offshoot of Britain's working-class Chartist movement; thirty years earlier, Thomas Spence and his disciples in England had preached similar ideas. Demands for land would continue to echo across the post–Civil War period, as Americans poured into the trans-Mississippi West, and groups ranging from formerly enslaved African Americans to Populist Party leaders echoed the call for the redistribution of land in ways that transcended the Civil War–era Homestead Act.[4]

In its basic outline, the National Reform program was a classic expression of the "safety-valve theory," later made famous by Frederick Jackson Turner,

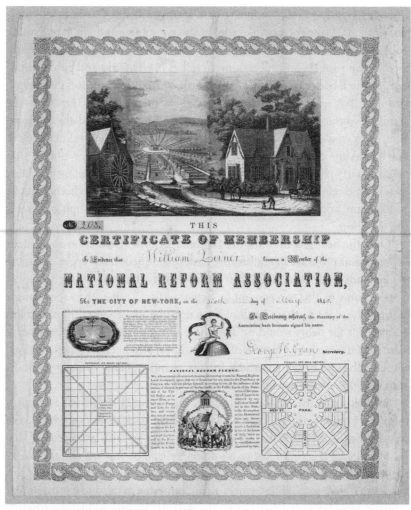

Figure 8. A certificate of membership in the National Reform Association, 1848. The plans for what National Reformers called "rural republican townships," probably created by former Owenite Lewis Masquerier, reflect the influence of utopian community planning on the land reform movement. The accompanying pledge was the only requirement for membership in the National Reform Association. The woodcut illustration at top depicts an idealized version of the township, complete with water-powered mill, a central town hall and meeting place, and a modest but comfortable-looking home. American Antiquarian Society.

which viewed settlement of western lands by wage earners and immigrants as the key to releasing social pressure and overcompetition for wages in crowded eastern cities. But contained within the three apparently straight-forward planks in the National Reform program were some genuinely new and genuinely radical ideas. National Reform ideology had received an injection of communitarian utopianism from the Associationists, with whom they increasingly made common cause, and from the Owenites—the latter mainly in the person of Lewis Masquerier, a former disciple of Owen who drew up ambitious plans for "rural republican townships" spiraling out from central plazas and connected by a series of roads and turnpikes, organized on a grid plan. But on a more basic level, the National Reform program was predicated on the idea that claims to certain forms of property, namely property in the soil, were illegitimate and therefore subject to intervention. Although Evans and other National Reform leaders claimed that their approach was "conservative" in the sense that it would not deprive anyone of their existing right to property, the third plank, referred to by land reformers as "limitation," struck not only at the heart of the economic inequalities created by excessive accumulations of landed property, but at the very idea of private property in land. As "the common inheritance of all mankind," National Reformers argued, all enjoyed an "equal right to the soil."[5]

Even if it was not yet self-evident to a majority of Americans that the institution of property in land was a violation of a sacred "right to the soil," it should have been clear, National Reformers held, that the public lands belonged to "the People"—not the individual states, as more orthodox Jacksonian Democrats insisted. In 1840, more than 800 million acres of public land existed, most of it in the Louisiana Purchase territories, but with substantial amounts of unsold lands in Florida, Mississippi, and Alabama, as well as the Old Northwest states of Illinois, Indiana, Ohio, and Michigan.[6] (The fact that much of this land was inhabited and claimed by Native Americans posed an ethical and moral dilemma for the National Reformers, but, as we will see, it was one for which they had a ready if not entirely convincing solution.) As opposed to the reigning ideas for dealing with federal government–held lands—"pre-emption" (allowing squatters to the right to first purchase of lands they occupied at a minimum price set by the government), "distribution" (distributing the proceeds of land sales to the states), and "cession" (ceding public lands to the states in which they were located)—the National Reformers believed that the public lands were held by the United

States "in trust" for its people and should be regarded as a "Capital Stock, which belongs, not to us only, but to posterity." Neither Congress nor any other branch of government had the right to sell them off to speculators, railroad companies, corporations, or any other private entities, but it *did* have the right, indeed the obligation, to grant them as homesteads. The National Reformers thus looked to federal government intervention to facilitate the division and redistribution of a form of property that most Americans considered to be matters of private property and "states' rights." No wonder that conservatives of all stripes—but slave owners in particular—denounced the National Reformers as "agrarians," "socialists," and "levellers."[7]

What, if anything, this all had to do with slavery may not seem obvious at first. But Evans and other land reformers made the connection repeatedly during the latter half of the 1840s, beginning in the second paragraph of one of its earliest tracts, a sixteen-page pamphlet entitled *Young America! Principles and Objects of the National Reform Association*. After a fairly standard reiteration of the well-rehearsed comparison between enslaved workers compelled by the lash and free ones compelled by the "*fear of want*," the pamphlet rhetorically asked readers whether it was "right, that any man should be *compelled*, by any sort of force, to work for any other man to obtain the means of existence." Although the "wage slavery" comparison once again inherently prioritized white workers at the expense of minimizing the suffering of enslaved people, the *Principles and Objects* made clear that the National Reformers stood opposed to any form of coerced labor. In their eyes, the recognition of a right to the land was the "*remedy*" not just for the ills plaguing white wage workers, but for all of "the evils that now afflict Humanity." Land reform, Evans believed, was "the common ground on which *all* reformers could meet."[8]

Whether its leading exponents intended it to or not, then, the National Reformers' land reform program was destined to become entangled with the conflict over slavery. Their demand that the public lands be turned into small, single-family homesteads worked by free laborers and their families directly threatened slaveholder expansionism, while their updated brand of "agrarianism" indirectly threatened slaveholders' demands for an ever more impenetrable security of their property in land and human beings. Worse yet from the perspective of slaveholders, the National Reformers invoked the power of the federal government to realize these goals, implying that Congress enjoyed broad, if not absolute, powers over the territories.

National Reform Ideology and the Politics of the 1840s

On the mastheads of his newspapers and in National Reform pamphlets, Evans evoked authorities from Moses to Mackenzie; Blackstone to Black Hawk; Paine, Spence, Jefferson, Jackson, Cobbett, and Carlile—all of whom, National Reformers claimed, had written in support of a natural right to the land.[9] But the most important influences to shape Evans's evolving agrarianism were those circulating within the radical workingmen's milieu with which he had long been associated. Although he claimed not to have encountered Paine's *Agrarian Justice* until the early 1840s, Evans clearly saw himself in the tradition of the author of *Common Sense* and *Rights of Man*; he had published several editions of Paine's works during the 1830s and had been a participant in the annual celebrations of Paine's birthday held by New York workingmen. He also acknowledged the influence of such diverse authorities as the French political economist Henri de Saint-Simon and the early English socialists John Gray, John Francis Bray, William Godwin, and Thomas Spence (whose 1796 pamphlet, *The Meridian Sun of Liberty*, Evans reprinted). The expatriate Evans claimed to have encountered all of these thinkers in an English "social paper," the *Working Bee*, in the early 1840s, and transatlantic influences continued to have an impact on the land and labor movements throughout the decade. Radical ideas growing out of the Chartist movement in Britain and physically transplanted Chartists like Thomas Devyr both played a significant role in the working-class movements of the United States in the 1840s, and the National Reformers' land scheme was of a piece with similar working-class plans in Britain, such as those of Feargus O'Connor's Chartist Co-Operative Land Company and William Evans's Potters' Joint-Stock Emigration Society. Surprisingly, given that they had been on opposite sides of the Working Men's Party factions in 1829–1830, Evans also recognized another influence in Thomas Skidmore's *The Right of Man to Property!*, which he now declared contained "more truths than any ten books which have since been published." Despite the leading National Reformers' roots in the secular freethinking tradition, they also drew from the ancient Jewish concept (rediscovered by Protestant Dissenters in the seventeenth century) of the Great Jubilee, in which slaves would be freed and lands restored to their original owners. Much as abolitionists viewed slavery, working-class land reformers like Evans and Devyr saw property in land as America's original sin, "the *root* of the evil" originating in "the most remote periods of time," that was responsible for the "vast inequality of condition now existing among us."[10]

The connection to Skidmore, whose support for abolition and Black rights had surpassed most of his fellow Working Men in the 1820s and early '30s, points to another, more unlikely source of Evans's land reform ideology. As we have seen, abolitionists like John A. Collins, William H. Channing, and Nathaniel P. Rogers, perhaps prompted by their scrutiny of slaveholders' claims to own property in man, also began to question the legitimacy of other forms of property, including property in land. Collins's *Bird's Eye View of Society* (1844) lamented that "ninety-nine hundredths of the human family are robbed of the land, and in their poverty and ignorance, [must] toil for bread," while the preamble to the constitution of his New England Social Reform Society declared that "individual interest has robbed the people of the soil and its products, their birthright" and concluded that "if man has an inalienable right to life, it legitimately follows that he has an inalienable right to that which can alone sustain life." If there were no "individual and absolute proprietorship in the earth," the preamble further proclaimed, there would be no "temptation to fraud, theft, slavery, piracy, or war." And Elizur Wright, Jr., the former national secretary of the American Anti-Slavery Society described in chapter 3, agreed with Collins and Evans that the system of land ownership in the so-called civilized world was "the worst system the world ever saw," although he gave a somewhat lower estimate (three-fourths) of the proportion of mankind forced into the market for wages by land monopoly. "Abolish land monopoly and you abolish at one blow idleness and poverty," Wright affirmed, before endorsing a modified version of the National Reformers' platform.[11]

The National Reformers' vision of free labor was predicated on related arguments about the nature of property rights, ones that flowed logically from the labor theory of value. As Evans explained, "the use of the LAND is the equal natural right of all citizens of this and future generations . . . land is not property, and, therefore, should not be transferable like the products of man's labor." This "error," according to Evans, made "labor subject to the landlords . . . and deprives it of its just reward."[12] John Pickering, a Cincinnati workingman and amateur political economist who became a leading spokesman for National Reform in that burgeoning border city, made perhaps the period's clearest connection between the labor theory of value and the natural right to the soil. In *The Working Man's Political Economy* (1847), Pickering concluded that legitimate "property consists of the products of human industry, or those things *only* which man creates, makes, or produces, by the energies of his physical capabilities." Therefore, the land was "never to be confounded with property upon it—land itself, *not* being a product of *human labor*, cannot, in justice, be valued by money." Nor were Pickering and the National Reformers alone in advancing such arguments. The same year that Pickering's work was published, Elizur Wright argued that land "does not and cannot come under the same category of other property, such as grain, cloth, metals, the product of industry." Every individual, Wright maintained, had "a peculiar right to the products of his own industry . . . a right which cannot extend to . . . the air, the water, the soil, the rocks, and the mines, [which are] given for the common benefit of all." To men like Evans, Pickering, and Wright, the idea of a property right in the "productions of nature" was (in Pickering's words) "a perfect absurdity."[13]

Perhaps taking a cue from the approaches utilized by abolitionists, National Reform members signed a pledge vowing not to vote for any candidate who would not pledge himself to "prevent all further traffic in the Public Lands," and quizzed politicians hoping to secure such a vow. But the land reformers' project, unlike that of the nonvoting Garrisonians, was an inherently political one. By the 1840s, the absorption of most former Workies and Loco Focos into the party of Jackson had solidified the Democrats' association with labor, even as the professional politicians within the Democratic Party showed little intention of taking their proposals seriously. But, despite their own Democratic proclivities, Evans, Commerford, and other leading National Reformers chafed at the attempts by Tammany Hall to co-opt land reform, and tried hard to avoid party alliances and steer an independent political path (other leading National Reformers, like Alvan Bovay, were Whigs). The response of the influential New England labor paper, the *Voice of Industry*, suggests that many wage workers, or at least those who claimed to speak for them, were ready for a third-party approach: the *Voice of Industry* cheered the National Reformers' political efforts as constituting the arrival of "a new party," which it alternately referred to as "the National Reform Party," "the Workingmen's Party," or "the Humanity Party." Other workers, no doubt, were drawn by the National Reformers' simple but effective slogan: "Vote Yourself a Farm."[14]

Initially, the National Reformers were forced to confront the fact that their biggest obstacle was their own lack of electoral power; in 1844, none of the candidates of either party running for state office in New York bothered to respond to a National Reform questionnaire. A series of relatively localized events in the mid-1840s, however, would soon bring the group a degree of national attention, and perhaps notoriety. The Anti-Rent movement, which had begun in the late 1830s in the counties of the Upper Hudson Valley region, presented itself as a test case for National Reform theories about the dangers of concentrated landholding. The anomalous pattern of landholding in the region, a remnant of legal claims dating to the time of the Dutch patroons, concentrated some two million acres of upstate land in the hands of the Van Rensselaers, the Livingstons, and a few other landlords. Perhaps a twelfth of the state's population, meanwhile, labored on their lands as tenants. Beginning in 1839, upstate tenants organized a movement to resist the unfair practices stemming from the landlords' monopoly on land, utilizing rent boycotts, lobbying, legal challenges to landholders' titles, and, most dramatically armed bands of men disguised as "Indians," who forcibly prevented evictions or seizure of property for nonpayment of rent. The movement was a natural fit for the National Reformers, who saw an opportunity to put their land reform principles into practice and consolidate a political base for a national land reform movement, while providing the Anti-Renters with a broader ideological underpinning for their struggle. Like the National Reformers, the Anti-Renters insisted that their independence could only be attained by the redistribution of landed property. As one Columbia County Anti-Renter suggested in a letter to *Young America*, the goals of the two movements overlapped, and might together form the basis for the substitution of wage labor with a system of cooperative exchange.[15]

By the time of the National Reform Association's formation, the Anti-Rent movement was transforming from an extralegal, grassroots protest movement to an organized political campaign. Both Thomas Devyr, an Irishborn former Chartist, and Alvan Bovay, the National Reform corresponding secretary and a future founder of the Republican Party, were instrumental in linking the Anti-Rent cause to land reform and in steering Anti-Renters into an electoral alliance with the National Reformers. Although it remains unclear to what extent Anti-Rent farmers embraced the radical agrarianism of the land reformers, the National Reformers won the backing of some of the most important Anti-Rent leaders. But a political backlash was not long in coming. Conservatives in both major parties denounced the "agrarianism" of the Anti-Renters, but it was to the Democrats—specifically, the Albany Regency, the political machine that dominated New York state politics—that the landowning class turned to defend their propertied interests. Much as they would during later struggles over the status of slavery in the territories, the majority of Democratic power brokers came to the aid of an entrenched landed aristocracy.

More surprising was the stance of Whigs such as Horace Greeley and New York governor William H. Seward. The *New-York Tribune* editor denounced the violence associated with the Anti-Rent movement but questioned the propriety of large concentrations of landholding; as we will see, he eventually became a staunch if somewhat inconsistent supporter of land reform. Seward, a future Republican presidential contender and U.S. secretary of state, complied with the landholders' demands to send in the state militia to restore order, but he appeared sympathetic to the Anti-Rent cause in his annual address, proposing to rewrite the state's land tenure laws in order to make them "more accordant with the principles of republican government." The Anti-Rent movement continued to gain strength, and a legislative committee convened by Seward concluded that the land tenure system in New York violated the public welfare, and that the state might use eminent domain to force the sale of parcels of land to tenants at a fair price. Seward, who also signed laws protecting the rights of fugitive slaves, free Black citizens, and abolitionists, would not abandon the causes of land reform or antislavery on entering the U.S. Senate in 1849, nor would the land reformers forget him.[16]

Further political shifts were hinted at by William L. Mackenzie, an expatriate Canadian and early National Reform supporter who had led the Upper Canada Rebellion in 1837, an event that in some ways prefigured and paralleled the Dorr Rebellion in Rhode Island. Appearing at Croton Hall, the site of numerous National Reform meetings not far from the notorious Five Points neighborhood, Mackenzie gave a speech on the "Distress of the Working Classes" that directly connected the freedom of the soil to slaveholder expansionism. Noting the millions of dollars spent on purchasing the slave territories of Louisiana, Florida, and now (as the Tyler administration proposed) Texas, Mackenzie denounced the expenditure of public funds for territory "to cut up into slave states" while doing nothing to promote "liberty in the north." The $45 million spent on the purchase of Florida and subsequent wars against Native Americans and runaway slaves, he suggested, could have instead purchased 225,000 160-acre farms. "Free trade is a fine thing," Mackenzie intoned, alluding to the economic orthodoxy of both northern Jacksonians and southern slaveholders, "but we first want *free labor*." Not only would the antitariff and nullification policies of southern-rights spokesmen like Calhoun and McDuffie do nothing for the "enslaved African," but their threats of secession implied that slaveholder politicians calculated the price of the Union "as if it were a bale of cotton."[17]

In 1844, the long-simmering question of Texas "annexation," as it was somewhat euphemistically termed, was threatening to boil over. The Republic of Texas, which by that time contained large numbers of slaveholders and enslaved people, had been independent for eight years, the issue of its relationship to the United States sidelined by a consensus among the political class that adding another slave state to the Union would upset the sectional balance, agitate abolitionists, and renew the conflicts over slavery. Evans endorsed bringing Texas into the Union, but only on two conditions: first, that the abolition of "*all* slavery" be provided for by reserving its remaining public lands for free settlers, and "second, that no human being shall be born a slave in Texas after the annexation"—an approach to gradual emancipation similar to the *post nati* or "free womb" laws adopted by several northern states and some Latin American countries. Similarly, the Oregon country could be safely annexed as long as war with Britain were avoided, and "the rights and existence of the Indian race" as well as "the natural rights of Universal Man" were respected by making its lands available free to both whites and Native populations.[18]

The stances of working-class land reformers in the conflicts over the Anti-Rent movement and Texas annexation thus revealed growing fault lines in labor reformers' longstanding loyalty to the Jacksonian Democrats—ones that in some ways anticipated the political realignments to come in the years between the outbreak of Mexican-American War in 1846 and the passage of the Kansas-Nebraska Act in 1854. Although usually depicted as anomalous in the political history of the "Jacksonian Era," the ad hoc alliances created by the Anti-Rent struggles would not be the last time that small farmers and urban workers made common cause with progressive antislavery nationalists. As they would in future debates over the issues of land, labor, and slavery, both radical former Democrats and progressive Whigs joined forces around an expansive conception of the "public welfare" and embraced unprecedented state interventions into the realm of private property to realize the broader social goals that their principles demanded. More concretely, the groundwork laid by National Reform activity in these struggles would contribute to one important base of support among urban land reformers, landless farmers, and antislavery activists—part of the broad coalition that would soon become loosely known as "free soil."[19]

"Slaves to the Land-Lord":
National Reformers, Race, and "White Slavery"

The National Reformers' path to coalition with abolitionists, however, faced at least one major ideological hurdle: their leaders' insistence that the state of landlessness, like that of working for someone else at wages, was a form of "slavery" comparable to chattel slavery. The now revived *Working Man's Advocate*, as well as Evans's new paper focused on land reform, *Young America*, were rife with articles expounding on "white slavery" and "wage slavery" comparisons. For Evans and other National Reformers, such comparisons were not simply metaphorical. Despite the support for abolition he had voiced in the 1830s, and his consistent claim that he supported abolition of "all slavery," Evans now insisted that landless white workers were slaves in all but name.[20] In Evans's case, this did not imply a growing acceptance of slavery; rather, he disagreed with abolitionists about which to prioritize, the "slavery" of poverty and landlessness or the chattel slavery of forced laborers considered to be human property by their enslavers.

In an 1844 letter to abolitionist Gerrit Smith (discussed in detail below), Evans wrote that "I was formerly, like yourself, sir, a very warm advocate of the abolition of slavery. This was before I saw that there was *white* slavery."[21] The quote has sometimes been used as an example of white workers' rejection of abolitionism as well as their emerging sense of a shared identity based on "whiteness"—or, less frequently, to illustrate a narrative of declension as labor leaders' early enthusiasm for antislavery waned over the Jacksonian period. But the truth is somewhat more complicated. On one hand, there is evidence that Evans never really abandoned his earlier abolitionism, even if the brand of gradual emancipation he favored had more in common with the abolitionists of a generation earlier. In a lengthy article written the same year as his exchange with Smith, Evans repudiated South Carolina's John Calhoun, by then known as the foremost exponent of the argument that slavery was a "positive good." Evans flatly rejected what he called Calhoun's "theory of holding the working classes of the South in perpetual slavery to all eternity because they happen to have dark skins and curly hair," and proposed that "the working classes of the North have intelligence enough to understand that most of the arguments that would apply in favor of Black Slavery would be equally applicable in favor of White Serfdom." If southerners failed to adopt a plan for the "gradual" but "progressive" abolition of slavery, Evans predicted, they would lose the support of northern workers for traditionally Democratic ideals of states' rights and free trade.[22]

Evans's understanding of slavery and abolition in the mid-1840s, then, was in some sense still grounded in the Jacksonian Era political struggles over tariffs and "equal rights," as well as in the founding generation's optimistic faith that slavery would inevitably and voluntarily be placed on a path to gradual extinction. Perhaps just as importantly, and in common with other "labor abolitionists," it was predicated on his own experience as a worker. Although they acknowledged the inherent injustice of claiming property in human beings, most labor reformers continued to view slavery not as a property regime but instead as a system of *labor*, one marked by a degree of dependence on employers (or the employing class) that was unacceptable and unsuitable for free citizens of a republic. Whereas abolitionists called for "the total repudiation of the Heaven-forbidden idea of property in man," working class reformers replied that it was "a gross error" to suppose that a man's body had to be claimed as property in order to be held as a slave. As Evans explained to Gerrit Smith, slavery consisted "in being subject to the will of a master, or a master class, by a deprivation of rights." This definition was closely tied to another common labor criticism of slavery, that it deprived the enslaved worker of the right to "the fruits of his labor." If, as labor intellectuals like Orestes Brownson had been arguing at least since the beginning of the 1840s, the wage system appropriated part of the product of labor to the employer or capitalist in the form of profit, then it, too, denied the laborer the fruit of his or her labor.[23] Just as abolitionists rejected the labor reformers' contention that wage labor (or landlessness) comprised a state of slavery, labor reformers rejected the emerging consensus that viewed "free labor"—defined as self-ownership and the freedom to compete in the market for wages—as the essence of freedom. Where defenders of the emerging liberal understanding of free labor saw freedom of choice and mobility, labor reformers saw compulsion and coercion, the freedom only to accept the wages offered by the employer—in other words, to "work, or starve." Where abolitionists saw white wage workers (and potentially, liberated slaves) as equals in the market for labor, labor reformers saw a vast asymmetry of power, in which the combined capital of employers rendered nominally free workers as dependent on them as slaves were on their masters. In their disputes over what comprised slavery, labor reformers and abolitionists were locked in a fundamental disagreement over the meaning of freedom itself.[24]

As time went on, however, the land reformers' critique of "land monopoly" led at least some of them to draw connections between property in land and property in man. As John Pickering explained in *The Working Man's Political Economy*, claims to property in land helped to "sustain . . . with the same propriety" slaveholders' claims to property in their enslaved workers. In fact, he explained, such misguided understandings of property rights were "the foundation of all kinds of slavery." The laws propping up property in human beings did not "make the transaction just or right," since even slaveholders knew deep down that their human property "had been stolen." The practice of buying and selling land, Pickering argued, was "precisely similar."[25]

But ironically, even as land reform ideology underscored the divergence of interests between northern workers and slaveholders and linked property in land to property in man, it also militated against more full-throated support for abolition. In the case of Pickering, his identification of the essential similarity between the two systems did not lead him to embrace abolitionism. Instead, in a twist on the proslavery argument that emancipation would undermine white workers by adding to the competition for low-wage jobs, Pickering claimed that the existing inequalities of property would only be exacerbated by the creation of a landless class of former slaves. Rejecting the conclusion that workers had to fight against an unholy alliance between (in Massachusetts senator Charles Sumner's famous quote) the "lords of the lash" and the "lords of the loom," Pickering believed that the fight over slavery was one best left to the "gentleman capitalists." For Pickering, writing in the late 1840s, the political contest over slavery appeared to be merely a battle to decide "which system is the best to suffer under."[26]

Evans, meanwhile, doubled down on and even expanded on white slavery comparisons. Responding to O'Connor's *Northern Star*, an influential radical newspaper in Britain, Evans declared that "we are no less opposed to slavery now than we ever have been. . . . But we have lived to learn that the slave to the land-*Lord* is in a worse, aye, a *worse* condition, than the slave who has a master of his own." While such claims were rightly denounced by abolitionists, they resonated with workers in an era before unemployment and accident benefits, health insurance, pensions, and retirement plans. Southern slaveholders, Evans explained, offered their oppressed labor force at least a minimum security of food, shelter, and protection in old age, none of which were enjoyed by the landless wage worker. It made little sense, then, to emancipate enslaved people before freedom of the soil had been established. To emancipate the enslaved would be merely to "reduce" them to "the level of the landless white," resulting in their "transfer ... from the one form of slavery to the other."[27]

The abolition of slavery in the British West Indies seemed to bear out these pessimistic conclusions. Notably, Evans rejected the claims by slavery's defenders that the experience of the West Indies proved the futility of emancipating "idle" and "ignorant" slaves; emancipation, he wrote, "has shown that the blacks can live and *pay rent*, and it has shown also that they are capable of improvement." But since "the whites retain most of the *land*," and since former slave owners were in the process of importing indentured servants from India and elsewhere in the Empire, emancipated Blacks would "eventually" regress into a situation akin to slavery, unless "the free land doctrine" were adopted. Citing a statistic from Antigua claiming that the advent of free labor there required only a third of the labor that had been employed during slavery, Evans predicted that the implementation of the "wages system" in the South would result in a similar proportion of former slaves being thrust into an overcompetitive market for wage labor. A relatively fortunate minority would be trapped in a race to the bottom, while the majority would be entirely without employment. Without access to land or other productive property, Evans argued, the mere "substitution" of slavery for free labor would do little to improve the material conditions of the enslaved.[28]

While it anticipated some of the criticisms of the limitations of liberal free labor ideology that that became apparent after emancipation, the labor reform critique of free labor also created an obstacle to the formation of an alliance with abolitionists, one that might have more effectively waged a unified campaign against "all slavery." Far from promoting solidarity with enslaved workers, "white slavery" comparisons diminished the suffering of enslaved Blacks and, somewhat counterintuitively, emphasized the gulf separating them from free white workers by implying that the "slavery" of white freemen was an inversion of the natural order of things. While he eschewed overt racism and emphasized that people of African descent were entitled to basic rights, including the right to land, Evans's frequent reliance on white slavery language bolstered white workers' growing understanding of themselves as a privileged caste with little in common with workers of color, whether enslaved or free. It would take someone whose commitment to both abolitionism and Black equality ran far deeper than Evans's to finally push Evans and the National Reformers to embrace a more robust brand of antislavery.[29]

Gerrit Smith, Black Abolitionists, and the Origins of the Antislavery–Land Reform Alliance

Today, Gerrit Smith is far less well-known than William Lloyd Garrison or Frederick Douglass, but in the 1840s he was one of the most prominent abolitionists in the United States. He was also one of its largest landowners; as the inheritor of a vast estate from his father, a land speculator and partner in John Jacob Astor's fur-trading business, Smith oversaw tens of thousands of acres in Upstate New York. For years, Smith had been using his considerable wealth to fund a number of antislavery and reform ventures, donating tens of thousands of dollars to the American Anti-Slavery Society, purchasing the freedom of enslaved people, and helping to found the antislavery Liberty Party. From his country estate in the rural hamlet of Peterboro, Smith exercised considerable influence over a faction of mostly New York–based abolitionists.[30]

Beginning in the summer of 1844, Smith embarked on an extraordinary exchange of letters with Evans that would change the course of both men's careers as reformers. The opening broadside in the exchange was a shot by

Figure 9. This portrait of Gerrit Smith by Matthew Brady captures the abolitionist's determination and uncompromising attitude. Smithsonian National Portrait Gallery.

Evans aimed across Smith's bow. In a Fourth of July open letter published in
the *Working Man's Advocate*, Evans bluntly informed the abolitionist that, as
the owner of some fifty thousand acres of land, "you are one of the largest
Slaveholders in the United States." More boldly still, Evans went on to suggest that Smith might rectify the situation and redeem himself by donating
his fifty thousand acres to "fifty thousand destitute inhabitants of the cities,"
who, by Evans's lights, were the "virtual slaves" of landowners like Smith.[31]
Smith's reply came two weeks later. To what must have been the land reformer's astonishment, Smith's reply informed Evans that he had "cherished for
years" the idea of large landowners dividing up their holdings to give away to
the poor. But Smith also held Evans's feet to the fire, chastising him and other
land reformers for their willingness to court the support of Democratic presidential candidate and slaveholder James K. Polk, their approval of armed
violence during the Dorr Rebellion, and their support for colonization. More
pointedly still, he offered a harsh indictment of Evans's "white slavery" rhetoric, arguing that it amounted to a de facto justification of slavery. Although
he knew that Evans would deny that references to the "slavery" of the landless
implied the justification of chattel slavery, "you do justify it, when you say
that poverty is as bad as slavery—nay, is even identical with it. Were you, and
your wife, and children, bought and sold and torn asunder, by Southern masters, and urged to your daily tasks by the Southern lash; and were I to answer
the appeals in your behalf with the cold-hearted and truthless remark, that
your condition is no worse than that of the Northern poor man, you would,
most properly, accuse me of justifying your enslavement."[32] Until land and
labor reformers adopted a more forthrightly antislavery position, Smith
could not support them. Moreover, until they embraced a vision of "human
rights" that included African Americans on a basis of equality, their project
was doomed to fail. Referring to Evans's occasional musings about the possibility of colonizing the formerly enslaved, whether in Haiti or in separate
colonies within the public lands of the United States, Smith urged him to
"give up all your notions of a separate dwelling place for colored people, and
of *first* looking after white slaves, and identify yourself with the whole human
family." "Every association in this land that would successfully prosecute a
benevolent scheme must first join the Abolitionists," Smith insisted. "Good
men cannot keep out of this partnership. Make the experiment."[33]

The experiment would be made—by both sides. Evans declared himself "more satisfied" by Smith's reply than any other communication he had
received, and he praised the abolitionist's "frankness and honesty." While he

stubbornly refused to relinquish his "white slavery" line of argument, Evans reaffirmed that "we believe the black has as good a right to be free as the white." As he explained to Smith, his proposals for separate "colonies" for former slaves had not stemmed from any bias of his own, but were in deference to the widespread "prejudice against color" among whites. Still, he emphasized that "we have *not* proposed to make the Public Lands free to any particular class of citizens, exclusively." Since "we live in the same *houses* with blacks" in New York City, Evans could not foresee "that there would be any more difficulty in living on contiguous farms or lots." For his part, Smith responded by quoting William Leggett's challenge to "convince me that a principle is right in the abstract, and I will reduce it to practice, if I can."[34]

Smith was soon convinced. Although the reasons for his sudden conversion remain unclear, his wife, Ann Carroll Fitzhugh Smith, may have played a behind-the-scenes role in precipitating the eventual collaboration between Evans and her husband.[35] Whatever the case, by 1846, Gerrit Smith was hailing land reform as "the greatest of all Anti-Slavery measures." "I am an Agrarian," he declared that year. Although he denounced the "lawless, violent and bloody" brand of revolutionary agrarianism, he now believed that "every man, who desires a farm, should have one," adding elsewhere that "men of true benevolence" should strive for a society in which "no man be rich, and no man be poor."[36] Although he continued to champion slave emancipation, Smith now viewed the relationship between abolition and land reform as mutually reinforcing: "The abolition of land monopoly in America," he wrote in 1847, "would be the abolition of Slavery in America." He saw clearly what the land reformers had only begun to articulate, that the implementation of land reform would essentially foreclose the further spread of slavery by "the breaking up of plantations—of tracts of several hundred, and in many instances, of thousands of acres—into farms of fifty or a hundred acres." Such a redistribution, Smith prophesied, "would leave but little room, little occasion for the employment of slaves." Sounding like Evans, Smith predicted that if slavery were abolished "to-morrow . . . Land Monopoly would pave the way for its re-establishment. But abolish Land Monopoly—make every American citizen the owner of a farm adequate to his necessity—and there will be no room for the return of slavery." Freedom of the soil was "the great basis reform," one which would pave the way for all others, including antislavery.[37]

Smith quickly sought to put his newfound theory into practice in a land reform scheme of his own—one that sought restorative justice for the victims of slavery and their descendants while demonstrating the efficacy of landed independence for those who suffered from its economic and social aftereffects. On August 1, 1846—the anniversary of West Indian emancipation—Smith announced a plan to give away some 120,000 acres of his lands to poor African Americans across New York State. Drawing on his contacts in New York's free Black community, Smith appointed Presbyterian minister Theodore S. Wright, *Colored American* publisher and clergyman Charles B. Ray, and the distinguished doctor James McCune Smith to oversee the plan as trustees. The three were placed in charge of selecting some three thousand African Americans in New York City to receive grants of between forty and sixty acres of land apiece, most of it located in the Adirondack wilderness region of Upstate New York.[38] A few years later, in 1849, Smith put Evans and the Quaker abolitionist Isaac T. Hopper on a committee charged with identifying an additional thousand poor men and women to receive similar grants of land—only this time the recipients would be white. Although the first round of grants had targeted African Americans, a group Smith identified as "the poorest of the poor, and the most deeply wronged class of our citizens," he ultimately concluded that he "could not put a bounty on color" in distributing his lands.[39]

The decision to allot his grants of land along racially bifurcated lines might seem strange, if not hypocritical, for Smith, a thoroughgoing believer in racial equality who cultivated deep friendships with Frederick Douglass and McCune Smith.[40] But regardless of whether Smith's intentions or execution was misguided, the response from the African American community to Smith's land grant plan, at least so far as can be gauged by the statements of its acknowledged leaders, was overwhelmingly positive. According to Amos Beman, a Black clergyman in New Haven, Connecticut, there was a "fever in this city among the colored people . . . to procure homesteads" after news of Smith's announcement reached town, an assessment corroborated by Elizur Wright, who reported that "a convention of the colored people" in Ithaca, New York, "enthusiastically" welcomed the news of Smith's land grants and resolved to settle on them. Douglass promoted the scheme in the *North Star*, while all-Black gatherings and conventions, like the Colored Conventions of the late 1840s and early '50s also endorsed Smith's land giveaway. No similar plan, Ray, Wright, and McCune Smith wrote elsewhere, had been "more full of hope to our down trodden portion of the human race."[41]

The statements of Ray, Wright, McCune Smith, and numerous other Black leaders of the period suggest that many free Blacks understood land reform as a bread-and-butter approach that spoke to the economic needs of the Black community, as well as, perhaps, the psychological needs of a group

Figures 10–12. (clockwise from top left) Ministers Charles B. Ray and Theodore S. Wright and the physician James McCune Smith became trustees of Gerrit Smith's plan to give away some 120,000 acres of land in Upstate New York to Black New Yorkers. (credits clockwise from top left) New York Public Library, Yale Beinecke Library, New-York Historical Society.

still emerging from the economic and social devastation of slavery and facing discrimination at every turn. "Once in possession of . . . *our own land*," Ray, Wright, and McCune Smith explained, "we will not only be independent, in ourselves, but will overcome that *prejudice against condition*, which has so long been as a mill stone about our necks." Sounding like the Owenites of the 1820s or the Fourierists of the 1840s, Wright et al. expressed their belief that "MUTUAL-RELIANCE must accompany self-reliance" and that a "Mutual system, thoroughly arranged, and rigidly adhered to will accomplish infinitely more than separate labour, and will bring out all the advantages, profits, pleasures, and advancement, which are beginning to dawn upon ORGANIZED

INDUSTRY."[42] The Colored Convention movement similarly extolled the importance of rural life, agriculture, and the skilled trades, and it articulated an alternative vision of "free labor" that shared much in common with that envisioned by white workingmen. At the Colored Convention in Troy, New York, in 1847, a committee on agriculture headed by Charles Ray and Willis Hodges thanked Smith for his "beneficent act" and went on to expound on the virtues of agrarian living. Resolutions passed by the Committee and signed by Frederick Douglass recommended that "our people ... forsake the cities and their employments of dependency therein, and emigrate to those parts of the country where land is cheap, and become cultivators of the soil, as the surest road to respectability and influence." "An Agricultural life," the convention proclaimed, "tends to equality ... by placing men in the same position in society." In self-sustaining rural communities, "all castes [would] fade away ... and an equality of rights, interests and privileges" would take their place. Other state and national Colored Conventions in the period recommended the formation of protective unions, of manual labor and "industrial" schools, and of organized communities of Black farmers in Canada or elsewhere outside the United States.[43]

But despite the well-documented evidence of a few long-lasting, self-sufficient communities of African Americans on the Smith land grants—most notably at North Elba, also known as Timbucto, where John Brown and his family lived for several years while Brown planned his raid on Harper's Ferry—most of the grant recipients, whether Black or white, never claimed their lands. As Smith himself occasionally admitted, the recipients of his land grants faced significant obstacles: apart from their location in remote wilderness areas, some of the land consisted of poor, rocky soil, and nearly all of the grantees, both white and Black, lacked the capital for basic provisions and start-up costs, as well as for the payment of taxes. Although National Reformer E. S. Manning claimed that "the greater part" of Smith's white land grant recipients had paid taxes, had signed deeds, and were "desirous of settling," he also pointed out that the isolated tracts, sometimes separated by large distances, entailed that settlers had to provide "more means" for their success and survival than most of them were able to furnish. As late as 1854, Ray and McCune Smith published an appeal urging Black New Yorkers to "Redeem your lands!!" by paying taxes and settling on them before they lapsed into ownership by the state. But such appeals seem to have come too little, too late; Smith himself guessed that "less than fifty" Black families remained on their Adirondack lands by 1857.[44]

However, Smith's land grant scheme may have served a different purpose altogether. Although only a handful of Black families ultimately remained as settlers, Smith estimated that approximately half the grantees retained ownership of their lands. Since New York's racist 1821 state constitution required Black voters to own at least $250 in property, while eliminating such requirements for whites, their ownership of Smith land grants meant an addition of 1,500 Black voters on New York's rosters by the late 1850s. While this number may seem relatively insignificant, it may have been enough to make the difference in places, including New York City and Brooklyn, where Black voters sometimes wielded the balance of power in tightly contested races. Perhaps just as importantly, it may have precipitated the shift of a number of New York's free Black leaders and voters toward an embrace of antislavery politics. By the late 1840s, free Black abolitionists like McCune Smith, Frederick Douglass, and Henry Highland Garnet were becoming frustrated with the Garrisonians' brand of antipolitics and their failure to promote what McCune Smith called the "Social Equality" of Black people. Smith's land grant scheme was instrumental in prompting such men to support land reform principles as well as Smith's wing of the Liberty Party.[45] Others, like the Virginia-born, Brooklyn-based abolitionist Willis Hodges, saw in the National Reform platform and Smith's land grant scheme an opportunity to realize their own long-cherished dreams of landed independence while cementing a political realignment in which Blacks held the balance of power. Considering the National Reformers' proposals in the pages of the newspaper he edited, the *Ram's Horn*, Hodges argued that since "the colored people are more oppressed than any other class," they should be "willing to make common cause" with the new movement, but only if "they carry out their principles" by "recogniz[ing] our manhood, and extend[ing] to us equal privileges." Alluding to the power of several thousand eligible African-American voters in New York State to make or break the new alignment's political fortunes, Hodges added that, "we will, of course, expect an equal participation with them *as equals.*" Hodges had long encouraged fellow Blacks to give up the economic competition and vice of city life and become farmers in small towns and villages, and in May of 1848 he took his own advice, settling on a tract of Smith's land with a group of Black families from Brooklyn.[46]

Neither the "equal participation" demanded by Hodges nor the grand coalition envisioned by Evans and Smith ever fully materialized, but by the time of Hodges's departure for the Smith lands, there were signs that land reformers and others within the early labor movement were moving toward a more forthright embrace of antislavery. By the turn of the revolutionary year 1848, the cover of the annual *National Reform Almanac* proclaimed that "a man has a right *to himself* [emphasis added] and to the use of enough of the earth's surface to sustain himself and family," while in a footnote to an essay by Smith, Evans preached that "a man has no more right to acquire 'landed property' than property in man."[47] A number of prominent Black abolitionists and activists continued to move toward support for both land reform and political abolition, and land reformers sometimes actively courted their support, with a small number of free Blacks even participating in white-dominated labor organizations and conferences. Gerrit Smith continued to promote land reform in the pages of antislavery periodicals and in his frequent open letters to the public, and—in a stunning turn of events that has gone largely unrecognized by labor historians—the National Industrial Congress, the National Reform Association, and a number of other labor organizations and spokespeople returned the favor by adopting the abolitionist as their candidate for president of the United States in 1848.

Seemingly, as the decade progressed, an increasing number of labor leaders and reformers were coming to the conclusion of National Reformer William West, that slave "emancipation and the redemption of the soil" were "indissolubly connected." And yet, Evans never completely relinquished his "white slavery" rhetoric, even amplifying it over the years, while Smith's equally stubborn and sometimes quixotic idealism made him a less than effective advocate for either antislavery or land reform during his various political campaigns. In some ways, then, Evans's single-minded dedication to land reform as a panacea and Smith's equally dogmatic commitment to a radically antislavery reading of the Constitution made them the mirror images of William Lloyd Garrison, whom both men professed to admire but whose brand of abolitionism they diverged from. Whatever their ideological blind spots and individual shortcomings, however, events would soon outpace Evans and Smith. Out of the circumstances of war, class conflict, and the fluctuating fortunes of democratic politics in the late 1840s would emerge the contours of an antislavery coalition that few could have anticipated when Evans first penned his letter to Smith in 1844.

CHAPTER 5

A "Union of Reformers":
The National Industrial Congress and
the Antislavery–Land Reform Alliance

In the earliest days of spring 1845, a little over a year after the organization of the National Reform Association, a call went out, addressed to reformers throughout the nation. Published first in the *Working Man's Advocate*, and later in such organs as the *Harbinger*, the *Voice of Industry*, and the *New-York Tribune*, the notice called on abolitionists, land reformers, temperance advocates, moral reformers, pacifists, and disenchanted Democrats to "unite their forces against the common enemy." Summoning "Farmers, Mechanics, and other useful classes," along with all other "friends of Reform," the call urged readers to send delegates to a national convention to be held in New York City, the purpose of which would be to lay plans and draft a constitution for a more permanent organization—what the reformers dubbed an "Industrial Congress."[1]

Although the announcement and subsequent annual meetings of the National Industrial Congress (NIC), as the new organization came to be known, aroused moderate interest among mainstream publications like the *Tribune* and *Niles' National Register*, the response from some quarters was nothing short of ecstatic. "The Revolution to be fought over again!" exclaimed the *New England Mechanic*. "A new Declaration of Independence! The work of '76 to be finished! Equality and Freedom to be achieved! The right to life, and to a free soil on which to toil for life, to be acknowledged! The toiling millions emancipated, and violated rights restored to all!" George Henry Evans, who probably penned the announcement and who played a leading role in launching the congress, thought its formation represented "more important work than . . . has ever been performed by any similar body in the Republic."

The *Voice of Industry* described the congress as an "Institution for concentrating the influence of all men of all parties who are struggling in the cause of Human Rights and Universal Brotherhood," while the Fourierist *Harbinger* thought it discerned in the new organization the potential to inspire a "grand movement," one whose object would be "the extirpation of the social causes of war, slavery, intemperance, licentiousness, and poverty."[2]

If measured against these grandiose, even millenarian, expectations, the achievements of the NIC seem modest indeed. Its meetings, comprising officers and delegates who were elected annually by local associations that pledged to abide by the NIC's core principles, accomplished little but the passage of resolutions and recommendations, and by its waning years in the mid-1850s, the meetings attracted only a handful of participants.[3] But the congress, which convened annually between 1845 and 1856 in cities from Boston to Chicago and as far south as Washington, DC, merits significance as the pre–Civil War era's longest-running labor organization. It both harkened back to the efforts in the 1820s and '30s to form a national "general trades union" organization and looked forward to the efforts to organize workers along the principles of "industrial" unionism, as represented by the Knights of Labor and the Congress of Industrial Organizations. Unlike the post–Civil War labor congresses and the industrial unionism that followed it, the NIC was "industrial" in the sense that it attempted to bring together and speak for not only factory operatives and wage workers across various trades, but farmers, artisans both urban and rural, and even a good number of employers and other professionals—all those who represented "the great producing and other useful classes of the country."[4]

And yet, the true significance of the Industrial Congress may lie less in its status as a precursor to the organized labor movement of the future than in its role in brokering an alliance between the early labor movement and antislavery, one that helped to pave the way for the broader, more potent antislavery coalition of the following decade.[5] Perhaps in an effort to break the impasse that had characterized relations between the antislavery and labor movements since the early 1830s, Evans appealed directly to abolitionists, whom he described as "sincere, ardent, [and] heroic," to join with labor and land reformers, temperance men, pacifists, and others in order to bring about what he called a "Union of Reformers."[6]

The Industrial Congresses, then, were no mere labor conventions. They solicited participation from abolitionists and trade unionists; temperance reformers and ten-hours law advocates; "no-government" men and representatives of the Democratic, Free Soil, and Liberty parties. The initial call to organize the NIC was signed by National Reformers George Henry Evans, Alvan Bovay, and Ransom Smith; radical Democrat and Associationist Parke Godwin; abolitionist and Universalist minister William H. Channing; the English-born Owenite abolitionist Benjamin D. Timms; and New England Workingmen's Association (NEWA) representative Albert Gilbert.[7] Gerrit Smith and John A. Collins served on its committee of correspondence, as did *New-York Tribune* editors Horace Greeley and Charles Dana, who published favorable op-eds and NIC proceedings in the *Tribune*; the venerable former Working Men's leader William Heighton sat on its executive committee. Smith was the congress's nominee for president of the United States in 1848, and Charles Durkee, an abolitionist congressman from Wisconsin, was chosen to preside over the 1852 session in Washington, DC. No wonder, then, that a handful of delegates disgusted with Smith's nomination denounced the congress as "an abolitionist convention."[8]

Despite this abolitionist presence, however, the industrial congresses rarely if ever spoke out directly against the institution of chattel slavery per se. The delegates and officers who assembled each June between 1845 and 1856 were far more concerned with such measures as the passage of ten-hours laws, the organization of producers' cooperatives and "protective" unions, and, above all, the recognition of the freedom of the soil in the form of free, government-provided homesteads.[9] But, for reasons both related and unrelated to its close ties to the land reform movement, the NIC did take a number of strongly antislavery stances over the course of its eleven-year existence. In its resolutions and statements about the annexation of Texas, the Mexican-American War, and the Kansas-Nebraska Act, as well as in its decidedly independent approach to politics (which mirrored that of its institutional cousin, the National Reform Association), the NIC aligned itself squarely with the new brand of antislavery politics that emerged from the crucible of the Mexican War and the Wilmot Proviso.

In one sense, is not difficult to see why the land and labor reformers who arrayed themselves within the NIC and the National Reform Association would be against the expansion of slavery; the spread of cotton plantations of thousands of acres, worked by "degrading" slave labor, posed a direct and existential threat to their plans (described in chapter 5) to preserve western lands as a safety valve for urban wage workers. But as we have already seen, the working-class land reformers who comprised the National Reformers articulated a far more radical version of "free soil" than that adopted by the Free Soil Party, which emerged in 1848 in direct response to the Mexican War. The "agrarian" version, as envisioned not only by Evans and his allies in the National Reform Association but by venerable labor leaders like John Commerford, Whiggish reformers like Horace Greeley, abolitionist converts like Gerrit Smith and Elizur Wright, Jr., and predecessors like Thomas Skidmore and Thomas Spence, called not only for keeping the territories free of enslaved labor, but for making them actually free for all labor, white or Black. Land was a resource to be held in common and enjoyed by all, and the land reformers believed that the right to occupy and work the land was a "natural right" as sacred as those to life, liberty, and property. Although they shared with the more progressive elements within the Free Soil Party the idea that keeping the territories free of slavery would cause slavery to die a gradual death—and although most seemed to agree with Evans that the establishment of "freedom of the soil" should precede the abolition of slavery—they also agreed with abolitionists that slavery was a moral and social evil, one that free white workers had a moral duty as well as a vested interest in helping to eradicate. Remarking on the formation of the Industrial Congress in 1845, one correspondent to the *New-York Tribune* placed an unfamiliar spin on familiar free labor arguments about the tendency of slavery to degrade all labor. Invoking a phrase that would become central to labor movement activism in later years, the writer argued that the seeming correlation between the declining fortunes of free wage laborers and the growth and expansion of slavery proved that a "mutual union and dependence"—what the author called "*solidarity*"—existed "between all classes" of workers, whether free or enslaved. The persistence of slavery and its debasing effect on both free and enslaved laborers were proof, for this correspondent, that "none can attain to a high state of elevation and happiness without the relative happiness and elevation of others."[10]

It was this understanding of the relationship between slavery and free labor, as much as their demands for free homesteads and their intrinsic dislike of slavery, that led the National Reformers and NIC to attempt to forge institutional and electoral links, not with the Free Soilers, but with the briefly lived but radically abolitionist Liberty League, and later, with the antislavery Free Democratic Party. Just as importantly, the Industrial Congress took a stance on racial equality that not only distinguished it from nearly every other labor organization at the time, but paved the way for what were likely the only examples of Black participation in a white-led labor organization before the 1880s (detailed in chapter 7).[11] In this sense at least, the reformers who dominated the NIC seemed genuinely committed to living up to the promise proclaimed in the body's constitution, "to establish Equality, Liberty, and Brotherhood among men of every Race." Regardless of whether the same can be said for the pre–Civil War labor movement as a whole, the Industrial Congress did much in both word and deed to foster the idea of a labor movement based on interracial solidarity, while promoting the formation of a political coalition between labor reformers and abolitionists.[12]

The Origins of the Industrial Congress: Land Reform, the Ten-Hours Movement, and Labor Abolitionism in New England

Much as the National Reformers' involvement with the Anti-Rent movement in upstate New York had helped to propel land reform into the political arena, the seeds for the Industrial Congress were sown by the arduous work of on-the-ground organizing. This time, the rocky New England soil would prove to be fertile ground for connections forged between land reformers, Associationists, trade unionists, and ten-hours law activists in the hardscrabble mill towns and shoemaking centers of Massachusetts. Since the 1830s, New England workers had been organizing around the issue of ten-hours laws— legislation limiting the legal workday to ten hours or fewer. In July 1844, the Mechanics' Association of Fall River, Massachusetts, issued a call for a national "general Convention" of trade unionists, ten-hours law supporters, and all who desired "the elevation of the Working Classes." Leaders of the newly organized National Reform Association saw an opportunity to consolidate support for land reform among wage workers outside of New York City. That October, National Reformers Evans, Alvan Bovay, and Thomas A. Devyr, together with *Subterranean* editor Mike Walsh, attended as delegates, traveling in the darkened second-class carriage of a passenger train to Boston. Once there, Evans and Devyr formally endorsed the main demand of the New England mechanics, the passage of ten-hours legislation. Walsh traveled to factory towns Fall River and Lowell, where he gave rousing speeches emphasizing the connections between ten-hours laws and land reform. Subsequently, demands for ten-hours legislation were added to the three National Reform planks in the organization's official publications. The

"Ten Hours System," Evans explained, was a *"means"*; freedom of the public lands was the *"end."*[13]

The famed textile mill town of Lowell, where slave-grown cotton was spun into fabric by low-paid (and usually female) operatives, was the site of a March 1845 meeting of the NEWA. Founded by the Fourierist Lewis Ryckman, *Voice of Industry* editor John Orvis, and *Boston Investigator* publisher Horace Seaver, the NEWA sought to build an inclusive labor organization along the lines of the New England Association of Farmers, Mechanics, and Other Working Men of the 1830s. The NEWA enjoyed a broad base of support among New England workers, and the new organization adopted the program of the land reformers nearly whole cloth. William Smith Wait, a founder of the New England Association of Farmers, Mechanics, and Other Working Men in the 1830s, presided at the Lowell meeting; the other members of the executive committee, including Evans, *New England Artisan* editor Dr. Charles Douglas, currency reformer Edward N. Kellogg, and Pittsburgh ten-hours movement veteran John Ferral, all had deep roots in the labor movement of the previous decade.[14] From this same meeting emerged the call to organize a national congress of labor reformers. The call was reiterated at the National Reform Convention in New York that May, attended by Robert Owen, Albert Brisbane, William H. Channing, and John A. Collins, among other reform luminaries, and again at the first annual meeting of the NEWA in Boston's Tremont Temple in June. The "Industrial Convention" that met in New York that October attracted a range of reformers with diverse approaches, including land reform, Association, and abolition. Although the reformers' visions for the industrial congress varied widely, and despite Horace Greeley's complaint that the plan for the NIC excluded employers in favor of representatives of "the Employed class, or those who labor for others," the Industrial Congress was now a reality.[15]

Perhaps unsurprisingly, given that this precursor to the NIC took place in New York and was organized by Evans and the National Reformers, the land reform issue dominated the October Industrial Convention and the early NICs.[16] Since the founding of the National Reform Association a little over a year and a half earlier, the land reform issue had gained widespread currency among northern workers. The same Lowell meeting of the NEWA in March 1845 that helped to launch the Industrial Congress issued an endorsement of "the two great fundamental Rights of Man—the Right of Labor and the Right to the Soil," which it equated with the rights spelled out in the Declaration of Independence. Independently, local committees of workingmen in

Boston and in the shoemaking center of Lynn also endorsed free homesteads as a solution to the condition of labor. With the fading of the Fourierist phalanxes, and perhaps fearful of losing their influence within the New England labor movement, the Associationists also moved toward an embrace of land reform.[17] Parke Godwin attended National Reform meetings in New York, and Albert Brisbane joined the land reformers in February 1845. Horace Greeley would also embrace the idea that land reform was "the basis of union and of the True Democracy" and would promote the cause extensively in the *Tribune*. By 1846, John Allen, the editor of the Lowell *Voice of Industry* who had helped to organize abolitionist meetings on Cape Ann, Massachusetts, was able to declare that "We have never yet known a [trade] Unionist, who was not in favor of National Reform."[18]

Meanwhile, there were further signs that the injustices of chattel slavery were beginning to penetrate the consciousness of the broader labor movement. In New York, at Robert Owen's "World's Convention," which took place the same month as the founding convention of the Industrial Congress, National Reform secretary Alvan Bovay announced his intention "to introduce the question of Slavery," and the aging father of English socialism was taken to task by another participant "for blinking the question about Negro Slavery." Despite what a reporter described as "a good deal of grumbling," a resolution was subsequently passed that prioritized the abolition of chattel slavery over "other forms."[19] In July 1844, the Lowell, Massachusetts, labor reformer Chauncey L. Knapp (soon to begin a successful career as an antislavery politician) and the abolitionist poet John Greenleaf Whittier launched the *Middlesex Standard*, a strongly antislavery newspaper that proclaimed as its motto "Slavery in all of its forms is anti-democratic, the natural enemy of the working man," a quote it attributed to Loco Foco Theodore Sedgwick.[20] Abolitionists considered female mill workers in Lowell and throughout New England to be a ready constituency for antislavery, since, as one entreaty to "the Factory Girls" put it, "while their fingers have been busy" spinning slave-grown cotton in the factories, "their minds have been in the cotton field— heard and felt its horrors." In 1845, one self-identified "Factory Girl" wrote to the *Voice of Industry* expressing her unwillingness to "keep quiet about slavery" when southern visitors toured the mills, "lest our pro-slavery friends should return to the South without having heard one word of anti-slavery truth." An announcement for a July Fourth "Great Mass Meeting of the Industrial Reformers" the following summer appealed to solidarity with enslaved people by declaring that "the hired laborer of the North deeply sympathizes with his brother slave at the South." Such considerations may have informed the highly qualified allusion to "wage slavery" that appeared on the *Voice of Industry*'s prospectus, which declared the paper "Devoted to the abolition of Mental, Moral, and Physical Servitude, in all their complicated forms."[21]

Neither the founding convention of the Industrial Congress in New York nor its first official session (held in Boston in 1846 and presided over by Evans and NEWA president David Bryant) mentioned slavery directly. But at the latter gathering, land reformers within the congress—still over a month away from the Wilmot Proviso and nearly two years before the formation of the antislavery Free Soil Party—began referring to their movement as "free soil" and recommended nominating independent candidates for president and vice president in the upcoming national elections of 1848.[22] Before that could take place, however, a seismic shift in American politics would reshape the political landscape and cause many northern workers and reformers to reconsider their movement's relationship to the South's peculiar institution. In the same summer that saw the inaugural Industrial Congress in Boston, the US Congress authorized the enlistment of some 75,000 American volunteers for twelve months' service in the lower Rio Grande Valley. The Mexican-American War, driven by slaveholder expansionism as well as by ordinary Americans' hunger for land and territory, would cast the expansionist ambitions of the Slave Power into stark relief and lead land and labor reformers into an alliance with antislavery politics.

The Mexican War, the Wilmot Proviso, and the Resurrection of Labor Movement Antislavery

On the evening of August 8, 1846, Pennsylvania congressman David Wilmot rose in the House of Representatives to propose what became known as the Wilmot Proviso, a resolution that would have made President Polk's request for $2 million in funds to secure the Treaty of Guadalupe Hidalgo's purchase of California and New Mexico contingent on the provision that "neither slavery nor involuntary servitude shall ever exist in any part of said territory." In so doing, Wilmot touched off a political firestorm that would ultimately rearrange existing party alliances and redefine the sectional conflict over slavery. As alarmed southerners noted at the time, the North and the West stood briefly united on preventing slavery's expansion westward, with congressmen from the states north of the Mason-Dixon line voting overwhelmingly in favor of the proviso; only in the Senate, where southerners continued to control a plurality of votes, was the measure defeated.[23]

That white northerners who supported Wilmot's Proviso saw the spread of slavery into the territories as antithetical to the interests of "free labor" has long been taken for granted in scholarship on the origins of the Civil War. The *Barnburner*, a Free Soil paper based in New York City, stated the problem succinctly. Noting that the combined territories accumulated by the Oregon Treaty and the Treaty of Guadalupe Hidalgo amounted to in excess of 1.6 million acres, the *Barnburner* predicted that "if slave owners seize the country, the poor whites will flee that region, and slavery will populate the land and exhaust the soil. Then this will be a land of slavery and not the abode of liberty."[24] More recently, many historians have concluded that anti-Black racism and white nationalism, rather than sympathy for the enslaved or a genuine desire to see slavery eradicated, lay at the heart of white northerners' opposition to slavery's expansion—a notion lent credence by Wilmot's own explanation that the proviso had been issued not of "morbid sympathy for the slave," but in the interest of "free white labor." Laws passed by numerous western states banning both slavery *and* settlement by free Blacks, such as those of the provisional government of the Oregon Territory in 1844 and 1849, not to mention the numerous discriminatory laws that disenfranchised African Americans and stripped them of basic civil rights and legal protections, further add to the period's well-deserved reputation as a nadir in the history of America's fraught relationship with race as well as an indication of the continued salience of the "white man's democracy" that had come into full fruition in the Jacksonian Era.[25]

To see white racism as the primary factor motivating northern support for the Wilmot Proviso and the Free Soil campaign that followed, however, risks minimizing the Free Soil movement's significance in precipitating the political realignment and sectional crisis of the 1850s that led to the Civil War, and ultimately to the end of slavery. Although the proviso was defeated in the Senate, the underlying ideas it unleashed had a much longer lineage, forming as they did the ideological basis of a broad antislavery political coalition—one that included political abolitionists, free Blacks, northern farmers and workers, and labor activists and social reformers of many different stripes. Moreover, many northerners, including the Proviso's author, supported the Wilmot Proviso because they viewed it as an essential first step towards slavery's complete eradication. Although David Wilmot stated that the proviso "does not propose the abolition of slavery, either in States or in

Territories," he predicted that "slavery has within itself the seeds of its own dissolution. Keep it within given limits, let it remain where it now is, and in time it will wear itself out." In this way, Wilmot explained, the restriction of slavery would "at no distant day . . . insure the redemption of the Negro from his bondage in chains."[26] A similar strategy would be adopted by antislavery Republicans in the 1850s, who hoped that by preventing the further expansion of slavery and by surrounding slave states with a "cordon of freedom," slavery would die a natural death, "like a scorpion girt by fire."[27] In the mid-1840s, however, Wilmot and other supporters of the proviso saw themselves as acting in the tradition of labor abolitionists and Loco Foco Democrats like William Leggett. Wilmot, who represented a Pennsylvania iron district and considered himself to be a champion of labor, thought of the struggle against the Slave Power as the logical extension of the Bank Wars of the 1830s. Viewing slaveholders as the "capitalists of the South, who hold a certain species of property," he depicted the conflict over slavery in the territories as essentially a struggle "between capital and labor." Jacob Brinkerhoff, the Ohio Democrat who coauthored the proviso, linked Free Soilism to the Loco Foco doctrines of a decade earlier, invoking Leggett's memory to make his point. Along with Thomas Jefferson, Leggett had been one of the "apostles" of "the Free Soil gospel," Brinkerhoff declared, and were he now alive, "he would be with us— his voice, calling us to combat the influence of slavery, would be heard, eloquent as of yore." Liberty Party founder Gamaliel Bailey, whose *National Era* proclaimed that the Buffalo Convention represented an epochal "Turn of the Tide" in favor of antislavery, likewise saw the advent of Free Soilism as the fulfillment of Leggett's prophecy of a "revolution" in northern public opinion on slavery. And the Quaker abolitionist Benjamin Lundy, nearing the end of his life and with his long-cherished hopes of establishing a colony for emancipated slaves in Texas or Mexico now dashed, joined the new political antislavery chorus to rage against the "cold blooded viper, tyranny or Texas," invoking an antislavery "Legion of Liberty" that included such Democratic-leaning champions of labor as Leggett, Theodore Sedgwick, Robert Owen, and Orestes Brownson.[28]

The history of the Free Soil movement is usually thought to begin with Wilmot's proviso and to have reached its full flowering with the founding of the Free Soil Party by Barnburner Democrats and antislavery Whigs at the Buffalo Convention of 1848. But what may have been the first body to call itself the Free Soil Party had been organized at a meeting of Anti-Renters, National

Reformers, and Liberty Party men in Albany, New York, in October 1846—
nearly two years before Buffalo.[29] Long before the Buffalo Free Soilers adopted
"free soil, free speech, free labor, and free men" as their slogan, land reformers
and political abolitionists had already begun the process of connecting opposition to the expansion of slavery to a radical vision of economic equality based
on the concept of man's natural right to the soil, a vision that was steeped
in these more traditionally Democratic views but that transcended them in
important ways. This vision entailed a general support for territorial expansion and settlement, but—crucially—diverged from the mainstream of the
Democratic Party when that expansion entailed the spread of slavery and the
displacement of the territory's occupants by force. Initially, National Reformers like Evans and the aging Jacksonian labor leader John Commerford had
supported the election of James K. Polk as the lesser of two evils, since Whig
candidate Henry Clay's policy of reserving the public lands for revenue was
anathema to their demand that they be divided into free homesteads. As discussed in the previous chapter, Evans also at first voiced cautious support for
Texas annexation, on the condition that slavery there be banned and its unset-
tled lands set aside for landless workers.[30] But after Texas was annexed by a
joint resolution of Congress in March 1845, it not only entered the Union as a
slave state, but retained control over its public lands rather than ceding them to
the federal government—thus becoming the only state, apart from those of the
original thirteen colonies, to do so.[31] Even before this development, Evans had
begun to renounce Polk and Texas in the pages of *Young America*. "The people
of Texas had a right to propose to come under our government," Evans suggested, "but they had no right to come in with a constitution tolerating slavery
either white or black, by monopolizing land or bodies."[32]

Even more unequivocal was the labor movement's response to the
Mexican-American War. After the annexation of Texas led to the declaration of war against Mexico in May 1846, some of the most strident voices
raised in protest came from those who spoke for labor. Far from viewing the
war as an opportunity for expansion that might hasten the advent of their
favored reform by the addition of thousands of square miles of public lands,
the land and labor reformers in the NIC denounced the war in no uncertain
terms, viewing it as a ploy by slaveholders to expand the sphere of slavery
rather than free labor. Evans's *Young America* turned fiercely against the war,
declaring that "If every man has a right to a home on earth, as we believe, we
have no right to invade the homes of others. . . . Can anything be imagined

more wickedly and stupidly absurd than to take advantage of the necessities of the poor lacklanders ... to send them to kill or be killed in Mexico because some of their citizens had wronged some of our own?" In the pages of his new weekly, the *Chronotype*, former American Anti-Slavery Society secretary Elizur Wright, Jr., a recent convert to land reform, declared that "every blow struck, every battle won over the poor degraded Mexican, has a direct tendency to undermine our free institutions, and serves to rivet still stronger the galling chains of slavery—to bring the free into subjection to the slave States." Wright urged poor volunteers to consider whether the war was being waged for their benefit or for that of "cunning villains ... who want vast landed estates, on which such men as you will either be driven to work by the whip, or will beg to work for wages that will just ward off starvation."[33] Nor were high-minded reformers like Evans and Wright the only ones to stand against the war. In the shoemaking town of Lynn, Massachusetts—a center of production for the cheap slave boots and brogans destined for the "southern trade"—an 1846 convention of workingmen pledged, seemingly against its members' own economic interests, that "we will not take up arms [in Mexico] to sustain the Southern slaveholders in robbing one-fifth of our countrymen of their labor," and urged northern laborers to "speak out in thunder tones" against slavery, "both as associations and individuals." The convention passed resolutions declaring its members' intention to be "consistent" by helping to secure "those rights and privileges for which we are contending for ourselves" for the "three millions of our brethren and sisters groaning in chains on the Southern plantations."[34]

A little under a month after the outbreak of hostilities between American soldiers and Mexican General Santa Anna's troops in the disputed zone north of the Rio Grande, and just over a week after Congress officially declared war, a group of New York City workers arrayed themselves in opposition to a "patriotic" rally in City Hall Park organized by Tammany Democratic mayor Andrew H. Mickle. The Working Men's demonstration, headed by Evans, Commerford, and National Reformers Ransom Smith and E. S. Manning, expressed their belief that the war had been brought about by "Texas landholders, and other speculators" who hoped to live in "luxurious idleness on the products of the working men." Noting the absence of authentic tradesmen on the roster of speakers and organizers at the competing prowar rally across the park, the reformers demanded the immediate withdrawal of American forces across the Rio Grande and the resumption of peaceful negotiations. For good measure, the meeting passed further resolutions demanding that "landless men" who volunteered for the war effort receive a raise in pay, and pointedly proposed that the organizers of the prowar demonstration should be the first to volunteer for military service.[35] A week later, at the National Reformers' regular meeting at Croton Hall, those assembled heard longtime Democrat John Commerford express his remorse at voting for Polk in 1844. Commerford described the conflict in Mexico as "discreditable" and "unjustifiable," since it placed the United States in the position of aggressor in a war waged against a "sister republic." Another speaker invoked the Magna Carta to denounce the war as a struggle for "the aggrandisement [*sic*] of individuals, to the exclusion of the people."[36]

The purpose of the Croton Hall gathering, however, was not to plan antiwar demonstrations, but to choose delegates for what would become the first official meeting of the NIC, then preparing to convene in Boston. The organization of the inaugural Industrial Congress was deeply intertwined with anti–Mexican War and antislavery activism. Although records of the proceedings of the first congress are scant, editorials in the *Voice of Industry* from the weeks surrounding its inaugural session denounced the war in unequivocal terms. In an article published the week after the congress met in Boston, the paper called on "Fellow Reformers" to stand opposed to "that hellish iniquity, the present Mexican War," which it blamed on "a slave-holding oligarchy" that had sparked the conflict "for the extension and perpetuation of Slavery." The same editorial voiced its objection to paying taxes in support of the war and put readers on notice that future editions of the *Voice* would adopt a similarly antiwar perspective.[37]

The following year, the NIC adopted an antiwar stance that was nothing short of astonishing. Gathered at Military Hall on New York City's Bowery— site of the old Workingmen's Party mass meetings of the 1820s and '30s—the congress issued an "Address to the Citizens of the United States" in which it depicted the war as having been "waged at the insistence and behalf of Southern Slavery and Northern Capital." A series of proposed resolutions demonstrated the lengths to which some delegates were willing to go to subvert the war effort. Declaring that any new territory added by the war would "inevitably . . . fall into the hands of speculators and monopolists, thereby extending and perpetuating wages and chattel slavery," the congress recommended that laborers use their influence to urge legislators to withhold supplies from the U.S. Army in hopes of bringing the war to a speedy conclusion. Other resolutions urged the adoption of a direct tax on property as means of forcing "Southern Slavery and Northern Capital . . . to bear the expenses" of the

war (passed unanimously) and another to abolish the "Standing Army" altogether (narrowly defeated). The congress then read a statement from William H. Channing, who urged his hearers to consider the ways in which "the
capital of the North and the South were leagued together" in bringing about
the war. Perhaps, Channing suggested to the congress, labor reformers would
do well to take "a more radical view of the question of Slavery."[38]

National Reform, the Industrial Congress,
and the Liberty–Land Reform Alliance

For many in the broader labor movement, then, the Mexican-American War
was a watershed moment that opened their eyes to the threat posed by slavery's expansion and helped to awaken what might be described as labor's
latent antislavery tendencies. Apart from the unjust aggression inherent to
what amounted to a war of conquest, the prospect of the expansion of slavery
into the millions of acres of new territory acquired from Mexico posed an
obvious and immediate threat to the proposals of the land reformers. But
unlike the more conservative elements within the Free Soil Party, land and
labor reformers saw no difficulty in combining appeals to the self-interest of
white worker and small farmer with humanitarian calls for the emancipation
of the enslaved. A few months after the 1847 congress in New York, the state
convention of the National Reform Association in Massachusetts, after passing measures in favor of land reform and the ten-hour working day, declared
slavery "a crime against Humanity so outrageous" that it "ought to be abolished immediately." The "present crisis" of the Mexican War, the convention
noted, had lent "peculiar force" to the question of what it might take to finally
abolish slavery. To that end, the convention urged abolitionists to cooperate
in ameliorating the condition of nonenslaved workers, and particularly urged
"our antislavery and 'no-voting' friends"—the Garrisonian immediatists—to
adopt "POLITICAL ACTION that shall secure to every disenthralled slave,
whatever their complexion . . . the peaceable and immediate possession of a
sufficient quantity of Land to enable them to procure the necessary means of
subsistence whenever their liberation is achieved." A final resolution restated
the organization's opposition to "Slavery at the South" as well as "oppression
at the North," and appealed to abolitionists to consider what "Political Principles" would best be suited to bringing about the "freedom as well as the
emancipation" of enslaved Blacks.[39]

To an extent not seen since the advent of the Working Men's parties in the late 1820s, the formation of the NIC signaled that workers were organizing with explicitly political intentions. Evans and the National Reformers had harbored political ambitions from the organization's earliest days. The land reform program, National Reform corresponding secretary Alvan Bovay argued, was inherently "political in its character," since meaningful land reform could only be effected "through the ballot box." Almost immediately after organizing in 1844, the National Reformers had begun their program of interrogating candidates for office and petitioning Congress, and Evans insisted that delegates to the NIC should focus on electing to local and national office representatives who were "thoroughly impregnated with the doctrine" of free soil.[40] Soon, the NIC and National Reformers were fielding their own candidates. In 1845, the National Reformers ran Bovay, a former Whig, as its candidate for the New York State Assembly; although he failed to win, this foray into electoral politics added legitimacy to the movement and launched Bovay on a political career that would reach its climax with his role in organizing the Republican Party in Ripon, Wisconsin, in the 1850s. The following year, at an Anti-Rent convention held in Albany in October, National Reformers questioned the Liberty Party candidate for governor of New York, Henry Bradley, on his support for National Reform measures. Bradley voiced strong support for all of the measures except land limitation, and even that gained his cautious endorsement—enough for Bradley to appear at the top of the National Reform ticket in the state elections of 1846. Although Bradley lost by a large margin, coming in third behind Whig John Young and Democrat Silas Wright, he defeated the Nativist candidate with more than double the number of votes, and Mike Walsh and another Democratic land reform supporter were elected to the State Assembly. The result seemed to bear out Evans's hopes that an alliance between land reformers and antislavery forces might wield the balance of power in future elections.[41]

Long before the Buffalo Convention of 1848 threw a firebrand into antebellum politics, Evans and like-minded reformers had been speculating on the "Power of a Third Party," convinced that a party that combined antislavery with land reform policies that appealed to the North's voting majority of small farmers and artisans could become a dominant force in politics. Such a possibility was suggested by the election of the dissident New Hampshire Democrat John P. Hale to the Senate in 1846. The antislavery, anti–Texas annexation Hale had lost his seat in the House of Representatives after Democratic Party regulars read him out of the party, "on a strong suspicion," as

Evans bitterly noted, "of being favorable to Human Rights." Hale ran for Senate anyway, winning election after Liberty Party voters and antislavery Whigs threw their support to him. If the Liberty Party and National Reformers could similarly be united, Evans hinted, "may they not reasonably expect for them the support of every friend of universal freedom?" Abolitionist and Liberty Party leader Gerrit Smith's embrace of land reform (discussed in the previous chapter) provided another source of the gravitational pull between National Reform and antislavery politics.[42]

Meanwhile, the NIC nominated its own candidates for U.S. president and vice president, an approach its organizers attributed to dissatisfaction with the Democratic Party, which they denounced as "corrupted by place and power" and "hostile to the principles of their constituents."[43] At the 1847 Industrial Congress in New York City, dominated by discussions of the Mexican War and by the presence of local land reformers, one delegate ventured to suggest that land reform efforts might "gain advocates in the abolition ranks. If the public lands were made free, we would get the entire abolition vote." As Bovay put it, "every National Reformer" was willing to admit that "Negro-Slavery" was "an enormous, and growing evil," even though most continued to view it as "only one of the many modes of oppression that the productive labor has to endure."[44] Even if Bovay exaggerated the extent of land reformers' commitment to abolition, pragmatic considerations propelled both sides toward the formation of a political coalition. Observing the decline of voting totals for the antislavery Liberty Party between 1843 and 1845, Evans wondered how "the Abolitionists ever hope to get the working classes to join a party for the single object of abolishing black slavery" when workers in general were so bereft of a basic recognition of their rights. By the same token, "how is an abolition party to succeed without the laboring masses?"[45]

Addressing Garrison directly, Evans suggested that the abolitionists, as an unpopular electoral minority, "cannot well afford to be divided in their forces." If antislavery remained, for the time being, the untouchable third rail of American politics, abolitionists "must sooner or later acknowledge that 'Free Soil'" was "the entering wedge to every great reform."[46] Given that the land reformers had popularized the term from which the new antislavery coalition took its name, the Free Soil Party might have seemed a natural fit for Evans and his allies in the National Reform Association and the NIC. Some contemporaries certainly thought so. Noting that the NIC had rejected the Democratic candidate, General Lewis Cass, "by an overwhelming majority," an anonymous source in the New York *Evening Post* optimistically suggested that if the "Barnburners" were true to their principles, "they will rally around them the strong men, the true men, of all parties, and will overwhelm all opposition." The same month as the Buffalo Convention in 1848, National Reformers Alvan Bovay and John H. Keyser wrote to Martin Van Buren in their official capacities as representatives of the Industrial Congress, requesting his views on land reform and asking him to sign the National Reform Pledge. But Van Buren's reply was a masterpiece of prevarication worthy of his nickname, the Little Magician, and did little to satisfy the land reformers.[47]

Partly for this reason, it was to the Liberty Party that the National Reformers increasingly turned. Founded in late 1839 by a group of political abolitionists, including Alvan Stewart, Myron Holley, Gerrit Smith, and Elizur Wright, Jr., the Liberty Party has generally been seen as more genuinely abolitionist than the Free Soil Party, despite the conviction of some Free Soilers that limiting slavery's expansion was tantamount to dooming its existence. Thanks in part to the involvement of former Democrats like Salmon Chase, Thomas Earle, and Gamaliel Bailey, as well as influence of financial backers like Smith, the Liberty Party also contained a strain of radically Democratic politics, as seen in its embrace of antimonopoly, antitariff, and other "free trade" policies.[48] Liberty Party spokesmen also made frequent use of economic arguments about the deleterious impact of slavery on free labor; Stewart, for example, blamed slavery for the "hard times" that followed the Panic of 1837, while the Liberty Party organ the *Philanthropist* identified "capitalists at the North, who own slave-property at the South, and others who from business, social connections or otherwise, are interested in perpetuating the supremacy of the slave-interest" as "constituent elements of the Slave-Power." By the mid-1840s, even more conservative party leaders like Joshua Leavitt had begun to acknowledge and publicize the Slave Power's deleterious effects on the fortunes of northern laborers, which they frequently expressed in terms of a conflict between "capital and labor."[49]

Although the Liberty Party never polled more votes than the 65,608 it garnered in the 1844 general election, it occasionally held the balance of power in states like New Hampshire, and Evans had come to view it as something of a model for the third-party pressure politics that he hoped that the National Reformers might be in a position to wield within a few years. In 1844, Liberty Party presidential candidate James G. Birney had been the only contender to respond to the National Reformers' attempt to interrogate the candidates on their positions on land reform (neither Whig Henry Clay nor Democrat James K. Polk had bothered to answer), and Evans had published

Birney's politely worded if ultimately equivocal reply in another of his journals, the *People's Rights*. In response, National Reformers Evans, Windt, and
Manning penned an open letter to Birney that attempted to present their
cause as the logical extension of the Liberty Party's antislavery. The land
reformers expressed their surprise that Birney, as the candidate of a party
"whose object is the delivery of a particular class from bondage," was not
more "familiar with the interests of labor and the rights of man," and reiterated their charge that to deprive a man of his natural right to the soil was tantamount to enslavement. But they added an affirmation of their conviction
that "no man, or class of men, have a *right* to hold slaves."[50]

Meanwhile, events within the Liberty Party itself were spurring one faction toward a coalition with the land reformers. As early as 1843, proponents
of a platform that embraced measures beyond the "one idea" of slave emancipation had proclaimed that the Liberty Party would "carry out the principle
of equal rights into all its practical consequences and applications, and support every just measure conducive to individual and social freedom." Frustrated by the party's lack of success at the polls and by the limited appeal of
the "one idea" of slave emancipation, Theodore Foster, the editor of a Liberty
Party paper in Ann Arbor, Michigan, wrote Birney that "I am more and more
convinced by reflection that the antislavery feeling alone will never bring
over to the Liberty Party a majority of all the voters of the United States.
We must have some other motives to present to people, which will appeal
directly to their own interests." Elizur Wright, now a Liberty Party organizer,
agreed that the idea of combining the "humanities" (reform movements) into
a single political party was "the true & only true one." Likewise, Gamaliel Bailey's newly launched Liberty Party paper, the *National Era*, hinted to readers
that the National Reformers had begun to show "a warm side" for the party,
and he speculated that Birney would be the candidate of the new alignment.[51]

New Liberty Party papers not only embraced labor and land reform,
but drew direct, specific connections showing how slavery undermined
the working man's right to land. In slaveholding Virginia, as the *Middlesex
Standard* pointed out, not only did landless men lack the franchise, but landholders could vote in as many counties as they owned land, an indication
of how "*Southern Democracy* . . . first makes slaves of its laborers, and next
disfranchises the poor, lest obtaining political power in the government they
should attempt agrarian legislation!" The debates then raging in Congress
and among presidential candidates over the best public lands policy provided
additional ammunition for political abolitionists who hoped to appeal to the

self-interest of workingmen. Land reformers had long opposed the policy, championed by Henry Clay and other Whigs, of the "distribution" of the proceeds of public land sales to the states, arguing that it not only denied the principle of a natural right to the soil, but would raise the price of public lands out of the reach of the poor, thereby trapping surplus labor in the crowded cities of the East. The Utica *Liberty Press* pointed out that distribution amounted to a "tax" on northern laborers to sustain the "'peculiar institutions' of the South," since the much more valuable lands of the free-labor North had already paid more than their fair share into the Federal Treasury. Worse, the distribution plan proposed by the Whig presidential candidate, slaveholder Henry Clay, would have paid out proceeds from land sales to the states in the proportion of the Constitution's notorious three-fifths clause, meaning that southern states would benefit disproportionately from the inclusion of their enslaved labor force—a position the *Press* called on "Freemen of the North—Republicans—Laborers" to reject.[52]

These and other ideas came to a head at the Macedon Convention in Macedon, New York, in June 1847. There, a breakaway faction of the Liberty Party that dubbed itself the Liberty League, led by William Goodell and Gerrit Smith, pledged itself to "universal reform" with a platform that included support for free homesteads, the repeal of tariffs, the restoration of lands taken from Mexico, and the abolition of monopolies (including the monopoly of the soil). Significantly, too, Goodell had been among the pioneers, along with Evans, Leggett, and others, of the antislavery interpretation of the Constitution in the 1830s. Now, the Liberty Leaguers (probably influenced by Smith) adopted a more radical version of antislavery constitutionalism, arguing that the nation's founding document did not recognize slavery anywhere, and therefore slaveholding was an illegal act akin to "piracy."[53]

Like the majority of Liberty Party leaders, however, Evans initially favored the antislavery ex-Democrat John P. Hale, but argued that since "these Liberty men adopt all the National Reform land measures . . . some means ought to be devised of uniting the strength of both parties on the same candidates."[54] Those means presented themselves during the 1847 Industrial Congress that June, when Appleton Fay reminded delegates that the Liberty League was meeting simultaneously at Macedon Lock, New York, and proposed sending a delegation "to enquire into the expediency of co-operating" with the Liberty men. The congress dispatched Hugh T. Brooks, a National Reformer and former Anti-Rent activist from Upstate New York, to Macedon Lock for the purpose of proposing unified action. At the Macedon Convention, an Industrial Congress resolution was read, pledging to support only those candidates who adopted the National Reform measures.[55] Subsequently, William Goodell's "Address to the Macedon Convention" added to the Liberty League's platform an endorsement of the "original right of every human being to occupy a portion of the earth's surface"—along with demands, in language similar to that used by the National Reformers, for land limitation, alienation of homesteads from debt, and the reservation of lands to "actual settlers."[56] Taking aim at "the cotton lords of the North" as well as the plantation owners of the South, Goodell claimed that the new platform offered "a connected and consistent system of political economy." The right to an inalienable homestead was "a Moral Law," Goodell argued; "to talk of a man's right to SELF-OWNERSHIP without a right to an inch of the earth's soil . . . is to talk self-contradiction and nonsense; for the right of self-ownership includes or implies the right of existence, of soil, and of free intercourse." A set of resolutions passed by the convention thus included one that appeared at last to reconcile the abolitionists' insistence on the right of self-ownership with workers' (including Black workers') demands for the fruits of their labor. "That we hope to secure for the colored people of this country and all others, *a self-ownership that implies the right to occupy space*," the convention's sixth resolution read, "*and includes the right to the products of their industry*, and the free disposal of those products" (emphasis added). The Macedon Convention then nominated Gerrit Smith, along with Massachusetts abolitionist and pacifist Elihu Burritt, known as "the learned blacksmith."[57]

That November, a National Reform convention in Massachusetts nominated an all-abolitionist slate of New England Anti-Slavery Society founders Samuel E. Sewall and Amasa Walker for governor and lieutenant governor and Gerrit Smith for president. The Industrial Congress had adjourned without nominating a candidate in 1847, but at its next meeting, in Philadelphia in 1848—after some wrangling led by Evans, H. H. Van Amringe, John Windt, and delegates from Pennsylvania and the Old Northwest—it, too, declared Smith its choice for president. Perhaps even more significantly, at that same gathering of the NIC, "after some rather exciting debates," the congress adopted a resolution making slaveholding a "test" for all NIC nominations to public office, declaring slaveholders ineligible. As the *Pennsylvania Freeman*, the antislavery paper published by the Pennsylvania branch of the AASS, reported, "a strong determination not to compromise anti-slavery, was manifested by some members of the Congress." "Every Northern laborer has a vital, personal interest in the question of slavery," the *Freeman* concluded elsewhere. "The issue is as directly between labor and capital, as between freedom and slavery."[58] Surveying the vastly altered political landscape of 1848, the *Voice of Industry* asked its readers whether any political party or candidate represented the true interests of workingmen: "Is there such a man for whom the working men may vote—and such a party with which they may act?" The answer, according to the *Voice*, was obvious: "Gerrit Smith is the man, and the National Reformers are the party. . . . He is the friend of the oppressed, of every color and clime, and a glorious Achilles in the ranks of the working men. . . . He is in favor of *Free Soil* in both senses in which it is now used—free from the contamination of slavery, and free to every human being who wishes to use it."[59]

Unfortunately, Smith's Liberty League faction garnered little actual support from the majority of political abolitionists. Mainstream Liberty leaders, including Leavitt, Henry Stanton, and Alvan Stewart, rejected the Macedon platform and nominated John P. Hale as the Liberty candidate at a separate convention in October 1847. Perhaps to these leaders' chagrin, many Liberty Party voters soon followed Hale into the new Free Soil Party, where he unsuccessfully vied for nomination against Martin Van Buren. The Liberty Party all but disintegrated after 1848, its remnants resurfacing in Smith's Radical Abolition Party and various other guises over the next decade, but the Free Soil Party, despite losing the presidential contest, was able to maintain the balance of power in several northern states. In the meantime, the first stirrings of a new mass politics of antislavery resulted in the election of a new crop of antislavery politicians, including Hale, Chase, Charles Sumner, and eventually Gerrit Smith, who would take up the antislavery cause in Congress.[60]

In some ways, however, the marriage between labor reform and political abolitionism was never fully consummated. The year 1848 would prove to be a year of revolution, both in the United States and in Europe, where new ideas about the rights of labor were combined with older ideals of republicanism, the rights of man, and national identity to topple kings from thrones. But the hopes of freedom's partisans on both sides of the ocean were quickly dashed, as Europe's monarchs regrouped and the promise of the antislavery third parties soon faded, temporarily displaced by an interlude marked by the growth of slaveholder power, a renewed campaign of terror against enslaved "fugitives," and a new set of explicitly proslavery presidents and implicitly proslavery "compromises."

Nonetheless, the short-lived alliance between National Reformers and the Liberty League represented an important step in the direction of a rapprochement between labor and abolitionism, as well as an important and overlooked building block in the construction of what would eventually become the antislavery political coalition of the 1850s. "Who would have thought it?" exclaimed the *Anti-Slavery Bugle*, commenting on Smith's nomination by a motley conglomeration of land reformers, radicals, and labor activists. The *Bugle*'s headline captured the astonishment felt by abolitionists and others at what, from their perspective, seemed a sudden and unexpected turn of events—but that a longer view suggests was the logical outcome of an ideological and political convergence years in the making.[61] Through the vehicle of the NIC, land reform had become the instrument by which the alliance between labor and antislavery, decades in the making, was finally if imperfectly cemented.

CHAPTER 6

_____

From Free Soil to Homestead:
Working-Class Land Reform
and Antislavery Politics

As the reformist fervor of the 1840s ran headlong into the stark political realities of the post-1848 world, National Reformer J. K. Ingalls took stock of the situation. "The movement of 1848 in Europe," he recalled, referring to the earthshaking, but ultimately unsuccessful, democratic revolutions of that year, "had stirred deeply the sentiment of fraternity and justice of the American people." But "the fiasco of the free soil party, and the success of the conservative spirit in the election of Taylor and Fillmore, brought on a re-action observed and felt everywhere." The National Reformers and the National Industrial Congress (NIC) both rejected the Democratic nominee that year, the Michigan ex-general Lewis Cass, who supported so-called popular sovereignty, i.e., allowing settlers in the territories to vote slavery up or down. Some land reformers had joined the Free Soil Party, contributing to the mass defection among ex-Democrats in states like Massachusetts and New York, which likely cost Cass the election, while others supported Gerrit Smith's Liberty League. But land reformers and abolitionists alike were dismayed by the election's outcome, which saw the Whig candidate, Mexican War hero Zachary Taylor, elevated to the presidency—only to be succeeded by his vice president, Millard Fillmore, after the former's untimely death in July 1850. Fillmore's support for the controversial "omnibus bill," then the subject of rancorous debate in Congress, virtually ensured that the western territories would continue to be a site of heated contestation over the issue of slavery. In its final form, the legislation spelled out the terms of the settlement later known as the Compromise of 1850, which attempted to settle the question of slavery's status in the territories by providing for the entry of California as a nonslaveholding state while leaving the status of slavery to be determined by popular sovereignty in the rest of the Mexican Cession. The new Fugitive Slave Act, arguably the compromise's most consequential provision, cast a pall over the lives of thousands of African Americans (both free and "fugitive"), threatening many with kidnapping or re-enslavement and outraging abolitionists and antislavery moderates alike.[1]

Meanwhile, most of the Associationist phalanxes had sputtered out after a few years of existence, along with similar efforts at forming cooperative communities, although a few would last into the new decade. Faced with mounting financial difficulties and mourning the premature death of his wife, Laura, George Henry Evans was forced to cease publication of *Young America* in 1850, retreating into semiretirement at his farm in Granville, New Jersey. Across the Atlantic, the defeat of democratic, class-tinged revolutions in France, Germany, Hungary, and elsewhere cast a pall over the hopes of radicals and republicans in both Europe and America. Ingalls, meanwhile, found employment as a journeyman in the New York City manufactory of John H. Keyser, an active National Reformer who played a key role in organizing the New York City Industrial Congress, an offshoot of the NIC with only tangential ties to the national organization. "My thought was all the while," Ingalls mused, "upon the question of the land and labor in the world."[2]

Despite this bleak picture, however, all was not lost. Ingalls soon found "the change to a workshop at wages ... disheartening" and threw himself back into the work of land reform organizing. He accepted a position (paid for by Gerrit Smith) to speak as a paid lecturer at public meetings in Madison, Cayuga, and Herkimer Counties in Smith's Upstate New York heartland, where Ingalls expounded on the virtues of combining antislavery with land reform. Unbeknownst to Ingalls at the time, the combination of land reform and antislavery he preached would soon gain a wider currency within the rapidly transforming political landscape of the 1850s, one that far transcended the limited audiences that Ingalls could have hoped to reach in his travels in the upstate hinterlands. In ways that were not yet obvious to Ingalls or other observers at the beginning of the decade, the Wilmot Proviso and the rise of antislavery third parties had forever transformed American politics. Although the Liberty Party continued to be a marginal force at the polls, and although the Free Soil Party would never surpass the 10 percent of the national vote it won in 1848, both the antislavery constitutionalism of the Liberty men and the antiextensionism of the Free Soilers would continue to make headway among antislavery northerners, ultimately recombining in a new and winning formulation after 1854. Despite signs of factionalization and fragmentation in both the abolitionist and labor reform movements and their continued marginalization in politics, these apparent weaknesses masked a new militancy on one hand and a slow but steady acceptance by mainstream political figures and broad swaths of northern voters on the other.[3]

In 1846, eight years before the founding of the party that would eventually adopt the name "Republican," George Henry Evans had predicted that there would soon exist "but two parties, the great Republican Party of Progress and little Tory Party of Holdbacks."[4] By 1852, it had become evident to Evans and many others within the labor movement that the Democratic Party with which they had so long been associated had evolved into something that more closely resembled the latter than the former. That year, the new Free Democratic Party, a short-lived venture that served as a bridge between the Free Soilers and the Republican Party, invited the NIC—then meeting in Washington, DC, with Wisconsin congressman and abolitionist Charles Durkee as chair—to send delegates. The NIC obliged, but it also expressed its own vision for a third party, "the party of masses, the Labor Party."[5]

While the failure of such a party to emerge in American political history has long posed an interesting counterfactual for historians and political scientists, in some ways the story of what *did* take place in the years between the end of the Mexican-American War and the passage of the Kansas-Nebraska Act has gone equally unrecognized.[6] Although neither a labor party nor the "union of reformers" envisioned by Evans and the Industrial Congress could be said to have coalesced during this period, the years 1848–1854 nonetheless pointed the way toward a reordered political landscape, one in which elements of antislavery constitutionalism, free soil antiextensionism, and radical demands for free labor on free homesteads would finally converge to form a critical mass for antislavery politics in the antebellum North.

The Fugitive Slave Act, Black Militancy, and Antislavery Interracialism in the Labor Movement

Reverberations from the Compromise of 1850 were felt almost immediately in the North—most acutely by African Americans, who found their freedom threatened in new and ominous ways by the Fugitive Slave Act, the compromise's most onerous provision. Long a key demand of slaveholders frustrated by "personal liberty laws" and other northern efforts to thwart the enforcement of the 1793 Fugitive Act, the 1850 act provided for special federal courts to try so-called fugitives (runaway slaves, who were not allowed to call witnesses or offer testimony), required state and local authorities as well as ordinary individuals to assist in the recapture of runaways, and criminalized giving aid to escaped slaves while mandating fines and other penalties for noncompliance. The passage of the act caused widespread outrage in the North, and a series of dramatic confrontations with authorities and rescues of fugitives over the next few years helped to revive the abolitionist movement, sparking a new militancy among Black and white abolitionists alike. In Colored Conventions, vigilance committees, anti–Fugitive Law meetings, and the pages of antislavery newspapers, free Blacks in the North resurrected and intensified a long-standing tradition of forceful resistance to kidnapping and the re-enslavement of fugitives, vowing to resist the Fugitive Act by any means necessary.[7]

At the same time, these forceful responses reignited debates between nonresistant abolitionists and those who sanctioned more violent forms of resistance. In some ways, these reflected earlier debates about the morality and utility of violence that had accompanied abolitionist responses to the 1848 revolutions, while mirroring similar divisions in the British Chartist movement, long split between proponents of moral force and physical force. Indeed, a handful of Black abolitionists had witnessed these debates over the use of force firsthand. Frederick Douglass, Charles L. Remond, and Henry Highland Garnet, who traveled throughout Great Britain during the 1840s, had been favorably impressed with the Chartists' militancy and demands for equal political rights. As Remond recalled, Douglass "openly recognized" the Chartists in England, and Remond himself had spontaneously joined a Chartist procession and "identified myself with them." Such experiences had convinced Remond that "the poor white man is as much interested . . . as the black man" in the success of the antislavery cause. Douglass's *North Star* was perhaps unique among African American papers in its ability to employ foreign correspondents based in Europe, enabling coverage of Chartist meetings in England and news of revolutionary events in France, Hungary, and Italy. The *North Star's* coverage of both Chartism and the 1848 revolutions was overwhelmingly sympathetic, although, in keeping with Garrisonians' commitment to nonresistance, it was more critical of those who resorted to violence, like the Physical Force Chartists or the working-class insurrectionaries who invaded the French National Assembly in May 1848. A few years later, however, Douglass would argue that it was "not only legal, but dutiful" to resist enforcement of the 1850

Fugitive Act by physical force, joining militant colleagues like Henry Highland Garnet and Martin Delany, who urged slave uprisings as well as resistance to the Fugitive Act.[8]

Other Black Americans chose to leave the United States altogether. In contrast to an earlier generation's focus on voluntary emigration to the Black republic of Haiti, many African Americans now set their sights on Canada, with perhaps forty thousand fleeing across the northern border in the decade before the Civil War. In places like Wilberforce, Dawn, and Elgin (all located in Canada West, now Ontario), free Black leaders like James C. Brown, Josiah Henson, and Mary Ann Shadd Cary, sometimes working in tandem with white abolitionists, sought to resettle African American migrants in tight-knit intentional communities. Although these lacked the cooperative and utopian aspirations of the Owenites or Fourierists, to some extent they reflected the same desire for agrarian independence and landed proprietorship that motivated working-class whites to join such communities, with the added impetus of overcoming racial prejudice and, for enslaved fugitives, securing basic freedom. Several of the Canadian communities formed by free African Americans mixed agriculture with light industry, such as sawmills and gristmills, and Dawn's biracial British-American Institute sought to educate Black children in manual labor or industrial schools. In 1855, the *Provincial Freeman*, the newspaper edited by Mary Ann Shadd Cary that served as a voice for African Americans in Canada, implored white workers "to feel how closely their interests, and those of the black working men are united." Under the heading "White and Black Slavery," the article argued that the persistence of chattel slavery had the inevitable effect of dragging workers of all races "downward to a condition of brutish ignorance, degradation, and slavish dependence."[9]

Of those free Blacks who remained in the United States, at least some proved open to the doctrines of the land reformers, perhaps because they resonated with African Americans' already existing emphasis on the independence and security provided by land ownership and community formation. A correspondent to the *North Star* from Salem, Massachusetts, reported that Black abolitionist Martin R. Delany had lectured on National Reform in that antislavery stronghold, home to the first female abolitionist society (founded by Black women in 1836). By the same token, some white land reformers made efforts to break down racial barriers and win over African Americans to their cause. Among the audiences J. K. Ingalls lectured to in 1848 were the members of a "colored congregation" in Little Falls, New York, who heard Ingalls wax eloquent on the subject of "land and freedom." Ingalls also reprinted Colored Conventions leader Willis Hodges's appeal to join forces with the National Reformers (quoted in chapter 5) in his own land reform paper, the *Landmark*.[10] That same year, the *Homestead Journal*, the local organ of National Reform in Salem, Ohio, was moved to publish an editorial refuting the charge that local National Reformers barred Blacks and women from membership. The *Journal*, which proclaimed that the land reformers aimed to secure "the greatest good to the greatest number . . . regardless of Color or Clime," noted that both African Americans and women had taken part in National Reform meetings in Salem. Moreover, the *Journal* insisted, "there is nothing in our Constitution or By-Laws which would prohibit any white or black person, male or female, from participating in our meetings, or prevent any one from aiding us to carry out our objects."[11] The constitution of the NIC declared that the organization was dedicated to the promotion of "Equality, Liberty, and Brotherhood among men of every Race," and in 1847 representatives debated the merits of a revision that explicitly recognized the rights of African Americans and women. Although the revision, proposed by Worcester National Reformer Appleton Fay, was ultimately sidelined, Fay believed that such a measure was not only "calculated to effect a union of reformers . . . garrisonians and others," but that it was "necessary to the success of the free soil doctrine."[12]

Such rhetorical pronouncements were put to the test in 1851, at the NIC in Albany. As the congress was preparing to convene, John C. Bowers, "a colored gentleman from Philadelphia," requested to be seated as a delegate to the convention. Bowers, a successful tailor, entrepreneur, and abolitionist active in the Colored Convention movement who seems to have been as passionately convinced of the need for Blacks to adopt skilled trades as he was an ardent opponent of colonization, arrived as a representative of an obscure organization known as the Philadelphia Land Association. According to the less-than-sympathetic coverage in the *New York Herald*, the ensuing debate over whether Bowers should be seated "threw the firebrand of slavery into the convention." Several letters, including one from Philadelphia labor leader John Campbell, were read that opposed recognizing Bowers's credentials. Campbell, an English immigrant and former Chartist, had bolted the congress in 1847 in response to its increasingly antislavery stances; his viciously racist manifesto *Negro-Mania*, a low-water mark of antebellum working-class racism, was published in the same year as the controversy over Bowers's seating. But a larger group, which the *Herald* labeled "abolitionists," and which

JOHN C. BOWERS,
Grand Master, 1870–71, G. U. O. of O. F., America.

Figure 13. John C. Bowers, a Black activist and abolitionist from Philadelphia who was active in the Colored Conventions movement and numerous other Black-led associations, participated in the 1851 National Industrial Congress in Albany, New York. New York Public Library Digital Collections.

included Evans, New York National Reformer E. S. Manning, Lucius Hine, and Charles Douglas of the New England Workingmen's Association, spoke in defense of Bowers's right to be seated. Perhaps the most compelling case was made by Bowers himself, who, as even the *Herald*'s hostile correspondent was forced to admit, made "an eloquent appeal in favor of his race, and . . . deserved more praise than those who called him their brother." Eventually, Bowers was seated, although at least "one delegate declared that he would not sit with a colored man, and left the congress."[13]

Remarkable as it was, Bowers's presence was not the only example of Black participation in the NIC. In 1855, Cleveland abolitionist and Colored Convention leader William H. Day not only was a delegate to the NIC, but served as one of the conference's secretaries. While the controversy over Bowers's seating certainly reflects the persistence of white racism in the antebellum labor movement, the precedent established by his participation may have reflected a growing desire among some labor reformers to take a more unequivocal stance against slavery and in favor of Black rights in the wake of the Fugitive Slave Act and the Compromise of 1850. As the implications of the compromise measures became apparent, land reformers and other workingmen's organizations began to respond. Like northerners generally, white workingmen resented their transformation into "slave catchers," as the law threatened to draft ordinary citizens into a national dragnet for fugitive slaves. Meeting in Boston in October 1850, a convention called by the New England Industrial League combined calls for land reform measures and a ten-hour day with resistance to the Fugitive Act. Although the convention called on workers to support whichever candidates they believed would most strongly support labor reform, it condemned both major parties as having "forfeited all claim to the confidence and support of the honest working classes." In the event, Massachusetts voters chose the antislavery Democrat George S. Boutwell for governor that November, the result of a coalition between Free Soilers and Democrats in the Bay State.[14] More strikingly, another convention of Massachusetts workers, representing twenty-two local labor organizations, passed a resolution proclaiming that to surrender "our fellow-workingmen to the Slave Hunters . . . dispensing with the trial by Jury" was an *"infamous act, fit only to be trampled under the feet of every lover of Liberty and Justice."*[15] Another group of Massachusetts "Friends of Industrial Reform" passed a resolution declaring that the Fugitive Act was not "binding in law or conscience on the people, and ought to be resisted, if necessary, to death, by every friend to our country, to humanity, and to justice." In Boston, Elizur Wright and John C. Cluer, a Chartist immigrant and local ten-hours law activist, took their opposition to the Fugitive Act to the next level, participating in civil disobedience and antislavery militancy. Both faced prosecution for resisting the law, Wright for helping Shadrach Minkins to escape in 1851, and Cluer for participating in the famous jailbreak that briefly liberated Anthony Burns in 1854.[16]

Outside the abolitionist hotbed of Massachusetts, the response from labor reformers to the 1850 Compromise was more muted, with some labor organizations explicitly disavowing any participation in the controversy over slavery.[17] In 1848, for example, some Baltimore delegates to the NIC were so disturbed by the organization's nomination of Gerrit Smith that on returning home, they denounced the congress as an "Abolition Convention."[18] But in 1851 and again in 1852, the New York City Industrial Congress reaffirmed its "hostility" to the Fugitive Act and urged its repeal, citing the case of Horace Preston, a fugitive from Baltimore recently arrested in Brooklyn. Separately, Philadelphia ironmonger and labor leader John Sheddon, Brotherhood of the

Union head George Lippard, and National Reformer August Duganne also spoke out against the Fugitive Law.[19] Somewhat more belatedly, in 1854, a group of signatories in Greenpoint, Brooklyn, led by the National Reform Association's Lewis Masquerier, expressed their disapproval of the idea that northern workers had "submitted to the degredation [sic] and meanness of becoming slave catchers." But the petitioners did not limit themselves to denouncing the Fugitive Act's deleterious impact on their status as northern freemen. The rancor created by the Fugitive Act, the petition continued, "prove[d] that the public conscience of the free states is outraged by the peculiar institution." The only "remedy" for the "evil" of slavery, the petitioners concluded, was "its ultimate abolition." By the middle of the decade, increasing numbers of ordinary northerners were ready to join the Greenpoint workingmen in reaching this conclusion.[20]

Land Reform and Antislavery in National Politics, Part One

The period between the passage of the Compromise of 1850 and the formation of the Republican Party in 1854 represented something of an interregnum in the development of antislavery politics, and the same held true for the alliance between antislavery and labor reform. Despite the growing antislavery sentiment among northern working men and women and the early promise suggested by the endorsement of Gerrit Smith as the presidential candidate of both the NIC and the National Reform Association, the anticipated merger of the land and labor reform and abolitionism in a "union of reformers" never fully materialized.

To some extent, this failure reflected the fragmented nature and diminished strength of the abolitionist movement, whether of the Garrisonian or political variety, at the beginning of the 1850s. Over the course of the previous decade, the movement had been repeatedly rocked by a number of schisms and divisions, including those between political abolitionists and nonvoting abstentionists; between supporters of women's rights and those who believed that the "woman question" should be left out of antislavery; and between those who defended Garrison's religious unorthodoxy and those who supported more traditional church structures and interpretations of scripture. By the middle of the 1840s, as political abolitionists like Gerrit Smith, William Goodell, Alvan Stewart, and Lysander Spooner were developing ever more complex arguments in favor of an antislavery Constitution, the Garrisonians embraced outright disunionism, a revolutionary strategy that, whatever its merits, led to many defections and caused the AASS to be further shunned by those who were unable or unwilling to sacrifice their devotion to their country.[21] Meanwhile, the Liberty League's Macedon Convention platform had won the accolades, but not the support, of many long-time Liberty Party supporters. After the already electorally marginal Liberty Party split in two—a Liberty League (later the National Liberty Party) led by Smith, and the remainder, which constituted the majority of the party—each faction tended to view the other's position as a surrender of principle. As one mainstream Liberty Party editor fumed, "I dispise [sic] the craven spirit of that man who will not vote the fetters of the slave off unless he can at the same time 'vote himself a farm'!"[22] But Smith's faction was, if anything, even more intransigent, a development in large part attributable to Smith's uncompromising political persona, which stemmed in part from his deep religious convictions and devotion to what he called "Bible politics." Rather than seeing land reform as part of a calculated appeal to white workingmen's self-interest, Smith viewed *both* immediate abolitionism and freedom of the soil as nonnegotiable stances based on principles of morality and natural rights. Although he welcomed the prospect of Van Buren's Free Soil Party as "tending to break up the great political parties, which . . . are the chief shelters and props of slavery," Smith explained to J. K. Ingalls that he could not vote for any presidential candidate who was not an outright abolitionist, or who did not embrace "the perfect equality of all men, in both their political and social rights"—a stance that, in the 1850s, virtually ruled out any major contender for the office.[23]

After the National Liberty Convention rejected most of the Liberty League's positions, Smith led his followers into a schismatic party based in New York, committed to land reform, antislavery constitutionalism, and what it considered "true" Liberty Party principles. But most Libertymen rallied behind the antislavery New Hampshire Democrat John P. Hale and, after Hale inconveniently declined the Liberty Party's nomination, drifted into support for the Free Soil Party. Although the Free Soilers made a strong showing under Van Buren in 1848, their success proved to be short lived, as most antislavery Barnburner Democrats and Conscience Whigs returned to the party fold. Smith's small faction launched a stirring but ultimately quixotic campaign that failed to catch fire even in its home base of New York, let alone nationally. Both Liberty factions combined garnered only a few thousand votes, continuing the party's precipitous decline.[24]

One important group of abolitionists, however, did seem to discern the potential of antislavery third parties to craft a successful mass movement from these disparate elements, while clearly expressing their preference for those who, like Smith, appealed to issues of economic equality without sacrificing antislavery principles. Both Frederick Douglass and Henry Bibb addressed the Free Soil Convention at Buffalo in 1848, and the National Colored Convention at Cleveland endorsed the Free Soilers that year. But Douglass's political compass nonetheless led him in the direction of the Liberty Party, where he found himself increasingly persuaded by the brand of antislavery constitutionalism developed by Goodell, Smith, and others.[25] In some cases, the move toward political abolitionism was paired with support for land reform, both as a political strategy and as a means of acquiring independence and self-determination for free Blacks and the formerly enslaved. Douglass's increasing contact with the Smith–Goodell wing of the Liberty Party as well as with local land reformers in Upstate New York may have contributed to a gradual transformation of his views on the subject. Although he continued to take issue with those who made "wage slavery" arguments, in early 1848, the *North Star* reprinted two lengthy articles on the public lands and land reform, as well as an extract from a speech by Gerrit Smith in which the latter predicted that land reform not only would "overthrow slavery" but would "make impossible, its resuscitation and repetition."[26] Later that year, the *North Star* again urged readers to vote for Smith and the Liberty Party, reprinting a notice for a Liberty convention in Smith's hometown of Peterboro featuring a speech by J. K. Ingalls, "who will present the cause of the Land Reform Party." Noting that the Liberty Party, the Liberty League, and land reformers all shared a candidate in Smith, the address expressed the hope that "the friends of the poor *white* man, as well as of the poor *black* man" would attend in large numbers.[27]

In an "Address to the Four Thousand Colored Voters of the State of New York," Samuel Ringgold Ward praised "the grand demonstration made at the Buffalo Convention for Free Soil," but urged Black voters to support the Smith wing of the Liberty Party, which best represented the "interests of the crushed, poor, black or white, bond or free." Ward criticized those Libertymen who had previously claimed to be too devoted to the cause of slave emancipation "even to listen to the discussion of Land Reform," only to abandon such principles in support of what Ward termed "the mere Wilmot Proviso" platform of Hale and Van Buren.[28] In 1847, Henry Highland Garnet had anticipated the shift to political abolitionism, clearly spelling out his reasons for embracing third-party antislavery. "If it were to save every mother's son of them from dying to-morrow," Garnet noted sardonically, neither Democrats nor Whigs could muster the political will to abolish the internal slave trade, let alone slavery itself. "When we unite in these northern states and go politically for the overthrow of the chattel slavery which has made merchandize of 3,000,000 of our fellow countrymen," Garnet wrote, "we want just such a man as Gerrit Smith to head the enterprise." Among other advantages, Smith's candidacy effectively neutralized the charges of hypocrisy then being leveled by slaveholders, who had by then adopted the language of "wage slavery" to use as a critique of northern free labor society. If abolitionists did not adopt land reform, Garnet intoned, "the slaveholders can very properly turn upon us and ask, How much worse are we than your *patroons*? How much better off will you make our slaves than your own beggarly hirelings? With Gerrit Smith at our head and Land Reform on our flag we can defy their logic and overwhelm their piratical law."[29]

Garnet's comment, while stopping short of endorsing comparisons between wage workers and slaves, points to the conclusion that wage slavery arguments had to be confronted and countered if antislavery was to make serious headway among an overwhelmingly white northern voting population, the majority of whom toiled as farmers, laborers, or artisans. After his final break with Garrison in 1851, Douglass complained to Smith that critics at the AASS's annual convention had stood "seven deep" against him for the *North Star*'s support of the Liberty Party and land reform. That spring, Douglass began to take steps to merge the *North Star*, now in financial difficulties after the withdrawal of support from the AASS, with the *Liberty Party Paper*, edited by Syracuse Libertyman and land reform supporter John Thomas. Initial funding for the new venture, emblazoned with the motto "All rights for All," was supported by Smith. As corresponding editor, Thomas used the columns of *Frederick Douglass' Paper* to champion the new Free Democratic Party and land reform, which it described as the most "interesting" subject then before the people. That same year, Douglass compared land reform favorably to colonization or emigration schemes before an antislavery audience, declaring that "the Land-Reform project, with its aim to elevate labor; to ameliorate the condition of the poor, to give homes to the homeless; and land to the landless" had "engaged some of the noblest heads, and most philanthropic hearts of this age."[30]

Although the outcome of Smith's quixotic campaign as the standardbearer of the Liberty League in 1848 had given little indication of political abolitionism's future success, garnering only a few thousand votes, it did provide evidence to militant abolitionists like Douglass and Garnet that a principled commitment to slavery's abolition and other radically transformative measures could be combined with an appeal to the economic self-interest of the majority of northern voters. Before that potential could be realized, however, the doctrines of land reform would have to be spread beyond the working-class urban wards, Hudson Valley tenant farms, and New England factory towns where it had first commanded the attention and votes of workingmen.

Land Reform Moves West: National Reform in Ohio, Wisconsin, and Beyond

Even as the National Reform Association began to decline in New York and other eastern cities after 1848, its radical brand of land reform continued to gain adherents in the burgeoning western cities of Cincinnati, Chicago, and Milwaukee, and among many humbler towns and pioneer settlements of the Old Northwest and the Middle West. Although their most diehard constituencies might have been among the radical artisan milieus of New York and New England, Evans and other National Reform leaders had always believed that land reform would be brought about "by the votes of the small farmers, who were the majority" in the North and throughout the country.[31] In recognition of the growing importance of the West, the NIC was held in Cincinnati in 1849, in Chicago in 1850, and in Cleveland in 1855. By the end of the 1840s, the National Reform Association claimed to have some fifty auxiliary associations, not only in industrializing eastern cities like Philadelphia, Boston, Albany, Rochester, and Lowell, but in Pittsburgh, Pennsylvania; Columbus and Cincinnati, Ohio; Louisville, Kentucky; Wheeling, Virginia; New Harmony, Indiana; and Milwaukee, Wisconsin. It also claimed that more than one hundred newspapers were "committed to the National Reform measures, in whole or in part," among which it counted not only Horace Greeley's *Tribune*, Elizur Wright's *Boston Daily Chronotype*, and the Lowell *Voice of Industry*, but also publications in Rochester and Auburn, New York; Cincinnati, Cleveland, Salem, and McConnelsville, Ohio; and Chicago and Chester, Illinois.[32]

Cincinnati, the boomtown on the free side of the Northwest Ordinance's dividing line between free and slave states, was a magnet for skilled artisans and laborers as well as for animal products, grain, iron, and other manufactured goods traveling by river and canal. It was also known for its hostility toward African Americans, who were subject to Ohio's discriminatory Black Codes, kidnappings of free people and runaways across Ohio's border with Kentucky, and anti-Black rioting. In one particularly notorious instance in Cincinnati in August 1829, white mobs largely comprising artisans, laborers, and Irish immigrants carried out attacks on Black homes and neighborhoods, forcing many to flee. As James C. Brown, a Black mason who organized the effort to found the Wilberforce colony in Canada in the aftermath of the riots, recalled, free Black artisans like himself had become "an object of jealousy to white mechanics, because I was more successful in getting jobs."[33] But by the 1840s, the atmosphere had become somewhat more favorable. Although tensions remained high, again flaring into riots in 1836, abolitionists gained a strong foothold in Cincinnati with the arrival of *Philanthropist* publisher James G. Birney, brothers Augustus and John O. Wattles, and the mass defection of the Lane Theological Seminary rebels, led by Theodore Weld. John Wattles was particularly notable for his combination of ideas derived from labor communitarianism and land reform with abolitionism; he ran the ill-fated Fourierist colony of Utopia (which he later sold to the protoanarchist labor reformer Josiah Warren), helped run a manual labor school for free Blacks with his brother in nearby Mercer County, Ohio, and published *Report on the Educational Condition of the Colored People of Cincinnati*. By the early 1850s, German immigrants in Cincinnati, many of them veterans of the European revolutions of 1830 and 1848, outnumbered the Irish. Although many of the German arrivals held conservative and racist views, the 1850s saw a remarkable degree of overlap and cooperation between German socialists, labor reformers, and abolitionists in the Queen City, perhaps most strikingly in the case of the interracial collaboration between '48er August Willich and Black socialist Peter H. Clark.[34]

National Reform also had a strong foothold in Cincinnati. John Pickering, author of *The Working Man's Political Economy*, was based there, and in 1848 he took the lead in collecting over two hundred signatures for a National Reform petition to Congress. Pickering's 1850 pamphlet *The Friend of Man, Being the Principles of National or Land Reform* seemed to abandon Pickering's earlier contention that land reform and slave emancipation were mutually exclusive, praising California's free soil constitution, ratified that year, as "a signal triumph of the principles we advocate." In 1850, Pickering was chosen by a group of local reformers to draft a document that would provide a working theory for the unification of various reform efforts, to be presented at that year's Industrial Congress at Chicago. The resulting document contained the usual denunciations of so-called fragmentary reforms, but also declared itself firmly against slavery's expansion and "the abridgement of the liberties" of free Blacks. Slavery, the NIC proclaimed that year, was an "evil, repugnant to the law of God," that "cannot exist without inevitably producing the destruction of a nation which permits it."[35]

Even more persuasive was Lucius A. Hine. The young and dashing Hine had studied law at the University of Cincinnati before adopting land reform and publishing his forceful but respectful argument against William Lloyd Garrison's rejection of political antislavery. Hine's *Lecture on Garrisonian Politics* (1853) also contained strident pleas for recognition of the rights of women and free Blacks, as well as one of the period's most original arguments in favor of an antislavery interpretation of the Constitution. Hine, who published a series of "Political and Social Economy" pamphlets throughout the decade, read Pickering's reform manifesto at the 1850 Industrial Congress (presided over that year by another westerner, the Fourierist and founder of the Wisconsin Phalanx, Warren B. Chase). For much of the 1850s, Hine traveled throughout Ohio, Michigan, Illinois, and Indiana lecturing on "Land Reform and Free Schools," holding hundreds of land reform meetings each year. "In no place," he reported, "have I failed to find staunch friends of Land Reform in its most radical import." Later, he resurfaced as a Lincoln supporter and a spokesperson for the various workingmen's organizations that coalesced after the Civil War.[36]

Land reformers joined forces with antislavery not only in Ohio, where Liberty Party leaders participated in that state's Free Territory convention, but throughout the states of the Old Northwest and greater West. In Michigan, the new, antislavery Free Democratic party demanded that public lands be "gratuitously distributed in limited quantities to actual settlers." Illinoisans organized the National Reform Democratic State Convention with the goal of showing that "the sons of toil" there were "acting in concert with those of other States" in the "great movement" then underway.[37] Iowa Free Soilers, denouncing the proslavery positions of Democrats and Whigs as "anti-Democratic, anti-Christian, and untrue," endorsed the Free Soil Party ticket as "the only political party who propose and sustain any great and good measures of National Reform in the present day." The Iowans nominated Free Soil Democrat John P. Hale for president, on the grounds that his efforts on the homestead bill then pending in Congress "entitled him to the gratitude and respect of the laboring classes." Indiana, Wisconsin, and California all incorporated homestead exemption clauses into their state constitutions; in

Indiana, the push for exemption was led by future Radical Republican Schuyler Colfax, who also gave his endorsement to the broader concept of freedom of the public lands.[38]

In California, David C. Broderick, an Irish immigrant stonecutter who had been associated with Mike Walsh's "Spartan gang" of working-class toughs in the lower wards of Manhattan, became the leader of the California Free Soilers against the conservative Hunker faction. Both Walsh and Broderick won election to their respective state legislatures in New York and California in the early 1850s, but unlike Walsh, who voted for the notorious Kansas-Nebraska Act, Broderick refused to become a dupe of the Slave Power. As a state legislator, Broderick opposed the passage of a bill barring the emigration of African Americans to California; later, as a US senator, Broderick's denunciations of northern "doughface" Stephen Douglas and the proslavery Lecompton Constitution in Kansas won him the esteem of many Republicans and the enmity of Hunker Democrats. Broderick would pay the ultimate price for his antislavery stances a few years later, when he was killed by California's proslavery former state supreme court justice David S. Terry in a duel.[39]

But it was in Wisconsin that the alliance between antislavery and land reform bore the most fruit. Even before attaining statehood in 1848, the brand of radical free soil promoted by the National Reformers had a solid foundation in Wisconsin. Despite the obvious but unstated irony—made more pungent by Evans's propensity to quote the Sauk leader Black Hawk— that the "freedom" of Wisconsin's soil was made possible by its recent appropriation from Native Americans, the influx of small farmers from New England, German '48ers, and Scandinavians with traditions of communal farming made the territory ripe for land reform proselytizing. As early as 1837, pioneers in the territory had sent petitions asking that Wisconsin's public lands be reserved for actual settlers rather than speculators. Beginning in the mid-1840s, National Reform lecturer H. H. Van Amringe traveled widely throughout the state, successfully extracting land reform pledges from local legislators and, in 1847, winning the inclusion of a homestead exemption clause in the new state constitution.[40] The following year, the state Free Soil convention in Janesville officially adopted the three National Reform planks alongside the Buffalo Free Soil platform, and in the national election, Wisconsin gave nearly a quarter of its votes to Free Soil candidate Van Buren—more than any other state besides Massachusetts and New York.[41] Most impressively—and to the horror of land speculators and probusiness conservatives, who viewed it as marking the advent of "agrarianism"—in 1851 a state measure limiting the size of individual landholdings to 320 acres (twice the National Reform recommendation) received the support of the governor and passed an initial vote in the state legislature, only to be defeated after the state's attorney general declared it unconstitutional. Nonetheless, the prospects for land reform in Wisconsin looked so promising that New York National Reformer Alvan E. Bovay, the organization's national secretary, relocated there that same year.[42]

Wisconsin land reformers also had an able mouthpiece in the form of the *American Freeman* (later the *Wisconsin Freeman*, and afterward the Milwaukee *Free Democrat*), edited by another transplant, Sherman M. Booth. Known as a "radical," "old-time abolitionist," the Western New York–born Booth had become involved in abolitionism as a Yale student assigned to teach imprisoned Africans from the *Amistad* rebellion how to read, and subsequently helped organize the Liberty Party in Connecticut. He arrived in Wisconsin in 1848, the year of Wisconsin's admission to the Union. With an assistant, Ichabod Codding, he established the *Freeman* in Waukesha, but soon moved to Milwaukee and became the paper's sole editor and proprietor. At first Booth was chary of the Free Soil movement, regarding it as an abandonment of Liberty Party principles, but after his election to the national Free Soil Convention in Buffalo (with instructions to "sustain no candidates except those who are not only pledged against the extension of slavery, but are also committed to the policy of abolishing it"), he played an important role in shaping the new party's platform.[43]

Back in Wisconsin, Booth became a vocal advocate of both the Free Soil party and the more radical version of "free soil" espoused by local National Reformers. In Milwaukee, Booth helped to organize a Free Soil league that included advocates of both antislavery and land reform, while German immigrant A. H. Biefeld publicized National Reform in the Milwaukee *Volksfreund*.[44] Booth's *Freeman*, which changed its name to the *Free Democrat* after the emergence of the breakaway party of the same name, also became an enthusiastic adopter of the land reform measures promoted by the National Reformers. Booth encouraged readers to travel to the Industrial Congresses in Chicago in 1850 and Washington, D.C., in 1852, and published notices of local National Reform lectures and meetings. At one of the latter, held before an overflow crowd at Madison's Assembly Hall, attendees listened to Van Amringe address "a full house on the subject of Free Soil," where Van Amringe "completely annihilated the arguments" against land reform. The *Free Democrat* announced that "the principles involved in those questions we unhesitatingly approve," noting that many of the same principles applied to the question of federal government intervention over slavery in the territories.[45]

Booth's version of Free Soil politics also took seriously the issue of Black equality. The *Free Democrat* devoted a column to denying the charge that local land reformers had voted against the election of an African American delegate to the NIC. The vote, the *Free Democrat* clarified, had been twenty to six in favor, rather than the reverse; furthermore, even some of the six who rejected the delegate came out "in favor of colored suffrage." Not far away, in Rosendale, Wisconsin, another local National Reform branch required that members take a pledge to end discrimination "on account of birth-place or color" in addition to the usual land reform pledges.[46] Booth also took National Reformers to task for failing to live up to the antislavery implications of their creed, splitting with a local National Reform leader after he attempted to bring followers back into the arms of the conservative Hunker Democrats. In May 1849, Booth republished an article from the like-minded *True Democrat*, chiding National Reformers for failing to pay attention to the importance of measures like the abolition of slavery in Washington, DC. The article agreed that a land limitation law would be "a blow . . . struck at the very root of all human slavery," but accused National Reformers of "an inconsistency . . . that operate[s] as a drawback to true, practical progress." Reversing the logic of land reformers' arguments prioritizing the abolition of land monopoly ahead of the abolition of slavery, Booth's *True Democrat* argued that "If we can not kill the root . . . we should not in our indignation, refuse to lop off its branches."[47]

Land Reform and Antislavery in National Politics, Part Two

The metaphor chosen by the *True Democrat* shows how, under the altered political conditions of the 1850s, the land reformers' insistence on striking at the roots of "all slavery" could be redirected in favor of abolitionism. At the same time, the associations between slavery, the exploitation of labor, and the appropriation of land helped bring about the dominance of "free soil" politics, in both their radical and more moderate guises, in states like Wisconsin. Not only was a more radical version of "free soil"—one that demanded a rough equality of landholding wealth and equal access to the soil—associated with a more militant form of political abolitionism there, but even conservative Whigs and Hunker Democrats were forced to adopt strong positions against the further spread of slavery. Such developments made Wisconsin, in the words of one historian, "more nearly anti-slavery than any similar area in the Union."[48]

Wisconsin may have been unique in both the ubiquity of free soil anti-slavery sentiment as well as the popularity of more radical land reform measures like land limitation, but its admission as a nonslave state—preceded by Iowa in 1846 and followed by California in 1850, Minnesota in 1858, and Oregon in 1859—was part of a wave of free soil sentiment in the West. In a sign of the political transformations wrought by the Wilmot Proviso and the Barnburner revolt as well as a harbinger of things to come, the period 1848–1851 also saw the election to Congress of antislavery champions Horace Mann and Charles Sumner from Massachusetts, Salmon P. Chase and Benjamin Wade from Ohio, William H. Seward from New York, George W. Julian from Indiana, and John C. Frémont from California. Seward, Chase, and Julian would all become strong supporters of land reform—which was then beginning to be referred to as "Homestead reform"—while Frémont would run for president as the candidate of the new Republican Party on the platform of "free soil, free labor, free men" in 1856.

Although far less well-known than Sumner or Seward, Wisconsin's Charles Durkee and I. P. Walker (both elected in 1848) would swell the ranks of both antislavery and land reform forces in Congress while fine-tuning the constitutional and legal arguments that sought to limit slavery's spread and contain its power. In the House, Durkee became a leading supporter of land reform and a vocal opponent of what he termed the Fugitive Act's "unrelenting war against the African race." In 1851–1852, Durkee was nominated by the remainder of the Liberty Party to serve as its vice presidential candidate; he declined that honor, but he did accept an invitation to preside over that year's NIC in Washington, DC, where he was appointed to serve as chair of the meeting.[49]

Walker, a Virginia-born lawyer who had rubbed shoulders with Abraham Lincoln in Springfield, Illinois, was chosen by state legislators as one of Wisconsin's first two senators along with another land reform supporter, former territorial governor Henry Dodge. The choice reflected the salience of land reform as well as the new state's penchant for democratic egalitarianism; known as a Loco Foco (as radical Democrats were still sometimes called), Walker was also a supporter of the Liberty Party and of the rights of women, immigrants, and Native Americans. Although Walker's efforts on behalf of the homestead bill he sponsored earned him the loyalty of land reformers nationwide, his antislavery legacy in Congress turned out to be somewhat more equivocal. Walker had been chosen in part due to his reputation as an uncompromising opponent of slaveholder expansion, and the state legislature, anticipating debate over the fate of slavery in the territories acquired from Mexico, had instructed its senators to oppose the admission of California, New Mexico, or "any other Territory" into the Union without an explicit provision permanently forbidding the introduction of slavery. Once in the Senate, however, Walker attempted to stake out a more nuanced position on the omnibus bill, submitting an amendment that extended constitutional authority to California and New Mexico without such a guarantee. Furious, free soil newspapers like Booth's *Free Democrat* and Greeley's *New-York Tribune* denounced the move, and—despite the senator's explanation that he feared the collapse of the union if no compromise with the South could be found—the Wisconsin legislature voted to censure him.[50]

Largely overlooked by antislavery contemporaries and later historians, however, were Walker's contributions to the legal and constitutional arguments that would soon be taken up by antislavery politicians as the national conflict over slavery wore on. During Senate debate on the status of slavery in California and New Mexico, Walker introduced a remarkable amendment arguing that, since slavery had already been abolished in Mexico, it did "not exist by law" in the lands taken after the Mexican-American War, nor could it be introduced into any of the territory acquired from Mexico "*without positive enactments*." The argument was a novel one so far as the Mexican Cession was concerned, but it rested on longstanding antislavery theory and precedent. Mexico's emancipation acts, Walker argued, had established the "free air" principle made famous by the 1772 Somerset decision in England, under which slaveholders who brought their enslaved chattels onto "free soil" found their claims to hold property in man rendered automatically null and void.[51] Combining the Somerset principle with familiar free labor arguments about the propensity of slave plantations to usurp large tracts of land and deprive hardworking settlers of access to the soil, Walker made a point that would soon become associated with the set of ideas associated with the antislavery theory of the Constitution sometimes known as "freedom national, slavery local," popularized by the abolitionist senator Charles Sumner and others. Slavery, Walker insisted, was "a purely *local* institution . . . it has no foundation in nature, or support in the laws of God . . . it exists, and can only exist, by virtue of the local laws of the States."[52]

Walker's efforts on behalf of free soil and Homestead legislation earned him the gratitude of land reformers, prompting the Industrial Congress to nominate him for president. But his Senate career soon fell victim to the perception—perhaps not entirely accurate—that he had capitulated to the South on the question of slavery's expansion, and in 1855 he was replaced by none other than Durkee, who had recently joined the new Republican Party.[53] Meanwhile, a new cohort of antislavery congressmen, including Sumner, Chase, and Seward, picked up on and refined ideas that stretched back to the Somerset decision and the antislavery constitutionalism of William Goodell, William Leggett, Gerrit Smith, and George Henry Evans—and which, under the rubric of "freedom national," would go on to become the most powerful unifying idea behind the antislavery politics of the second half of the 1850s.[54]

While the full fruits of these developments would have to await the formation of the Republican Party in the aftermath of the Kansas-Nebraska debacle, events in the meantime seemed to hold promise for a reunion of land and labor reformers with political abolitionists. After the passage of the Compromise of 1850, elements of the old Free Soil Party had regrouped and threatened to break off from the Democratic Party, now widely seen as being in thrall to the Slave Power. In June 1852, Ohio congressman Samuel Lewis issued a call for a convention to be held by the "friends of the principles declared" at the 1848 Free Soil convention, made up of what Lewis called "Delegates of the Free Democracy." When the newly christened Free Democratic Party convened in Pittsburgh that August, it invited the NIC, then holding its annual meeting in Washington, DC, to send delegates. At the same time, in New York, a city convention of "Independent Democrats," after passing the by now requisite resolutions on land reform, elected a delegation consisting of National Reformers William West, Lewis Masquerier, and William J. Young to attend the new party's inaugural meeting. At the Pittsburgh convention, land reformers rubbed shoulders with the likes of Gerrit Smith, Joshua Giddings, Lewis Tappan, Frederick Douglass, Charles Francis Adams, Owen Lovejoy, and Henry Wilson (the antislavery Massachusetts Senator known as the "Natick cobbler" for his humble artisan origins). Convening on August 11, 1852, only a day after the defeat of I. P. Walker's homestead bill in the Senate, the convention's majority report added a plank declaring that "the public lands of the United States belong to the people, and should not be sold to individuals nor granted to corporations, but should be held as a sacred

trust ... [and] granted in limited quantities, free of cost, to landless settlers"
to resolutions denouncing slavery and the 1850 Compromise.[55]

But the majority report's positions on both slavery and land reform
failed to satisfy the backers of the minority report, read by Smith and Lowell National Reformer William Young. Although, unlike the 1848 Free Soil
platform, the convention's majority report did not deny the authority of the
federal government to intervene in preventing the spread of slavery in the
territories, neither did it explicitly recognize the constitutional authority of
Congress to do so. The minority report's position went further, characteriz-
ing slavery as an "atrocious and abominable" form of "piracy" and declaring
it "entirely incapable of legislation"—that is to say, illegal. Echoing the language of the Massachusetts workingmen in 1850, Smith and Young vowed
that the fugitive law should not only be defied but "trample[d] under foot."
As far as the public lands were concerned, the minority report pushed for the
recognition that the "right to the soil is the right of all men." In the ensuing
debate over the "legality" of slavery that followed, land reform emerged as the
middle ground on which both sides could meet; one Pennsylvania delegate
thought it could serve as an "entering wedge" in bringing about the demise
of slavery. In the end, the convention not only adopted the majority report's
acceptance of the three National Reform planks, but added a resolution submitted by Sherman Booth affirming a "natural right" to a portion of the soil,
which was adopted almost unanimously. The convention then renominated
the perennial hope of antislavery Democrats, John P. Hale, for president and
a relative newcomer, George W. Julian of Indiana, for vice president.[56]

Back in New York, however, National Reform support for Free Democracy proved to be far from a foregone conclusion, as the remaining core
of the National Reform leadership continued to debate the best course of
action. By the early 1850s, politicians ranging from William H. Seward to
Horace Greeley to Tennessee's Andrew Johnson to Tammany Hall operatives were tripping over themselves to show support for the homestead bill.[57]
Much as they had in 1848, when National Reformers found themselves torn
between the faint promise of the Liberty League and the "sham free soil" of
the Van Burenites, in 1852 the group found itself divided over the efficacy of
supporting third-party candidates. That August, convinced that they held
the balance of power over the decisive New York State vote in the upcoming
election, the National Reformers held a public meeting in Broadway's Military Hall to debate strategies and weigh the merits of each new party alignment. Strikingly, the land reformers' rejection of the Democratic nominee

that year, the New Hampshire proslavery doughface Franklin Pierce, was unanimous. Reporting back from Pittsburgh, William West declared the Free Democracy platform to be "perfect," although he found its candidate, John P. Hale, to be unsatisfactory (Hale had never formally endorsed land reform, nor for that matter had he agreed to be the Free Democrats' candidate). Noting that a small group of prominent Whigs, persuaded by editorials in Horace Greeley's *Tribune*, had all endorsed land reform, West explained that he had attended the Pittsburgh conference mainly in the hopes of getting the Whig candidate, General Winfield Scott, nominated on the national ticket. But William Young protested the tilt toward the Whigs, describing the Free Democrats' platform as "one of the greatest that ever was," and insisting that land reformers had a "duty" to vote for them. A Mr. Crawley agreed, believing that a vote for the new party would do more to damage the Democrats and fearing that support for the Whigs would alienate strongly Democratic Irish and German immigrants. Evans, meanwhile, counseled caution, insisting that "the wisest policy of all" would be to vote only for candidates pledged to land reform. But the overall thrust of the meeting was in favor of support for the Whigs—a startling turnaround for an organization rooted in the party of Jefferson and Jackson. Even the once staunchly Democratic Thomas Devyr acknowledged that the northern Democracy was now clearly operating "in collusion with the South." Devyr now favored throwing National Reform votes to the Whigs in order to "fire a volley into the democrats, so that when the smoke clears away they will not know where to find themselves."[58]

Even if it was largely strategic, then, the shift of land reformers' support to the Whigs represented a significant reversal of the political order that had obtained at least since the ascendance of Andrew Jackson in 1828. Unlike the coalition between land reformers and the Liberty League in 1847–1848, however, a formal political alliance between the National Reformers and the Whigs or the Free Democratic Party was not to be. Free Democracy would itself prove to be a short-lived phenomenon, with many of its leading lights going into the new Republican Party; militant abolitionists, led by Smith, formed a Radical Abolition Party, while others returned to the Democratic fold. Coinciding roughly with the eclipse of National Reform as a political movement, the demise of the Free Democrats after 1852 in some ways represented the last gasp of the Barnburner revolt and the old Free Soil and Liberty parties.[59] But although the antislavery parties and social reform movements of the 1850s would continue to undergo this process of fragmentation, co-optation, and coalition during the remainder of the decade, a new political party would prove much more successful at building a mass politics based on antislavery constitutionalism, free soil antiextensionism, and appeals to free labor, while incorporating a radical strain from the abolitionist, labor, and land reform movements of previous decades. In the years immediately before the Civil War, this broad coalition would become a force to be reckoned with in an American political landscape newly divided along lines of sectionalism and slavery.

CHAPTER 7

Antislavery, Labor, and the *Res Publica*: The Rise of the Republican Party

In 1855 and early 1856, Parke Godwin, a founding member of the National Industrial Congress (NIC) who had been one of Fourierism's most prominent supporters in the 1840s, penned a series of influential essays in *Putnam's Magazine*. Although Godwin had left behind the utopian socialism of his earlier days, he had become an enthusiastic supporter of the National Reformers' approach to land reform, and his ongoing commitment to the labor movement was reflected in his election as vice president of the Typographers' Union, which represented typesetters and print workers. Beginning with an attack on the Kansas-Nebraska Act, the controversial measure passed by Congress in 1854 that opened the territories north of the 36°30' line to slavery, Godwin lamented the substitution of ideals of democratic equality for "a dogma about the natural superiority of certain races" and the tendency of the slaveholding class "to defend the subjugation of labor as a just and normal condition." For Godwin, the Kansas-Nebraska controversy demonstrated once again that "the fundamental and vital question" was the contest between "the two social systems of the North and South," a conflict that Godwin depicted in terms that anticipated William H. Seward's famous speech of a few years later, as destined to lead to an "irrepressible crisis." As far as Godwin was concerned, "the results of [the] two social experiments" were already in and had been demonstrated amply in favor of freedom. Citing an array of sources, from Henry Carey's *Principles of Political Economy* and Frederick Law Olmsted's *A Journey in the Seaboard Slave States* to the 1850 census statistics and southerners' own words about the condition of poor whites there, Godwin argued that in the slave societies of the South, "the masses . . . cannot rise above the lowest level." The choice, as Godwin saw it, was a stark one:

whether the future of the nation would more closely resemble "the pens and plantations of slavery" or "the factories and free-schools of freedom."[1]

If this former radical and soon-to-be ex-Democrat sounded like a Republican, the similarity was not coincidental. In June 1856, the same year that the *Putnam's* articles were published under the straightforward title *Political Essays*, Godwin served as a clerk for the committee on the platform at the Republican Party's first national convention in Philadelphia. Although the exact nature of Godwin's contribution to the platform remains unclear, at least one later chronicler noted that it bore a significant resemblance to the principles laid out in the *Essays*. George Haven Putnam, the publisher of *Putnam's Magazine*, would later assign to this former Fourierist much of the credit for this early formulation of Republican Party principles.[2]

Out in Wisconsin, radicals played a similarly decisive role in the birth of the new party. Sometime in the early 1850s, National Reform Association national secretary Alvan E. Bovay had traveled West to join the Wisconsin phalanx at Ceresco, headed by Warren B. Chase. After the phalanx disbanded, the town was renamed Ripon, and in February 1854, Bovay found himself chairing anti–Kansas-Nebraska meetings in the local schoolhouse and Congregational church. At one such meeting in Milwaukee, abolitionist and land reformer Sherman Booth helped secure the passage of a series of resolutions that were then adopted by other anti-Nebraska meetings throughout the state, including one vowing to forgo former party affiliations and organize a new party dedicated to the nonextension of slavery. Bovay's Ripon group approved this resolution at the village schoolhouse on March 20—an event that many historians have cited as marking the founding of the Republican Party. When questioned why he had advocated calling the new party "Republican," Bovay explained in terms that hearkened to the egalitarian promise of the early nation: for Bovay, the name captured "the thing we wish to symbolize—*Respublica*—the common weal."[3]

Observing the strength of the Republicans' appeal to social reformers of nearly all stripes, its enemies, northern and southern, rushed to exploit them. Political cartoons lampooned the followers of Frémont and Lincoln as a motley collection of abolitionists, agrarians, Fourierists, and devotees of spiritualism and "free love," while southern conservatives attempted to brand the new party as "red republicans," alluding to their alleged support for the radical new social ideas emanating from the 1848 revolutions.[4] The reality, of course, was far different; the new party's base consisted primarily of small farmers, small and middling businessmen, and an emerging class of

THE REPUBLICAN PARTY GOING TO THE RIGHT HOUSE.

Figure 14. This political cartoon highlights the radical origins of the early Republican Party, depicting it as a motley conglomeration of radicals, reformers, and cranks. Presidential candidate Abraham Lincoln is being run out on a rail into the lunatic asylum, carried by *New-York Tribune* editor Horace Greeley and accompanied by a train of followers including African Americans, women's rights activists, Fourierists, free lovers, agrarians, and working-class rowdies. Library of Congress.

manufacturing and financial capitalists. Like most successful political parties in American history, the Republicans were a "big tent" party, and its success in winning elections and governing was dependent on its appeal to broad swaths of northern voters, drawing its strength from a coalition of mobilized supporters that included those who belonged to the above groups as well as political abolitionists, social reformers, and certain elements within the labor movement. While it would be going too far to describe the early Republican Party as "radical" in any but the most general sense, then, the early party did contain an undeniably radical element derived not only from its assimilation of various social reform elements, antislavery Democrats, and former Free Soilers, but from its absorption of ideas and ideologies long championed by political abolitionists and labor reformers. As the following pages show, this appeal was based chiefly on an idea that, by the mid-1850s, enjoyed a broad consensus in the North: a commitment to preventing the further extension of slavery and, conversely, to keeping the territories open to settlement by "free labor." But as recent work on the Republicans' brand of antislavery politics has demonstrated, mixed in among these consensus understandings of free labor and the nonextension of slavery was a set of ideologies and strategies that contained a genuinely radical potential for the both the "ultimate extinction" of slavery and the emancipation of free labor.[5] By the 1850s, long-germinating ideas about antislavery constitutionalism, the illegitimacy of slaveholders' claims to property in their enslaved workers, and the incompatibility of slavery with free labor had at last come to full fruition, both in and outside of labor-reform circles.

Working-Class Reformers and the Politics
of Slavery and Antislavery

The rapidly changing nature of the northern economy in the 1850s presented workers with unprecedented opportunities, but also unprecedented challenges. Even in the midst of general prosperity, nonfarm manual workers in the North were hard hit by declining wages and rising rents and food prices after 1847, a "hidden" economic recession between 1853–1855, and then again by the Panic of 1857. Workers responded to the latter with massive demonstrations of the unemployed in New York City, Philadelphia, and Newark, New Jersey, which to some observers recalled the June Days of the 1848 revolution in France. Throughout the country, workers went out on strike, renewed the agitation for hours of labor laws, demanded government-sponsored work programs, and formed new unions organized by trade as well as organizations that cut across craft lines, like the Amalgamated Trades Convention, the American Labor Union, and the various city industrial congresses (not to be confused with the NIC, which sputtered out by the mid-1850s, only to meet for a final "irregular session" on the eve of the Civil War).[6]

Tensions between white and African American workers probably intensified during the first half of the 1850s and remained high throughout the period, especially among dockworkers and other "unskilled" trades. Proslavery Democratic organs like the *New York Herald* attempted to exploit these racial tensions, warning Irish and German workers that, should Lincoln be elected, "the North will be flooded with free Negroes, and the labor of the white man will be depreciated and degraded."[7] Although they did so far less frequently, Republican and prolabor propaganda also occasionally succumbed to various forms of racial demagoguery. An anonymous 1856 pamphlet addressed to workingmen in New Haven, Connecticut, was typical in oscillating between claims about the dignity of free labor and racially charged warnings about what it alleged was the ulterior motive behind the Kansas-Nebraska Act, to bring "NEGROES to drive out free labor in the United States Territories" and force white laborers to "work side by side with *negro slaves*." But the pamphlet also put a strong emphasis on class conflict, urging supporters of the "true democracy" to spurn the efforts of "artful men" who "live mostly in handsome houses and wear fine clothes" but "care little how poor you may be, if they can only get you to vote away your rich lands in the West to the slaveholders whom they serve." The true policy, the New Haven pamphlet affirmed, was that of the Republicans, who "declare and maintain that while *Slavery is sectional*, FREEDOM IS NATIONAL."[8]

An "Address of the Working Men of Pittsburgh," published the same year as the New Haven pamphlet, likewise urged workers to abandon the Democratic Party, but prioritized class solidarity over racial politics. The several hundred Pittsburgh workingmen who signed the address were convinced alike both that "our interests as a class are seriously involved in the present political struggle" and that the rights of free labor were "in great peril." The South lay in the hands of "a practical aristocracy, owning Labor. . . . With them, Labor is servitude, and Freedom is only compatible with mastership." After this aristocracy had finished extending the slave system over the territories and gained control of the government, the Working Men warned, "they will extend it over us." Combining older free soil notions with a heightened awareness of the class interests at stake, the "Address" further warned that slaveholder expansionism threatened to "cover thousands of acres with slave tillage" with the "baneful system" of slavery. Shut out from "Slave Territories, and with the "refuge" of the "broad Western plains" gone, the "free working man" would be abandoned to European-style low wages and dependence on employers, so "that slavery may be profitable!" The Pittsburgh workingmen concluded that slavery was now the "overshadowing issue, dwarfing all minor questions," and its eradication required rejecting the Democratic Party and uniting with "the friends of Freedom of whatever name or party." Even more radical was the platform of the Free Germans (known as the Louisville Platform), drafted by '48er radicals and workingmen under the leadership of Karl Heinzen in the slaveholding border state of Kentucky. Although the Free Germans declined to advocate immediate abolition, they put the "slavery question" at the top of their platform, calling for gradual abolition, the repeal of the fugitive law, and equal rights for free African Americans. First among their proposed "Measures for the Welfare of the People" was "the free cession of the Public Lands to actual settlers," together with demands for laws establishing a minimum wage and maximum hours of labor, aid to immigrants, and the abolition of land speculation and large inheritances.[9]

In the wake of the 1854 Kansas-Nebraska Act, which potentially opened up millions of acres in the western territories to slavery, many were not content to await the U.S. government's recognition of "the freedom of the soil." Ohio's Thomas Sutherland formed the Nebraska Emigration Association with the goal of consolidating local land reform organizations and establishing a free labor community in the territory that was soon to become the subject of so much controversy. And in 1856, J. K. Ingalls's employer, the New York manufacturer and inventor Thaddeus Hyatt, traveled to Kansas with a party of ninety former Free Soilers in order to "furnish them with useful employment" by organizing the free-labor community of Hyattville in Anderson County. It was in "Bleeding Kansas" that Hyatt encountered John Brown; he would later be jailed for refusing to offer testimony about his possible involvement in planning Brown's raid at Harpers Ferry. Although the precise nature of Hyatt's involvement with Brown remains a mystery, as Ingalls later put it, "many a squattor [sic] in Kansas, and many a working man in New York" had cause to remember him. Brown himself, of course, had lived for a time among the African American community of Timbucto (North Elba) on Gerrit Smith's land in the Adirondacks, and his "Provisional Constitution" for the interracial society he envisioned there included a provision for the common ownership of all property that was "the product of the labor of those belonging to this organization and their families."[10]

A number of free Black leaders, too, had moved steadily toward an embrace of land reform principles. By 1856, Frederick Douglass, who had previously expressed skepticism about the movement and criticized its use of white slavery rhetoric, was publishing articles in favor of "the abrogation of land monopoly" in *Frederick Douglass' Paper*, which proclaimed that the earth, like air, fire, and water, should be "free to all." If land were treated as a free commodity and the size of landholdings limited, an article now claimed, the causes of poverty could "at once be removed." Criticizing government land giveaways to "soulless railroad corporations," *Frederick Douglass' Paper* believed that genuine land reform would promote education and temperance, free child workers from a lifetime of toil in factories, and reduce large estates to "moderate dimensions." Best of all, "with land limitation Slavery would be impossible," since "your slaveholder is ever a land monopolist." And on the eve of the Civil War, the New York *Anglo-African Magazine* predicted that "two ideas recently organized into facts—two ideals reduced to practice, will, within the lifetimes of some now born, change the whole face of American society, and break down, forever, the power of gold. We mean land-reform, and the association of social economies and of labor." Just as white land reformers described the advent of their favored reform as the "Jubilee"—the ancient Jewish and Biblical term for the coming of a time when debts would be forgiven, slavery abolished, and landholdings broken up and distributed— free Black abolitionists and intellectuals understood the moment as one with truly revolutionary potential, and looked forward to a time when the world might start anew.[11]

The Kansas-Nebraska Act: Northern Workers Respond

The passage of the Kansas-Nebraska Act, on May 30, 1854, ushered in a new era of antislavery militancy in the North. The brainchild of Illinois Democrat Stephen Douglas, who cherished ambitions to drive a Pacific railroad from his home state of Illinois through the same expanse of territory that land reformers envisioned for free homesteads, the act threatened to open millions of acres of land to slavery by what was called "popular sovereignty"—a vaguely defined, ostensibly democratic approach by which the (white) settlers of a given territory would vote the existence of slavery up or down. Not only Kansas and Nebraska, but all of the remaining Louisiana Purchase territories on either side of the 36°30' line dividing slave territories from free (established by the Missouri Compromise in 1820) were potentially affected by the measure, which threatened to greatly expand the political control of the Slave Power and make slavery a national institution. In response, Ohio congressman Salmon P. Chase, assisted by Charles Sumner, Joshua Giddings, Edward Wade, Alexander De Witt, and Gerrit Smith, fired off the *Appeal of the Independent Democrats*, which revived the old Wilmot Proviso and Free Soil arguments and injected them with fresh outrage at the audacity of the Slave Power. (Always willing to go further than his colleagues, Smith made a passionate speech against the bill in which he elaborated his theory of slavery as an "outlaw" institution.)[12]

Along with antislavery politicians like Chase, Sumner, and Smith, skilled workers and prolabor, antislavery newspapers, like the *New-York Tribune* and the *National Era*, were vocal in their opposition to Kansas-Nebraska. An analysis of anti-Nebraska petitions from a handful of industrializing towns and cities in New York and Massachusetts shows that, as they had in the 1830s, skilled workers made up the largest percentage of antislavery petition signers, while those who owned no appreciable real estate or other property were a solid majority.[13] Signs of northern workers' discontent over the legislation were evident even before the bill became law. On February 17, as the Nebraska bill was being discussed, the *Tribune* published a call, signed by a host of workingmen who appended their trades next to their names, for a "People's Meeting" in opposition at the Broadway Tabernacle, a frequent site of abolitionist gatherings. The notice specifically called on "the mechanics, artisans and laboring masses of this metropolis" to voice their dissatisfaction. The next day, an "immense assembly" of perhaps five thousand workers met in the Tabernacle to protest the proposed legislation's "base breach of compact" and "attempt to degrade free labor." The workingmen loudly applauded a speech by former Free Soil and Liberty Party candidate John P. Hale, who phrased the great question of the day in terms of the threat it posed to the dwindling supply of free soil in the west. If northern workingmen and recent immigrants would only look to their interest in "free farms (enthusiastic cheers)," and "free houses (loud cheers)," Hale explained, they would recognize that the expansion of slavery threatened their ability to claim this rightful "inheritance." The famed abolitionist minister Reverend Henry Ward Beecher informed the working-class audience that "it lies with you" whether the coming political conflict would end in "a victory of Slavery or a victory of Liberty." The assembly responded by resolving that "we the mechanics and workingmen of New York heartily concur in the stern protests against the threatened repeal of the Missouri compromise."[14]

Although urban immigrants in general, and the Irish in particular, remained largely unreceptive to antislavery appeals, German-born workers were at the forefront of the opposition to Kansas-Nebraska. In February, the New York German American *Arbeiterbund* (workers' league) held a mass meeting where resolutions were passed describing the law as the triumph of "capitalism and land speculation . . . at the expense of the mass of the people" and branding its supporters as "traitors[s] against the people." Two days later, an anti-Nebraska meeting organized by the *Arbeiter Verein* (a voluntary association for German-speaking workers) drew a crowd of two thousand to hear speakers at Washington Hall on Elizabeth Street. The German American speakers scarcely hesitated to connect the Nebraska bill's potential to nationalize slavery with the homestead bill, then once again making its way through

Congress. Gottlieb Kellner, a '48er refugee from Kassel who edited the Marx-inflected *Reform*, spoke of "the interests which the laboring classes have in the question now before the meeting," focusing on the Kansas-Nebraska Act's attempt "to exclude free labor from this soil in order to devote it to Slavery." A Mr. Rosenstein insisted that "there has never been a German, who really *was* a German, who desired to be a slaveholder," and prayed that the territories be kept free from "the curse of Slavery." Wilhelm Schlutter blamed the obstructionism of southern congressmen for the current watered-down version of land reform in the homestead bill then before the Congress, and argued that the whole notion of land reform had been undermined by Douglas's Nebraska bill. Likening Douglas to the monarchs and despots of Europe, Schlutter called for "Revolution!" to cheers from the audience, before clarifying the kind of revolution he had in mind: the election of men to Congress "that will dare to tell the slave-breeders to their faces who they are." In a separate meeting on March 1, several thousand German workers endorsed a resolution by Joseph Weydemeyer, a compatriot of Marx and the founder of New York's Kommunist Klub, blaming the bill on "capitalist land speculation" and asserting that German Americans "have, do now, and shall continue to protest most emphatically against both black and white slavery." Even George Dietz, the editor of the Democratic and antiabolitionist *Staats Zeitung*, was forced to disavow his former southern allies, blaming them for bringing on "the storm that now shakes the very foundation of this Union." Nor was New York's German immigrant community atypical; in Cincinnati, German workers dominated the city's first anti-Nebraska meeting in February 1854, and a meeting a month later organized by former '48ers and workingmen added resolutions in favor of the complete eradication of slavery and the distribution of free homesteads "irrespective of color." In Saint Louis, Chicago, and other parts of the North, the West, and even the border South, German workers and radicals rallied around the slogan "*Kansas gehört der Arbeit, nicht der Sklaverei.*"[15]

The fallout over Kansas-Nebraska continued to reverberate long after the bill's passage, with anti-Nebraska meetings organized by and consisting primarily of manual workers in at least ten northern states. A group of cigar makers meeting in a state convention in New York expressed their fear that "if Nebraska became a slave region, the negroes, who live in uncarpeted houses, on plain fare . . . would . . . produce a ruinous competition" with efforts to grow tobacco there using free labor.[16] But although many northern workers may have been motivated primarily by a desire to keep the territories open to "free white labor," the fact that anti-Nebraska petitions were often

coupled with resolutions calling for the repeal of the Fugitive Slave Act and/
or the complete abolition of slavery complicates this assumption. A Fourth of
July petition signed by 870 citizens of the shoemaking center of Lynn, Massachusetts, called for the repeal of both laws, while National Reformer Lewis
Masquerier's memorial on behalf of the "democratic citizens of Greenpoint
and Bushwick," described previously, demanded their "instant repeal" as well
as the "ultimate abolition" of slavery. On the eve of the Civil War, large numbers of signatories in the working-class cities of Fall River and Lynn urged
the Massachusetts legislature to "put an end to SLAVE HUNTING" by refusing to enforce the terms of the fugitive act, while a group of "German Workmen" in Cincinnati decried the use of meetings of ersatz "workingmen" to
demonstrate in favor of compromise with slavery. Separately, Elihu Burritt,
the "learned blacksmith" who had been the National Reform/Liberty League
choice for Vice President, insisted that "we should have no more 'Missouri
Compromises, Fugitive Slave Bills, or Nebraska Bills'," concluding that "no
measure short of the total extinction of slavery can establish a Union on this
Continent worth saving."[17]

The records of the NIC highlight the divisions between workers and labor
reformers over the slavery issue, but also reflect the ongoing presence of committed and determined labor abolitionists as well as a broad consensus over
free soil. At the NIC's 1854 meeting in Trenton, New Jersey, the organization
was finally forced to confront the now unavoidable issue of slavery head-on.
With Yorkshire-born Philadelphia tailor John Sheddon presiding, the NIC
passed the usual resolutions in favor of freedom of the public lands, alongside those supporting term limits and the direct election of senators—the latter a clear sign of dissatisfaction with the political ruling class in the wake of
the Senate's approval of Kansas-Nebraska and failure to pass homestead legislation.[18] But the most heated debate at the NIC that summer was reserved for
resolutions that responded directly to Kansas-Nebraska. As New Jersey delegate and *Trenton Daily News* editor Franklin S. Mills explained, the delegates
"were all agreed that Kansas and Nebraska ought to be settled by free people."
But a series of strongly worded resolutions introduced by Philadelphian
T. W. Braidwood and a Mr. Henderson of New York created considerable rancor within the body. After a preamble that proclaimed that "the moral sense of
this nation is outraged, and the spirit of freedom . . . lies smothering beneath
the suffocating grasp of Slavery," the resolutions demanded the immediate
repeal of both Kansas-Nebraska and the Fugitive Act and the resignation
of those northern congressmen who had helped to pass them, and insisted

that all future state and national representatives pledge themselves "to resist the aggression of the Southern Slave power." Another resolution framed the fugitive issue in terms of states' rights—specifically, *northern* states' rights, which Braidwood, like many northerners, felt had been violated by the Fugitive Act's imposition of federal power on behalf of slave catchers. Another declared the body's sympathies with both the "oppressed" southern slave and the "fugitive freeman," "whom we swear to protect by the rights of our States and the strength of our arms." A separate resolution, offered by Henderson, proposed the formation of "Emigrant Associations" to resettle "fellow industrials" and newly arrived immigrants from Ireland and Germany in Kansas and Nebraska, "as a preventative to the extension of the piratical system of Slavery in those vast regions."[19]

Reaction to the resolutions was swift, but far from unanimous. N. W. Brown of Massachusetts was opposed to "any action upon such inflammatory resolutions," while delegate Franklin Mills considered it "injudicious" for the NIC to "mix itself up in the political broils of the country." Delaware's Saxe Gotha Laws similarly felt that if the resolutions were passed as worded, "this Congress would be resolving itself into an Abolition Society, under a false name" (Laws ultimately resigned from the congress in protest). But New York's David Marsh, citing the recent anti-Nebraska demonstration of German workingmen as proof that the tide of northern sentiment had turned against slavery, thought that the congress should be free to "give expression" to its antislavery impulses, "feeling as they all should, that wherever Slavery was allowed free labor was degraded." A Pennsylvania delegate likewise overcame his initial reservations and "now believed that the Congress would do best by openly avowing its principles on the Slave question," since "they could gain nothing by temporizing with an institution that was inimical to all the rights of free labor." George F. Gordon of Philadelphia had what proved to be the last word. Any attempt to "engraft upon this Congress the doctrines of the Abolitionists" would be voted down, he believed; still, it seemed to him that "the constitution of their body did not forbid the discussion of questions in favor of universal freedom." "As Land Reformers," Gordon continued, the members of the Industrial Congress "had more to do with Slavery than they might at first think." The passage of Kansas-Nebraska represented a direct threat to their interests, since "any State given over to the Slave power was rendered unfit for free labor."[20]

In the end, only the resolutions demanding Kansas-Nebraska's repeal and censuring lawmakers for undoing the Missouri Compromise were passed.

The latter was stripped of some of its more inflammatory language, and other, more conservative resolutions framed the slavery issue in terms of states' rights and blamed immigrant voters for "sustaining Southern tyranny." But Henderson's resolution in favor of forming associations to assist workingmen in emigrating to the West passed with additional language about rescuing Kansas and Nebraska from "the machinations of the Slave power," making clear that the congress "consider[ed] the system of involuntary servitude inimical to the interests of the laboring man." A majority report by the business committee resolved to send the NIC's compliments to antislavery Republicans William Seward, Salmon Chase, Charles Sumner, Benjamin Wade, and Gerrit Smith, prevailing over a minority report that favored recognizing only Democrat Andrew Johnson. A public meeting subsequently vindicated the congress's course, eliciting approval from the people of Trenton. And the body chose to inscribe its banner with a slogan similar to that of the Free Soilers in 1848 and the Republican party organizations then just beginning to take shape, which read, in part, "Free Homes, Land Limitations, Free Schools, Free Speech, [and] a Free Soil for Free Men."[21]

The radical tenor of Braidwood's resolutions suggest that the Industrial Congress might have taken an even more unequivocally antislavery stance, had circumstances been more favorable. Several factors likely prevented the Trenton congress from doing so. First, and most obviously, the leadership, and even the rank-and-file membership, of the NIC in 1854 was almost entirely different from that of even a few years earlier. As a reporter for the *New York Times* noted, "a few only of the old officers were about"; indeed, with the possible exception of Sheddon, old-guard labor leaders whose roots lay in the workingmen's movements of the 1820s and '30s, like Evans and John Commerford, were entirely absent. Likewise missing were former Fourierists and social reformers, like L. W. Ryckman and Lewis Masquerier, and abolitionists who had attended previous congresses, like William H. Channing, Alvan Bovay, and Charles Durkee. Although several delegates represented organizations, like the secretive Brotherhood of the Union, that supported land reform, only one represented the National Reform Association per se. Also significant is the fact that the sponsor of the most stringent antislavery resolutions, T. W. Braidwood, was known as a confirmed nativist. Whatever their prosouthern or antiabolitionist prejudices, Braidwood's antagonists may have feared further alienating their immigrant constituencies, already chary of abolitionism.[22] Finally, the Congress's location in New Jersey, the last northern state to abolish slavery, meant that delegates from the state's strongly Democratic central and southern counties, as well as from slave-holding Delaware next door, wielded an outsize influence over the proceedings. Whatever the case, by the time of the Trenton congress, the NIC had begun to go into decline, never again attaining the numbers of attendees or national coverage it had briefly enjoyed in the late 1840s and early '50s. Although the congresses would straggle on until 1860—and would later be revived, in altered form, after the war—by 1856 the NIC was a shadow of its former self. Held in New York that year, it attracted only eleven attendees.[23]

The history of the NIC thus highlights several of the factors that make it difficult to trace a linear progression toward an antislavery consensus within the early labor movement. The disruptions created by economic upheaval and the arrival of millions of immigrants, along with the looming specter of disunion, the persistence of wage slavery rhetoric, and the fluctuating fortunes and fragmented nature of the labor movement itself, all greatly complicate any effort to find working-class reformers speaking with a single voice on slavery, even in the years immediately preceding the Civil War. What is clear, however, is that the furor over the Kansas-Nebraska Act served as a watershed moment for many workers and working-class reformers—who, like other northerners alarmed by the aggression of the Slave Power and dismayed by the spinelessness of northern politicians, saw in the prospect of slavery's further expansion a direct threat to their own interests. Labor activists who had formerly denounced slavery mainly in the abstract now confronted a clear and unambiguous challenge to their declared principles, as well as an existential threat to one of their most cherished reforms—the availability of free homesteads on the public lands. The threat to the long-held goal of land reform, effected by southern proslavery expansionists and their northern allies, made slavery's expansion an inherently political proposition. It was inevitable, therefore, that working-class reformers would once again turn to political solutions.

The Republican Appeal to Labor:
Homesteads and Tariff Reform

Before antislavery could become what William H. Seward termed "a respectable element" in politics, then, it had to be linked to the self-interest of the majority of ordinary northern voters. But, more often than not, these interests were inextricably bound up with the future of slavery in the nation. The fortunes of the second major attempt to pass a homestead bill in 1854, for example, were closely tied to the debates over Kansas-Nebraska. Homestead measures had previously been supported by a number of southerners, including Georgia's Felix McDonnell, Texas's Sam Houston, and Tennessee's Andrew Johnson. But by 1854, southern congressmen had become implacably opposed to the bill, for one overwhelming reason: they feared that farmers and immigrants from the North would overwhelmingly be the ones to take advantage of the bill's provision for the creation of small, 160-acre farms, precluding any possibility for slave owners and plantations to gain a foothold in areas still potentially open to slavery by popular sovereignty.[24] Andrew Johnson, who came from humble origins and despised the slaveholder class, was one important exception, yet Johnson's proposed homestead legislation failed to place limits on the size of landholdings or make them inalienable from seizure for debt, for, as the Tennessee congressman was quick to clarify, he was "no agrarian, no leveller." Just as importantly, these early bills mandated both the retrocession of the public lands and the control over parceling out grants to the individual states, rather than to "the people" or "the nation"—a distinction with important implications for parallel arguments over the fate of slavery in the territories and the constitutional and legal nature of slavery as either a "national" or "local" institution.[25] Other southerners, in an echo of the Nullification Debates of 1832, pointed to what they claimed was the disproportionate burden on the South of the costs of giving away free land. The southern slave economy's underdeveloped manufacturing sector and dependence on imports meant that it paid more than its share of the revenue that would have funded the land giveaway, while a homestead act would drain southern population by luring away landless and non–slave-owning farmers to the West. Even the minority of southern congressmen who continued to support homestead measures, like Robert Johnson of Arkansas, refused to vote for the bill until after the Kansas-Nebraska Act had been passed, after which they assumed that Kansas-Nebraska's sanction to slavery north of the 36°30' line provided a sufficient counterweight to the threat posed by free farms.[26]

The fate of the 1854 homestead bill thus reflects the increasing sectionalization and the subordination of all other political issues to slavery that characterized the decade before the Civil War, as well as the racism, nativism, and antiradicalism that transcended sectional and party lines. In echoes of the hysteria that accompanied Skidmore's *The Rights of Man to Property!* and the rise of the Workies in the late 1820s, opponents of homestead reform made arguments based on what they viewed as the "agrarianism" behind the bill's "radical, revolutionary" proposal to give away the public domain to immigrants and "ragamuffins." But in the end, it was race that helped sink the 1854 bill, after a northern Democrat, Pennsylvania representative Hendrick Wright, added a last-minute amendment restricting the bill's benefits to whites only. Outraged, Gerrit Smith, then serving his term as a representative from New York, angrily turned against the bill. But Smith's principled stance—along with his equally idealistic, but perhaps unwise, decision to allow a procedural vote on Kansas-Nebraska—ultimately led to the end of his career in Congress. After a nasty dispute with Horace Greeley, in which the *Tribune* editor and homestead bill supporter falsely claimed that Smith had voted in favor of the Kansas-Nebraska bill, Smith was forced to issue a series of rebuttals as well as a letter to his constituents explaining his course of action. Frederick Douglass leapt to Smith's defense, arguing that "a true land reformer from principle . . . is, whether he knows it or not, an abolitionist at heart." But the damage had been done, and Smith resigned from Congress, thereafter abandoning any hope that a political solution could bring about a "bloodless termination of American slavery."[27]

In any event, the 1854 homestead bill passed the House, only to be stymied in the Senate. In response, Horace Greeley and other land reform supporters stepped up efforts to blame southern intransigence for the impasse, while prodding the newly formed Republican Party to incorporate support for Homestead into its platform. Greeley's earlier efforts to pass a homestead bill during his brief tenure in Congress had come to naught, but he had continued to serve as an effective and tenacious advocate of land reform measures in the pages of the *Tribune*. In 1855, Greeley sat on the platform committee of the Republican state convention in Syracuse, New York, where he penned a resolution that demanded free land for actual settlers. Although the Syracuse resolution was defeated, and although Homestead was absent from the Republican national platform in 1856, the new party's national convention in Philadelphia that year cemented opposition to the further extension of slavery and upheld the constitutional authority of Congress over the territories. It also nominated John C. Frémont, a figure popularly associated with free soil and the West, for president.[28]

Four years later, in Chicago, Greeley and other pro-Homestead Republicans had more success. Although Greeley's precise role in writing the 1860 platform remains unclear, he claimed shortly thereafter that the Homestead plank it contained was "fixed exactly to my own liking."[29] Without outlining

FREEDOM AND SLAVERY, AND THE COVETED TERRITORIES.

Figure 15. The frontispiece to an 1856 Republican campaign biography of John C. Frémont juxtaposed a portrait of the candidate with this abolitionist image contrasting free states in light and slave states in darkness, with the "coveted territories" hanging in the balance. Division of Rare and Manuscript Collections, Cornell University Library.

a specific proposal, Article 12 made it clear that the party stood "against any sale or alienation to others of the Public Lands held by actual settlers" and demanded the passage of the latest version of the homestead bill, then pending in the Senate. Although the 1860 platform failed to enshrine access to the soil as a natural right, it echoed the land reformers' dissatisfaction with more moderate homestead proposals by placing itself in opposition to "any view of the Homestead policy which regards the settlers as paupers or suppliants for public bounty."[30]

A homestead bill again made it through the House in 1859, only to be killed in the Senate. Again, Greeley and other Republicans blamed the failure of Homestead squarely on the Slave Power. The bill, which the *Tribune* had described as "a moderate and cautious one" (it provided for the sale of quarter sections of public land at $1.25 and acre, without limitation or alienability), had passed by an overwhelming margin in the House, only to be defeated by southern senators who outvoted a measure to consider it. As the *Tribune* observed, only two southerners and only nine Democrats had voted to take up the bill in the Senate; twenty-three of the twenty-nine votes against consideration had come from southern senators. Although the *Tribune* remained confident that the passage of the Homestead Act was only a matter of time, it suggested that "if there be any one not yet convinced that Gov. Seward was correct in affirming an 'irrepressible conflict' in this country between the Free Labor and Slave Labor systems . . . we beg him to study closely the history of the struggle for Land Reform."[31] The following year, yet another homestead bill finally made it past both houses, only to be vetoed by President James Buchanan, a prosouthern "doughface" Democrat. A similar fate awaited the Morrill Act, which proposed setting aside a portion of the public lands within each state for the establishment of colleges to provide the sons of farmers and workers with education in "such branches of learning as are related to agriculture and the mechanic arts." Greeley claimed that both vetoes were the work of "Mr. Buchanan's Southern masters" and contrasted the president's lack of "sympathy with the poor" with the Republican presidential candidate whose humble origins had already become the stuff of Republican mythmaking. "Does anybody suppose," the *Tribune* rhetorically asked, "that Abraham Lincoln would ever veto such a bill?"[32] Other Republican orators, like New Hampshire's James A. Briggs, attacked Democrats, "who affect to be above all aristocratic notions, [and] sneer at Lincoln, because he was a rail splitter," and suggesting that "Uncle Sam was rich enough to give us all a farm but if he filled up his territories with servile hosts he crowds out freemen."[33]

In response to Buchanan's veto, Greeley had antislavery Republican Galusha Grow's House speech on Homestead from that February printed up in pamphlet form; the pamphlet's introduction framed Grow's oration as an example of "the Republican policy of granting the Public Lands in limited tracts to actual settlers." Just as Gerrit Smith and William Goodell had urged the Liberty Party to adopt land reform in 1847–1848, Greeley now relentlessly pushed the Republicans to publicize their progressive position on land reform. The *Tribune* informed readers that "the best single step" that friends of the party could take to persuade northern farmers and laborers to vote Republican "is, in our judgment, the circulation of documents which show just where the two great parties stand on the vital question of LAND REFORM"; the *Tribune* recommended the publication of "One Million copies" of an expanded tract on the subject, and Republican campaign organs like the *Rail Splitter* published column after column emphasizing the Republicans' commitment to a homestead bill. "There is not a shoemaker's shop in America, much less a machine-shop or foundry," the *Tribune* claimed, "in which that tract alone will not make votes for the Republican ticket, provided there be any voters there who are not already Republicans. . . . We can carry the Election on Land Reform alone, if we shall only have made nearly every voter see and realize just what Land Reform is, and how the two great parties respectively stand upon it." But it was not merely electoral victory that Republican backers sought by promoting homestead reform. As E. Smalley, who identified himself as "one of the originators of the 'Land Reform Party'" in Chicago, wrote in the *Rail Splitter*, land reformers were "fully satisfied that the passage of a liberal Homestead Law would settle the question of slavery in the territories."[34]

Greeley was also instrumental in effecting the transformation of another long-cherished measure into something the new party hoped would prove palatable to both urban workers and northern farmers in the hinterlands. He had been prescient in his perception that the Whigs needed to modernize their economic program in order to accommodate the changing economic realities of the day, which included the growth of wage and factory labor, the influx of massive numbers of immigrants, and a shift in the orientation of the northern economy away from the Cotton South and toward a growing interdependence with producers and markets in the West. Such perceptions had long fueled his support for land reform, a departure from Whig orthodoxy for which he had nearly been read out of the party, but also undergirded his support for a longstanding pillar of the Whig's political economy: protective tariffs. Both Greeley's faith in the "harmony of interests" between labor and capital and his longstanding belief that government had an active role to play in promoting employment undergirded his push for higher tariffs. For Americans like Greeley, the new social thought emanating from the 1848 revolutions in Europe had reinforced such convictions. (Meanwhile, more radical elements, like the German Marxists led by Joseph Weydemeyer, also turned toward support for tariffs as a means of completing the ascendancy of northern capitalism, which, along with the abolition of slavery, they believed was a necessary precondition for bringing about a worker's revolution.)[35] Building on the work of Whig political economist Henry Carey, Greeley defended the tariff's violation of *laissez-faire* economic theory, just as he had with issues like ten-hours laws, land reform, and other measures, by emphasizing its benefits to workers. Although northern farmers were arguably the most important constituency to be won over to pro-tariff arguments, Greeley and other Republicans also hammered on the tariff's potential benefits to urban wage earners, viewing them, along with homestead reform, as part of grand bargain that would combine the interests of manufacturers, wage workers, and farmers alike in a mutually beneficial exchange between western settlers and eastern producers.[36]

Largely as a result of such efforts by Greeley and others, the Republicans' 1860 platform emphasized the tariff's mutual advantages to both employers and producers and recommended a foreign trade policy "which secures to the working men liberal wages, to agriculture remunerating prices, to mechanics and manufacturers an adequate reward for their skill, labor, and enterprise." In its broadsides and campaign material, the party gave its policy of "Protection to American Industry" a prominent place alongside support for Homestead and the nonextension of slavery. One 1860 appeal to "Working Men" summed up this approach: "the Republicans," it announced, "hold that the natural condition of all the Territories is freedom, and that they should be kept free; that the landless should have free homes in the Territories and that American industry should be protected." These ideas, long connected in the minds of many workers and labor reformers, were united as never before in a powerful appeal to the self-interest of the laboring masses of the North.[37]

"White Slavery" Versus Free Labor, Redux

Perhaps unsurprisingly, given the salience of white racism and the ways that racial tensions were exploited in the context of economic and political upheaval, the language of white slavery not only refused to disappear from the national discourse about labor in the 1850s, but may have even intensified. Unlike in an earlier period, however, in the decade before the Civil War the most conspicuous adopters of white slavery comparisons were not labor leaders or land reformers, but southern slaveholders. In a reprise of statements made in the 1830s by George McDuffie and John Calhoun, southern politicians and intellectuals revived and sometimes doubled down on their comparisons between northern wage workers and slaves. Among the most notorious was that of South Carolina senator (previously governor and congressman) James Henry Hammond, who, in the same March 8, 1858, speech that helped to popularize the phrase "King Cotton," described "the manual, hired laborers of the North, the operatives" as "the mudsills of society," no better off than slaves. In his *Sociology for the South* (1854), Virginian George Fitzhugh described slavery as "the natural and normal condition of the laboring man" and argued that the North's "servile" class of mechanics and laborers were unfit for self-government. Echoing the arguments made by West India slaveholders seventy-five years earlier—and by the labor reformers who were their unwitting abettors—Fitzhugh, Hammond, and other slaveholding politicians, like Louisiana's Solomon W. Downs and Alabama's Jeremiah Clemens, argued that the North's "hireling" laborers were more poorly treated and worse off than southerners' enslaved workers. This proved that the idea of free society was a "delusion," Fitzhugh claimed—a point echoed by a quote attributed to an Alabama newspaper, which described the working population of the North as "*a conglomeration of* GREASY MECHANICS, FILTHY OPERATIVES, SMALL FISTED FARMERS, and moon-struck THEORISTS," unfit to serve as "A SOUTHERN GENTLEMAN'S BODY SERVANT."[38]

Fitzhugh specifically repudiated the notion of a natural right to land and denounced the homestead bill, which he equated with an attack on property rights. In his view, the "agrarian" disregard for property rights was the ideology that bound together a host of disparate antislavery figures, from Garrison and Gerrit Smith to William H. Seward. Although Fitzhugh was an outlier in his extremism, he was not alone; southern politicians and proslavery ideologues frequently cited land reform as a particularly insidious expression of the "agrarianism" that they believed lurked behind a sinister conspiracy among abolitionists and labor agitators. Speakers at the Virginia secession convention in 1861 identified "exemption and homestead laws, and the cry of land for the landless" as among the radical measures that menaced northern society, and one correspondent of Andrew Johnson's from Alabama condemned homestead reform as a plan to "abolitionize" the West by encouraging the non–slave-owning followers of southern antislavery author Hinton Helper to migrate there.[39]

Republicans who represented large constituencies of urban mechanics and small farmers, including Henry Wilson, William H. Kelley, and, most famously, Abraham Lincoln, jumped at the chance to exploit the high-handed offensiveness of the so-called mudsill theory while promoting their own optimistic vision of free labor society. Wilson, a former Massachusetts shoemaker known as the "Natick cobbler," drew on his own experience to emphasize the "equality" and dignity that Republicans believed resided in free labor relationships. Wilson described slavery as "the one enemy of the free laboring men of America" and posited the brewing conflict between free labor and slavery as one between "the interests and claims of a few" and the rights of "millions of toiling men who eat their bread in the sweat of their faces." Just as pointedly, Wilson summoned reams of statistics to refute Hammond's claim that the northern economy was dependent on southern cotton, a belief that led Hammond to arrogantly suggest that southern plantation owners might one day "discharge" their northern "employees" at will. In reality, Wilson argued, northern "mudsills," together with enslaved workers like those who toiled on Hammond's cotton plantations, were the true producers of the nation's wealth. In an imagined dialogue that revealed Wilson's alignment with the producerist values of the labor movement while also serving as a pointed inversion of slavery's racial hierarchy, Wilson imagined one of Hammond's enslaved workers telling him, "Massa, you only sells de cotton. . . . 'Spose we discharge *you*."[40]

Another figure who redirected white slavery rhetoric back at the slaveholders was William Goodell. Having pioneered the antislavery interpretation of the Constitution that now provided the foundation of the Republicans' approach to the slavery issue, the former Liberty Party organizer spent much of the 1850s compiling learned tracts on the history and political economy of slavery. In 1856, he warned workingmen that "the efforts of one class to secure *their own* liberties shall avail them nothing, without an equal effort to ensure the liberties of their equal brethren." Then, on the eve of the Civil War, he launched a new periodical, the *Principia*, which contained a detailed, fifteen-part series dedicated to explaining the foundations of slaveholders' power. Building on his earlier arguments about the "aristocracy" of northern capitalists and southern slaveholders, Goodell now emphasized the latter, who he believed constituted an "American Oligarchy." But the economic might on which the Slave Power was predicated, Goodell argued, was largely illusory. Utilizing statistics from Hinton Helper's *The Impending Crisis of the*

South and other sources, he argued that the South was an economic paper
tiger, one that was rapidly losing ground to the economic dynamism of the
North. More controversially, he undertook a refinement of his earlier "chattelization" thesis, warning that if slavery continued to grow unchecked, along
with enslaved populations of mixed African and slaveholder blood, a white
skin would no longer serve as a guarantee against enslavement. Although the
racial implications of such an argument were uncomfortable, and although
Goodell was apparently unique in making them so explicitly, in other ways
his racial rhetoric was not far outside the abolitionist mainstream. Throughout the period, abolitionists made use of the trope of the fair-skinned "white
slave" (usually female or a child) as a means of making the realities of slavery
more relatable to white northerners.[41]

Others picked up on "white slavery" arguments to appeal to working-
class audiences even more directly. Framing "the Issue" before voters in 1856
as "WHITE SLAVERY!," the Frémont and Dayton Tenth Ward Club of Philadelphia warned that slavery's extension threatened not only "FREE SOIL,"
but "FREE MEN." Noting that some proslavery organs had shifted from
"apologies" for the perpetuation of racial slavery to a defense of the institution in principle, the campaign's propaganda echoed Goodell, alerting
readers in all caps that slavery was not dependent "UPON DIFFERENCE OF
COMPLEXION" and that southern state laws could "JUSTIFY THE HOLD-
ING OF WHITE MEN IN BONDAGE." Quoting the same sources from
southern politicians and newspapers, another Republican broadside that election year described "the new 'Democratic doctrine'. . . now openly avowed and
defended" by Buchanan supporters, that slavery was "no longer to be confined to the negro race, but to be made the universal condition of the laboring
classes of society."[42]

Despite their problematic racial overtones and propagandistic sensation-
alism, such arguments were apparently deemed both legitimate and effective by a wide range of antislavery figures, as evidenced by their adoption by
abolitionists like William Lloyd Garrison and Charles Sumner. During the
war, in the aftermath of Gettysburg and the draft riots in 1863, the antislavery
poet and reformer William Oland Bourne, who signed a series of broadsides
as "a Democratic Workingman," revisited Hammond's 1858 Senate speech to
prove to presumably working-class readers in New York that the "rebellion"
of southern "traitors" was part of an effort "to build up forever a system by
which '*Capital shall own Labor*,'" and predicted that its success would prove
"a death-blow to the interests of Free Workingmen, North and South." And

Henry Clarke Wright, a former hatmaker turned radical abolitionist, published a compendium of slaveholders' most egregious "mudsill" arguments in the *Liberator*, depicting the conflict between Union and Confederacy then underway as a "Rebellion of Capital against Labor, to Enslave the Laborer."[43]

However clever—or crude—and whatever their effectiveness in swaying working-class voters, the Republican reversal of southerners' proslavery white slavery rhetoric constituted only a small part of their appeal to northern wage earners, mechanics, and small farmers. The Frémont and Dayton Club, for example, published numerous pamphlets emphasizing the antidemocratic nature of the Slave Power's political machinations, which prioritized the demands of "350,000 slaveholders and their capital" over "the interests of TEN MILLIONS OF FREE LABORING MEN." Other Republicans, along with abolitionists of both the political and nonvoting varieties, emphasized slaveholders' attacks on free speech and freedom of the press, pointed to the abuses of accused fugitives as a denial of the fundamental rights of habeas corpus and trial by jury, and argued that the presence of slavery lowered workingmen's wages. But perhaps the most frequently made argument had to do with a set of ideas, assumptions, and understandings that had been articulated and challenged by workers and labor reformers for decades—and that now gained new traction, albeit in altered form, under the Republican rubric of "free labor."[44]

The Republican Reconstruction of Free Labor

On September 30, 1859, less than a year after his defeat by Stephen Douglas for Illinois's Senate seat and still more than a year away from his election as president, Abraham Lincoln gave a speech to attendees at an agricultural fair in Milwaukee, recently the site of one of the nation's most heated battles over the issue of land reform. Lincoln's address before the Wisconsin State Agricultural Society offers one of the clearest distillations of Republican free labor ideology. But it also highlights the ways in which Republican understandings of free labor both aligned with and diverged from more radical understandings of the term as articulated by labor reformers and radicals over the previous several decades. Although the contrast Lincoln drew between free labor and slavery aligned with labor reformers' producerist ideology and longstanding dislike of slavery, Lincoln's speech was a repudiation of "wage slavery" arguments. Notably, however, Lincoln's critique was aimed not at labor radicals, but at those who promoted what Lincoln derided as "the mud-sill theory"—the idea, recently expressed by Hammond, Fitzhugh, and others, that those who worked for someone else composed a permanent underclass in northern society. According to Lincoln, the flaw in the mudsill theory lay in its assumption that the hired wage laborer was "fatally fixed in that condition for life." Far more typical of the northern free labor economy was the scenario Lincoln spelled out for his listeners, in which "the prudent, penniless beginner in the world, labors for wages awhile, saves a surplus with which to buy tools or land, for himself; then labors on his own account another while, and at length hires another new beginner to help him. This, say its advocates, is free labor—the just and generous, and prosperous system, which opens the way for all—gives hope to all, and energy, and progress, and improvement of condition to all."[45]

This optimistic expression of the American faith in the promise of social mobility no doubt resonated with many workers, including those among the small farmers, businessmen, and agricultural improvers who likely made up Lincoln's audience, many of whom, as he observed, had "doubtless" once been hired laborers themselves. But it likely would have failed to convince those, like the immigrant hod carriers and canal diggers, New England textile mill workers, or pieceworkers in New York's clothing sweatshops, for whom the promise of upward mobility rang hollow. Nor would it have satisfied the radical land reformers or '48er refugees who were a conspicuous presence in Milwaukee, where Lincoln delivered his address. In his address, Lincoln seemed to conceive of free labor in an anachronistic, almost Jeffersonian sense, based on an ideal of the free yeoman farmer that was already rapidly receding into the past, thanks to innovations in agriculture that made it possible to cultivate many more acres of farmland while making farmers increasingly dependent on far-flung networks of credit and transportation. Furthermore, Lincoln's claim that "a large majority" of northerners "neither work for others, nor have others working for them" was already probably incorrect in 1859; economic historians have concluded that by the Civil War, perhaps 40 to 60 percent of all Americans worked for wages, a percentage that was no doubt higher outside the slave South.[46] More egregiously from the standpoint of labor reformers, Lincoln reiterated common myths, rooted in Anglo-American Protestant morality, that drew a distinction between the "deserving" and "undeserving" poor, suggesting that "if any continue through life in the condition of the hired laborer," it was their own fault, rather than the fault of "the system." As would become apparent during Reconstruction and after, the limitations of this liberal-individualist understanding of free labor, which presumed that self-ownership and formal legal equality made employers and employees equals in the marketplace, ignored the asymmetries of power created by large concentrations of capital as well as the persistence of various forms of class and racial privilege.[47]

Nevertheless, Lincoln and the Republicans' conception of free labor was calculated to appeal to a broad swath of Americans, including those who worked with their hands. Republicans made the appeal to ordinary workers a central part of their electoral strategy, and frequently emphasized the modest occupational backgrounds of their candidates and their experience as manual laborers. The most famous exemplar of this was, of course, Lincoln himself, whose humble origins as a common laborer on the Illinois frontier were emphasized throughout the 1860 campaign, notably by his most common early nickname, "the Rail Splitter" (not coincidentally the name of a short-lived Republican newspaper that emphasized Homestead and other issues appealing to laboring men). Lincoln's running mate in 1860, Maine's Hannibal Hamlin, had worked as a farm laborer, while another influential Republican, former shoemaker Henry Wilson of Massachusetts, had once been an indentured servant.[48]

More substantively, Republicans emphasized aspects of free labor thought that enjoyed broad consensus in the North (including among labor reformers and wage workers), while articulating them in new and sometimes radical ways. In describing labor as "the source of all our wealth, of all our progress, of all of our dignity and value," New York Republican William Evarts was reiterating the producerist labor theory of value, championed by labor leaders like William Heighton and George Henry Evans since at least the 1820s. Others, like Maine representative Israel Washburn, updated the Loco Foco attack on special privilege and built on the foundations created by radical Democrats like Thomas Morris and William Leggett in the 1830s, rhetorically connecting the Money Power to the Slave Power—an approach pioneered by the abolitionist senator Charles Sumner. Leading Republicans, from former Democrat William D. Kelley to former Whig William H. Seward, emphasized the class dimensions of the conflict with slavery, with Seward as "between the few privileged and the many underprivileged—the eternal question between aristocracy and democracy." Another Maine Republican, George M. Weston, revisited Adam Smith's familiar arguments about slavery's intrinsic inefficiency, but added a new twist, claiming that "southern slavery reduces northern wages." Far from being doomed to die a natural death as a result of its inferiority to free labor, Weston explained, slavery's unchecked expansion had breathed new life into the institution, and southern experiments with the use of slave labor in manufacturing provided mounting evidence that slave owners and free laborers were now "direct competitors with each other." Slavery's "system of reducing the laborer to a bare subsistence" would force down the wages paid to free laborers, and slave owners would "hereafter regulate the wages of the workingmen of the North and West," if not reduce them to actual slavery. Similarly, former National Reform vice presidential nominee Elihu Burritt explained to a working-class audience that the persistence of slavery not only "degraded" free labor, but allowed northern capitalists to conceive of slavery as "the base point" that "somehow . . . must determine the compensation and honor for free labor." "We earnestly hope that the working men of every free country will awake to the importance of this subject; that they will see the bearing of slavery upon their own condition," Burritt wrote in the Philadelphia *Citizen of the World*, "then they will perceive the length and breadth of the meaning of FREE LABOR." Seemingly persuaded by such arguments, workingmen marched in torchlight processions in 1856 carrying banners proclaiming "Free Soil, Free Labor, Frémont" and "We Won't Work for 10 Cents a Day."[49]

Echoing the language of labor reformers, Republicans frequently expressed the belief that all capital was "the fruit of labor," an idea Lincoln reiterated in his Wisconsin address, adding that therefore labor was "the superior . . . greatly the superior to capital." These statements and others have led some observers to depict Lincoln as an incipient radical, while his cautious support for striking workers before and during his presidency led to his adoption by the trade union movement of the late nineteenth and early twentieth centuries as a champion of labor. In reality, the extent of Lincoln's support for the labor movement is less clear. During an 1860 speaking tour of New England, he gave his tacit approval to the actions of striking shoemakers in New Haven, seemingly endorsing their right to strike. Disclaiming any direct knowledge of the circumstances surrounding the strike, Lincoln proclaimed that "I am glad to see that a system of labor prevails in New England under which laborers CAN strike when they want to," and that he wished to see such a system "prevail everywhere." A moment later, however, Lincoln seemed to conflate the right to strike with the more basic right to quit, and he framed both in essentially laissez-faire terms, describing as the ideal society that in which each individual engaged in "the race of life" was "free to acquire property as fast as he can."[50] But in the context of the period, perhaps the more significant aspect of Lincoln's insistence on the right to the "fruits of one's labor" was that he extended it to include African Americans. In the same address on the shoemaker's strike in New Haven quoted above, Lincoln explained that "I want every man to have the chance—and I believe a black man is entitled to it—in which he *can* better his condition—when he may look forward and hope to be a hired laborer this year and the next, work for himself afterward, and finally to hire men to work for him!"[51] Earlier, at a speech in Hartford, he had confronted the issue of competition between white wage earners and emancipated slaves directly, describing "the proposition that there is a struggle between the white man and the negro" as a "falsehood." And during his speech on the infamous Dred Scott decision in 1857 and again during the course of his famous series of debates with Stephen Douglas the following year, Lincoln repeatedly insisted that "in the right to eat the bread . . . which his own hand earns," African Americans were "my equal and the equal of Judge Douglas, and of every living man."[52]

At this point, Lincoln expressed less certainty about whether Blacks were entitled to voting rights, or to what he called "social" equality. But if Lincoln's economic egalitarianism seems radical only in hindsight—or in contrast to the unabashed white supremacism and race-baiting of his opponent—there is evidence to suggest that the Republican iteration of free labor held a good deal of appeal for free Black workers as well as whites. In his *Narrative*, Frederick Douglass glowingly recalled his first experience of being able to keep the "fruits of his labor" he earned as a ship caulker in New Bedford, despite encountering discrimination from racist workers there, while Henry Highland Garnet cited self-ownership, security of household and family, and freedom of movement as the factors that distinguished free wage workers from "chattels personal." Peter Wheeler, a former slave who had worked for wages as a sailor, drew the line somewhat differently; slavery, he explained, entailed not only the theft of body and soul, but "a kind of theft which is worse than all the others . . . to steal the wages of the poor, three hundred and sixty-five days in the year!" If a rich man were to steal the wages of a "poor day laborer," Wheeler pointed out, he would surely be an object of opprobrium, "and yet every slaveholder as absolutely steals the slave's wages every night—for he goes to his dwelling and family, if he have one, pennyless after a day of hard toil." For free Black workers like Wheeler, the Republican reconstruction of free labor held more than merely rhetorical value, despite the absence of some of the more economically egalitarian aspects that had long constituted labor reformers' understanding of the term.[53]

Despite its overwhelmingly capitalist and middle-class orientation, then, the Republican Party in the late 1850s and early 1860s could reasonably lay claim to be the "People's Party" (as it was referred to in Pennsylvania) or the "Workingman's ticket" (as it appeared on ballots in other areas). Lincoln's refusal to court the Know-Nothing element and his rejection of the Nativist "Massachusetts Amendment" also helped win him the votes of German Americans, like those of the working-class Turner Bund, whose newspaper endorsed Lincoln, and the German workers who endorsed the Republicans in mass meetings in New York and Chicago.[54] Not for nothing, then, did the workingmen who attended the Lincoln-Douglas debates in Galesburg, Illinois, in 1858 carry banners that read, in a direct rebuke to the slavocracy, "SMALL-FISTED FARMERS, MUDSILLS OF SOCIETY, GREASY MECHANICS, FOR A. LINCOLN."[55]

Conclusion: Workingmen, Reformers, and the Coming of the Civil War

Ultimately, the Republicans' combination of free soil antislavery and homestead reform proved sufficient to win the support of the most prominent land and labor reformers, along with majorities of northern voters. Although the Republicans' winning formula had many antecedents and contributors, the figure arguably most responsible for the homestead policy, George Henry Evans, did not live to see his efforts come to fruition. Caught in a snowstorm while returning to New Jersey, where he had become involved in a land reform campaign with fellow labor veteran William Heighton, Evans took ill and succumbed to a "nervous fever" in February 1856.

Evans's potential future political trajectory therefore remains a matter of speculation. What remained of the National Reform Association, however, had endorsed John C. Frémont for president earlier that year, and Evans's longtime collaborator, the ex–Brook Farmer Lewis Ryckman, ran for state assembly on the Republican ticket. J.K. Ingalls and Lewis Masquerier also became stalwart Republicans, as did Ingalls's employer, the artisan-cum-manufacturer John Keyser, who served as a delegate to the 1856 Republican National Convention.[56] At the final prewar Industrial Congress in 1860, the body's acting president acknowledged the success of the land reform movement in bringing their cause into the political mainstream, arguing that "it would not be wise to form a new and distinct political party in view of the success of the outside pressure of the land reformers upon the republican party as to the Homestead bill."[57] Others, however, stuck to third-party approaches. Having finally abandoned the Democratic Party, Thomas Devyr campaigned for Gerrit Smith's quixotic 1858 run for New York governor, even as he continued to urge Democrats to adopt homestead as a campaign issue. But most northern Democrats—at least those who had not already fled the party for the Republicans—refused to budge, instead doubling down on pro-southern, proslavery positions and a reliance on racist rhetoric. If it was not necessarily obvious that the Republicans were the great "party of Progress" that George Henry Evans had predicted back in 1849, then, it was becoming increasingly clear, even to diehards like Devyr, that the Democrats had become "the little Tory party of Holdbacks." Perhaps the biggest coup among New York labor radicals was the defection of John Commerford, one of the original leaders of the New York Working Men's revolt of 1829. Some thirty years later, on the eve of the election of 1860, Commerford warned southern Democrat and homestead supporter Andrew Johnson that "in the next Presidential Contest, I shall have to cast my ballot for the Republican Candidate" as a result of Democrats' lukewarm support for land reform and ongoing obeisance to the Slave Power. The following year, Commerford made good on that threat, and more: in October 1860 he won his district's nomination as the Republican candidate for Congress. Although he ultimately lost the race, Commerford's campaign stirred up enthusiasm among New York's radical workingmen, with a torchlight procession featuring delegations from groups like the German Kommunist Klub and the Italian American Garibaldi Wide-Awakes.[58]

Throughout 1860, pro-Republican mass meetings of "workingmen and mechanics" were held in Philadelphia, Pittsburgh, Boston, Newark, Cincinnati, and Indianapolis, and even in border South cities like Saint Louis, Richmond, Memphis, and Louisville. Nonetheless, more precise measurements of working-class support for the Republicans are difficult to ascertain. The available evidence, moreover, suggests that Republican appeals to urban workingmen were only partially effective. Party strategists, while never abandoning the hope of capturing large cities, realized that the Republicans' strength lay among "the farmers and mechanics . . . moral & religious men" in the "*rural districts*."[59] Lingering associations with Nativism kept many Catholic immigrants away, and racist demagoguery by Democrats, who stoked fears of competition from emancipated Blacks and relentlessly portrayed Lincoln as the candidate of the "Black Republican" party, seemed to have the desired effect on many white workers. In New York City, the successful Democratic mayoral candidate Fernando Wood combined a prosouthern platform (even going so far as to propose that New York might join secessionists in the event of the collapse of the Union) with a public works program aimed at providing work for the unemployed, an idea he co-opted from the city's labor movement.

Yet among certain groups of workers, the Republicans made significant gains. German immigrant votes for Republicans increased substantially between 1856 and 1860, and German Americans, most of them skilled workers and small farmers, may have provided the margin of victory in Indiana, Illinois, and Pennsylvania, as well as in border state cities like Saint Louis (where Lincoln won 40 percent of the vote). A group of "German workmen" in Cincinnati wrote to President Lincoln in 1861, assuring him of having earned their votes "as a Champion of free labor and free homesteads" and hailing his election as a victory already won by "freedom over Slavery." But the most important divisions may have lain along lines of skill and property rather than ethnicity: in Cincinnati, the largest percentages of both skilled laborers and those owning only modest amounts of property voted for the Republicans by significant margins in 1856 (a margin that probably increased in 1860), while the unskilled and least wealthy voted Democratic. Other locales present a still more mixed picture. Democrats probably retained the votes of most wage workers in large cities like New York, Philadelphia, and Boston in both 1856 and 1860. But in the latter year, Lincoln increased his vote tally substantially over Frémont's in all three cities, a proportion which grows more impressive if one looks at the industrializing surrounding counties of Kings and Queens (New York), Montgomery and Delaware (Philadelphia), and Suffolk (Boston). More noteworthy still is the fact that both skilled and unskilled workers (particularly the native-born but also substantial numbers of British, German, and Scandinavian immigrants) helped the Republicans triumph in the mill towns and shoemaking centers of Massachusetts, in the canal towns and burned-over districts of Upstate and Western New York, and in the manufacturing and farming regions along the Great Lakes and points further west. In 1860, Lincoln won by 60 percent or more in the counties of Bristol (Fall River), Essex (Lawrence and Lynn), and Worcester in Massachusetts; Hartford County in Connecticut; Onondaga (Syracuse) in New York; Allegheny (Pittsburgh) in Pennsylvania; and Cuyahoga (Cleveland) in Ohio. He took 50 percent or more of the vote in Philadelphia as well as in Chester and Bucks Counties in Pennsylvania; Oneida (Utica) and Rensselaer (Troy) in New York; Middlesex (Lowell) in

Figure 16. This Civil War recruiting poster capitalizes on southern insults of northern working men as "greasy mechanics," appealing to workers in a variety of specifically named trades to enlist in an "engineers' and artisans'" regiment in the Union Army. "Greasy Mechanics, Attention!" circa 1861–1865. M1975.815, Brooklyn Public Library, Center for Brooklyn History.

Massachusetts; New Haven and New London in Connecticut; Providence in Rhode Island; Cook (Chicago) in Illinois; and Waukesha (outside Milwaukee), Wisconsin.[60]

Despite this necessarily incomplete picture, a few things remain certain. Working-class reformers and workers contributed powerfully to the ideas and understandings that formed the foundation of the Republicans' appeal to voters, allowing them to forge a politics of antislavery that was capable of winning large majorities of northerners for the first time. Those who worked with their hands, particularly farmers and skilled workers but also large numbers of lower-skilled and propertyless workers, formed a vital and significant part of the Republican coalition. And those who combined one or more of these characteristics undoubtedly made up the largest part of the North's fighting force in a war made unavoidable by developments that working-class reformers and ordinary workers helped to bring about.

After southern states began to secede from the Union in 1860–1861, abolitionists and Republicans stepped up their efforts to depict the slaveholders'
rebellion as a war of "capital against labor." After the firing on Fort Sumter,
a Union Army recruiting poster in New York City made good use of the
slaveholders' "mudsill" language, redirecting it to spur support for the Union
war effort. Calling attention to "Greasy Mechanics" in bold, large-point type,
the broadside urged "Machinists, Blacksmiths, Carpenters, Masons, Boiler-
Makers, Railroaders, Wagon-Makers, and Mechanics of all kinds" to form
an "Engineers' and Artisans' regiment." Enlistees were promised forty cents
per day over regular infantry "when on mechanical work," and the broadside appealed to laborers in terms similar to Lincoln's and Wilson's refutation
of the mudsill theory, framing the Confederate rebellion as an effort by the
"Southern Chivalry" to "degrade Honest Labor."[61]

On December 14, 1861, Companies A, B, C, D, and E of the Engineers
and Artisans Regiment, comprising men from New York City, Newark, and a
number of smaller towns and villages along the Hudson River Valley and in
Pennsylvania, sailed for James Henry Hammond's home state of South Carolina. It was to be a long war, during the course of which slavery would be
destroyed forever, and the meaning of "free labor" forever changed.

Epilogue

The coming of the war changed everything. With slave-owning legislators from seceded states out of Congress, Republicans were able to secure the passage of progressive legislation, including the long-awaited Homestead Act, the Morrill Tariff, and the Morrill Land-Grant Act, all passed in 1862 (the latter responded to another long-cherished demand of workingmen by providing for agricultural and mechanical state colleges on federally owned land). At the same time, the outbreak of war further complicated northern workers' already complex relationship to slavery and emancipation. Working-class responses to secession and the outbreak of war ranged from that of the Philadelphia labor convention that voted to endorse the Crittenden Compromise (which would have extended the Missouri Compromise's 36°30' line to the Pacific and guaranteed slavery's existence below it) to that of the German Free Working-men of Cincinnati, who declared themselves opposed to all compromises with the Confederacy and expressed their willingness to give their lives "to maintain the victory already won by freedom over slavery" in an address to the newly elected President Lincoln. But the overwhelming response of northern workers, after the firing on Fort Sumter of April 12, 1861, was one of loyalty to the Union and the effort to suppress the rebellion. The self-described Mechanic's Phalanx of Lowell won a prize for being the first unit ready for military camp, while Philadelphia iron molder and future labor leader William H. Sylvis organized one of the first regiments to defend the nation's capital against a Confederate invasion. German '48ers with fighting experience and members of German socialist and Turner societies proved particularly valuable to the Union effort, producing such distinguished members of the Union officer corps as Carl Schurz, August Willich, Joseph Weydemeyer, and Franz Sigel. The story of Union Army regiments organized along ethnic lines, like Sigel's XI Corps or the Irish Brigade under Colonel Thomas Francis Meagher, is well known, but less familiar are those units that organized themselves by occupation or even union affiliation. In some cases, as in the company of the Second Wisconsin (made up entirely of iron foundry workers), or the printers of the Michigan Twenty-Fourth, men of a single trade formed fighting units, while in others, workers organized under banners like that of the Salem Mechanic Grays or the Lynn Mechanic's Phalanx (led by the abolitionist and leader of the 1860 shoemakers' strike, Captain Alonzo Draper). Mark A. Lause has estimated that more than one hundred members of the Typographers' Union fought at Gettysburg, of which perhaps one-third died there, together with Carpenters' Union leader and land reformer turned Union Army captain Benjamin Price. Even before the numbers of casualties began to mount, trade unions and labor organizations voted to dissolve themselves as their rank-and-file memberships were decimated by men volunteering for the war; some contemporary sources estimate that urban mechanics and laborers made up between 38 and 54 percent of the Union Army, a figure that was probably higher in industrialized states like Massachusetts and Connecticut. Whatever the true figure, it is clear that workers, whether industrial or agricultural, made up the majority of the Union's fighting forces.[1]

Few, perhaps, took their loyalty to the Union more seriously than Michael Shiner, an African American block maker at the Washington Navy Yard who may have been the first Black man in that city to take the oath of allegiance to the United States. As Shiner recalled in his diary, the oath was administered "to the mechanics and Laboring Class of working men without DistincSion of Colour ... that oath still remains in my heart and when I had taken that oath I Taken it in the presence of God without prejudice or enmity to any man And I intend to Sustain That oath with The assistance of the Almighty God until I die for when a man takes an oath For a Just cause it is more then [sic] taking a Drink of water." Even in secession-mad Washington, on the borders of a seceded state and a Union slave state, only 37 of Shiner's 400-plus fellow Navy Yard workers refused to take the oath of allegiance. A few years later, however, such solidarity was in short supply. In 1863, Black workers at the Navy Yard had a leading role in one of the dozens of labor actions that took place during the war, when twenty-nine "colored hands" at the Yard's anchor foundry attempted to strike for higher wages—only to find themselves replaced by white strikebreakers, in a reversal of the racial pattern that generally obtained during the period.[2]

If solidarity was lacking at the Navy Yard, however, it was in ample supply among the slave plantations of the South, where enslaved workers took part in work stoppages, sabotaged crops and equipment, negotiated with masters and owners, and ran away in what has been described as a "general strike." While the concept of a coordinated general strike among slaves remains a matter of debate among labor historians and historians of emancipation, what is clear is that enslaved people relied on their own agency to free themselves in a symbiotic process that both provoked and took advantage of the emancipation policies emanating from the Lincoln administration, the Republican-controlled Congress, and the United States Army.[3]

Although white workers had always been susceptible to racism, the advent of slave emancipation as an official Union war aim lent plausibility to long-standing fears about emancipated Blacks flooding north to compete for jobs. Pro-Confederate Copperheads and those who favored fighting to preserve "the Union as it was" stoked the flames of these racial animosities, doubling down on openly racist appeals to working-class voters. Meanwhile, as battle-field casualties mounted, the appalling human toll of the war tested the limits of even its most adamant supporters, perhaps nowhere more so than among the ranks of the working classes, who suffered losses disproportionate to their numbers. Even so, Copperheads and so-called Peace Democrats (northern Democrats who wanted to negotiate an end to the war with the Confederacy, leaving slavery intact) found it difficult to persuade workers. Again, labor newspapers played an important role, with social reformer William Oland Bourne's *Iron Platform* and Philadelphia Machinists and Blacksmiths Union president Jonathan Fincher's *Fincher's Trades' Review* taking the lead in urging workingmen to remain loyal to the Union and pursue the war to its ultimate conclusion. In New York, land reformers J. K. Ingalls and Henry Beeny raised volunteers for the war, while Lewis Masquerier helped create Republican campaign materials. Although John Commerford had lost his election as the Republican candidate for New York's Fourth Congressional District in 1860, he busily organized a circle of the secretive Brotherhood of the Union as well as a new National Industrial Congress, which passed resolutions in favor of forming a new labor party but agreed to work with the Republicans.[4]

Economic hardships created by the war, however, soon exacerbated already simmering ethnic and racial tensions. Labor shortages led to higher wages for many workers, but these gains could not keep pace with the price increases caused by wartime inflation, which saw the prices of basic goods like milk, butter, beef, and coal skyrocket out of the range of many workers and their families.[5] This led in turn to a resurgence of trade union organization and a wave of strikes during the war years. Among the latter were turnouts for higher wages and shorter hours at facilities directly involved in the war effort. At times, Union Army commanders issued prohibitions against unionization and striking, and federal troops were used to put down labor actions in Pennsylvania, Tennessee, Saint Louis, and Cold Spring, New York. One exception to this approach was that of General Benjamin Butler in Union-held New Orleans, who instituted price fixes and a work relief program for the poor there. Another was Lincoln himself. At the Brooklyn Navy Yard, striking ship carpenters, sailmakers, joiners, plumbers, blacksmiths, boilermakers, machinists, carpenters, and others formed a committee to appeal directly to the president. Perhaps they were encouraged by Lincoln's response to the shoemakers' strike in Lynn, Massachusetts, in 1860, described in chapter 7. In November 1863, Lincoln granted the Navy Yard workers' committee a personal hearing, during which he expressed his "sympathies" with the strikers, but regretted that "he could do nothing as President," and advised them to appeal to the secretary of the Navy, Gideon Welles. If Lincoln's polite reception was enough to convince the workers, as the New York Times reported, that he had "not left all his sympathy for laboring men with his maul and wedges in the prairie State," Secretary Welles's response must have been even more gratifying: he instructed the commandant of the yard to reduce the men's hours and pay them wages in comity with private establishments in the vicinity, as per law. Similarly, Lincoln told a delegation from the Working Women's Relief Association representing subcontracted female workers at a Philadelphia arsenal that he could not interfere with private war contracts, but he nonetheless intervened to raise the women's pay.[6]

Not far away from the White House, however, Michael Shiner must have looked at the labor unrest of 1863 with some trepidation. The last time workers at the Washington Navy Yard had gone on strike, in 1835, they had been replaced with Black strikebreakers brought in from Baltimore, and local whites had retaliated by attacking and looting Black homes. Unfortunately, the infamous Draft Riots in New York City of July 1863 recalled the worst of the anti-Black riots of the 1830s, while far exceeding them in terms of destructiveness and lives lost. The riots had been presaged by a series of labor conflicts that pitted white workers against African Americans. In 1855 and again in April 1863, just months before the riots, racial violence had broken out on New York's waterfront, as mostly Irish American longshoremen tried to enforce an all-white rule against Black strikebreakers. Almost a year to the day before the Draft Riots, African American tobacco workers in a Brooklyn cigar-rolling plant had been chased from their workplace by a mob of white workers, some barely escaping with their lives. Then, beginning on July 13, 1863, what started as a protest against the class-based provisions of the Union Army draft (those so inclined could hire a substitute to fight in his place for $300, the equivalent of a year's salary for the average workingman) devolved into a three-day orgy of destruction, arson, and anti-Black violence, with lower-skilled workers and Irish-born immigrants playing a conspicuous role. Along with such targets as the Colored Orphan Asylum and the homes of wealthy Republicans, the rioters attacked and partially destroyed the Colored Seamen's Home, the headquarters of the American Seamen's Protective Union Association, one of the first all-Black unions. In response, William O. Bourne's Workingmen's Democratic-Republican Association, formed earlier that year to consolidate working-class support for Lincoln in the war across partisan boundaries, issued series of broadsides urging workers to "Stop and Think!" Bourne's subsequent offerings, rendered in large-character boldface type and signed "A Democratic Workingman," denounced northern and southern "traitors," reminded Irish Americans of Irish liberation hero Daniel O'Connell's pronouncements in favor of abolition, and resurrected the specter of "WHITE SLAVES" to warn workingmen of their supposed fates in the event of a Confederate victory.[7]

The "Democratic Workingman's" appeals may have had some effect; although scattered evidence suggests that proletarianized workers, including day laborers and iron foundry and dock workers, were responsible for much of the violence, skilled artisans took the lead in quelling the disturbances.[8] Ultimately, however, the riots had to be suppressed with federal troops from the 152nd New York, the 26th Michigan, the 27th Indiana, and other regiments, at the cost of an unknown number of lives. Less than six months later, the Democratic-Republican Workingmen's Association elected President Lincoln as an honorary member, sending him an address in which they emphasized their loyalty to the Union. In a lengthy reply, Lincoln defended the existence of inequalities of property, but agreed with the committee's characterization of the Confederacy's rebellion as "a war upon the rights of all working people," and went on to quote his own address to the Wisconsin State Agricultural Society, with its message that labor was "prior to, and independent of, capital." Lincoln concluded by saying that his views in 1864 remained unchanged, and that he had little to add. What followed, however, proves that the president understood that the context had changed dramatically since 1859. In the former year, he had addressed farmers and others dedicated to reducing the burdens of frontier agriculture; now he addressed urban workers in the midst of a brutal civil war and in the aftermath of a deadly riot carried out by those of their own class. "The most notable feature of a disturbance in your city last summer was the hanging of some working people by other working people," Lincoln observed. "It should never be so. The strongest bond of human sympathy, outside of the family relation, should be one uniting all working people, of all nations, and tongues, and kindreds."[9]

The Democratic *New York World*, which supported Peace Democrat (and former Union Army commanding general) George McClellan in the decisive wartime election of 1864, pounced on Lincoln's words as evidence that the president supported "amalgamation" (or racial intermixing, a common charge made by Copperheads and Peace Democrats). After disparaging the Workingmen's class credentials, the *World* complained that Lincoln "overlooks all difference of race and regards the whites and blacks simply as laborers," a policy bound to "excite all the worst prejudices of our white laboring population," who were bound to vote for McClellan. In the event, however, the *World*'s predictions were not borne out. When a Workingman's Congress was held in New York's City Hall (paid for by ex-mayor and Peace Democrat Fernando Wood), the painters' union leader Patrick Keady (himself a vocal critic of the Republicans) led a walkout in protest of its antiwar, pro-Copperhead stance. Keady and others then formed the rival, independent United Organization of Workingmen, while the Workingman's Congress changed its name to the Workingmen's Central Association and received the endorsement of Peace Democrats and the proslavery, white-supremacist *Weekly Caucasian*. The ultimate test of northern workers' loyalties, however, came later that fall. Although McClellan won many urban districts in the North, including Manhattan, Lincoln won the election handily, including in all of the counties of Massachusetts and Vermont; all but one county in Maine and Connecticut; and those containing the burgeoning industrial population centers of Chicago, Saint Louis, Cincinnati, Cleveland, and Baltimore.[10]

Apart from their general support for the Union and the war effort, however, the complexity of working-class politics, as well as the scarcity of reliable statistics, makes it difficult to assess northern workers' political preferences during the war years. Perhaps to a greater extent than they had been during the antebellum period, so-called workingmen's meetings and organizations were often in reality dominated by professional politicians and employers, further muddying the waters. It is clear, however, that working-class support for the Republicans remained scattered, particularly in large cities where Democrats remained in control. The reasons for this are complicated and involve

UNION AND LIBERTY!   AND   UNION AND SLAVERY!

Figure 17. This 1864 Republican campaign image appeals to working-class voters by juxtaposing "Union and Liberty!" with "Union and Slavery!" On the left, a workingman with the tools of his trade and wearing an artisan's cap shakes hands with Lincoln, while Black and white children emerge from an integrated schoolhouse in the background; on the right, the Democratic candidate, former Union commander George McClellan, shakes hands with Jefferson Davis against a backdrop of enslaved people at the auction block. American Antiquarian Society.

a combination of cultural, political, economic, and class factors, which have been well-documented elsewhere. Irish immigrants, and to a lesser extent German immigrants, remained largely aloof from the Republicans due to their association with Nativism as well as the party's generally middle-class, Protestant orientation. The Protestant morality that lay at the heart of Republican ideology, including its embrace of a laissez-faire version of free labor and support for reforms such as temperance, made it anathema to many Irish and German workers, for whom socializing in taverns and beer gardens was a staple of social life, and who resented what they perceived as interference in their domestic and religious lives. It remains unclear, however, to what extent urban workers resented the advent of government intervention in *economic* life, since many welcomed and called for the expansion of the secessionist ex-mayor and Peace Democrat Fernando Wood's introduction of city government–run public works projects and work relief schemes. Indeed, such approaches, which a few ex–land reformers likened to an "'urbanized' version of a national Homestead Act," attracted strong support from working-class New Yorkers, and probably helped to lure the disaffected among them to the Peace Democrat cause.[11]

In many ways the Homestead Act, passed by the Republican Congress and signed by Lincoln on May 20, 1862, represented the culmination of workers' long-held demands for the freedom of the public lands. But despite the Homestead Act's revolutionary potential—it would eventually facilitate the distribution of 270 acres, or 10 percent of the United States' total land area—it failed to live up even to the relatively modest hopes of the progressive Republicans who supported it, let alone the expectations of a "Jubilee" cherished by land reformers. In its final form, the Homestead Act provided 160 acres of free land to anyone twenty-one years of age or older, or the head of a family, who was a citizen of the United States or who had declared an intention to become one. Potential homesteaders had simply to pay a filing fee of $10 and live on and cultivate the land for five years to validate the claim; alternatively, one could pay $1.25 an acre and validate the claim after occupancy of only six months. With southerners from the seceded states out of Congress, the act passed easily, by a vote of 107 to 16 in the House and 33 to 7 in the Senate. Within nine months of the law's passage, more than 1,450,000 acres of the public lands had been filed for.[12] But almost immediately, those with profit on their minds and capital to spare began the process of exploiting the Homestead Act. To some extent, this was the fault of loopholes created by the legislation's ambiguous language. One ploy, at least according to legend, was to take advantage of the law's failure to specify whether the "12-by-14 dwelling" that was required by the law to be erected on the property was constructed in feet or inches. More frequently, land speculators simply hired phony claimants to buy up the land or occupy it for six months only to sell it back at a higher price (in violation of the National Reformers' concept of "inalienability," which would have forbidden such resale). Of the 500 million acres dispersed by the General Land Office between 1862 and 1904, only an estimated 80 million acres went to "actual settlers," with the rest acquired by railroad companies, speculators, cattle ranchers, mining corporations, and other highly capitalized interests that sprung up during the Gilded Age. The underfunded and overburdened Land Office lacked the manpower to investigate claims spread amid millions of acres and thousands of local land offices, and its agents were often susceptible to bribes.[13]

Urban workers, meanwhile, often lacked the start-up capital or the agricultural skills to escape the crowded wage labor market of the eastern cities and take advantage of the Homestead Act. But even the disadvantages faced by northern wage workers and immigrants paled before those that confronted some four million newly emancipated former slaves. Here, the land reformers' warnings that emancipation without access to land would trap formerly enslaved people in a state of slave-like dependency proved all too prescient. Throughout the Reconstruction South, the formerly enslaved expected and demanded access to the soil. After all, as an Alabama freedmen's convention put it, the wealth amassed by former slaveholders "was nearly all earned by the sweat of *our* brows." But most freed people not only failed to receive the "forty acres and a mule" that many had believed promised to them by General William Tecumseh Sherman's Special Field Order No. 15, they ended up remaining on the same land they had worked as slaves—not as proprietors, but as sharecroppers or in other semidependent capacities.

In 1863, Secretary of War Edwin Stanton created the American Freedmen's Inquiry Commission—comprising abolitionists James McKaye and Samuel Gridley Howe, along with Robert Dale Owen, the son of the famous socialist and now an Indiana congressman—which was charged with investigating the status and condition of formerly enslaved people and recommending ways to aid the process of the transition from slavery to freedom. Howe traveled to Canada to visit communities formed by former slaves there, while Owen insisted that, if treated justly and offered "temporary aid and supervision," former slaves would remain in the South and become good and loyal citizens.[14] As a direct result of the commission's work, Congress in 1865 passed a bill creating the Bureau of Refugees, Freedmen, and Abandoned Lands, more commonly known as the Freedmen's Bureau. When the bureau's one-year charter expired the following year, the bill to recharter it initially included a proposal, devised by a group of Radical Republicans that included George W. Julian and Thaddeus Stevens, to allot three million acres of public lands in the South for homesteading by the formerly enslaved. During congressional debate on the bill, Senator Lyman Trumbull included a provision affirming former slaves' right to the lands in coastal South Carolina and Georgia set aside for them by General Sherman, and Stevens added a clause turning the "forfeited estates of the enemy" into potential land for Black homesteaders. Ironically, Lincoln's successor, President Andrew Johnson—one of the few prominent southern supporters of land reform before the war, who had been chosen as Lincoln's vice-presidential candidate in 1864 for his strong support of homestead reform and his reputation for hostility toward the slave-owning class—now became one of the biggest obstacles to land redistribution for

African Americans. Johnson refused to recognize the validity of the Sherman grants and eventually oversaw the restoration of the vast majority of
them to former slave owners. But even before Johnson vetoed the Freedman's
Bureau bill, Stevens's clause was overwhelmingly defeated by the Republican-
dominated House. As Eric Foner explains, "Republicans were quite willing
to offer freedmen the same opportunity to acquire land as whites already
enjoyed under the Homestead Act of 1862, but not to interfere with planters'
property rights."[15]

The subsequent Southern Homestead Act, sponsored by Julian and
intended to provide former slaves and loyal whites with access to public lands
in the South, largely ended in failure. Slaveholding plantations had long since
monopolized the best lands, leaving mainly swampy, barren, or mountainous
soil; only four thousand Black families applied for land under the act's provisions, and much of the land ended up in the hands of white-owned timber
companies. Although Black land ownership existed in the Reconstruction
South, with success stories in Florida and South Carolina, where perhaps
10 percent of Black families lived on land of their own, perhaps only one in
twenty Black families in the cotton states managed to acquire land by the
end of the Reconstruction period.[16] In 1869, Frederick Douglass proposed the
formation of a "national land and loan company" to enable freedmen to purchase land on easy credit terms, and in a few places, such as Colleton County,
South Carolina, and Davis Bend, Mississippi—the plantation formerly owned
by Confederate president Jefferson Davis's brother Joseph Emory Davis and
managed by Davis's formerly enslaved foreman Benjamin T. Montgomery as
a cooperative community into the 1880s—Blacks utilized cooperative labor
schemes with some success. But such success stories remained the exception,
and by the late 1870s, African American "exodusters" and other migrants
were seeking refuge in Kansas and elsewhere in the North and West.[17]

Meanwhile, a new generation of postwar labor leaders, like Ira Steward,
who before the war had been a machinist and antislavery labor organizer,
urged urban workers to change their slogan from "Vote Yourself a Farm" to
"Vote Yourself an Eight-Hour Day."[18] The emphasis on hours of labor laws by
the Knights of Labor and other postwar labor organizations has been seen
by labor historians as indicating a turn toward "bread and butter" unionism—the focus on fundamental issues of hours, conditions, and wages—in
the years after the Civil War. But the fact that many workers continued to
cherish revolutionary, even utopian, ambitions for social change, and that
they viewed them as compatible with so-called bread and butter issues, is

reflected by the 1865 call of the Boston Labor Reform Association to combine "the reconstruction of our dinner tables" with the overthrow of the "whole Social System." Clearly, many workers and labor leaders—many of whom, like Steward, now proudly proclaimed their abolitionist credentials—viewed the Reconstruction period as a potentially revolutionary moment, pregnant with possibilities for both sweeping social change and more modest but tangible gains. As they had before the war, labor organizations would work with political parties and politicians to devise legislative solutions to the problems faced by workers, while continuing to espouse more radical responses to the increasing division of labor and mechanization imposed by industrialization, including calls to reorganize the nation's political economy into what they called a "cooperative commonwealth," and demands for greater control over the pace and output of work.[19]

But labor reformers faced a different world than the one they had confronted before 1860. Within a decade of the close of the war, both the free labor vision espoused by Lincoln and the radical agrarian version championed by labor reformers had receded irretrievably into the past. By the end of the Reconstruction period, the number of nonagricultural laborers would exceed that of farmers for the first time in the country's history. Between 1865 and 1873, industrial production increased by 75 percent, and more miles of railroad track were laid than had existed in the entire country before the war. In an earlier moment of revolutionary possibility, in the heady days of 1848, land reformers had stormed a meeting at the Broadway Tabernacle held by merchant and railroad entrepreneur Asa Whitney, who called for the use of funds from public land sales to fund a transcontinental railroad. The land reformers effected a hostile takeover, accusing Whitney of "betraying a trust" by "endowing Railroad Companies, or Syndicates with the inheritance of the people," and Whitney and his fellow businessmen had hurriedly left by the back door.[20] By the time Whitney's dream of a transcontinental railroad became a reality in 1869, men of his class practically ran the Republican Party, which had rather quickly shed its radical origins and become identified with big business, big finance, and new corporations like the Union Pacific and Central Pacific Railroad companies. Both of the latter had been chartered by the Pacific Railway Act, passed by Congress in the same year as the Homestead Act, and both received a total of 100 million acres of land and millions of dollars in subsidies from the Republican Congress, whose members in turn received shares of stock and other ethically dubious rewards. The completion of a transcontinental railroad network united far-flung regions of the country and spurred a commercial and transportation revolution, but at a terrible cost—not only to the dreams of would-be homesteaders but to the Plains Indians and other Native groups, who were decimated by the U.S. Army, white settlers, and the environmental havoc they wrought.[21]

As the conflicts over Reconstruction raged in the South, a series of panics and depressions, the demise of the Radicals and the emergence of the Liberal Republicans, and the increasingly vicious suppression of strikes and other worker's activities would drive many workingmen into the arms of the Knights of Labor, the Greenback-Labor, and finally the Socialist Labor Party. Simultaneously, rising land prices, issues of money supply and inflation, the advent of large-scale mechanized agriculture and the crop-lien system, and the intervention of banks, middlemen, and commodities brokers would propel southern and western farmers to embrace the Grangers, Farmers' Alliance, Greenback, and People's Parties. In 1880, the Greenback-Labor platform, the product of a short-lived political alliance between southern and western farmers and urban workingmen, echoed the earlier pronouncements of labor abolitionists and abolitionists-cum-laborites such as George Henry Evans, Nathaniel P. Rogers, and Elizur Wright Jr., by declaring that the "land, air, and water are the grand gifts of nature to all mankind, and the law or custom of society that allows any person to monopolize more of these gifts of nature than he has a right to, we earnestly condemn and demand shall be abolished."[22] Out in California, a young journalist, Henry George, noted in 1871 that the state had already become "not a country of farms," but of large "plantations and estates," sometimes worked by Chinese indentured servants or Mexican migrant workers. In his *Progress and Poverty*, published eight years later, George proceeded from the same propositions that had actuated National Reformers almost forty years earlier: that land, like other natural resources, was the common inheritance of all and could not be legitimately the property of any individual or corporation, but rather belonged to the public trust. "Political liberty, when the equal right to land is denied," George concluded, "becomes . . . merely the liberty to compete for employment at starvation wages." George's "single-tax" plan, which called for a tax on land, but not on the improvements or revenue produced from it, became the basis of his nearly successful run for mayor of New York City in 1886, as well as of a strain of populist economic thought that motivated farmers, workingmen, and others throughout the period.[23]

Such ideals also continued to inspire former abolitionists and their ideological (and sometimes literal) descendants. In 1898, a compendium of

George's works was published that included an overview of Gerrit Smith's thoughts and writings on land monopoly; the introduction, written by William Lloyd Garrison, Jr., imagined Smith as "a Forerunner of Henry George." Other former abolitionists, perhaps none more prominent than Wendell Phillips, emerged as strong advocates of the right to labor in the post–Civil War period. Whether or not Phillips actually uttered the words attributed to him in the 1840s, that "the great question of Labor, when it shall fully come up, will be found paramount to all others," his postwar activities largely bore out that prediction. By 1865, Phillips had repudiated his earlier embrace of laissez-faire free labor, and throughout the 1870s and '80s he became known as a champion of the eight-hour movement and a vocal supporter of former Union general Benjamin Butler's campaigns for Massachusetts governor as the candidate of the Labor Reform and Greenback parties.[24]

Veterans of the workingmen's struggles of the 1820s through '50s also reemerged to champion their vision for the postemancipation United States. Ex–National Reformer William V. Barr and former New England Workingmen's Association leader John Orvis both ran for office on joint Socialist Labor Party-Greenback-Populist tickets, and Union Army general James B. Weaver, who had been involved with land reform in Iowa and who commanded the Second Iowa infantry at Shiloh, ran for president on the Greenback-Labor and Populist tickets.[25]

But perhaps the most surprising encore performance of the period was that of William Heighton. Early in 1865, Heighton, the aging former leader of the Philadelphia Working Men, resurfaced after decades of obscurity to pen a letter to George L. Stearns, an abolitionist John Brown supporter turned Radical Republican. Heighton's letter was published in a pamphlet on *The Equality of All Men before the Law, Claimed and Defended*, with contributions from Wendell Phillips, Frederick Douglass, Elizur Wright, Jr., and Pennsylvania Republican William D. Kelley. Stearns had solicited Heighton's aid "to organize the anti-slavery men of the country," and to consider "the reconstruction of the social and political institutions of the Rebel States," including the "remodel[ing of] our financial system, in order to correct abuses growing out of slavery." The request must have been surprising to those who remembered Heighton from the 1820s and '30s, since, although his *Mechanic's Free Press* had published a number of articles against slavery, he was hardly known as an abolitionist or as a vocal champion of racial equality. But Heighton's recommendations for reconstructing the former Confederate states "upon the basis of liberty and equal rights" emphasized "the Unity and Essential Equality of the Human

Race," which included not only a right to "life and liberty," but the "right to *property* in the common elements of nature,—light, air, water, and the land."[26]

Heighton's other points stressed the "Responsibility of Government" to secure these rights, attacked monopolies, and upheld the sanctity of the elective franchise. But Heighton felt that his proposition about the right to property was "so important" that he spent much of the rest of his letter elaborating on it. "Immense landed estates," Heighton intoned, "are death to Democracy"; even when cloaked in "republican forms," they were capable of subverting the democratic process and becoming "an element of jarring and perpetual discord." "The landed estates, therefore, of all the prominent and active rebels . . . should be confiscated and broken up." After the leading Confederates had been duly punished, their heirs who pledged an oath of allegiance might be given "so much land as would constitute a moderate homestead," but "an equal homestead should be apportioned to each colored family." "These," Heighton concluded, "have the first and highest right, since the clearing and improvements have been done mainly by their labor."[27]

Like so much of what the pre–Civil War labor reformers had stood for, Heighton's final contribution to the public record serves more as a reminder of what might have been than as a prediction of what actually came to pass. But by providing a glimpse of the alternate routes that fed into the main path of history, Heighton and others like him nonetheless helped to alter its course at a critical fork in the road, while pointing the way for future generations of radicals and reformers.

NOTES

Introduction

1. "The International Industrial Assembly of North America, 1864," in John R. Commons et al., eds., *A Documentary History of American Industrial Society*, Vol. 9 (Cleveland: Arthur H. Clark, 1910), 118–25.

2. Brian Kelly, "Mapping Alternate Routes to Antislavery," *Labor: Studies in Working-Class History in the Americas* 5, no. 4 (2008), 69.

3. Bruce Laurie arrives at a somewhat different conclusion in his excellent 2008 review essay in the same volume of *Labor* cited above, emphasizing that workers embodied a spectrum of views "from proslavery to antislavery to abolitionist, with the weight shifting towards the second two over time." Laurie, "Workers, Abolitionists, and the Historians: A Historiographical Perspective," *Labor: Studies in Working-Class History in the Americas* 5, no. 4 (2008), 17–55.

4. Marx first made this statement in an 1866 letter to François Lafargue, and later repeated it in the first volume of *Capital*. Saul K. Padover, ed., *Karl Marx: On America and the Civil War (New York: McGraw-Hill, 1972)*, 275; Karl Marx, *Capital: A Critique of Political Economy*, Vol. 1 (New York, 1967), 301.

5. Mark A. Lause has pointed to the Typographical Union's inclusion of a handful of African American members, an exception that proves the rule. See Lause, *Free Labor: The Civil War and the Making of an American Working Class* (Urbana: University of Illinois Press, 2015), 60.

6. Key works in the literature on whiteness include David R. Roediger, *The Wages of Whiteness: Race and the Making of the American Working Class* (New York: Verso, 1991); Noel Ignatiev, *How the Irish Became White* (New York: Routledge, 1995); Alexander Saxton, *The Rise and Fall of the White Republic: Class Politics and Mass Culture in Nineteenth Century America* (New York: Verso, 2003).

7. David Brion Davis, *The Problem of Slavery in the Age of Revolution 1770–1823* (Oxford: Oxford University Press, 1999); Aileen Kraditor, *Means and Ends in American Abolitionism: Garrison and His Critics on Strategy and Tactics, 1834–1850* (New York: Pantheon Books, 1969), 247.

8. The Louisville Platform hedged on the question of immediate abolition, deeming it "neither possible or advisable," but described slavery as a "political and moral cancer" and called for its "gradual extermination." The platform can be found in Don

Heinrich Tolzmann, ed., *The German-American Forty-Eighters, 1848–1998* (Bloomington: Indiana University, 1997), 98–105.

9. "National Convention—Union of Reformers—Industrial Congress," *Young America*, October 4, 1845.

10. W. E. B. Du Bois first coined the term "wages of whiteness" to describe the psychological advantage that white workers derived from their skin color; see Du Bois, *Black Reconstruction in America, 1860–1880* (1935), 700. For a critique of the way that Du Bois's idea has been used by whiteness studies scholars, see Adolph Reed, Jr., "Du Bois and the 'Wages of Whiteness': What He Meant, What He Didn't Mean, and Besides, It Shouldn't Matter for Our Politics Anyway," June 29, 2017, https://nonsite.org/du-bois -and-the-wages-of-whiteness/.

11. For recent studies of antislavery that reject the emphasis on Garrisonianism for political abolitionism, see Bruce Laurie, *Beyond Garrison: Antislavery and Social Reform* (Cambridge: Cambridge University Press, 2005), and Corey M. Brooks, *Liberty Power: Antislavery Third Parties and the Transformation of American Politics* (Chicago: University of Chicago Press, 2016). For recent work on Black politics and political antislavery in the Early Republic and antebellum periods, see Stephen Kantrowitz, *More Than Freedom: Fighting for Black Citizenship in a White Republic* (New York: Penguin, 2021); Kate Masur, *Until Justice Be Done: America's First Civil Rights Movement, from the Revolution to Reconstruction* (New York: W. W. Norton, 2021); Van Gosse, *The First Reconstruction: Black Politics in America from the Revolution to the Civil War* (Chapel Hill: University of North Carolina Press, 2021); Christopher James Bonner, *Remaking the Republic: Black Politics and the Creation of American Citizenship* (Philadelphia: University of Pennsylvania Press, 2020); Van Gosse and David Waldstreicher, eds., *Revolutions and Reconstructions: Black Politics in the Long Nineteenth Century* (Philadelphia: University of Pennsylvania Press, 2020).

12. Works that emphasize the importance of land ownership and the lack thereof for former slaves during Reconstruction include Eric Foner, *Reconstruction: America's Unfinished Revolution, 1863–1877* (New York: Perennial, 1988); Steven Hahn, *A Nation Under Our Feet: Black Political Struggles in the Rural South from Slavery to the Great Migration* (Cambridge, MA: Harvard University Press, 2003); Adrienne M. Petty, *Standing Their Ground: Small Farmers in North Carolina Since the Civil War* (Oxford: Oxford University Press, 2013).

13. John Thelwall, "The Connection between the CALAMITIES of the PRESENT REIGN, and the SYSTEM of BOROUGH-MONGERING CORRUPTION—LECTURE THE THIRD. —*The Connection between Parliamentary Corruption and Commercial Monopoly; with Strictures on the* WEST-INDIA SUBSCRIPTION, &c. Delivered *Wednesday, Oct. 14, 1795. in the Tribune*, No. XXXV (Vol. 3, pp. 73–52), in Gregory Claeys, ed., *The Politics of English Jacobinism: Writings of John Thelwall (University Park: Pennsylvania State University Press, 1995)*, 285–292; [Charles Hosmer], *The Condition of Labor: An Address to the Members of the Labor Reform League of New England; in a Speech in Support of Some Resolution Offered at Their Late Convention in Boston, By*

One of the Members (Boston: Published by the Author, 1847), 7–8, 21; Hudson quoted in Christopher Clark, *The Communitarian Movement: The Radical Challenge of the Northampton Association* (Amherst: UMass Press, 1995), 99–100; "Our Principles," in *Working Man's Advocate*, April 6, 1844; Gerrit Smith, *Letter to J. K. Ingalls, Editor of the Landmark* (Peterboro, NY, August 15, 1848); "The Land Reformer," *Frederick Douglass Paper*, August 15, 1856.

14. Evans to O'Connor; "Young America—National Reformers" (from Osh-kosh *True Democrat*), *Wisconsin Free Democrat*, May 2, 1849. I am grateful to Madeline Lafuse of the CUNY Graduate Center for her insights into abolitionists' use of the metaphor of the upas tree.

15. Robert Owen, *A New View of Society, or, Essays on the Formation of Human Character . . .* 2nd ed., (London: 1816); Thomas Paine, *Agrarian Justice, Opposed to Agrarian Law . . .* (London, 1797); George Fitzhugh, *Cannibals All!, or, Slaves Without Masters* (Richmond: A. Morris, 1857).

16. Daniel R. Mandell, *The Lost Tradition of Economic Equality in America, 1600–1870* (Baltimore: Johns Hopkins University Press, 2020).

17. Smith, Circular Letter; Abraham Lincoln, "First Debate: Ottawa, Illinois," August 21, 1858, quoted in Roy Basler, ed., *Collected Works of Abraham Lincoln*, Vol. 3 (New Brunswick, NJ: Rutgers University Press, 1953), 1–37. On nineteenth-century ideas about the right to the fruits of labor, see James L. Huston, *Securing the Fruits of Labor: The American Concept of Wealth Distribution, 1765–1900* (Baton Rouge: Louisiana State University Press, 1998); Jonathan A. Glickstein, *Concepts of Free Labor in Antebellum America* (New Haven: Yale University Press, 1991); Eric Foner, *Free Soil, Free Labor, Free Men: The Ideology of the Republican Party Before the Civil War* (Oxford, UK: Oxford University Press, 1995).

18. Table 3, in Trina Williams, "The Homestead Act: A Major Asset-building Policy in American History," working paper, Center for Social Development (Saint Louis: Washington University, 2000), 18.

19. In the interest of brevity, I have limited this discussion of the historiography on labor and abolitionism to focus primarily on work that has emerged since 2000. For a rich discussion of the older historiography on this subject, see Laurie, "Workers, Abolitionists, and the Historians."

20. I am indebted to Ariel Ron for this insight; see Ron, *Grassroots Leviathan: Agricultural Reform and the Rural North in the Slaveholding Republic* (Baltimore: Johns Hopkins University Press, 2020), 216–217.

21. Key works in the recent literature on slavery and capitalism include Walter Johnson, *River of Dark Dreams: Slavery and Empire in the Cotton Kingdom* (Cambridge, MA: Harvard University Press, 2013); Edward E. Baptist, *The Half Has Never Been Told: Slavery and the Making of American Capitalism* (New York: Basic Books, 2014); Sven Beckert, *Empire of Cotton: A Global History* (New York: Alfred A. Knopf, 2015); Joshua Rothman, *Flush Times and Fever Dreams: A Story of Capitalism and Slavery in the Age of Jackson* (Athens: University of Georgia Press, 2014); Caitlin Rosenthal, *Accounting for*

Slavery: Masters and Management (Cambridge, MA: Harvard University Press, 2018). See also the recent collection edited by Sven Beckert and Seth Rockman, *Slavery's Capitalism: A New History of American Economic Development* (Philadelphia: University of Pennsylvania Press, 2016). The modern debate on the relationship between capitalism and slavery was inaugurated by Eric Williams, *Capitalism and Slavery* (Chapel Hill: University of North Carolina Press, 1944), and to some extent by W. E. B. Du Bois in *Black Reconstruction*. For a critique of recent scholars' use, or misuse, of Williams's scholarship, see H. Reuben Neptune, "Throwin' Scholarly Shade: Eric Williams in the New Histories of Capitalism and Slavery," *Journal of the Early Republic* 39, no. 2 (Summer 2019), 299–326. For a broader critique of the recent literature, see John J. Clegg, "Capitalism and Slavery," *Critical Historical Studies* 2, no. 2 (Fall 2015), 281–304.

22. James Oakes, "Capitalism and Slavery and the Civil War" (review), *International Labor and Working-Class History* 89 (Spring 2016), 195. For the now-standard interpretation of the economic origins of the Civil War, see Foner, *Free Soil, Free Labor;* Bruce Levine, *Half Slave and Half Free: The Roots of the Civil War* (New York: Hill and Wang, 1992).

23. Williams, *Capitalism and Slavery;* Davis, *The Problem of Slavery in the Age;* Davis, Thomas Haskell, and John Ashworth, in Thomas Bender, ed., *The Antislavery Debate: Capitalism and Abolitionism as a Problem in Historical Interpretation* (Berkeley: University of California Press, 1992). For old and new criticisms of the "Davis thesis," see Eric Foner, *Politics and Ideology in the Age of the Civil War* (Oxford, UK: Oxford University Press, 1980), 57–76; Seymour Drescher, *Capitalism and Antislavery: British Mobilization in Comparative Perspective* (Oxford, UK: Oxford University Press, 1986); Manisha Sinha, *The Problem of Slavery in the Age of Revolution 1770–1823,* by David Brion Davis (review essay), *American Historical Review* 124, no. 1 (February 2019), 144–163.

24. Foner, *Free Soil, Free Labor,* ix–xxxix.

25. Recent work on slavery/antislavery, race, and class in the Civil War Era includes Bruce Laurie, *Beyond Garrison;* Mark A. Lause, *Young America: Land, Labor, and the Republican Community* (Urbana: University of Illinois Press, 2005); Lause, *Free Labor;* Keri Leigh Merritt, *Masterless Men: Poor Whites and Slavery in the Antebellum South* (Cambridge: Cambridge University Press, 2017). On wage slavery/white slavery, see Roediger, *Wages of Whiteness,* 65–92, passim; Lause, *Young America,* 74, 77, 83, 129; Gunther Peck, "Labor Abolition and the Politics of White Victimhood: Rethinking the History of Working-Class Racism," *Journal of the Early Republic* 39, no. 1 (March 2019), 89–98; Peck, "White Slavery and Whiteness: A Transnational View of the Sources of Working-Class Radicalism and Racism," *Labor: Studies in Working-Class History of the Americas* 1, no. 2 (2004), 41–63; Peck, *Trafficking in Race: White Slavery and the Rise of a Transatlantic Working Class, 1660–1860* (forthcoming).

26. Bruce Laurie, "Workers, Abolitionists, and the Historians," 55. Recent work on political antislavery includes Corey M. Brooks, *Liberty Power;* James Oakes, *Freedom National: The Destruction of Slavery in the United States, 1861–1865* (New York: W. W. Norton, 2013); Manisha Sinha, *The Slave's Cause: A History of Abolition* (New

Haven: Yale University Press, 2016); Matthew J. Karp, *Millions of Abolitionists: The Republican Party and the Political War Against Slavery* (forthcoming).

27. Nonetheless, the change from 6 percent urban in 1810 to 20 percent by 1860 means this period saw the highest rate of urbanization in U.S. history. Eric Foner, John Ashworth, and David Montgomery all rely on the work of economist Stanley Lebergott to arrive at an estimate that 40 percent of the American adult population were wage workers by 1860, but as Ashworth has pointed out, the low numbers of wage workers in the South mean that the majority of workers in the North worked for wages by the Civil War. See Foner, *Free Soil, Free Labor,* xv – xvi; David Montgomery, *Beyond Equality: Labor and the Radical Republicans, 1862–1872* (Urbana: University of Illinois Press, 1981), 28–30; John Ashworth, *Slavery, Capitalism, and Politics in the Antebellum Republic: Volume 2: The Coming of the Civil War* (Cambridge: Cambridge University Press, 2007), 297, n244. See also Stanley Lebergott, "Labor Force and Employment, 1800–1960," quoted in James McPherson, *Battle Cry of Freedom,* 9.

28. The literature on the origins of capitalism and the debates on that subject are vast, but important entries that emphasize agrarian transformation as a precursor to capitalist development include Maurice Dobb, *Studies in the Development of Capitalism* (London: George Routledge and Sons, 1946); Rodney Hilton, Introduction to *The Transition from Feudalism to Capitalism* (London: New Left Books, 1976); T. H. Aston and C. H. E. Philpin, eds., *The Brenner Debate: Agrarian Class Structure and Economic Development in Pre-Industrial Europe* (Cambridge: Cambridge University Press, 1985); Ellen Meiskins Wood, *The Origin of Capitalism: A Longer View* (New York: Verso, 1999). Works that have examined the "agrarian origins" theory in an American setting include Alan Kulikoff, *The Agrarian Origins of American Capitalism* (Charlottesville: University of Virginia Press, 1992), and most recently, Ariel Ron, *Grassroots Leviathan.*

Chapter 1

1. "Forrester" [Thomas Paine] to the *Pennsylvania Journal,* April 24, 1776. My interpretation of Paine has been particularly informed by Eric Foner, *Tom Paine and Revolutionary America,* updated ed. (Oxford: Oxford University Press, 2004); Seth Cotlar, *Tom Paine's America: The Rise and Fall of Transatlantic Radicalism in Early America* (Charlottesville: University of Virginia Press, 2011); and Staughton Lynd, *Intellectual Origins of American Radicalism,* 2nd ed. (Cambridge: Cambridge University Press, 2009).

2. Paine to Benjamin Rush, March 16, 1790; and [Thomas Paine and Joseph Priestley], *Old Truths and Established Facts: Being an Answer to A Very New Pamphlet Indeed!* (London, 1792). On the reevaluation of Paine's antislavery and the scholarly controversy surrounding authorship of the essays in the *Pennsylvania Journal* and other writings attributed to Paine, see James V. Lynch, "The Limits of Revolutionary Radicalism: Tom Paine and Slavery," *Pennsylvania Magazine of History and Biography* 123, no. 3 (July 1999), 177–199.

3. "E. Rushton's Letter to T Paine, on the Slave-trade," *Belfast Monthly Magazine* 3, no. 17 (December 31, 1809), 417–419. The anonymous author who included the

contents of Rushton's letter noted that he had received a copy from Rushton in 1807, but it is unclear when Rushton originally wrote it.

4. "Biographical Sketch of Edward Rushton, Written By His Son," *Belfast Monthly Magazine* 13, no. 77 (December 31, 1814), 474–478. See also Betty Fladeland, *Abolitionists and Working-Class Problems in the Age of Industrialization* (Baton Rouge: Louisiana State University Press, 1984), 20–27, passim.

5. Fladeland, *Abolitionists and Working-Class Problems, 26*; John Epps, *The Life of Thomas Walker* (London, 1832), quoted in Lynch, "The Limits of Revolutionary Radicalism," 196.

6. Mercure Conway's late-nineteenth-century biography of Paine, while a valuable effort to recover and resuscitate the reputation of the then-forgotten founder, undoubtedly bears much of the responsibility for Paine's somewhat undeserved reputation as an abolitionist. See Conway, *The Life of Thomas Paine*, 2 vols. (New York: G. P. Putnam's Sons, 1893). On the relationship between Paine, *The Rights of Man,* cosmopolitan internationalism, and antislavery, see Lynd, *Intellectual Origins*, 130–138. On Paine's birthday celebrations, see *An Oration Delivered in Tammany Hall, in Commemoration of the Birthday of Thomas Paine* (New York: Evans and Brooks, 1832); see also Sean Wilentz, *Chants Democratic: New York City and the Rise of the American Working Class, 1788–1850* (Oxford: Oxford University Press, 1984), 70-74; 153-55; 224-25.

7. Paine, *Rights of Man, Being an Answer to Mr. Burke's Attack on the French Revolution* (London: J. S. Jordan, 1791), 30; Paine, *Rights of Man, Part the Second* (1792), 414; Wilentz, *Chants Democratic*, 70, 224, 335.

8. Foner, *Tom Paine and Revolutionary America*, 214–219. See also Simon P. Newman and Peter S. Onuf, eds., *Paine and Jefferson in the Age of Revolutions* (Charlottesville: University of Virginia Press, 2013); Gregory Claeys, *Thomas Paine: Social and Political Thought* (Boston: Unwin Hyman, 1989); Carine Lounissi, *Thomas Paine and the French Revolution* (London: Palgrave Macmillan, 2018).

9. Cotlar, *Tom Paine's America*, 57–64.

10. "To the Honorable Congress of the United States . . . ," in *Memorials Presented to the Congress of the United States by the Different Societies for Promoting the Abolition of Slavery* (Philadelphia: Francis Bailey, 1792), 23–27; Cotlar, *Tom Paine's America*, 56–57. For an example from the early United States, see Humanitas, "To the Editor of the Chronicle" (notice of formation of the Washington County, Pennsylvania, Society for the Relief of Free Negroes and Others Unlawfully Held in Bondage), *United States Chronicle*, March 18, 1790.

11. "To the Inhabitants of Stamford," *Stamford Mercury*, March 9, 1792; *Philadelphia Daily Advertiser*, September 17, 1791, September 14, 1792; *Dunlap's Daily Advertiser*, June 1, June 15, October 13, 1792; *Hereford Journal*, May 7, 1794; Jean Jacques Dessalines, "Liberty or Death! Proclamation," in *The New Annual Register, or General Repository of History, Politics, and Literature for the Year 1804* (1805), 192–195. The Irish marchers credited the French revolutionary Comte de Mirabeau, at that time associated with the Jacobin faction, for his opposition to the slave trade.

12. James Harrington, *The Commonwealth of Oceana and a System of Politics* (Cambridge: Cambridge University Press, 1992), 34; John Locke, *Second Treatise of Government* (London, 1689), 217; Ashcraft, "Lockean Ideas," in Brewer and Staves, eds., *Early Modern Conceptions*, 43–61; Mandell, *The Lost Tradition*, 14–20, 56–58.

13. On "agrarianism" and the contemporary meanings and uses of the term in the eighteenth- and nineteenth-century Atlantic world, see Thomas P. Govan, "Agrarian and Agrarianism: A Study in the Use and Abuse of Words," *Journal of Southern History* 30, No. 1 (February 1964), 35–36; Arthur E. Bestor, Jr., "The Evolution of the Socialist Vocabulary," *Journal of the History of Ideas* 9, No. 3 (June 1948), 259–302; Cotlar, *Tom Paine's America*, 123–125, 134–135; Mandell, *Lost Tradition*, 104–107.

14. Thomas Gordon, "Of Public Spirit," *Cato's Letters*, 7th ed., 4 vols. (1755; Indianapolis: Liberty Fund, 1995); Jefferson and Webster quoted in James L. Huston, *Securing the Fruits of Labor: The American Concept of Wealth Distribution, 1765–1900* (Baton Rouge: Louisiana State University, 1998), 3, 47; Cotlar, *Tom Paine's America*, 115, 125, 129; Lynd, *Intellectual Origins of American Radicalism*, 34–37.

15. Peter Linebaugh and Marcus Rediker, *The Many-Headed Hydra: Sailors, Slaves, Commoners, and the Hidden History of the Revolutionary Atlantic* (Boston: Beacon Press: 2000), 105–106, 118.

16. Sharp chaired a meeting of the Constitutional Society in which excerpts from Paine's *Rights of Man* were read aloud. See "Trial of John Horne Tooke," *Northampton Mercury*, November 22, 1794.

17. On the ideology of the LCS, see *To the Parliament and People of Great Britain, an Explicit Declaration of the Principles and Views of the London Corresponding Society* (London: Citizen Lee, 1795); *Account of the Proceedings of a Meeting of the London Corresponding Society, Held in a Field Near Copenhagen House, Monday, Oct. 26, 1795* (London: Printed for Citizen Lee, at the Tree of Liberty); Gregory Claeys, "Introduction," in Claeys, ed., *The Politics of English Jacobinism*, xiii–lix; Thompson, *Making of the English Working Class*, 152–157, passim. John Binns, an LCS member who later emigrated to the U.S., recalled that the group's membership was made up primarily of "small shopkeepers, artisans, mechanics, and labourers," while "Citizen Groves," a government spy, reported that a larger number came from "the very lowest order of society." See E. P. Thompson, *Making of the English Working Class* (New York: Vintage Books, 1966), 153.

18. James Walvin, "The Impact of Slavery on British Radical Politics: 1787–1838," in Vera Rubin and Arthur Tuden, eds., *Comparative Perspectives on Slavery in New World Plantation Societies* (New York: New York Academy of Sciences, 1977), 44–45.

19. *Memoir of Thomas Hardy, Founder of, and Secretary to, the London Corresponding Society* . . . (London: James Ridgway, 1832), 102, quoted in Walvin, "The Impact of Slavery on British Radical Politics," 344; Hardy to unnamed British Corresponding Society, April 14, 1792, quoted in Cotlar, *Tom Paine's America*, 57.

20. Ryan Hanley, *Beyond Slavery and Abolition: Black British Writing, c. 1770–1830* (Cambridge: Cambridge University Press, 2019), 13–22, 71, 180–187; Nini Rodgers,

"Equiano in Belfast: A Study of the Anti-Slavery Ethos in a Northern Town," *Slavery and Abolition* 18, no. 2 (1997), 73–89.

21. Thomas Hardy to "Reverend Sir" [Thomas Bryant], London, March 8, 1792, in *Memoir of Thomas Hardy*, 14–15; William Hodgson, *The Commonwealth of Reason* (London: 1795). An earlier version of the letter retains Hardy's less literate, but probably more authentic, spelling and diction. Patricia Hollis has argued that, despite the anti-slavery of early radicals like Hardy, the story of the relationship between abolitionism and British radicalism was essentially one of declension over time. See Hollis, "Anti-Slavery and British Working-Class Radicalism in the Years of Reform," in Christine Bolt and Seymour Drescher, eds., *Anti-Slavery, Religion and Reform: Essays in Memory of Roger Anstey* (London: William Dawson & Sons, 1980), 294–315.

22. Gerrald held memberships in both the SCI and the LCS. For examples of Britons and other Europeans as "slaves," see [Thomas Hardy and Maurice Margarot], "Address to the French National Convention," September 27, 1792, reprinted in *The Sun*, December 5, 1794, D. McPherson [Poem on Thomas Hardy] on frontispiece to Hardy, *Memoir of Thomas Hardy* (London, 1832); "A Friend," *Authentic Biographical Anecdotes of Joseph Gerrald, a Delegate to the British Convention in Scotland from the London Corresponding Society* (London: Daniel Isaac Eaton, 1795). On the British Convention, see Kenneth R. Johnston, "The First and Last British Convention," *Romanticism* 13, no. 2 (2007), 119.

23. On the origins of white slavery language, see Roediger, *The Wages of Whiteness*, especially 19–40 and 65–92; Peck, "Labor Abolition and the Politics of White Victimhood"; Peck, "White Slavery and Whiteness; Ryan Hanley, "Slavery and the Birth of Working-Class Racism in England, 1814–1833, *Transactions of the Royal Historical Society* 26 (December 2016), 103–123; Hanley, "Slavery and the British Working Class, 1787–1833," paper read at the British History in the Long Eighteenth Century Seminar, Institute for Historical Research, Senate House, London, February 2, 2017.

24. Paine, *Rights of Man;* Samuel Johnson, *Taxation No Tyranny* (London, 1775). I have borrowed the phrase "gold standard of oppression" from James Oakes; see Oakes, "The New Cult of Consensus," *nonsite* 20 (January 25, 2017), https://nonsite.org/the -new-cult-of-consensus, accessed March 13, 2020.

25. "A Friend to the West India Colonies, and Their Inhabitants" [James Tobin], Cursory Remarks Upon the Reverend Mr. Ramsay's Essay on the Treatment and Conversion of African Slaves in the Sugar Colonies (London: G. and T. Wilkie, 1785), 69, 85–90; William Beckford, *Remarks Upon the Situation of Negroes in Jamaica, Impartially made from local experience of nearly thirteen years in that island* (London: 1788); Hanley, "Slavery and the British Working Class," 5–9. Tobin's rebuttal to Ramsay proved the occasion for a pamphlet war between the abolitionist and the slave owner that prefigured the "wage slavery" debates between Garrisonians and labor reformers in the 1840s, with the famed abolitionist Thomas Clarkson as well as the former slaves turned Afro-British abolitionists Ottobah Cugoano and Olaudah Equiano all weighing in over the rest of the 1780s.

26. "A Plain Man, who signed the petition at Derby," *The True State of the Question, Addressed to the Petitioners for the Abolition of the Slave Trade* (London: J. Bell, 1792), 4–5, 13. As Hanley points out, Bell's "class ventriloquism" mirrored the approach of groups like the antiradical Loyalist Association, which directed tracts against Paine and Jacobinism to working-class audiences. See Hanley, "Slavery and the British Working Class," 15, n28.

27. M. J. D. Roberts, "The Society for the Suppression of Vice and Its Early Critics, 1802–1812," *Historical Journal* 26, no. 1 (March 1983), 159–176; Hanley, "Slavery and the Birth of Working-Class Racism," 116.

28. Davis, *The Problem of Slavery in the Age of Revolution*, 364–365; Patrick Rael, *Eighty-Eight Years: The Long Death of Slavery in the United States, 1777–1865* (Athens: University of Georgia Press, 2015), 108–109; Sinha, *The Slave's Cause*, 101–103. Robin Blackburn provides a detailed account of the impact of the Napoleonic Wars on British abolitionism, but concludes that they ultimately "boosted the strategic case for abolition." Blackburn, *The American Crucible: Slavery, Emancipation, and Human Rights* (London: Verso, 2011), 221–28.

29. Hanley, *Beyond Slavery and Abolition*, 220–221; Hanley, "Slavery and the Birth of Working-Class Racism in England," 116; E. P. Thompson, *The Making of the English Working Class* (New York: Vintage Books, 1963), 103–105, 146; Roberts, "The Society for the Suppression of Vice."

30. "Slaves to Common People," *Tribune* 167 (1795); "Letter I. Introductory Remarks; On the Spirit and Temper of Burke's Letters on the Prospect of a Regicide Peace," in Thelwall, *Rights of Nature, against the Usurpations of Establishments. A Series of Letters to the People, in Reply to the False Principles of Burke. Part the Second* (London and Norwich: H. D. Symonds and J. March, 1796), in Claeys, ed., *The Politics of English Jacobinism*, 478.

31. "To Dr. Joseph Priestley. Address of the Republican Natives of Great-Britain and Ireland, Resident in the City of New York," [New York] *Diary*, June 14, 1794; Priestley to the Republican Natives, in the [New York] *Daily Advertiser*, June 16, 1794. Priestley had published an antislavery *Sermon on the Subject of the Slave Trade* in 1788. On Binns and Branagan, see Padraig Riley, *Slavery and the Democratic Consciousness: Political Life in Jeffersonian America* (Philadelphia: University of Pennsylvania Press, 2015), 61–71, 73–79, passim.

32. Thomas Yarrow, *An Oration Delivered at Mount-Pleasant, State of New-York, on the Fourth of July, 1798* (Mount Pleasant, NY: William Durell, 1798); *American Universal Magazine*, December 5, 1797, quoted in Seth Cotlar, *Tom Paine's America*, 152.

33. The *Aurora* warned readers that if competition in an unregulated market for wages reduced skilled workers to poverty, the result would be the creation of "a breed of *white slaves*" who would take the places of formerly enslaved Blacks, then completing the process of acquiring freedom under the terms of Pennsylvania's 1780 Gradual Emancipation Act. The decision in *Commonwealth v. Pullis*, declared the shoemakers' strike a criminal conspiracy and sentenced eight members of the Federal Society of Journeyman

Cordwainers to fines that bankrupted their union. The decision left the status of labor unions in a precarious legal position until it was partially overturned by *Commonwealth v. Hunt* (1842). See Thomas Lloyd, *The Trial of the Boot & Shoemakers of Philadelphia* (Philadelphia: B. Graves, 1806), 130; Commons, et al., *A Documentary History of American Industrial Society, Vol.* III, 6; Ronald Schultz, *The Republic of Labor: Philadelphia Artisans and the Politics of Class, 1720–1830* (New York: Oxford University Press, 1993), 153–154. Lloyd's notes on the trial, taken in shorthand and later published, are the only surviving documentary evidence of this landmark labor decision.

34. Iain McCalman, ed., *The Horrors of Slavery and Other Writings by Robert Wedderburn* (Princeton, NJ: Markus Weiner, 1991); Wedderburn quoted in Hanley, *Beyond Slavery and Abolition*, 213–215, 232.

35. Ryan Hanley, "A Radical Change of Heart: Robert Wedderburn's Last Word on Slavery," *Slavery & Abolition* 37, no. 2 (2016), 1–23.

36. Thelwall, "The Connection between the CALAMITIES," in Claeys, ed., *The Politics of English Jacobinism*, 285–292; Ottobah Cugoano, *Thoughts and Sentiments on the Evil and Wicked Traffic of the Slavery and Commerce of the Human Species* (London, 1787); Hanley, *Beyond Slavery and Abolition*, 184–187; Claeys, ed., *The Politics of English Jacobinism*, 285–297. Thelwall's contention that anti–slave trade sentiment was "almost unanimous" among the British public was an exaggeration, but evidence suggests that large numbers of ordinary Britons in the 1790s were opposed to the trade. In 1792, a total of 519 anti–slave trade petitions were sent to Parliament containing as many as four hundred thousand signatures—an estimated 5 percent of the British population of around 8 million in 1790 (if counting only adult males, the proportion grows to nearly 13 percent). Many of these came from the new industrial centers where growing numbers of unskilled laborers and operatives toiled in factories, many of them churning out textiles spun from cotton, an increasing although not yet dominant portion of it grown by American slaves. See Rael, *Eighty-Eight Years*, 108.

37. John Locke, *Second Treatise of Government* (London, 1689), 217; Ashcraft, "Lockean Ideas," in John Brewer and Susan Staves, eds., *Early Modern Conceptions of Property*, 43–61; Mandell, *Lost Tradition*, 14–20, 56–58.

38. Thomas Paine, *Agrarian Justice*, in M. Beer, ed., *The Pioneers of Land Reform: Thomas Spence, William Ogilvie, Thomas Paine* (London: G. Bell and Sons, 1920), 185, 194–199.

39. Gregory Claeys, "Paine's Agrarian Justice and the Secularization of National Jurisprudence," *Bulletin of the Society for Labour History* 52, no. 3 (November 1987), 21–31; Claeys, ed., *Social and Political Thought*, 33, 198, 200, 202; Lynd, *Intellectual Origins*, 74–77; Eric Foner, *Tom Paine*, 94–95, 100, 105–106, 249–251; Brent Ranalli, "Thomas Paine's Neglected Pamphlet: *Agrarian Justice*" (unpublished essay), 5, 8–9. On struggles over land and their significance for wage earners and laborers in the Early American Republic, see Reeve Huston, "Land Conflict and Land Policy, 1785–1841," in Andrew Shankman, ed., *The World of the Revolutionary American Republic: Land, Labor, and the Conflict for a Continent* (New York: Routledge, 2014), 324–345.

40. Cotlar, *Tom Paine's America*, 117–119, 125, 129, 156; A Pennsylvanian [Benjamin Rush], *An Address to the Inhabitants of the British Settlements in America Upon Slave-Keeping* (Philadelphia, 1773), 7; St. George Tucker, *Cautionary Hints to Congress Respecting the Sale of the Western Lands Belonging to the United States* (Philadelphia: Matthew Carey, 1796); Tucker, *A dissertation on slavery, with a proposal for the gradual abolition of it, in the state of Virginia* (Philadelphia: Printed for Matthew Carey, 1796); Mandell, *Lost Tradition*, 104–105. On Native American ideas of property and landholding and their influence on Euro-Americans, see Mandell, *Lost Tradition*, 32–55.

41. Thomas Spence, "Conclusion," in *The Rights of Infants* (London: 1796). Spence's ideas were described by a contemporary as "another *Rights of Man* . . . that goes farther than Paine's," and his *Rights of Infants*, which proposed an early form of universal basic income drawn from the proceeds of socialized lands, was intended as an answer to Paine's *Agrarian Justice*.

42. *The Axe Laid to Root or a Fatal Blow to Oppressors, Being an Address to the Planters and Negroes of the Island of Jamaica*, no. 1 (1817), in McCalman, *The Horrors of Slavery*, 81–87; Hanley, *Beyond Slavery and Abolition*, 203–239.

43. Table II, in Sharon V. Salinger, "Artisans, Journeymen, and the Transformation of Labor in Late-Eighteenth Century Philadelphia, *William and Mary Quarterly* 40, no. 1 (January 1983), 67; Gary B. Nash, "Slaves and Slaveowners in Colonial Philadelphia," *William and Mary Quarterly* 30, no. 2 (April 1973), 223–256; Gary B. Nash and Jean R. Soderlund, *Freedom by Degrees: Emancipation in Pennsylvania and Its Aftermath* (New York: Oxford University Press, 1991), 115–118.

44. Cotlar, *Tom Paine's America*, 19, 33, 57–60.

45. William Duane, *A Letter to George Washington, President of the United States . . .* (Philadelphia, 1796), 46–48; *Aurora*, September 24, 1800, December 23, 1806; Duane to Thomas Jefferson, "William Duane's Notes on the Expediency of Using Black Troops" (enclosure, ca. August 11, 1814), Thomas Jefferson Papers, National Archives Founders Online, https://founders.archives.gov/?q=Author%3A%22Duane%2C%20William%22 &s=1111311111&r=69, accessed May 18, 2020.

46. Kim T. Phillips, "William Duane, Philadelphia's Democratic-Republicans, and the Origins of Modern Politics," *Pennsylvania Magazine of History and Biography* (1977), 370, 384–386. For other examples of Duane's "producerism" and ideas on political economy, see *Aurora*, December 23, 1806; January 7, 9, 1807.

47. *Aurora*, December 27, 1806.

48. On the attitudes of political parties and factions toward slavery, antislavery, and Black voting in the Early National period, see Van Gosse, *The First Reconstruction*; Riley, *Slavery and the Democratic Consciousness*; Paul J. Polgar, *Standard Bearers of Equality: America's First Abolition Movement* (Williamsburg, VA: Omohundro Institute of Early American History and Culture, 2019); Sarah Gronningsater, "'Expressly Recognized by Our Election Laws': Certificates of Freedom and the Multiple Fates of Black Citizenship in the Early Republic," *William and Mary Quarterly* 75, no. 3 (July 2018); David Waldstreicher and Stephen R. Grossbart, "Abraham Bishop's Vocation: or, the Mediation of

Jeffersonian Politics," *Journal of the Early Republic* 18, no. 4 (Winter 1998), 617–657; Ingersoll, "Riches and Honour Were Rejected By Them as Loathsome Vomit: The Fear of Leveling in New England," in Carla Gardina Pestana and Sharon V. Salinger, eds., *Inequality in Early America* (Hanover, NH: University Press of New England, 1999), 60–61. As Ingersoll points out, Federalists were not above resorting to racialized depictions that stigmatized the democratic leanings of the Democratic-Republicans as leading to an unnatural blurring of racial and class hierarchies.

49. Riley, *Slavery and the Democratic Consciousness*, 235–236.

Chapter 2

1. "W" (Samuel Whitcomb) to the Editor, *Liberator*, January 29, 1831.

2. *Liberator*, January 29, February 5, 1831.

3. Among the many important works to engage with these questions are Davis, *The Problem of Slavery*; Bender, ed., *The Antislavery Debate*; Eric Foner, *Politics and Ideology*; Jonathan Glickstein, "'Poverty Is Not Slavery': American Abolitionists and the Competitive Labor Market," in Lewis Perry and Michael Fellman, eds., *Antislavery Reconsidered: New Perspectives on the Abolitionists* (Baton Rouge: Louisiana State University Press, 1979), 195–218; Marcus Cunliffe, *Chattel Slavery and Wage Slavery: The Anglo-American Context, 1830–1860* (Athens: University of Georgia Press, 1979); Drescher, *Capitalism and Antislavery*. See also Manisha Sinha's retrospective on David Brion Davis and the "Davis thesis," in her review essay on *The Problem of Slavery in the Age of Revolution, 1770–1823, American Historical Review*.

4. Table 4.1: Cotton Production in the United States, in Edward E. Baptist, *The Half Has Never Been Told: Slavery and the Making of American Capitalism* (New York: Basic Books, 2014), 114.

5. Thomas Dublin, *Women at Work: The Transformation of Work and Community in Lowell, Massachusetts, 1826–1860* (New York: Columbia University Press, 1979), 98–99, 127; Dublin, "Women, Work, and Protest in the Early Lowell Mills: 'The Oppressing Hand of Avarice Would Enslave Us,'" in Neil Shumsky, ed., *The Working Class and Its Culture* (New York: Routledge, 1996), 127–145; Roediger, *The Wages of Whiteness*, 69, 71, 82–84.

6. On the role of whiteness and white supremacy in the period, see Roediger, *The Wages of Whiteness*; Saxton, *The Rise and Fall of the White Republic*, 153–154; Ignatiev, *How the Irish Became White*.

7. The phrase "gentlemen of property and standing" was a common trope in antebellum literature used to refer to the upper- and upper-middle-class men who often comprised the civic leadership of American cities and towns. It was frequently adopted by abolitionists who wanted to make a point about the class background of many of the leaders of antiabolition riots. See Leonard L. Richards, *Gentlemen of Property and Standing: Anti-Abolition Mobs in Jacksonian America* (New York: Oxford University Press, 1970).

8. For examples of references to British "factory slavery" in this period, see Thompson, *The Making of the English Working Class*, 681–691, 696–697, 709–710; Drescher,

"Cart Whip and Billy Roller: Antislavery and Reform Symbolism in Industrializing Britain," *Journal of Social History* 15, no. 1 (Autumn 1981), 3–24; Hollis, in Bolt and Drescher, eds., *Anti-Slavery, Religion and Reform*; Hanley, "Slavery and the British Working Class, 1787–1833."

9. William Cobbett, *Rural Rides* (London, 1830), 262; Cobbett, *Cobbett's Legacy to Labourers* (London, 1835); Speech of William Cobbett, in HC Deb 18 March 1833 vol. 16 cc729–30, https://api.parliament.uk/historic-hansard/commons/1833/mar/18/abolition-of-slavery#S3V0016P0_18330318_HOC_26; John Brown, *A Memoir of Robert Blincoe, An Orphan Boy . . .* (1828); *The Lion* I, no. 5 (1828), 145; "White and Black Slavery Contrasted," *Working Man's Friend and Political Magazine*, February 2, 1833; Hanley, *Transactions of the Royal Historical Society* 26 (December 2016),121–122. For an example of Cobbett's influence on American labor radicals, see Thomas Brothers, ed., *Nineteen Numbers of the Radical Reformer, and Working Man's Advocate* (Philadelphia: Coates, 1836).

10. John R. Commons, ed., *History of Labour in the United States*, Vol. 1 (New York: Macmillan, 1918), 285–301; Joshua Greenberg, "Radicalism in the Age of Jackson," in Sean Patrick Adams, ed., *A Companion to the Era of Andrew Jackson* (Chichester, UK: Wiley-Blackwell, 2013), 412–432.

11. Seth Luther, *Address to Working Men of New England, on the State of Education, and On the Condition of the Producing Classes in Europe and America* (New York: George H. Evans, 1833); see also the (Boston) *New England Artisan and Farmer's, Mechanic's, and Laboring Man's Repository*, September 5, October 10, 1833; the "coffin handbill" was quoted in the *Commercial Advertiser*, June 7, 1836. Luther's "Ten Hour Circular," one of the most important documents of the early labor movement, was notable for its use of "wage slavery" metaphors, but elsewhere, Luther evinced sympathy with a Black man he encountered in prison, describing him as an "equal." See Luther, *An Address on the Origin and Progress of Avarice . . .* (Boston, 1834), 31. Examples of wage slavery and white slavery metaphors in labor periodicals are too numerous to mention, but for a representative sampling, see (Providence, Rhode Island) *New England Artisan, and Laboring Man's Repository*, June 7, 1832; (Boston) *New England Artisan and Farmer's, Mechanic's, and Laboring Man's Repository* (from the *Religious Enquirer*), August 1, 1833; (Woodstock, Vermont) *Working Man's Gazette* (from the *Genius of Universal Emancipation*) September 23, 1830; "Who Are the Slaves," "A Democrat of the Old School" to the editor of the *Working Man's Gazette*, May 3, 1831. On laborers' responses to economic changes in this period, including the ideology of "artisan republicanism," see Sean Wilentz, *Chants Democratic: New York City and the Rise of the American Working Class, 1788–1850* (Oxford: Oxford University Press, 1984); Schultz, *The Republic of Labor*; Bruce Laurie, *Working People of Philadelphia, 1800–1850* (Philadelphia: Temple University Press, 1980).

12. Maria W. Stewart, "Lecture Delivered at the Franklin Hall, Boston, September 21, 1832," in *Meditations from the Pen of Maria W. Stewart* (Washington, 1879), 55–59.

13. Langton Byllesby, *Observations on the Sources and Effects of Unequal Wealth* (New York: 1826), 50–51.

14. "Difference Between a Free Laborer and a Slave. To the Free Laboring Men and Women of the United States" ("Truth Teller" to the editors of the *Liberator*), December 1, 1837; "Manifest of the Principles of the Working Men of New York," (Boston) *Working Man's Advocate*, January 22, 1831.

15. *Investigator*, May 29, 1829; "Worse Than Negro Slavery?" and "A Seasonable Hint," *Emancipator*, January 29, 1834; "What They Would Do If They Could. Addressed to the Free Laborers of the United States," *Emancipator*, December 1835; Jonathan A. Glickman, "The Chattelization of Northern Whites: An Evolving Abolitionist Warning," *American Nineteenth Century History* 4, no. 1 (Spring 2003), 25–58; Paul Goodman, *Of One Blood: Abolitionists and the Origins of Racial Equality* (Berkeley: University of California Press, 1998), 69–80.

16. *Philanthropist*, January 1, 1836; *Philanthropist*, quoted in the *Liberator*, February 4, 1837; "An Operative" to the editor of *American Manufacturer*, in the *New England Artisan and Farmer's, Mechanic's, and Laboring Man's Repository*, February 23, 1833; "Who Are the Slaves?" (Woodstock, VT) *Working Man's Gazette*, May 3, 1831; *Proceedings of the Rhode Island Anti-Slavery Convention*, 40, quoted in Goodman, *Of One Blood*, 155–156. See also *Friend of Man*, December 1 and 22, 1836.

17. On the ways that nineteenth-century Americans understood the relationship between property rights, commodification, and slavery, see James Oakes, *Slavery and Freedom: An Interpretation of the Old South* (New York: W. W. Norton, 1990), 43–45, 71–72; Amy Dru Stanley, *From Bondage to Contract: Wage Labor, Marriage, and the Market in the Era of Slave Emancipation* (Chicago: University of Chicago Press, 1998). On the importance of the "chattel principle" for both abolitionists and historians, see Moses Finley, "Between Slavery and Freedom," *Comparative Studies in Society and History* 6, no. 3 (1964).

18. Samuel Whitcomb, unpublished speech, n.d., p. 3, Folder 4, Samuel Whitcomb Papers, Massachusetts Historical Society; Whitcomb, *Two Lectures on the Advantages of a Republican System of Society, For the Promotion of the Arts, and the Cultivation of Science* (Boston: Marsh, Capen, & Lyon, 1833), 3.

19. *Antislavery Quarterly* 2 (October, 1836), 61–73, quoted in Goodman, *Of One Blood*, 156; Quincy quoted on 141.

20. Ronald Schultz, "Small Producer Thought in Early America, Part I: Philadelphia Artisans and Price Control," *Pennsylvania History: A Journal of Mid-Atlantic Studies* 54, no. 2 (April 1987), 115–147.

21. "A Fellow Laborer" (William Heighton), *Address to the Members of Trade Societies, and to the Working Classes Generally . . .* (Philadelphia, 1827), 17–22. See also, "Competition," *Mechanic's Free Press*, February 20, 1830; May 8, 1830. On Heighton, see Edward Pessen, *Most Uncommon Jacksonians: The Radical Leaders of the Early Labor Movement* (Albany: State University of New York Press), 12–14, passim; Laurie, *Working People of Philadelphia*, 75–76; Sean Wilentz, *The Rise of American Democracy: Jefferson to Lincoln* (New York: W. W. Norton, 2005), 282–286, 357–358, 794. Laurie describes

Heighton as "the most influential working-class activist and intellectual" in Philadelphia in the 1820s and early '30s.

22. *Mechanic's Free Press*, April 24, 1830.

23. "The Dying Slave" (from the *Genius of Universal Emancipation*), *Mechanic's Free Press*, June 26, 1830; "The Slave" (Robert Dale Owen), March 27, 1830; "Liberty and Slavery," January 17, 1829; unattributed story, November 8, 1829; "Horrors of the Slave Trade," November 7, 1829 (from the Plymouth, UK, *Journal*); untitled article on the slave trade to Brazil, and editorial on the domestic slave trade from the (Wheeling, Va.) *Eclectic Observer, and Working People's Advocate*, both January 9, 1830; "Slave Traders" (from the *American Spectator*), June 11, 1830.

24. "Biography" (from *Journal of the Times*), *Mechanic's Free Press*, January 3, 1829; May 30; June 5, 1830. The letter writer was Simon Snyder, Jr., son of the former Democratic-Republican governor of Pennsylvania.

25. Simon Snyder, Jr., to Messrs. Editors, *Mechanic's Free Press*, June 5, 1830.

26. Letter to the Editors, from "Vertical," *Mechanic's Free Press*, January 10, 1829.

27. "Freedom and Slavery" (from the Boston *Working Man's Advocate*); "Slave Traders" (from *American Spectator*), both in *Mechanic's Free Press*, September 11, 1830. David Roediger, citing Bernard Mandel, uses this source to suggest that Heighton and *Mechanic's Free Press* endorsed wage slavery claims and that this example was the "first such direct and significant" comparison between free labor and slavery in the American labor movement, without noting either the article's origin in a different labor newspaper or the article condemning the slave trade that followed it. Roediger, *Wages of Whiteness*, 77.

28. The literature on abolitionism and Protestant religious convictions is well-known, and too vast to be included here. On the Second Great Awakening and workers, see John B. Jentz, *Artisans, Evangelicals, and the City: A Social History of Abolition and Labor Reform in Jacksonian New York* (PhD diss., City University of New York, 1977).

29. Unsigned letter to the editor, *Mechanic's Free Press*, August 23, 1828; "Mahometan and Christian Slavery," *Mechanic's Free Press*, July 5, 1828.

30. "A New York Negro and a Kentuckian" (reprinted from the *New York Constellation*), "Anecdote," both in *Mechanic's Free Press*, November 13, 1830. Heighton told an audience of workingmen that "when we consider drinking, gaming, and frolicking as our highest enjoyments, we shall never obtain any useful knowledge, nor hold a rank in society but little above the African slave." See The Unlettered Mechanic [William Heighton], *An Address, Delivered Before the Mechanics and Working Classes Generally* . . . (Philadelphia, 1827), 1.

31. *Liberator*, January 29, 1831 (clipping with Whitcomb's manuscript signature printed under his letter), Samuel Whitcomb Papers, Massachusetts Historical Society.

32. "Memorial to Congress," *Mechanic's Free Press*, October 25, 1828; in John R. Commons and Helen L. Sumner, eds., *A Documentary History of American Industrial Society* V, pt. 1 (Cleveland: Arthur Clark, 1910), 43–45. See also the series of open letters

"To Industrious Mechanics who possess small available capitals," *Mechanic's Free Press*, May 22, 29, June 5, 12, 1830.

33. *Mechanic's Free Press*, May 22, 29, 1830. On the Philadelphia Working Men's demands for publicly funded education, see "The Report of the Working Men's Committee," *Working Man's Advocate*, March 6, 1830 (reprinted from the *Mechanic's Free Press*), in Commons and Sumner, *A Documentary History* V, 94–107.

34. Eva Sheppard Wolf, "Early Free-Labor Thought and the Contest over Slavery in the Early Republic," in John Craig Hammond and Matthew Mason, eds., *Contesting Slavery: The Politics of Bondage and Freedom in the New American Nation* (Charlottesville: University of Virginia Press, 2011), 32–48; Andrew Shankman, "Neither Infinite Wretchedness nor Positive Good: Matthew Carey and Henry Clay on Political Economy and Slavery During the Long 1820s," in Hammond and Mason, 247–267; Esther Lowenthal, *The Ricardian Socialists* (New York: Columbia University Press, 1911).

35. A Yankee [Stephen Simpson], *A Glance at the Times. Including an Appeal for the Greeks, &c. In a Poetical Epistle Addressed to De Witt Clinton. Part I* (Philadelphia: Richard R. Small, 1827), 12; Edward Pessen, "The Ideology of Stephen Simpson, Underclass Champion of the Early Philadelphia Workingmen's Movement," *Pennsylvania History* 22, no. 4 (October 1955), 328–340; Pessen, *Uncommon Jacksonians*, 75–79, 105–108; Wilentz, *Rise of American Democracy*, 211–213, passim; Alex Gourevitch, *From Slavery to the Cooperative Commonwealth: Labor and Republican Liberty in the Nineteenth Century* (Cambridge: Cambridge University Press, 2015), 87–88.

36. Stephen Simpson, *The Working Man's Manual: A New Theory of Political Economy* (Philadelphia: Thomas L. Bonsal, 1831), 15–17, 85–86, 135.

37. Simpson, *The Working Man's Manual*, 15n, 16–17, 30–31, 49, 85–86, 135; *Mechanic's Free Press*, December 4, 1830; Samuel Whitcomb, Jr., *An Address Before the Working-Men's Society of Dedham, Delivered on the Evening of September 7, 1831* (Dedham, MA: L. Powers, 1831), 7–8.

38. New York *Morning Courier*, April 25, 30, 1829; *Working Man's Advocate*, October 31, 1829; Commons and Sumner, *A Documentary History* V, pt. 1, 146–156; Wilentz, *Chants Democratic*, 191–194; George Henry Evans, "History of the Origins and Progress of the Working Men's Party of New York," *Radical*, January 1842. The last quote from the report is from Evans's history of the New York Working Men in the *Radical*, February 1843.

39. Thomas Skidmore, *The Right of Man to Property! Being a Proposition to Make it Equal Among the Adults of the Present Generation* (New York: Alexander Ming, Jr., 1829). Although several historians have evinced a fascination with Skidmore and his proposal for wealth redistribution, few have paid serious attention to his antislavery proposals. See Wilentz, *Chants Democratic*, 184–188; Gourevitch, *From Slavery to the Cooperative Commonwealth*, 78–82.

40. Gregory Claeys, ed., *A New View of Society and Other Writings* (New York: Penguin Books, 1991), 1–10; Arthur Bestor, *Backwoods Utopias: The Sectarian Origins and*

the Owenite Phase of Communitarian Socialism in America: 1663–1829 (Philadelphia: University of Pennsylvania Press, 1950), 96, n 9; Robert Owen, *Discourses on a New System of Society as Delivered in the Hall of Representatives of the United States* (Lexington, KY: 1825), quoted in Holly Jackson, *American Radicals: How Nineteenth-Century Protest Shaped the Nation* (New York: Crown Books, 2019), 23; John Gray, *A Lecture on Human Happiness, To Which Is Added a Preamble and Constitution of the Friendly Association for Mutual Interests, to be Located in Valley Forge, Pennsylvania* (Philadelphia: J. Coates, Jr., 1826). Reynolds's *Equality* was published in the *Temple of Reason*, a Deist weekly published by another radical Irish immigrant, Denis Driscoll, in 1802.

41. Skidmore, *Rights of Man to Property!*, 4–5, 15, 24–25, 205, 227, 231, 239, 249, 255, 272, 333, 337, 382, 388.

42. Ibid., 54–55, 269–271.

43. Ibid., 54–55, 58–59, 158, 270–271.

44. On Wright's career as a radical and sometime antislavery activist, see Jackson, *American Radicals*, 6–12, 24–46, passim; Celia Morris Eckhardt, *Fanny Wright: Rebel in America* (Cambridge, MA: Harvard University Press, 1984), 182–191, 216–220; Wilentz, *Chants Democratic*, 176–183; Sean Griffin, "Antislavery Utopias: Communitarian Labor Reform and the Abolitionist Movement," *Journal of the Civil War Era* 8, no. 2 (June 2018), 243–268; Gail Bederman, "Revisiting Nashoba: Slavery, Utopia, and Frances Wright in America, 1818–1826," *American Literary History* 17, no. 3 (Autumn 2005), 438–459.

45. On the Cook faction of Working Men, see Wilentz, *Chants Democratic*, 189–190; for the occupational breakdown of the various factions of New York Working Men, see Table 18, 409. Significantly, Evans sided with the Owen-Wright faction in the dispute. Wilentz, *Chants Democratic*, 180–183, 192–208; Commons and Sumner, *Documentary History* V, pt. 1, 149–182. Evans's connections to Owenite reform are explained in chapter 4.

46. *Evening Journal*, December 30, 1829; *Morning Courier and New York Enquirer*, November 4, 1829; Wilentz, *Chants Democratic*, 203. Skidmore claimed, and Wilentz seems to support the conclusion, that George Henry Evans played a role in writing the handbill. See also "To the Mechanics and Working-Men of the Fifth Ward, and those friendly to their Interests" (New York: n.d.), which informed voters that "*Infidelity* and *Agrarianism*" were the "leading principles" of the Owen-Wright faction.

47. Wilentz, *Chants Democratic*, 209–210. On the rise and fall of the New York Working Men, see Wilentz, *Rise of American Democracy, 353–355;* H. (Hobart) W. Berrian, *Brief Sketch of the Origin and Rise of the Workingmen's Party* (Washington, DC, 1840?); George Henry Evans, "History of the Origin and Progress of the Working Men's Party in New York," in the *Radical*, January 1842–April 1843.

48. On the 1834 riots, see Richards, *Gentlemen of Property and Standing*; Linda Kerber, "Abolitionists and Amalgamators: The New York City Race Riots of 1834," *New York History* 48 (January 1967), 28–39. On the Utica riot and Gerrit Smith's reaction, see

John Stauffer, *The Black Hearts of Men: Radical Abolitionists and the Transformation of Race* (Cambridge, MA: Harvard University Press, 2001), 100–101.

49. *History of Pennsylvania Hall* (Merrihew and Gunn, 1838), 6; Lewis C. Gunn, *Address to Abolitionists* (Philadelphia: Merrihew and Gunn, 1838), 4; *Minutes of Proceedings of the Requited Labor Convention* (Philadelphia: Merrihew and Gunn, 1838). Gunn's speech was also published in the convention's minutes, pp. 22–36. See also Carol Faulkner, "The Root of Evil: Free Produce and Radical Antislavery, 1820–1860," *Journal of the Early Republic* 27, no. 3 (Fall 2007), 377–405.

50. Richards, *Gentlemen of Property and Standing*, 113–122, 152–155; [William Goodell], "Hints on Anti-Abolition Mobs," *Anti-Slavery Record* II, no. 7 (July 1836); "Why Do the Aristocratic Encourage Mobs?" *Emancipator*, July 1836. See also Goodell, *Slavery and Anti-Slavery; A History of the Great Struggle in Both Hemispheres; with a View of the Slavery Question in the United States* (New York: William Harned, 1852), 407.

51. Thomas Brothers, ed., *Nineteen Numbers of the Radical Reformer*, 271; "Speech of David Paul Brown," in *History of Pennsylvania Hall* (Philadelphia: Merrihew and Gunn, 1838), 23. Brothers was, to say the least, a paradoxical figure; a master hatmaker, he repudiated radicalism and democracy after returning to Britain, an about-face occasioned in part by his disgust with American hypocrisy over slavery. See Brothers, *The United States of North America as They Are; Not as They are Generally Described: Being a Cure for Radicalism* (London: 1840); Edward Pessen, "Thomas Brothers: Anti-Capitalist Employer," *Pennsylvania History* 24, no. 4 (October 1957), 321–330.

52. John B. Jentz, "The Antislavery Constituency in Jacksonian New York City," *Civil War History* 27, no. 2 (June 1981), 101–122; Goodman, *Of One Blood*, 142–152; Edward Magdol, *The Antislavery Rank and File: A Social Profile of the Abolitionists' Constituency* (New York: Greenwood, 1986), 61–99, see especially Tables 6.4 through 6.13. Jentz found that at least seventy signers of antislavery petitions collected in New York in the 1830s had participated in the Working Men's Party movement of the previous decade.

53. *The Man*, June 9, July 17, 19, 1834; *Evening Post*, July 8, 1834; Richards, *Gentlemen of Property and Standing*, 113–122. Notably, Evans printed the AASS executive committee's letter with a disclaimer noting his objection to their "measures tending to a union of Church and State," such as the banning of Sunday mail. The *Working Man's Advocate* also printed materials expressing more conventional northern views on slavery, such as a notice of an August 1835 "Meeting in the Park" in which the speakers affirmed the abolitionists' right to free speech while denying that slavery was "in all cases necessarily immoral" and alluding to a constitutional duty of noninterference with the institutions of the South. See "The Slave Question. Meeting in the Park" (from the *New York Transcript*), in *Working Man's Advocate*, August 29, 1835. On the antislavery careers of Evans and Leggett, see Jonathan H. Earle, *Jacksonian Antislavery and the Politics of Free Soil, 1824–1854* (Chapel Hill: North Carolina University Press, 2004), 19–37, passim. For a different interpretation of Evans's views on slavery and race, see Roediger, *Wages of Whiteness*, 77–80.

54. Wilentz, *Chants Democratic*, 197–201, 240; Earle, *Jacksonian Antislavery*, 29–30; *Working Man's Advocate*, October 15, 1831; "The Slave Trade," *The Man*, May 27, 1834; "A Parallel," *The Man*, June 6, 1834; "Effects of Slavery," *Working Man's Advocate*, October 24, 1835; "Slavery," *The Man*, June 9, 1834; "Anti Slavery Society," *Working Man's Advocate*, October 10, 1835; "The Abolitionists," *The Man*, July 19, 1835. In an article mocking the efforts of a "Moral Improvement Association" aimed at young mechanics, Evans opined that "the true path of 'moral improvement'" was "wide enough for every son and daughter of a republican, *without distinction of sex, class, or colour.*" *Mechanic's Free Press* (reprinted from the *Working Man's Advocate*), March 6, 1830.

55. *Working Man's Advocate*, October 1, 15, 1831; Earle, *Jacksonian Antislavery*, 30–32. For Garrison's views on the Turner Rebellion, see *Liberator*, September 3, 10, October 29, November 5, 12, 1831, and Manisha Sinha, *The Slave's Cause*, 219.

56. *Working Man's Advocate*, October 1, 1831.

57. Ibid.; *Working Man's Advocate*, October 15, 1831; *The Man*, June 9, 1834; Earle, *Jacksonian Antislavery*, 33–35. Despite his opposition to the American Colonization Society, Evans continued to publish other authors who endorsed colonization, and later developed his own ideas for a Black colony located within the territorial United States.

58. *Evening Post*, July 8, 1834; September 3, 4, 1835; *Plaindealer*, January 14, February 11, 25, July 29, December 3, 24, 1837; Theodore Sedgwick, ed., *A Collection of the Political Writings of William Leggett*, Vol. 2 (New York: Taylor & Dodd, 1849), 50–55, 327–330.

59. Sean Wilentz, *No Property In Man: Slavery and Antislavery at the Nation's Founding* (Cambridge, MA: Harvard University Press, 2018), 210–222.

60. Earle, *Jacksonian Antislavery*, 23–25; "The Anti-Slavery Society," *Evening Post*, September 9, 1835; "The Power of Congress Over Slavery in the District of Columbia," *Plaindealer*, February 25, 1837; "The Question of Slavery Narrowed to a Point," *Plaindealer*, April 15, 1837; "Abolition Insolence," *Plaindealer*, July 29, 1837. Weld's editorials on slavery in the District of Columbia were published in the *Evening Post* beginning December 28, 1837, and continued throughout early 1838.

61. The *Washington Globe* and the *New York Times* quoted in Fitzwilliam Byrdsall, *The History of the Loco-Foco, or Equal Rights Party, Its Movements, Conventions and Proceedings, with Short Characteristic Sketches of Its Prominent Men* (New York: Clement & Packard, 1842), 18–19, 29. See also the *Liberator* on "Jacobinism," September 8, 1837, May 3, 1839.

62. Byrdsall, *The History*, 20, 32; Earle, *Jacksonian Antislavery*, 25–26.

63. Leggett to Theodore Sedgwick, Jr., October 24, 1838, in Leggett, *Political Writings*, 2: 335–36; Julius Rubens Ames and Benjamin Lundy, *The Legion of Liberty!: And Force of Truth, Containing the Thoughts, Words, and Deeds of Some Apostles, Champions and Martyrs* (New York: American Anti-Slavery Society, 1842), 64; Earle, *Jacksonian Antislavery*, 161–162.

64. Skidmore, *Right of Man to Property!*, 270–271.

65. Morris quoted in Eric Foner, *Free Soil, Free Labor*, 91.

Chapter 3

1. Orestes Brownson, "The Laboring Classes," *Boston Quarterly Review* (July 1840); Albert Brisbane, *Social Destiny of Man: or, Association and Organization of Industry* (Philadelphia: C. F. Stollmeyer, 1840). On Brownson's debates with William Lloyd Garrison, see Sinha, *The Slave's Cause*, 349; Kraditor, *Means and Ends in American Abolitionism*, 235–260. For an abolitionist response to Brownson's class analysis, see "Prospects and Projects of the Democracy," *Emancipator*, December 31, 1840.

2. Carl J. Guarneri, *The Utopian Alternative: Fourierism in Nineteenth-Century America* (Ithaca, NY: Cornell University Press, 1991), 3, 60; see also Tables 1–5 in the appendix, 407–411. On Fourierism's relationship to Transcendentalism, see Guarneri, *Utopian Alternative*, 44–57, 86, 103, 132; Jackson, *American Radicals*, 95–106, 107–122; Peter Wirzbicki, *Fighting for the Higher Law: Black and White Transcendentalists Against Slavery* (Philadelphia: University of Pennsylvania Press, 2021), 102–104, 110, 122–123, passim. Jackson persuasively ascribes some of the impetus for communitarianism to the "come-outer" movements within abolitionist churches; see Jackson, *American Radicals*, 87–94.

3. Important exceptions include Guarneri, *Utopian Alternative*; Clark, *The Communitarian Movement*; and John L. Thomas, "Antislavery and Utopia," in Martin Duberman, ed., *The Antislavery Vanguard: New Essays on the Abolitionists* (Princeton, NJ: Princeton University Press, 1965), 240–269.

4. Friedrich Engels famously distinguished between "utopian" and "scientific" socialism in his 1880 book *Socialism: Utopian and Scientific*. The American Fourierists' somewhat more pragmatic approach was captured by the subtitle of Brisbane's follow-up to *The Social Destiny of Mankind*, 1843's *Association, Or, A Concise Exposition of the Practical Part of Fourier's Social Science* (New York: Greeley and McElrath, 1843).

5. On the Fourierists' criticisms of capitalism and their proposed solutions, see Guarneri, *Utopian Alternative* 10, 65–66, 100–101, 139–140, 283–289, 292–320, 344–345, passim; Jackson, *American Radicals*, 111–122; Mandell, *The Lost Tradition of Economic Equality*, 200–203, 226–227, 249–251; Bestor, *Backwoods Utopias*, 52–59.

6. Charles Dain, ed., *De l'abolition de l'esclavage* (Paris: Bureau de la Phalange, 1836).

7. Bailey quoted in the *Cincinnati Morning Herald*, June 28, 1845. On the schism within the abolitionist movement, see Sinha, *The Slave's Cause*, 256–265, and below. The phrase "genius of integral emancipation" appears in a resolution of the American Union of Associationists, signed by Greeley, Channing, Dana, George Ripley, John S. Dwight, and others; see "Anniversary of the American Union of Associationists," *New-York Tribune*, June 3, 1850. The term may have been inspired by abolitionist Benjamin Lundy's newspaper, *The Genius of Universal Emancipation*.

8. MG 285, Raritan Bay Union and Eagleswood Military Academy Papers, 1809–1923, New Jersey Historical Society; A. J. Macdonald Writings on American Utopian Communities, Yale Beinecke Library, Box 2, Folder 31. See also the Philadelphia *North American*, November 30, 1852, and *Liberator*, March 11, 1853 (advertisement); Thomas, "Antislavery and Utopia," 263. Manisha Sinha has noted that the American Union of Associationists, which aspired to be the national umbrella organization for American

Fourierism, modeled its organizational structure after that of the AASS; see Sinha, *The Slave's Cause*, 355. On Collins, see Sinha, *The Slave's Cause*, 350; Caleb McDaniel, *The Problem of Democracy in an Age of Slavery* (Baton Rouge: Louisiana State University Press, 2013), 147, 153; Lester Grosvenor Wells, "The Skaneateles Communal Experiment, 1843–1846: A Paper Read Before the Onondaga Historical Association, February 13, 1953 (Syracuse, NY: Onondaga Historical Association, 1953).

9. G. W. S. (George W. Stacy) to Edmund Quincy, in the *Liberator*, October 9, 1846.

10. "Social Reform Convention at Boston," *Phalanx* I, January 5, 1844, 46–47; John Humphrey Noyes, *History of American Socialisms* (Philadelphia: J. P. Lippincott, 1870), 161; Frederick Douglass, "What I Found at the Northampton Association," in Charles A. Sheffeld, ed., *The History of Florence, Massachusetts, Including a Complete Account of the Northampton Association of Education and Industry* (Florence, MA: The Editor, 1895), 130; *Cincinnati Morning Herald*, June 28, 1845; Guarneri, *Utopian Alternative*, 25–27, 40–44, 254–255; Thomas, "Antislavery and Utopia," 254–259, 249–263. On numbers of Associationist communities and members, see Table 1 in the appendix, Guarneri, *Utopian Alternative*, 407–408; Norman Ware, *The Industrial Worker, 1840—1860: The Reaction of American Industrial Society to the Advance of the Industrial Revolution* (Boston: Houghton Mifflin, 1924), 167; Noyes, *History of American Socialisms*, 11–13. Ware, citing Noyes, estimated a number of between three thousand and eight thousand members of between thirty-four and forty-two Fourierist communities during the 1840s. Carl J. Guarneri, in the most exhaustive survey of the movement to date, uses a more conservative estimate of approximately four thousand people in twenty-nine communities.

11. For the older labor history on Association, see Commons et al., *History of Labour in the United States*, Vol. I, 496–506; Ware, *The Industrial Worker*, 163–179.

12. Carl Guarneri has found that several of the most important phalanxes had majorities or near-majorities of artisans and craftsmen, including 67 percent at Brook Farm and 49 percent at Alphadelphia. See Guarneri, *Utopian Alternative*, 170–171, Tables 11 and 12, Appendix, 415. A number of Associationists also played a leading role in the National Reform movement, most notably Albert Brisbane, Lewis Ryckman, and H. H. Van Amringe. The connections between and collaboration among Associationists and National Reformers are discussed in greater detail in the following chapter.

13. Guarneri, *Utopian Alternative*, 10, 368–369. In Guarneri's terms, American Fourierists "shifted their reform energies from the attack on 'wage slavery' to the crusade against chattel slavery" (3).

14. 14. Rebecca T. Pool to Isaiah Coffin Ray, September 5 (n.d., 1846?), American Antiquarian Society, Slavery in the United States Collection, Box 1, Folder 10. Both Allen and Orvis lived at Brook Farm, combined Associationism with and antislavery, and took turns editing the Voice of Industry. See David A. Zonderman, *Uneasy Allies: Working for Labor Reform in Nineteenth-Century Boston* (Amherst: University of Massachusetts Press, 2011), 54–55, 57–60; the *Liberator*, January 21, 1842, February 3, 1843. I am indebted to Lise Breen for the information on Allen's abolitionist activism.

15. Sinha, *The Slave's Cause*, 256–265, 347–355, 468, 482; McDaniel, *The Problem of Democracy*, 68–85, 143–158. Garrison himself later denied that Paine had been the

inspiration for the *Liberator*'s motto, but both men used the phrase in much the same sense. The phrase "citizen of the world" may have been coined by the British Quaker abolitionist Granville Sharp in 1776. See Lynd, *Intellectual Origins*, 133–135.

16. "A Call to the Friends of Social Reform in New England," *Phalanx* I, no. 3 (December 5, 1843), 44; see also the *Present*, December 15, 1843; "Social Reform Convention at Boston" (from the *Tribune*), *Phalanx* I, no. 4 (January 6, 1844), 46–47; Ballou quoted in Thomas, "Antislavery and Utopia," 249–253. Both Bassett and Buffum were Quaker "come-outers" and small business owners from Lynn, Massachusetts.

17. See, for example, *Liberator*, June 18, 1847, June 14, 1850.

18. Frederick Douglass, *Life and Times of Frederick Douglass, Written By Himself* (Hartford, CT: Park Publishing, 1882), 266–267; *Ninth Annual Report of the Board of Managers of the Mass. Anti-Slavery Society, Presented January 27, 1841; With an Appendix* (Boston: Dow and Jackson, 1841), 32–33.

19. Collins to Garrison, December 7, 1840, in Anti-Slavery Collection, Boston Public Library; Thomas, "Antislavery and Utopia," 253–259.

20. Address of Glasgow workingmen to John A. Collins, in *Tenth Annual Report of the Board of Managers of the Mass. Anti-Slavery Society. Presented January 26, 1842* (Boston: Dow and Jackson, 1842), 54–56. The address was given at "great public meeting" in Glasgow on April 26, 1841, and signed by William Patison, Malcolm M'Farlane, and Charles M'Ewer.

21. Douglass, *Life and Times*, 283; Garrison quoted in Wells, "The Skaneateles Communal Experiment," 1; *Liberator*, February 17, 1843. A second "Property Convention" was held in June at the Chardon Street Chapel in Boston, site of an 1840 anti-Sabbatarian and antisectarian convention promoted by Garrisonians that had scandalized conservatives. On Collins's evolving ideology, see Collins, *Bird's Eye View of Society As It Is, and As It Should Be . . .* (Boston: J. P. Mendum, 1844); Collins, *Preamble and Constitution of the New England Social Reform Society* (Boston: 1844).

22. Mass Anti-Slavery Society resolution quoted in Noyes, *American Socialisms*, 163; Douglass, *Life and Times*, 283; Noyes, *American Socialisms*, 163; Wells, "The Skaneateles Communal Experiment." Douglass may have been influenced by James Needham Buffum, who accompanied him on a lecture tour of Britain in 1845–1846. See Sinha, *The Slave's Cause*, 468, 482.

23. The Skaneateles Community's short lifespan has been blamed on several factors, ranging from the hostility of local residents, problems stemming from freeloaders and hangers-on, and the machinations of Collins's partner, lawyer Quincy A. Johnson. Collins himself blamed the community's failure on its tendency to attract "two extremes of character from motives diametrically opposite," the "dedicated" and the "indolent." See Noyes, *American Socialisms*, 170–171; Thomas, "Antislavery and Utopia," in Duberman, ed., *The Antislavery Vanguard*, 259. Noyes speculated that Collins became a mine owner in California, while the abolitionist Samuel J. May similarly reported that Collins became a "brazen-faced" businessman. See Samuel J. May, Jr., to Richard D. Webb, in Thomas, "Antislavery and Utopia," 259; see also Douglass, *Life and Times*, 554.

24. Clark, *Communitarian Moment*, 20–21, 49, 66, 98–108. Clark cites a list of those who had taken the "one dollar pledge" to support the AASS in the *National Anti-Slavery Standard* in 1841 as evidence for his calculation, identifying twelve signatories who became Northampton members.

25. Ibid., 48, 57, 64, 173–176; Northampton Association of Education and Industry, *Preamble and Articles of Association* (1842), quoted in Clark, 60.

26. See A. J. Macdonald on the Prairie Home Community, in Noyes, *American Socialisms*, 319. Adin Ballou's Hopedale Community, despite being open to membership "without distinction of sex, age, color, birth-place, or money qualification," had only one black resident, Rosetta Hall, who left after a short stay. Ballou, *A Concise Exposition of the Hopedale Community: Descriptive, Statistical, Historical, and Constitutional* (1853), 5; Clark, *Communitarian Moment*, 71, 239 n31.

27. Douglass in Sheffeld, *History of Florence*, 130–131; Clark, *Communitarian Moment*, 31, 49, 64–67, 126; Northampton Association of Education and Industry, *Constitution and Articles of Association* (1842), Northampton Association Records, American Antiquarian Society.

28. Clark, *Communitarian Moment*, 15, 71–78, 88–89; Douglass in Sheffeld, *The History of Florence, Massachusetts*, 120–121, 132, 134–135; Stephen C. Rush to Hall Judd, Northampton Association, July 17, 1846. Truth arrived after wandering the highways as an itinerant preacher after her association with the Kingdom of Matthias and Millerism, while David Ruggles was guided to the community by William Lloyd Garrison after falling into poor health and losing his eyesight. Most, if not all, members were subjected to a trial period before being subjected to a vote taken to determine their acceptance as members; in the case of Stephen Rush, members voted unanimously to waive the two-week requirement for admission, perhaps in deference to Rush's status as a fugitive.

Although the association resolved in November 1842 to let Ruggles "come among us and remain with us as a member, without being admitted until better acquainted," he does not seem to have become an official member. Rush is listed as "entering" in November 1843, but the "membership commenced" fields for both Rush and Ruggles are blank. Truth's name does not appear in the register, despite her stay until the very end and Frederick Douglass's recollection of her as "one of the most useful members of the community." All three, however, appear in the association's account book. See Northampton Association of Education and Industry, Membership Register, Folio Volume 1, and Laborers' Account Book, Folio Volume 3, Northampton Association Records, American Antiquarian Society. For Rush's admission to the community, see the entry for November 4, 1843, in Record of Proceedings, Folio Volume 2, 84.

29. Horace Greeley to the Anti-Slavery Convention, June 3, 1845, in the *New-York Daily Tribune*, June 20, 1845 (originally published in the *Cincinnati Morning Herald*). The letter was reprinted in Greeley, *Hints Toward Reforms*, 352–357.

30. On Greeley and the *Tribune*'s treatment of both antislavery and labor reform, see Adam Tuchinsky, *Horace Greeley's* New-York Tribune: *Civil War-Era Socialism and the Crisis of Free Labor* (Ithaca, NY: Cornell University Press, 2009).

31. "The Question of Slavery," *Harbinger* I, no. 2 (June 21, 1845).

32. *Northampton Democrat*, quoted in *Voice of Industry*, August 13, 1847; *Awl*, October 25, 1845; Walsh quoted in Roediger, *The Wages of Whiteness*, 77; see also "Legislature of New-York," *Subterranean*, February 13, 1847. For an extended discussion of the pro- and antislavery uses of the terms "wage slavery" and "white slavery" by workers in the 1840s, see Roediger, *Wages of Whiteness*, 65–72, 77–80.

33. Rebecca T. Pool to Isaiah Coffin Ray, September 5. As Guarneri points out, the members of the North American Phalanx failed to incorporate the formerly enslaved people living on the estate purchased for the site into their community; see Guarneri, *Utopian Alternative*, 258.

34. For an exposition of the Associationists' understanding of the origins of chattel slavery in feudalism and other forms of oppression, see *Harbinger* V, no. 20 (October 23, 1847), 329–330.

35. Greeley, *Hints Towards Reform*, 28–29; [Hosmer], *The Condition of Labor*, 21; *Harbinger* II, no. 20 (April 25, 1846), 318–319; *Harbinger* V, no. 21 (October 30, 1847), 325–326, 329–330; Mischa Honeck, *We Are the Revolutionists: German-Speaking Immigrants and Abolitionists After 1848* (Athens: University of Georgia Press, 2011), 57–58.

36. "Waltham Celebration," *Liberator*, July 16, 1847; *National Anti-Slavery Standard*, August 5, 1847 (reprinted from the *Lowell Journal*). I have reconstructed Channing's speech from the accounts given in these two sources. Channing's speech preceded Charles Sumner's similar comparison between southern "lords of the lash" with northern "lords of the loom" by about a year. Sumner's comparison first appeared in a speech given at a gathering of antislavery Whigs in Worcester, Massachusetts, on June 28, 1848; see Edward L. Pierce, ed., *Memoir and Letters of Charles L. Sumner*, Vol. 3 (Boston: Roberts Brothers, 1893), 179. On Channing, see also Guarneri, *Utopian Alternative*, 54–55, 259; "A Typical American: Memoir of William Henry Channing," *New York Times*, December 5, 1886; and the papers of the Religious Union of Associationists, Massachusetts Historical Society.

37. On the origins of the "chattel principle" idea, see Moses I. Finley, *Ancient Slavery and Modern Ideology* (New York: Viking Press, 1980); John Blanton, "This Species of Property: Slavery and the Properties of Subjecthood in Anglo-American Law and Politics, 1619–1783" (PhD diss., CUNY Graduate Center, 2015).

38. "Garnet's Plea for the Bondsman," *Christian News*, October 17, 1850; James W. C. Pennington, *The Fugitive Blacksmith, or Events in the Life of James W. C. Pennington, Pastor of a Presbyterian Church, New York, Formerly a Slave in the State of Maryland, United States (London: Charles Gilpin, 1849)*, iv–v; *National Anti-Slavery Standard*, August 5, October 14, 1847. The *Standard* may have been referencing a notorious pamphlet published by National Reformer John Windt. See Windt, *The Slavery of Poverty, Together with a Plan for Its Abolition* (New York: The New-York Society for the Abolition of All Slavery, 1842). For a more in-depth discussion of the ideological differences between abolitionists and labor reformers, see Glickstein, "Poverty is not Slavery," in Perry and Fellman, *Antislavery Reconsidered*, 195–218.

39. *Liberator*, July 9, 1847; "The Question of Labor" [Wendell Phillips to the editors of the *Liberator*], in *Harbinger* V, no. 6 (July 17, 1847), 87.

40. Ibid.; "The Liberator on the Question of Labor," *Harbinger* V, no. 6 (July 17, 1847), 92–93.

41. Dana in the *Harbinger*, quoted in the *Voice of Industry*, September 18, 1845; *Harbinger* V, no. 21 (October 30, 1847), 331; [Charles Hosmer], *The Condition of Labor: An Address to the Members of the Labor Reform League of New England; in a Speech in Support of Some Resolution Offered at Their Late Convention in Boston, By One of the Members* (Boston: Published by the Author, 1847), 7–8, 21.

42. Hudson, quoted in Clark, *Communitarian Moment*, 99–100.

43. Wells, "The Skaneateles Communal Experiment," 6, 9; "Social Reform Convention at Boston" (from the *Tribune*), *Phalanx* I, no. 4 (January 6, 1844), 46–47; Collins to Elizabeth Pease, February 2, 1843, Garrison papers, BPL; Nathaniel P. Rogers, "Property" (from the *Herald of Freedom*, March 15, 1844), in *A Collection of the Miscellaneous Writings of Nathaniel P. Rogers* (Manchester, NH: W. H. Fisk, 1849), 285–288. Although Rogers was atypical, and his editorial control of the *Herald of Freedom*, the official organ of the New Hampshire Anti-Slavery Society, was taken away from him shortly after his articles on "Property" were published, Garrison continued to defend Rogers until his early death in 1846.

44. "The Associationists and the Abolitionists" [reprinted from the *National Anti-Slavery Standard*], *Harbinger* V, no. 20 (October 23, 1847), 325–326; "The Anti-Slavery Standard," *Harbinger* V, no. 21 (October 30, 1847), 329–330.

45. "The Liberty League," *Harbinger* V, no. 20 (October 23, 1847), 331–332.

46. "Convention in Boston—Organization of the 'American Union of Associationists,'" *Harbinger* II, no. 26 (June 6, 1846), 410–411; *Harbinger* V, no. 20 (October 23, 1847); "Annual Meeting of the American Union of Associationists," *Harbinger* V, no. 2 (June 19, 1847); "Waltham Celebration," *Liberator*, July 16, 1847; *National Anti-Slavery Standard*, August 5, 1847 (reprinted from the *Lowell Journal*); Guarneri, *Utopian Alternative*, 258; Guarneri, "Two Utopian Socialist Plans for Emancipation in Antebellum Louisiana," *Louisiana History* 24, no. 1 (Winter, 1983), 8. Channing had previously expressed this conviction in a letter to Maria Weston Chapman; see Channing to Chapman, September 29, 1846, Weston Collection, Boston Public Library. The resolution was, however, narrowly rejected by the gathering.

47. "Anniversary of the American Union of Associationists," *New-York Tribune*, June 3, 1850; *Voice of Industry*, January 22, 1847, quoted in Commons et al., *A Documentary History*, Vol. VIII, 126; *Voice of Industry*, February 19, 1847; Herbert Aptheker, *A Documentary History of the Negro People in the United States: From Colonial Times to the Civil War* (Citadel, 1960), 112. I have found no evidence to support Bernard Mandel's conclusion, reiterated by Eric Foner, that the New England Labor Reform League's resolution was proposed at the behest of abolitionists who supposedly "packed the meeting." It is unclear whether the resolution was ever voted on. See Mandel, *Labor: Free and Slave*, 93; Foner, *Politics and Ideology*, 67.

48. "Appendix: Checklist of Communitarian Experiments," in Bestor, *Backwoods Utopias*, 277–284.

49. Frances Wright to Julia Garnett, June 8, 1825, in Cecilia Helena Payne-Gaposchkin, ed., "The Nashoba Plan for Removing the Evils of Slavery: Letters of Frances and Camilla Wright, 1820–1829," *Harvard Library Bulletin* 23 (July 1975), 288–299; Gail Bederman, "Revisiting Nashoba: Slavery, Utopia, and Frances Wright in America, 1818–1826," *American Literary History* 17, no. 3 (Autumn 2005), 438–459; and Sean Griffin, "Antislavery Utopias: Communitarian Labor Reform and the Abolitionist Movement," *Journal of the Civil War Era* 8, no. 2 (June 2018), 243–268.

50. *National Era*, quoted in *Voice of Industry*, February 19, 1847. On Robert Dale Owen's later activities, see Robert Dale Owen, *Emancipation Is Peace* (New York: Loyal Publication Society of New-York, 1863); Owen, *The Wrong of Slavery, the Right of Emancipation, and the Future of the African Race in the United States* (Philadelphia: J. B. Lippincott, 1864); and the epilogue in the current volume.

51. Dain, *De l'abolition de l'esclavage* (1836).

52. Parke Godwin to Charles Dana, September 8, 1845. Bryant-Godwin Collection, New York Public Library. Godwin had earlier outlined a Fourierist plan for emancipation in "The Slavery Question," *Pathfinder*, no. 10 (April 29, 1843), 145–146.

53. Carl J. Guarneri, "Two Utopian Socialist Plans for Emancipation in Antebellum Louisiana," *Louisiana History* 24, no. 1 (Winter 1983), 5–24.

54. Albert Brisbane and Osborne Macdaniel, "Dangers Which Threaten the Future," *Phalanx* I, no. 2 (November 4, 1843), 19; *Harbinger* IV, no. 26 (June 5, 1847), 407; Guarneri, *Utopian Alternative*, 262–267. In formulating his plan, Macdaniel apparently drew on his connections to a handful of Louisiana Fourierists, among them sugar planters John D. Wilkins, Robert Wilson, and Thomas May, and New Orleans lawyers Thomas J. Durant and T. Wharton Collens. Certain aspects of Macdaniel's plan may have been borrowed from John McDonogh, a paternalistic Louisiana planter who allowed his slaves to purchase their freedom by working for wages. See Guarneri, *Utopian Alternative*, 262.

55. I am in full agreement with Guarneri's conclusions about Macdaniel and Lazarus's plans in Guarneri, "Two Utopian Socialist Plans," 17–21.

56. "The Liberty League," *Harbinger* V, no. 20 (October 23, 1847), 319–320.

57. *Harbinger* V, no. 16 (September 25, 1847); "Mr. Macdaniel's Lecture," *Harbinger* V, no. 2 (June 19, 1847); "Our Policy—Slavery—Letter from Mr. Macdaniel," *Harbinger* V, no. 6 (July 17, 1847); *Boston Daily Chronotype*, January 9, 1850.

58. Channing quoted in *Liberator*, June 14, 1850.

Chapter 4

1. For details of the initial meeting of the National Reform Association and the backgrounds of its founders, see "Workingmen's Meeting," *Working Man's Advocate*, March 16, 1844; Lause, *Young America*, 9; Helene Zahler, *Eastern Workingmen and National Land Policy, 1829–1862* (New York: Columbia University Press, 1941), 36–37; Lewis Masquerier, *Sociology, or, the Reconstruction of Society, Government, and Property*

(New York: 1877), 95. The exact date of the initial meeting in Windt's print shop is unclear; Zahler, apparently following Masquerier, describes it as a Sunday in February, while Lause gives the date as Friday, March 8, 1844. A different account of the original meeting of the National Reformers is given by Thomas Devyr, who claimed the "National Reform Party" had first been organized in his offices, and mentions only Evans and Windt as being present. See Thomas Ainge Devyr, *The Odd Book of the Nineteenth Century, or "Chivalry" in Modern Days* ... (Greenpoint, NY: 1882), 39–41.

2. Lause, *Young America*, 16–17. In addition to Lause's definitive work on the National Reformers, see the citations for Evans above on the land reform movement more generally. On issues and controversies surrounding the public lands in the Early Republic and antebellum periods, see Daniel Feller, *The Public Lands in Jacksonian Politics* (Madison: University of Wisconsin Press, 1984). Older works on this subject include Zahler, *Eastern Workingmen*, and Roy Marvin Robbins, *Our Landed Heritage, the Public Domain, 1776–1936* (Princeton, NJ: Princeton University Press, 1942).

3. "To the People of the United States," *Working Man's Advocate*, July 6, 1844; "A Member," *Young America! Principles and Objects of the National Reform Association, or Agrarian League* (New York: 1845), 2–6. I refer to this pamphlet as *Principles and Objects* below, to avoid confusion with Evans's newspaper *Young America*. Evans had laid out these basic planks of National Reform, along with a theoretical basis for the abolition of property in land, justified in the language of natural rights, as early as January 1841. See "To the Working Men of the United States," *Radical* I, no. 1 (January 1841).

4. On land reform and the importance of access to the land for various groups in nineteenth-century America, see Jamie L. Bronstein, *Land Reform and Working-Class Experience in Britain and the United States, 1800–1862* (Stanford, CA: Stanford University Press, 1999); Reeve Huston, *Land and Freedom: Rural Society, Popular Protest, and Party Politics in Antebellum New York* (Oxford: Oxford University Press, 2000); Feller, *The Public Lands*; Earle, *Jacksonian Antislavery*, 36–37, passim; Mandell, *The Lost Tradition*, 140, 149, 173, 175, 192–222, passim.

5. On the land reformers' relationship to the Associationists, see the *Working Man's Advocate*, April 6, 20, June 15, July 13, 20, August 21, September 7, 1844, February 22, 1845; *Young America*, May 10, October 4, 1845, February 28, 1846, and see chapter 6. On plans for "rural republican townships" and Masquerier's role in them, see *Principles and Objects*, 3–6; *National Reform Association Certificate of Membership*, American Antiquarian Society; Masquerier, *Sociology: or, The Reconstruction of Society, Government, and Property, Upon the Principles of the Equality* ... (New York: 1877), 12–13, 19, 74–77.

6. Table 1.1, "Acquisition of the Public Domain, 1781–1867," in U.S. Department of the Interior, Bureau of Land Management, *Public Land Statistics 2021*, Vol. 206 (Washington, DC, 2022), 3.

7. *Principles and Objects*, 2–3. On public land policy in the Early National and antebellum periods, see George M. Stephenson, *The Political History of the Public Lands, from 1840 to 1862* (Boston: Richard G. Badger, 1917); Zahler, *Eastern Workingmen*,

109–126; John Van Atta, *Securing the West: Politics, Public Lands, and the Fate of the Old Republic, 1785–1850* (Baltimore: Johns Hopkins University Press, 2014).

On contemporary discussions by workingmen's groups on the importance of land limitation, see "To Workingmen—Land Limitation—the New Party," *Mechanic's Advocate*, January 28, 1847; "Land Limitation, & c.," *The Subterranean*, April 24, 1847; "Labor Movements," *New-York Tribune*, June 27, 1850; *Spirit of the Times*, July 26, 1853. For denunciations of the National Reformers and related land reform schemes, see, for example, *New York Herald*, May 7, October 18, 1845; Rep. Thomas H. Averett (Va.), in *Congressional Globe*, April 8, 1852, 1018–1020; Reps. Thomasson of Kentucky and Sutherland of New York, quoted in Bronstein, *Land Reform and Working-Class Experience*, 235, 236–237; New York *Sun* and *Commercial* quoted in Commons et al., *History of Labour in the United States*, Vol. I, 533; Milwaukee *Daily Sentinel and Gazette*, quoted in Commons et al., *A Documentary History*, VIII, pt. 2, 57. Thomasson's quote can be found in the *Congressional Globe*, 28th Congress, 2nd session, HR, Appendix, p. 309.

8. National Reform Association, *Principles and Objects*, 2; and *Young America*, October 18, 1845.

9. For an indicative sampling of the political thinkers cited by Evans, see George H. Evans, ed., *Working Man's Advocate*, Vol. I, New Series, 1845, bound volume held at American Antiquarian Society; see also "People's Right to the Land," *Working Man's Advocate*, March 16, 1844. Beginning in 1845, *Young America*, the official organ of the National Reform Association published simultaneously with the *Working Man's Advocate* by Evans, added quotes by Black Hawk, John Gray, and William Henry Channing to its masthead.

10. *Principles and Objects*, 11–14; *The Jubilee: A Plan for Restoring the Land of New-York or (Incidentally) Any Other State to the People* (New York: 1845); "To the Working Men of the United States," *Radical* I, no. 1 (January, 1841), 1–2.; "Man's Inalienable Right to Land," *Radical* I, no. 4 (April, 1841); "Our Principles," *Working Man's Advocate*, April 6, 1844; "Explanation," *Subterranean, United with the Working Man's Advocate*, I, no. 34 (November 16, 1844). For further evidence of the National Reformers' influences, see also the mastheads of *Young America* and the *Working Man's Advocate*, 1844–52. Evans' National Reform partner, John Windt, had been among the organizers of Paine birthday celebrations. On Spence, see the *Radical*, July 1841; *Working Man's Advocate* March 16, 1844; June 8, 1844. Norman Ware and some other early biographers claimed that Evans's father had been "a disciple of Thomas Spence" in England, but no evidence for this assertion can be found. See Norman Ware, *The Industrial Worker*, 181; Jeffrey Newman, "Social Origins of George Henry Evans," 151. Evans also credited Fourier, St. Simon, John Gray, and Moses Jacques as being among the forerunners of his land reform ideas. For an early exposition of Evans's agrarian thought, see "Man's Inalienable Right to Land," *Radical* I, no. 4 (April 1841), 1. For a list of works published by Evans, including those of Paine, see "Works, Published and For Sale Wholesale and Retail, by George H. Evans," *Radical* I, December 31, 1841; *Radical* I, no. 7 (July 1841). On the concept of the Jubilee and its connections to nineteenth-century social reform,

see Mandell, *Lost Tradition*, 2, 5, 19, 215, passim. On connections to Chartism, Bronstein, *Land Reform and Working-Class Experience*. Among the notable former Chartists who became involved in labor and/or land reform causes in the U.S. were Thomas A. Devyr, John C. Cluer, and John Campbell.

11. Collins, *Bird's Eye View*; Collins, *Preamble and Constitution*; *Daily Chronotype*, September 9, 16, 1847; see also September 19, October 6, July 15, 1847, May 27, 1848. Evans cited Collins and Channing on the frontispiece to the collected volume of the *Working Man's Advocate* for 144–145; see Evans, ed., *Working Man's Advocate* Vol. I. See also "The Skaneateles Community" (from the *Onondaga Standard*), *Working Man's Advocate*, July 13, 1844.

12. "To the Working Men of the United States," *Radical* I, no. 1 (January 1841), 2.

13. John Pickering, *The Working Man's Political Economy, Founded on the Principle of Immutable Justice, and the Inalienable Rights of Man; Designed for the Promotion of National Reform* (Cincinnati: Thomas Varney, 1847), 37, 46–48, 28–31; *Boston Daily Chronotype*, quoted in the *Voice of Industry*, October 15, 1847.

14. *Working Man's Advocate*, July 6, 1844; "The New Party," *Voice of Industry*, November 6, 13, 1846, November 19, 1847; Lause, *Young America*, 42; "Interrogation of Candidates," *American Freeman*, September 1, 1847; John Ashworth, *"Agrarians" and "Aristocrats": Party Political Ideology in the United States, 1837–1846* (Cambridge: Cambridge University Press, 1983), 92–99. Ashworth makes the case that the National Reformers in particular were "neo-Jacksonian" in their outlook and that they "retained far more than they rejected" of Democratic ideology. While there is a sense in which Ashworth's assertion rings true, it ignores the fact that many National Reformers, including Evans, later rejected the Democratic Party entirely. For an older but still influential alternative view, see Pessen, *Most Uncommon Jacksonians*. Pessen argues that radical workingmen were as far away from mainstream Democrats as they were from the Whig Party.

15. Reeve Huston, the author of the most thorough recent study of the New York Anti-Rent movement, concludes that Devyr "revived in a new and more radical form what most anti-renters had quietly dropped: a challenge to prevailing definitions of property as derived from paper title." Huston, *Land and Freedom*, 113–114, 138–143, 158, 163–166. Huston speculates that conflicts over the nature of landed property may have contributed to a split among the rural middle-class Anti-Rent constituency, and offers statistical data correlating support for National Reform based on property holdings and occupation. See Appendix 15, 16, 17, p. 228. See also Tuchinsky, *Horace Greeley's New-York Tribune*, 131; *Young America*, May 10, June 21, August 2, 9, 16, 23, 30, September 6, 13, 14, November 8, 1845; *Freeholder*, July 9, August 6, 1845, January 21, February 25, August 26, 1846; *Anti-Renter* January 31, February 14, 21, June 6, 1846.

16. Typically, Greeley framed the issue in terms of the labor theory of property while attempting to strike a balance between the legal property rights of landholders and the broader principle of a right to the soil. Both upstate poltroons and western speculators effectively denied future generations of settlers access to the land by artificially usurping it for posterity, but rather than a forced redistribution, Greeley averred

that "we would so shape the legislation and policy of the country as to discourage the *future* concentration of land into vast estates or manors and encourage its division into small freeholds." Tuchinsky, *Horace Greeley's New-York Tribune*, 130–131. On Seward, see Huston, *Land and Freedom*, 98–100, 214.

17. "Distress of the Working Classes: The Cause and the Remedy," *Working Man's Advocate*, March 16, 1844.

18. *Working Man's Advocate*, April 20, May 11, August 10, 1844; *People's Rights*, July 27, 1844. Although he frequently reiterated his opposition to slavery in Texas, at times Evans seemed to accept the arguments of Polk's treasury secretary Robert J. Walker that annexation would lead to the abolition of slavery by providing a ready outlet for the South's enslaved workers by means of emigration to Mexico or Central America. See "How to Abolish Slavery," *Young America*, December 18, 1847. On organized labor's response to the Mexican-American War, see chapter 5.

19. Earle, *Jacksonian Antislavery*; Tuchinsky, *Horace Greeley's New-York Tribune*, 130–131; Huston, *Land and Freedom*, 169–170; Zahler, *Eastern Workingmen*, 44–46. I here use the term "free soil" to refer to the broad coalition of antislavery northerners that coalesced around the Wilmot Proviso and that included, but was not synonymous with, the Free Soil Party. As mentioned above and described further in chapter 6, the National Reformers' version of "free soil" diverged from that represented by the Free Soil Party in important ways.

20. *Working Man's Advocate*, May 25, 1844; "That Land Question Again," [Ohio] *Friend of Man*, in *Young America*, January 24, 1846; *Liberator*, April 2, 1847; and *Working Man's Advocate*, June 1, 1844. The best discussion of Evans's use of and relationship to "white slavery" rhetoric remains Roediger, *The Wages of Whiteness*, 65–92. The staying power of the debates on class and "whiteness" and their relevance to twenty-first-century social issues is indicated by Ta-Nehisi Coates's invocation of Roediger and Evans to explain the election of Donald Trump; see Coates, "The First White President," *The Atlantic* (October 2017).

21. "To Gerrit Smith," *Working Man's Advocate*, July 6, 1844. The exchange of letters with Smith is discussed in detail below.

22. *Young America*, December 13, 1845.

23. Evans to Gerrit Smith, *Working Man's Advocate*, July 6, 1844; Smith to Evans, Peterboro, July 29, 1844, published as "Second Letter from Gerrit Smith. For the *People's Rights*," *Working Man's Advocate*, August 10, 1844; "Slavery. To Feargus O'Connor," *Working Man's Advocate*, June 22, 1844.

24. On competing views of free labor in early America, see Eric Foner, *Free Soil, Free Labor, Free Men*, xv–xvi, 9, 11–39, 43–48, 59–61, 63–64, 266–267; Huston, *Securing the Fruits of Labor*, 155–162; Glickstein, *Concepts of Free Labor*; Glickstein, "Poverty Is Not Slavery," 195–218; Robert J. Steinfeld, *The Invention of Free Labor: The Employment Relation in English and American Law and Culture, 1350–1870* (Chapel Hill: University of North Carolina Press, 1991); Stanley, *From Bondage to Contract*; William Forbath, "The Ambiguities of Free Labor: Labor and the Law in the Gilded Age," *Wisconsin Law Review* 4 (1985).

25. Pickering, *Political Economy*, 46.

26. Ibid.

27. *Working Man's Advocate*, May 25, 1844.

28. "The Memphis Convention—Mr. Calhoun—Democracy of South Carolina—Universal Emancipation," *Young America*, December 13, 1845; "Consistency of Reformers," *Young America*, June 28, 1845. Evans rehashed the argument about free labor in Antigua from an earlier article published in April 1845, citing the *Antigua Observer* as the source of the statistic; see *Young America*, April 26, 1845.

29. The *Slavery of Poverty* pamphlet was printed by John Windt, Evans's early collaborator in National Reform, although it is unclear whether he was its author. See *The Slavery of Poverty, with a Plan for Its Abolition* (New York: The New-York Society for the Abolition of All Slavery, 1842); "Dialogue on Free and Slave Labor," *Working Man's Advocate*, June 8, 1844; John Campbell, *Negro-mania: Being an Examination of the Falsely Assumed Equality of the Various Races of Men* (Philadelphia: Campbell and Power, 1851).

30. John Stauffer's *The Black Hearts of Men* and Octavius Brooks Frothingham's late-nineteenth century biography remain the best available accounts of Smith's life and antislavery activities. A complete and thorough new biography of this critically understudied figure is long overdue.

31. "To Gerrit Smith," *Working Man's Advocate*, July 6, 1844. The letter was also printed in the *People's Rights*, July 24, 1844.

32. Gerrit Smith to George H. Evans, July 8, 1844, published as "Gerrit Smith's Reply," *Working Man's Advocate*, July 20, 1844. Significantly, although there are no extant copies, Smith's letter (or letters) were also published in pamphlet form, together with an article from Wright's *Chronotype* and a letter from the communitarian abolitionist John O. Wattles. See "National Reform Tracts," *Young America*, September 23, 1848.

33. "Gerrit Smith's Reply" (Smith to Evans), *Working Man's Advocate*, July 20, 1844; *The Rural Code of Haiti, Literally Translated from a Publication by the Government Press; Together with Letters From That Country, Concerning Its Present Condition, By a Southern Planter* (Granville, NJ: George Henry Evans, 1837); "Indian State," *Young America*, November 15, 1845.

34. "Rejoinder to Gerrit Smith," *Working Man's Advocate* (published as the *People's Rights*), July 24, 1844; *Working Man's Advocate*, July 20, 1844.

35. The National Reformers credited "a Lady," described as "the Wife of a distinguished Philanthropist and large Land-holder of New-York" with inspiring and helping to fund the publication of the group's *Principles and Objects*, an assertion later echoed by Henry Highland Garnet. See *Principles and Objects*, 1; Garnet in the *National Watchman*, quoted in the *Daily Chronotype*, September 16, 1847.

36. Smith to Theodore S. Wright, Charles B. Ray, and James McCune Smith, Peterboro, August 1, 1846; Smith to Evans, August 27, 1846, GS Papers. The land grants included parcels in Franklin, Essex, Hamilton, Fulton, Oneida, Delaware, Madison, and Ulster counties.

37. "Letter of Gerrit Smith" [from *Young America*], *Voice of Industry*, November 20, 1846; Smith to J. K. Ingalls, August 15, 1848; "Gerrit Smith on Land Monopoly," letter

dated July 17, 1847, initially published in the *Christian Recorder*, in *National Reform Almanac for 1848* (New York: 1848), 3 (pages numbered nonconsecutively); Smith to Beriah Green, Peterboro, April 4, 1849.

38. [Gerrit Smith, Theodore S. Wright, Charles B. Ray, and James McCune Smith], *An Address to the Three Thousand Colored Citizens of New-York, Who Are the Owners of One Hundred and Twenty Thousand Acres of Land . . .* (New York, 1846); Smith to Theodore S. Wright, Charles B. Ray, and James McCune Smith, Peterboro, November 14, 1846, GS Papers. Both Wright and Ray were active in New York City's Vigilance Committee, a militant organization aimed at preventing the kidnapping of free blacks and the return of fugitive slaves, by force if necessary. Ray, who had once labored as a blacksmith, combined his ministry and editorship of the *Colored American* with a position as a secretary of the Liberty Party. McCune Smith, who had attended medical school in Scotland to become the first African American to hold a medical degree, not only was a practicing physician and a radical abolitionist, but led an active intellectual life as a frequent contributor to literary pursuits as well as medical, scientific, and statistical journals. Smith had a long-standing correspondence and friendship with McCune Smith; see Stauffer, *Black Hearts of Men*; Richard H. Sewell, *Ballots for Freedom: Antislavery Politics in the United States, 1837–1860* (New York: W. W. Norton, 1980), 101. On Ray, see M. N. Work, "The Life of Charles B. Ray," *Journal of Negro History* 4, no. 4 (October 1919), 361–371.

39. "Circular," Gerrit Smith to Unknown, Peterboro, May 1, 1849. Smith made clear that his specification that the recipients in this case be white was predicated on the fact that he had already made allowances for the distribution of three thousand grants to African Americans. Smith specified that the new recipients be "white inhabitants of the State of New York . . . between the ages of 21 and 60; must be virtuous, landless, and poor; and must be entirely clear of the vice of drinking intoxicating liquors." Aside from the obvious factor of race, these criteria were identical to the ones Smith had specified for black recipients, with the exception that the requirement of total abstinence from alcohol was imposed for whites.

40. Stauffer, *Black Hearts of Men*, 148–152, passim.

41. *North Star*, March 2, 1849; *Weekly Chronotype*, January 21, 1847; Wright, Ray, and Smith, *An Address to the Three Thousand Colored Citizens of New-York*, 10.

42. Wright, Ray, and Smith, *An Address to the Three Thousand Colored Citizens of New-York*, 10–13; "Report of the Committee on Agriculture," *Proceedings of the National Convention of Colored People and Their Friends; Held in Troy, N.Y., on the 6th, 7th, 8th, and 9th of October, 1847* (Troy, NY: 1847), 29–30.

43. "Report of the Committee on Agriculture," *Proceedings of the National Convention of Colored People and Their Friends; Held in Troy, N.Y., on the 6th, 7th, 8th, and 9th of October, 1847* (Troy, NY: 1847), 29–30; "State Council of the Colored People of Massachusetts, Convention January 2, 1854," *Meeting of the [Massachusetts] State Council, in Behalf of Colored Americans*, coloredconventions.org/items/show/263, accessed March 27, 2015. See especially the resolutions of Charles L. Reason and H. O. Remington.

44. *North Star*, March 2, 1849; *Weekly Chronotype*, January 21, 1847; Charles B. Ray and James McCune Smith, *Gerrit Smith Grantees, Redeem Your Lands!!* (New York, 1854); Stauffer, *Black Hearts of Men*, 156–157; Smith quoted in the *New-York Tribune*, August 10, 1857.

45. Stauffer, *Black Hearts of Men*, 139, 153–158; Van Gosse, *The First Reconstruction*, 447–448. Smith himself seemed to include overcoming the $250 freehold requirement as a barrier to Black voting in his initial letter to the plan's trustees. Douglass himself was a recipient of one of Smith's land grants, located on a tract next to those of Black abolitionist leaders William Wells Brown, William Nell, Charles Remond, and Henry Bibb. The eight counties where Smith lands had been granted saw a sixfold increase in the number of Black taxpayers between 1845 and 1855.

46. "National Reform and People of Color," *Landmark* (reprinted from the *Ram's Horn*), June 3, 1848; Willard B. Gatewood, ed., *Free Man of Color: The Autobiography of Willis Augustus Hodges* (Knoxville: University of Tennessee Press, 1982).

47. *National Reform Almanac for 1848* (New York: 1848); "That Land Question Again," [Ohio] *Friend of Man*, in *Young America*, January 24, 1846. Evans's footnote, signed "Editor of Young America," appears on page 2 of Gerrit Smith's essay on Land Monopoly (pages numbered separately).

Chapter 5

1. *Working Man's Advocate*, March 8, 1845; "National Convention—Union of Reformers—Industrial Congress," *Young America*, October 4, 1845; reprinted in *Young America*, October 18, 1845; *Voice of Industry*, June 11, 1847; *Harbinger* I, no. 9 (August 9, 1845), 144; *New-York Tribune*, September 17, 1845. See also "The Convention—Industrial Congress," *Young America*, May 10, 1845, and the *Harbinger's* commentary on "the Union of Reformers" in the issue cited above and *Harbinger* I, no. 11 (August 23, 1845), 169–170.

2. *New England Mechanic*, quoted in *Young America*, October 4, 1845.

3. For the NIC's organizational structure and manner of electing delegates, see "Constitution of the Industrial Congress," *Young America*, October 25, 1845. For details about the NIC and its significance, see Commons, *History of Labour*, Vol. I, 547–551; Lause, *Young America*.

4. "Constitution of the Industrial Congress," *Young America*, October 25, 1845.

5. For a full list of the NIC annual meetings with locations and dates, see Appendix B in Lause, *Young America*, 156–157. Lause's list includes the "National Convention" held in New York in October 1845. As Lause points out, the Industrial Congresses that flourished briefly after the Civil War were organized by a new generation of labor reformers and bore little direct connection to their predecessors.

6. "National Convention—Union of Reformers—Industrial Congress," *Young America*, October 4, 1845; reprinted in *Young America*, October 18, 1845; *Voice of Industry*, June 11, 1847; *Harbinger* I, no. 9 (August 9, 1845), 144; *New-York Tribune*, September 17, 1845. Although Evans's appeal went mostly unheeded by Garrison and the abolitionists associated with the AASS, it mirrored Garrison's own call for "A CORDIAL

UNION OF EFFORTS" among different factions of abolitionists. See Sinha, *The Slave's Cause*, 481.

7. "National Convention—Union of Reformers—Industrial Congress"; "Industrial Convention," *Young America*, October 18, 1845. Evans claimed that the 1845 convention that birthed the Congress, held at an unspecified location in New York, brought together "Anti-Slavery men, Associationists, Communitists, Temperance Men, Peace Men, Free Trade Men, and Free Land men" from New York, New Jersey, Pennsylvania, Ohio, Massachusetts, Connecticut, Rhode Island, Illinois, and beyond. The activities of Bovay, Godwin, and Channing are described in detail below. Smith has been described as a clockmaker and former Loco Foco; see Lause, *Young America*, 32. Timms was a founder of the New York branch of the Universal Community Society of Rational Religionists, formed by British immigrant Owenites in 1840. See Lause, *Young America*, 35–36; J. F. C. Harrison, *Robert Owen and the Owenites in Britain and America: The Quest for the New Moral World* (New York: Routledge, 1969), 110, n3.

8. J. E. Snodgrass to the editor of the *National Era*, July 20, 1848; Devyr to Andrew Johnson, December 9, 1859, Johnson-Patterson Papers, quoted in Zahler, *Eastern Workingmen*, 104 n57. Snodgrass informed readers of the *Era* that he attended to the congress for the specific purpose of promoting Smith's nomination, but he feared that the actions of antiabolition delegates had "destroyed whatever prospects there might have been of a National Reform ticket" in Baltimore.

9. For a fairly representative statement of the NIC's goals and ideology, see Lucius Hine to the editors of the *Boston Protective Union*, Cincinnati, March 9, 1850, in the *New-York Tribune*, April 10, 1850.

10. "The Industrial Congress," (letter of "B." to Horace Greeley), *Harbinger* I, no. 17 (October 4, 1845), 260 (reprinted from the *New-York Tribune*).

11. Frank J. Ferrell, an African-American member of the Knights of Labor, appeared at that organization's national convention in Richmond, Virginia, in 1886.

12. "Constitution of the Industrial Congress," *Young America*, October 25, 1845; "National Convention—Union of Reformers—Industrial Congress," *Young America*, October 4, 1845. In addition to its statement in favor of racial equality, the NIC constitution added to the Declaration's formulation of "natural rights" the insistence that among these were the rights to "the fruits of labor," access to the soil, education, and "paternal protection from society."

13. "Circular: To the Mechanics of New England," *People's Rights*, July 24, 1844; "New England Convention," *Working Man's Advocate*, July 20, 1844; *Working Man's Advocate*, October 19, 1844, November 2, 1844; February 15, March 22, 1845; "The Ten Hours System," *Young America*, July 11, 1846; Lause, *Young America*, 24–25; Zahler, *Eastern Workingmen*, 58–63. The Circular calling for the convention was printed in the *Mechanic* (Fall River), the *Laborer* (Boston), the *New England Operative* (Lowell), the *Manchester Operative* (Manchester, NH), the *Olive Branch* (Boston), the *Investigator* (Boston), the *Vox Populi* (Lowell), and the *Phalanx* (New York), as well as the *Working Man's Advocate* and *People's Rights*. Several thousand copies of the *Circular* were also

printed and distributed by Evans. See also Devyr, *The Odd Book of the Nineteenth Century*, 41.

14. Kellogg's writings on banking and currency reform provide one of the few links between the pre- and postwar Industrial Congresses. A New York merchant and one-time member of the Modern Times community on Long Island, in 1849 he published a plan to replace banks with a "National Safety Fund" that was later adopted by the National Labor Union. See Kellogg, *Labor and Other Capital* (1849); Montgomery, *Beyond Equality*, 426. On Douglas, see Commons, *History of Labour*, Vol. I, 384; on Ferral, see Lause, *Young America*, 25, 36, 39, 41.

15. Commons, *History of Labour*, Vol. I, 547–549. *The Operative*, March 22, 1845; *New-York Tribune*, March 24, 1845; "The Convention—An Industrial Congress," *Young America*, May 10, 1845; "First Annual Meeting of the N.E. Working Men's Association," *Harbinger* I, no. 1 (June 14, 1845), 15; "Appendix B: The National Industrial Congresses," in Lause, *Young America*, 156. The 1845 gathering, which took place from October 14 to 16 in New York, was billed as a "National Industrial Convention"; the first official session of the NIC did not meet until June, 1846, in Boston.

16. William S. Wait, a founder of the NEWA who later became a judge in Illinois, was the October meeting's president, while Evans was one of its secretaries. Commons, *History of Labour*, Vol. I, 550.

17. On the collaboration between National Reform and Association, see Lause, *Young America*, 34–39; Guarneri, *Utopian Alternative*, 296–297, 306–309, passim; Mandell, *The Lost Tradition of Economic Equality*, 214; *Working Man's Advocate*, March 22, 1845; *Voice of Industry*, January 23, 1846; Greeley to Schuyler Colfax, April 22, 1846, Horace Greeley Papers, New York Public Library; *New-York Tribune*, September 29, 1847.

18. *Voice of Industry*, June 19, 1846; Zahler, *Eastern Workingmen*, 61–63, nn10 and 13. John Allen, a Universalist minister, and John Orvis had both been in residence at Brook Farm; both combined Associationism with land reform and antislavery, and both took turns in editing the *Voice of Industry*. Orvis later became prominent in the Knights of Labor and other postwar labor organizations. See David A. Zonderman, *Uneasy Allies: Working for Labor Reform in Nineteenth-Century Boston* (Amherst: University of Massachusetts Press, 2011), 54–55, 57–60; Montgomery, *Beyond Equality*, 414. On Allen's and Orvis's activities at Brook Farm, see "Brook Farm Correspondence," Middlebury College Special Collections & Archives. On Allen's antislavery activities in and around Rockport, Massachusetts, see the *Liberator*, January 21, 1842, February 3, 1843. I am indebted to Lise Breen for the information on Allen's abolitionist activism.

19. *Voice of Industry*, September 25, 1845; "B" to Horace Greeley, *New-York Tribune*, September 10, 1845; *Liberator*, June 6, 1846; *Niles' National Register*, October 25, 1845; Lause, *Young America*, 77.

20. *Middlesex Standard*, July 25, 1844. The quote seems to have been attributed to Sedgwick by Whittier; see John Greenleaf Whittier, *Old Portraits and Modern Sketches: Personal Sketches and Tributes: Historical Papers* (Boston: Houghton Mifflin, 1866), 189. On Knapp, see Laurie, *Beyond Garrison*, 5, 130, 136–140, 149, 151.

21. *Circular. To Those in Rhode-Island Who Love Liberty* (Providence, June 8, 1847); *Voice of Industry*, September 25, 1845, June 19, 1846.

22. "The Industrial Congress—Its Laws & c.," *Voice of Industry*, June 19, 1846. Evans had been using the term "free soil" since at least 1844. See the *Workingman's Advocate*, September 14, November 23, 1844; *Young America*, April 19, June 28, 1845.

23. *Congressional Globe*, 29th Congress, 1st session, 1217–1218. Twenty-two northern Senators voted with the South against the proviso on March 3, 1847, but as Jonathan Earle has pointed out, none were members of the Van Buren-Wilmot wing of the party, and all but four were lame duck congressmen serving the final day of their terms. Earle, *Jacksonian Antislavery*, 137.

24. *Barnburner*, July 1, 1848.

25. Wilmot quoted in *Congressional Globe*, 29th Congress, 2nd session, 1847, Appendix, p. 317. For the "whiteness" interpretation of the Wilmot Proviso and the Free Soil movement, see Saxton, *The Rise and Fall of the White Republic*, 153–154; Roediger, *The Wages of Whiteness*, 43–95. See also Eric Foner, "Racial Attitudes of the New York Free Soilers," in Foner, *Politics and Ideology*, 77–93.

26. *New York Courier and Enquirer*, August 11, 1847, quoted in Joseph G. Rayback, *Free Soil: The Election of 1848* (Lexington: University Press of Kentucky, 1970), 60; Wilmot quoted in Earle, *Jacksonian Antislavery*, 124, 133. Wilmot's comments were made at the Herkimer Free Soil convention in 1847.

27. James Oakes, *The Scorpion's Sting: Antislavery and the Coming of the Civil War* (New York: W. W. Norton, 2014), 13–14, 25–26. As Oakes points out, both the "scorpion's sting" metaphor and the plan to choke off slavery by surrounding it with free states were developed by abolitionists beginning in the mid-1840s.

28. "The Turn of the Tide," *National Era*, August 31, 1848; [Benjamin Lundy, ed.], *The Anti-Texass Legion. Protest of Some Free Men, States, and Presses against the Texass Rebellion, Against the Laws of Nature and of Nations* (Albany, 1844); Julius Reubens Ames and Benjamin Lundy, eds., *The Legion of Liberty! And Force of Truth, Containing the Thoughts, Words, and Deeds, of Some Prominent Apostles, Champions and Martyrs*, 10th ed. (New York: American Anti-Slavery Society, 1847); Earle, *Jacksonian Antislavery*, 139, 142. On Leggett's influence on Wilmot personally, see Earle, *Jacksonian Antislavery*, 127.

29. Huston, *Land and Freedom*, 170; Lause, *Young America*, 77.

30. "Texas," *Working Man's Advocate*, April 27, 1844; "Great Texas Meeting in the Park," *Working Man's Advocate*, May 11, 1844; "Texas—A Development," *People's Rights*, July 27, 1844. Unbeknownst to the land reformers, Polk had dismissed their questionnaire with a note deeming it "not worthy of an answer." At least one prominent National Reformer, New York's John Keyser, voted for Birney in 1844, suffering a beating at the hands of local Democrats as a result. Lause, *Young America*, 27, 43; Zahler, *Eastern Workingmen*, 94–95.

31. Texas General Land Office, "History of Texas Public Lands," http://www.glo.texas.gov/history/archives/forms/files/history-of-texas-public-lands.pdf, accessed July 18, 2017.

32. John L. O'Sullivan, "Annexation," *United States Magazine and Democratic Review* 17, no. 1 (July–August 1845); "Congress," *Young America*, December 27, 1845; "Wholesale Robbery of the People's Lands—Sacrifice of the Lacklanders—War for Slavery" [from *Young America*], *Voice of Industry*, November 27, 1846. Most recently, Yonatan Eyal has conflated the two versions of "Young America," implying that Evans and the land reform movement were closely identified with the movement associated with O'Sullivan and exaggerating the extent to which so-called "New Democrats" endorsed the land reformers' program. See Yonatan Eyal, *The Young America Movement and the Transformation of the Democratic Party, 1828–1861* (Cambridge: Cambridge University Press, 2012), 148–150. Mark Lause's *Young America*, which focuses on the National Reform Association, makes the distinction between the two movements clear, even if he somewhat confusingly titles his work after Evans's newspaper.

33. *Weekly Chronotype*, January 14, 28, 1847; *Young America*, quoted in the *Chronotype*, January 28, 1847.

34. Quoted in George E. McNeill, ed., *The Labor Movement: The Problem of To-Day* (Boston: 1887), 107.

35. "Tremendous War Gathering in the Park," *New York Herald*, May 21, 1846.

36. "Meeting of the National Reform Society," *New York Herald*, May 28, 1846. Commerford's anti-Mexican War stance did not arise from nowhere; he had been among the seventy or so Working Men's Party members who had signed antislavery petitions in the 1830s. See John B. Jentz, "The Antislavery Constituency in Jacksonian New York City," *Civil War History* 27, no. 2 (June 1981), 101–122.

37. "The War," *Voice of Industry*, June 12, 1846. The *Voice* was then edited by Lowell Female Labor Reform Association organizer Sarah G. Bagley.

38. *Voice of Industry*, June 11, 18, 1847; "Taxation and the War," *Liberator* July 9, 1847. The resolution on direct taxation was offered by Charles Hosmer, the New England Associationist whose address to the Labor Reform League of New England is quoted above. The 1847 congress was also notable for the participation of a female delegate, Fanny Lee Townsend of Providence, Rhode Island. See also the *New-York Daily Tribune*, June 4, 7, 1847; *Harbinger* V, no. 3 (June 26, 1847), 48; *Niles' National Register*, July 10, 1847, for accounts of the proceedings of the 1847 congress.

39. "National Reform Convention," *Voice of Industry*, November 5, 1847.

40. "National Reform Convention. First Day" (from the *New York Herald*), *Young America*, May 10, 1845. The *Herald* complained that its reporter was excluded from afternoon proceedings in favor of a reporter from the *New-York Tribune*, in what may be taken as a sign of the convention's distaste for the proslavery, Democratic paper.

41. Lause, *Young America*, 77–78.

42. *Voice of Industry*, June 19, 1846.

43. Ibid.

44. "Letter of Alvan E. Bovay to the Auburn Convention," *Albany Patriot*, January 26, 1848; quoted in Lause, *Young America*, 73.

45. "Unpaid Toil," *Young America*, December 27, 1845; *Liberator*, September 4, 1846.

46. "Unpaid Toil," *Young America*, December 27, 1845; *Liberator*, September 4, 1846.

47. "Industrial Congress—Gen. Cass. Extract of a letter dated Philadelphia, June 9, 1848," *Evening Post*, June 10, 1848; Alvan E. Bovay and John H. Keyser to Martin Van Buren, and Buren's reply, in the *Barnburner*, July 29, 1848. See also Van Buren to Rochester National Reformers, *Evening Post*, September 21, 1848.

48. Richard H. Sewell, *Ballots for Freedom: Antislavery Politics in the United States, 1837–1860* (New York: W. W. Norton, 1980), 83, 103–107, 115. On the Liberty Party generally, see Reinhard O. Johnson, *The Liberty Party, 1840–1848: Antislavery Third Party Politics in the United States* (Baton Rouge: Louisiana State University Press, 2009). On Smith's commitment to free trade, see Smith to William H. Seward, January 1, 1843; "To the Liberty Party," May 7, 1846, GS Papers. It should be cautioned that, unlike later free-trade and laissez-faire ideologues, but in common with a significant strain of American political economy in the Early Republic and antebellum period, the free trade views of Smith and other Liberty Party members did not preclude them from criticizing predatory forms of capitalism or the hoarding of resources and wealth, or from embracing land limitation, hours of labor laws, or other measures that utilized the power of government to bring about the common good.

49. Sewell, *Ballots for Freedom*, 87–99; Laurie, *Beyond Garrison*, 135–136; Brooks, *Liberty Power: Antislavery Third Parties*, 59–60, 82–83, 107–08, passim. For a sampling of writings on political economy by Liberty Party leaders, see Alvan Stewart, *Tract No. 4. The Cause of the Hard Times* (Boston 1843); Joshua Leavitt, *The Financial Power of Slavery: The Substance of an Address Delivered in Ohio, in September, 1840* (1841); *Philanthropist*, February 16, 1842; Gerrit Smith, *To the Friends of Political Reform, In the County of Madison* (Peterboro, n.d.); *To the Poor Men of the County of Madison* (Peterboro, NY, October 17, 1846); *Homes for All. Speech of Gerrit Smith, on the Homestead Bill. In Congress, February 21, 1854* (Washington, DC: Buell and Blanchard, 1854).

50. "Mr. Birney's Letter" and "Reply to Mr. Birney," *People's Rights*, July 27, 1844.

51. Sewell, *Ballots for Freedom*, 117–120; Elizur Wright, Jr., to Gerrit Smith, February 18, 1848, Gerrit Smith Papers; *National Era*, quoted in the *American Freeman*, June 9, 1847. Smith himself seems to have embraced the conclusion that the Liberty Party needed to expand its platform only reluctantly, as he was still arguing against this position as late as May 1846. See Smith, *To the Liberty Party* (Peterboro, NY, May 7, 1846), GS Papers.

52. *Middlesex Standard*, August 15, September 12, 1844.

53. Sewell, *Ballots for Freedom*, 117–120; Brooks, *Liberty Power*, 135–136; Johnson, *Liberty Party*, 64–65; Elizur Wright, Jr., to Gerrit Smith, February 18, 1848, Gerrit Smith Papers; Goodell, *Address of the Macedon Convention by William Goodell; and Letters of Gerrit Smith* (Albany: S. W. Green, 1847). For Smith's understanding of the antislavery interpretation of the Constitution, see *Gerrit Smith's Constitutional Argument* (Peterboro, NY: Jackson & Chaplin, 1844). For recent interpretations of the significance of antislavery constitutionalism to the history of antislavery politics, see Wilentz, *No Property In Man*; Oakes, *Freedom National*. The site of the Liberty League meeting was

referred to as "Macedon Lock," although no such community existed by that name. The "lock" likely referred to the Erie Canal lock that existed in the town of Macedon.

54. *National Era*, quoted in the *American Freeman*, June 9, 1847.

55. *Voice of Industry*, June 25, 1847; *Niles' National Register*, July 10, 1847.

56. *National Era*, June 24, 1847; Goodell, *Address of the Macedon Convention*, 3–5; Lause, *Young America*, 89.

57. "Resolutions Passed by the Macedon Convention," *Voice of Industry* (from the *Albany Patriot*), July 7, 1847; "Industrial Congress—Annual Session at Philadelphia," *New-York Tribune*, June 21, 1848. The 1848 congress in Philadelphia also sent a memorial to the US Congress praying for laws prohibiting traffic in the public lands. Records of the 30th Congress, National Archives. On Burritt, see Sinha, *The Slave's Cause*, 549–550, and Burritt, *A Plan of Brotherly Copartnership of the North and South for the Peaceful Extinction of Slavery* (New York: Dayton and Burdick, 1856), as well as the epilogue in the current volume. Burritt's peace activism, organized into the League of Universal Brotherhood in 1846, united abolitionists like Garrison and Joseph Sturge with "moral force" Chartists and the economic approaches of the free labor produce movement.

58. "National Reform Convention," *Voice of Industry*, November 5, 1847; "Industrial Congress—Annual Session at Philadelphia," *New-York Tribune*, June 21, 1848; *Pennsylvania Freeman*, June 15, 1848, January 17, 1850; Joshua King Ingalls, *Reminiscences of an Octogenarian in the Fields of Industrial and Social Reform* (Elmira, NY: Gazette Company, 1897), 26; Lause, *Young America*, 92–93. The abolitionist members of the NIC compromised with elements who preferred a "practical working man" by substituting William S. Wait for Burritt as the vice-presidential candidate. In the event, both Wait and Burritt declined the nomination.

59. "Where Are We?" *Voice of Industry*, June 29, 1848.

60. Brooks, *Liberty Power*, 135–136.

61. *Anti-Slavery Bugle*, July 21, 1848. The Garrisonian *Bugle* was writing to criticize the National Reformers' choice for vice president, Illinois judge William S. Wait, who declined the nomination. The *Bugle* claimed that Wait had resigned out of opposition to Smith, an "ultra abolitionist," but failed to offer any evidence for this conclusion, admitting that it had not yet seen Wait's resignation letter. *Niles' Weekly Register* also recorded Wait's resignation, without offering any reason; see *Niles' Weekly Register 74* (July 1848–January 1849), 19. Regardless, Wait was replaced by the Michigan abolitionist Charles C. Foote. On Wait, see *Portrait and Biographical Record of Montgomery and Bond Counties, Illinois* (Chicago: Chapman Bros., 1892), 486–487.

Chapter 6

1. Ingalls, *Reminiscences*, 44–45. For the National Reformers on Cass, see "Industrial Congress—Gen. Cass," *Evening Post*, June 10, 1848; "The Democratic Nomination," *Landmark*, June 3, 1848.

2. Ingalls, *Reminiscences*, 44–45.

3. Ibid., 45.

4. *Young America*, March 21, 1846.

5. Schuyler C. Marshall, "The Free Democratic Convention of 1852," *Pennsylvania History: A Journal of Mid-Atlantic Studies* 22, no. 2 (April 1955), 146–167; and *National Era*, June 10, 1852.

6. The question of why the United States, in contrast to other industrialized countries, failed to develop either a Labor Party or a robust tradition of socialism was first raised by the German sociologist Werner Sombart, in Patricia M. Hocking, trans., *Why Is There No Socialism in the United States* (London: Macmillan Press, 1976; originally published 1906). See also Eric Foner, "Why Is There No Socialism in the United States," *History Workshop*, no. 17 (Spring 1984), 57–80.

7. For recent work on free Black resistance to the Fugitive Act, see Kellie Carter Jackson, *Force and Freedom: Black Abolitionists and the Politics of Violence* (Philadelphia: University of Pennsylvania Press, 2019); Bonner, *Remaking the Republic*; Van Gosse, *The First Reconstruction*; Eric Foner, *Gateway to Freedom: The Hidden History of the Underground Railroad* (New York: W. W. Norton, 2015).

8. *North Star*, May 5, June 21, June 30, July 14, August 11, 1848, August 17, September 7, 1849, April 26, 1850; *Frederick Douglass' Paper*, April 29, 1852; *Frederick Douglass' Paper*, August 20, 1852, quoted in Bonner, *Remaking the Republic*, 96; McDaniel, *The Problem of Democracy*, 143–152, 183–203.

9. *National Era*, November 18, 1847; *Frederick Douglass' Paper*, December 31, 1852; *Provincial Freeman*, December 29, 1855. On free Black intentional communities before the Civil War, see William H. Pease and Jane Pease, *Black Utopia: Negro Communal Experiments in America* (Madison: State Historical Society of Wisconsin, 1963); Nikki Marie Taylor, *Frontiers of Freedom: Cincinnati's Black Community, 1802–1868* (Athens: Ohio University Press, 2005). On the Elgin community, see William King, Manuscript Autobiography, Public Archives Records Center, Canada, 1846–1916 (available at Yale University Beinecke Library).

10. Ingalls, *Reminiscences*, 28–35; Amos Gilbert to the editor, March 22, 1848, in the *North Star*, May 12, 1848; "National Reform and People of Color," *Landmark* (reprinted from *Ram's Horn*), June 3, 1848; Gatewood, *Free Man of Color*.

11. A. H., "Misrepresentations," *Homestead Journal*, reprinted in *Anti-Slavery Bugle*, March 31, 1848. The *Bugle's* response seems to reflect its editor's Garrisonian bias against political antislavery; according to the *Bugle's* logic, the fact that the National Reform Association was an explicitly political organization meant that women and Blacks could not participate as equals even if invited to do so. The *Bugle* also noted that the Salem National Reformers had refused to pass a resolution admitting antislavery disunionists to the organization.

12. *Niles' National Register*, July 10, 1847, 296–297. Other delegates opposed the measure on the basis that freedom of the public lands alone would be enough to win "the entire abolition vote" and that "the more simple our measures the better," but at least part of the opposition stemmed from William Wait's concern that it "did not recognize the rights of women or of colored people; if adopted, therefore, offence would

be taken by the liberty party and other reformers." Among the women who participated in the NIC were Lowell labor leader Sarah Bagley; Eliza Edwards, a Philadelphian who served as one of the meeting's vice presidents in 1851; and Fannie Lee Townsend, the editor of the *Monthly Jubilee* (later the *Jubilee Harbinger*).

13. *New York Herald*, June 6, 7, 1851; Cincinnati *Daily Nonpareil*, June 11, 1851; *National Reform Almanac for 1848*; *New-York Tribune*, June 8, 1855, *Cleveland Morning Leader*, June 8, June 6, 1855; Lause, *Young America*, 107. The letter writer, J. L. Kingsley, claimed that Bowers's arrival had been paid for and promoted by "the Quaker abolitionists of Philadelphia," and accordingly gave up his nomination for secretary in protest of Bowers' seating. Given its well-known hostility to abolitionism and racial equality, however, it is possible that the *Herald* exaggerated the level of opposition to Bowers and amplified the concerns of those, like Kingsley, who opposed his seating. See also the *Herald, June 8, 10, 13 1851*. For more sympathetic coverage, see the *New-York Tribune*, June 6, 9, 13, 14, as well as Lucius Hine's letters (as "H") to the Cincinnati *Daily Nonpareil*, June 11, 13, 16, 17, 1851. On Bowers, see Julie Winch, *The Elite of Our People. Joseph Wilson's Sketches of Black Upper-Class Life in Antebellum Philadelphia* (State College: Pennsylvania State University, 2000), 153, n78; *Philadelphia Inquirer*, October 8, 1873.

14. Zonderman, *Uneasy Allies*, 68–69.

15. *Liberator* (from the *Boston Protective Union*), October 25, 1850.

16. Lause, *Young America*, 115; *U.S. vs. John C. Cluer*, U.S. Circuit Court for the District of Massachusetts, Record Group 21: Records of the District Courts of the United States, 1685–2009, Case Files, 1790–1911, National Archives. Cluer was a Glasgow weaver and Chartist organizer who emigrated to the United States in 1839, where he became active in the National Reform and ten-hours movements.

17. John R. Commons et al., eds., *History of Labour in the United States*, Vol. II (New York: Macmillan, 1918), 619.

18. J. E. Snodgrass to the editor of the *National Era*, July 20, 1848; Devyr to Andrew Johnson, December 9, 1859, Johnson-Patterson Papers, quoted in Zahler, *Eastern Workingmen*, 104, n57.

19. *National Era*, July 15, October 14, 1852.

20. "Proceedings of the State Convention of the friends of Industrial Reform," *New-York Weekly Tribune*, October 26, 1850, 329; *New York Herald*, April 7 and 15, 1852; "Memorial for the Support of Liberty!" July 4, 1854. A recent account of the Preston case can be found in Foner, *Gateway to Freedom*, 133–134.

21. William Goodell, *Views of American Constitutional Law In Its Bearing upon American Slavery* (1844); Alvan Stewart, "A Constitutional Argument on the Subject of Slavery"; Lysander Spooner, *The Constitutionality of Slavery* (1845). See also Goodell's reply to Phillips in the *National Anti-Slavery Standard*, March 18, 1847.

22. Westley Bailey to GS, June 5, 1847, Smith Papers, quoted in Sewell, *Ballots for Freedom*, 120.

23. Smith to J. K. Ingalls, Peterboro, August 15, 1848, GS Papers. See also Gerrit Smith, *Address to the Voters of the United States*, Peterboro, July 15, 1851, GS Papers.

24. Brooks, *Liberty Power*, 129–153, 155–160; Johnson, *The Liberty Party, 1840–1848*. See also Goodell, "Address of the Convention at Honeoye," in the *Liberty Leaguer*, March 1, 1849. According to Johnson, the Smith faction probably commanded less than 20 percent of the overall Liberty Party vote even in New York. The League's candidate for Lieutenant Governor, Charles O. Shepard, fared somewhat better with 4.1 percent of New York's total vote, a fact Johnson attributes to National Reform support in that state.

25. Douglass, "Slavery, the Free Church, and British Agitation against Bondage: An Address Delivered in Newcastle-upon-Tyne, England, on 3 August 1846," in John W. Blassingame, ed., *The Frederick Douglass Papers: Series One: Speeches Debates, and Interviews Vol. 1: 1841-46* (New Haven: Yale University Press, 1979); Sinha, *The Slave's Cause*, 468, 482. Buffum's career is briefly described in Blassingame, Vol. 1, 38, n1.

26. *North Star*, February 25, April 21, 1848.

27. "To the Liberty Party of the County of Madison," *North Star*, September 15, 1848. Notices for conventions of the "true" Liberty Party were also published in *Young America* and the *Model Worker;* see *Young America*, September 23, 1848.

28. Samuel Ringgold Ward, "Address to the Four Thousand Colored Voters of the State of New York," in the *North Star*, September 1, 1848. Willis Hodges and his brother William, Henry Highland Garnet, and William Hamilton all served as delegates to the 1844 Liberty Party convention in Kings County, New York. On African Americans and the Liberty Party, see Gosse, *The First Reconstruction*, 150–157, 416–417, 438, 458–459, *passim*.

29. Ward quoted in Sinha, *The Slave's Cause*, 468; Garnet quoted in *The Weekly Chronotype*, September 16, 1847. Although the *Chronotype* published a long excerpt from Garnet's letter in reply to the editors of the Albany *Evening Journal*, his original words in the *National Watchman* have apparently been lost.

30. *Frederick Douglass' Paper*, April 1, 1852; "Persecution on Account of Faith, Persecution on Account of Color: An Address Delivered in Rochester, NewYork, on 26 January 1851" (published in the *North Star*, January 30, 1851); Sinha, *The Slave's Cause*, 492–496; Frederick Douglass to Gerrit Smith, May 15, 1852, in Blassingame, *Frederick Douglass Papers* I, 536–537.

31. "Industrial Congress," *Niles' National Register* (July 10, 1847), 296.

32. *National Reform Almanac for 1848* (New York: Office of Young America, 1848), 44–45. The National Reform Association claimed to have organizations in "about" twenty of the thirty states by this time, nearly all of them in the North.

33. Brown quoted in Benjamin Drew, *A North-Side View of Slavery: The Refugee: Or the Narratives of Fugitive Slaves, Related By Themselves, with an Account of the History and Condition of the Colored Population of Upper Canada* (Boston: John P. Jewett, 1856), 239–248. For a contemporary African American source on the Cincinnati riots, see the *Rights of All*, September 18, 1829.

34. "Letter from John O. Wattles," *National Reform Almanac for 1848* (New York, 1848), 4 (pages numbered inconsecutively); Wattles, *Report on the Educational*

Condition of the Colored People of Cincinnati (Cincinnati: John White, 1847); Honeck, *We Are the Revolutionists*, 71–103. An earlier version of Wattles's report found, out of a population of a little over 2,000 Cincinnati Blacks, that only 34 qualified as "mechanics," while a greater number (158) were "laborers"; "many" were said to own local farms, and significant numbers toiled as barbers, whitewashers, river workers, carters, or draymen (wagon deliverers). See "Colored People of Cincinnati" (from the *Cincinnati Herald*), *Herald of Freedom*, May 16, 1845.

35. National Reform Association of Cincinnati [John Pickering], *The Friend of Man; Being the Principles of National or Land Reform; Clearly Stated, Together With Answers to the Various Objections that Have Been Urged Against It* (Cincinnati: William McDiarmid, 1850), 3–7, 11; Lause, *Young America*, 104–105; *New-York Daily Tribune*, June 12, 13, 15, 17, 1850; "Petition of John Pickering, John White, James Gibson and 228 other citizens of Cincinnati praying Congress to cause the public lands to be laid out in tracts and to be occupied without charge by landless persons," January 31, 1848, Records of the 30th Congress, National Archives. Little biographical information about Pickering is available, but a "J. Pickering" is described as the Mechanic's Institute librarian in Charles Cist, *Cincinnati in 1841: Its Early Annals and Future Prospects* (Cincinnati, 1841), 133.

36. L. A. (Lucius Alonzo) Hine, *A Lecture on Garrisonian Politics Before the Western Philosophical Institute, Delivered in Cincinnati, Sunday, April 24th, 1853* (Cincinnati: Longley and Brother, 1853); L. A. Hine to the *New-York Daily Tribune*, March 1, 1853, in Commons, Doc. Hist. Vol. VIII, Part 2, 60–61; Lause, *Young America*, 63, 104, 113, 130–133. See also Dayton Kelley, "L.A. Hine, Prophet of the Rights of Man" (manuscript biography, n.d.), Ohio History Connection.

37. "A Free Soil—Progress of the Cause," *Young America*, July 5, 1845; *Wisconsin Free Democrat*, September 3, 1851.

38. "Free Soil Ratification Meeting," *National Era*, September 30, 1852; Paul Goodman, "The Emergence of Homestead Exemption in the United States: Accommodation and Resistance to the Market Revolution," *Journal of American History* 80, no. 2 (September 1993), 487; Zahler, *Eastern Workingmen*, 98 n44.

39. "Sketch of the Life and Political Career of the Late D. C. Broderick," *New York Times*, February 25, 1860. Terry blamed Broderick for his defeat in state elections in 1859. See *Journal of the Senate*, 1857, 1st session 372–373, and especially the speech in 35th Congress, 1st session, Cong. Globe, 191–193. See also David A. Williams, *David C. Broderick: A Political Portrait* (San Marino, CA: Huntington Library, 1969).

40. *Wisconsin Argus*, November 16, 1847; quoted in Lena London, "Homestead Exemption in the Wisconsin Constitution," *Wisconsin Magazine of History* 32, no. 2 (December 1948), 184.

41. Rayback, *Free Soil: The Election of 1848*, 282.

42. Merle Curti, "Isaac P. Walker: Reformer in Mid-Century Politics," *Wisconsin Magazine of History* 34, no. 1 (Autumn 1950), 4–5; Lause, *Young America*, 63, 87; *New-York Tribune*, May 1, 1849.

43. Theodore Clarke Smith, "The Free Soil Party in Wisconsin," *Wisconsin State Historical Society Publications* 42 (December 1894), 112–114, 150; Rayback, *Free Soil*, 215, 250.

44. Rayback, *Free Soil*, 282.

45. *Wisconsin Free Democrat*, September 3, 1851, February 7, 1849, February 26, 1851.

46. *Wisconsin Free Democrat*, June 25, 1851; Lause, *Young America*, 79–80. See also Van Amringe's regularly published column on national reform in the *Wisconsin Freeman*, especially January 19, 26 and March 22, 1848.

47. *Wisconsin Free Democrat*, September 3, 1851, February 7, 1849, February 26, 1851; "Young America—National Reformers," (from Osh-kosh *True Democrat*), *Wisconsin Free Democrat*, May 2, 1849.

48. Rayback, *Free Soil*, 282.

49. *The Fugitive Slave Law, Etc. Speech of Charles Durkee, of Wisconsin, in the House of Representatives, August 6, 1852, on the Fugitive Slave Law as a 'Finality' and the Present Position of Parties* (Washington, DC, 1852); *National Era*, June 10, 1852. See also *New-York Herald*, June 7, 1852.

50. Curti, "Isaac P. Walker," 58–59.

51. Isaac P. Walker, *The Compromise Resolutions. Speech of Hon. I. P. Walker, of Wisconsin, in Senate of the United States, March 6, 1850, On the Compromise Resolutions submitted by Mr. Clay, on the 25th of January* (Washington, DC: Government Printing Office, 1850), 3–11, 13; *Milwaukee Sentinel*, October 10, 1849; *Congressional Globe*, 31st Congress, 1st session, Vol. 19, Part I, pp. 439–440, cited in Curti, "Isaac P. Walker," 60.

52. Walker, *Compromise Resolutions*, 3–11, 13; Charles Sumner, *Freedom National, Slavery Sectional: Speech of Hon. Charles Sumner, of Massachusetts, on His Motion to Repeal the Fugitive Slave Bill: In the Senate of the United States, August 26, 1852* (Boston: Ticknor, Reed, and Fields, 1852). Walker's antagonist in these debates was the Mississippi Senator and future president of the Confederacy, Jefferson Davis.

53. On a single day in 1852, Walker presented petitions in favor of the homestead bill on behalf of the citizens of the state of Wisconsin, Indiana County, Pennsylvania, and the National Reform Association of Monmouth County, New Jersey, all of which were referred to as the Committee on Public Lands. See the *Congressional Globe*, 32nd Congress, 1st session (June 8, 1852). In 1854, Walker was one of only thirteen senators to vote against the Kansas-Nebraska Act; see the *Congressional Globe*, 33rd Congress, 1st session, 1321 (May 25, 1854). The final debate on the Nebraska Bill can be found in the appendix, pp. 755–796.

54. Oakes, *Freedom National*.

55. The Free Democratic Party's platform, along with Smith's minority report, was printed in full in *Frederick Douglass' Paper*, August 27, 1852. See also Marshall, "The Free Democratic Convention of 1852," 146–167; Zahler, *Eastern Workingmen*, 100, n48. Smith, Goodell, and James G. Birney issued a competing call for a Liberty Party convention in Buffalo to be held on September 1; eventually, the remaining Liberty Party

members held a convention in Syracuse on September 30. See "To the Public," *Frederick Douglass' Paper*, June 24, 1852.

56. Marshall, "The Free Democratic Convention of 1852," 159, 160–164; Bronstein, *Land Reform and Working-Class Experience*, 242. See also the report in the (London) *People's Paper*, 18 (September 4, 1852). Young had been the vice president of the Massachusetts workingmen's convention that met in Boston in October 1850.

57. Mandell, *The Lost Tradition*, 217–221. In March 1846, New York's Richard Herrick became the first congressman to publicly support land reform by presenting a National Reform petition in the House, followed on the same day by a homestead proposal from Georgia's Felix McConnell. Seward also presented memorials from the New York City Industrial Congress seeking to prevent speculation in the public lands and asking for a change of U.S. foreign policy to intervene on behalf of "the oppressed subjects of other countries seeking to shake off tyrannical and despotic governments"; see *Journal of the Senate* 43, 42 (December 9, 1851), 79 (December 20, 1851). At one "Great Land Reform Meeting" in New York's City Hall Park in May 1852, supporters were addressed by Horace Greeley, Andrew Johnson, and Sherman Booth and heard letters of support from William H. Seward, Stephen Douglas, and I. P. Walker. See the *Evening Post*, May 28, 1852. Tammany Hall also hosted a land reform meeting in 1851, but largely dropped the issue as it became associated with antislavery; see the *New-York Tribune*, May 30, 1851; *National Era*, June 12, 1851, and chapter 7.

58. "Land Reform Meeting at Military Hall," *New York Herald*, August 19, 1852; Tuchinsky, *Horace Greeley's New-York Tribune*, 147–151. See also the *New-York Tribune* of the same date for an alternative account of the meeting. Gerrit Smith's faction of the Liberty Party had earlier made the distinction between the "truthful" free soil of the National Reform Association and "sham" free soil of the Free Soil Party in a call for a convention at Canastota, New York, in September 1848; see "State Convention. To the Liberty Party of the State of New York" (from the *Model Worker*), *Young America*, September 23, 1848.

The path taken by the National Reform Association becomes harder to follow at this point; *Young America* stopped publishing in 1849, although the association's activities in the early 1850s were covered by the (mostly hostile) *New York Herald* and the (somewhat more sympathetic) *Tribune*.

59. Although some state organizations of the Free Soil/Free Democratic Party survived until 1854, as a national movement the Free Soil Party did not long outlast its relatively strong (but nonetheless ineffectual) electoral showing in 1848 (when the party gained thousands of votes in New York, Pennsylvania, and elsewhere, but failed to carry a single state). On former Free Soilers in the Republican Party, see Foner, *Free Soil, Free Labor*, 149–185.

Chapter 7

1. Parke Godwin, *Political Essays* (New York: Dix, Edwards & Co., 1856), 48, 55, 254–255, 283–297, 320–321.

2. George Haven Putnam, *Memories of a Publisher, 1865–1915* (New York: Putnam, 1915), 12–13.

3. Frank A. Flower, *History of the Republican Party, Embracing Its Origin, Growth, and Mission, together with Appendices of Statistics and Information Required by Enlightened Politicians and Patriotic Citizens* (Springfield, IL: Union Publishing, 1884), 147–156; Diane S. Butler, "The Public Life and Private Affairs of Sherman M. Booth," *Wisconsin Magazine of History* (Spring 1999); Lause, *Young America*, 113–114. Francis Curtis, *The Republican Party: A History of its Fifty Years' Existence and a Record of its Measures and Leaders, 1854–1904*, Vol. 1 (New York: G. P. Putnam's Sons, 1904), 174–178.

4. *The Great Republican Reform Party, Calling on their Candidate* (New York: N. Currier, 1856); [Louis Maurer], *The Republican Party Going to the Right House* (New York: Currier & Ives, 1860); *The Black Republicans at their Devotions* (n.p., 1856); Andre Fleche, *The Revolution of 1861: The American Civil War in the Age of Nationalist Conflict* (Chapel Hill: University of North Carolina Press, 2012).

5. Classic works on the Republican Party and its ideology include Foner, *Free Soil, Free Labor*, William E. Gienapp, *The Origins of the Republican Party, 1852–1856* (Oxford: Oxford University Press, 1987). For more recent work, see Graham A. Peck, *Making an Antislavery Nation: Lincoln, Douglas, and the Battle over Freedom* (Urbana: University of Illinois Press, 2017); Oakes, *Freedom National*; Matt Karp, "The Mass Politics of Antislavery," *Catalyst* 3, no. 2 (Summer 2019), 130–178; and Karp, *Millions of Abolitionists: The Republican Party and the Political War Against Slavery* (forthcoming).

6. Robert Fogel, *Without Consent or Contract: The Rise and Fall of American Slavery* (New York: W.W. Norton, 1989), 354–362; Commons et al., *History of Labour in the United States*, Vol. 1, 564; Foner, *History of the Labor Movement*, 219–248.

7. *New York Herald*, quoted in Foner, *Organized Labor*, 12. On competition between African American and white workers in the antebellum and Civil War periods, see Foner, *Organized Labor*, 10–16; Roediger, *The Wages of Whiteness*, 147–150.

8. Leaflet addressed to the "Workingmen of New Haven" (ca. 1856), collection of Yale University, quoted in Philip S. Foner and Herbert Shapiro, eds., *Northern Labor and Antislavery: A Documentary History* (New York: Praeger, 1994), 245–246. For a recent interpretation of Lincoln and the Republican Party's de-emphasis of racial equality and its relationship to Republican antislavery, see Manisha Sinha, "Lincoln's Competing Political Loyalties: Antislavery, Union, and the Constitution," in Nicholas Buccola, ed., *Abraham Lincoln and Liberal Democracy* (Lawrence: University Press of Kansas, 2016), 164–191. For an older interpretation of the Free Soilers, see Eric Foner, "Racial Attitudes of the Free Soil Party," in *Politics and Ideology in the Age of the Civil War*, 77–95.

9. "Address of the Working Men of Pittsburgh to Their Fellow Working Men of Pennsylvania," *New York Tribune*, October 31, 1856; quoted in Foner and Shapiro, *Northern Labor and Antislavery*, 242–244; Union of the Free Germans, *To All True Republicans in the Union* (Louisville, KY, 1854), quoted in "Appendix A: The Louisville Platform," in Ann Kathryn Fleming, "Galvanizing Germantown: The Politicization of

Louisville's German Community, 1848–1855" (PhD diss., University of West Virginia, 2020), 146–153.

10. Ingalls, *Reminiscences*, 45–48; John W. Geary to William L. Marcy, in Kansas Historical Society, "Thaddeus Hyatt Papers, 1843–1898: Biography," in *Selections from the Hyatt Manuscripts*, Vol. 2 (1880), 203–221; Article XXVIII, in John Brown, *Provisional Constitution and Ordinances for the People of the United States* (1858).

11. "The Land Reformer," *Frederick Douglass' Paper*, August 15, 1856; "A Word to Our People," *Anglo-African Magazine* (September 1859), 297. I am grateful to Matt Karp for bringing the *Frederick Douglass' Paper* article to my attention. On the concept of the Jubilee, see Mandell, *The Lost Tradition*, 2, 92–93, 215, 236–238, *passim*.

12. Salmon P. Chase, Charles Sumner, J. R. Giddings, Edward Wade, Gerrit Smith, and Alexander De Witt, *Appeal of the Independent Democrats in Congress, to the People of the United States: Shall Slavery Be Permitted in Nebraska?* (Washington, DC: Towers' Printers, 1854); *No Slavery in Nebraska, No Slavery in the Nation, Slavery an Outlaw: Speech of Gerrit Smith, on the Nebraska Bill, in Congress, April 6, 1854* (Washington, DC: Buell & Blanchard, 1854); James L. Huston, *Calculating the Value of Union: Slavery, Property Rights, and the Economic Origins of the Civil War* (Chapel Hill: University of North Carolina Press, 2003), 194–197.

13. Foner, *Free Soil, Free Labor*, 126–127; Magdol, *The Antislavery Rank and File*, 117–135; see especially Tables 8-1 and 8-4.

14. "Voice of the Workingmen of New York," *National Anti-Slavery Standard*, February 25, 1854; quoted in Foner and Shapiro, *Northern Labor and Antislavery*, 247–250; Foner, *History of the American Labor Movement*, Vol. 1, 281–282.

15. "The Nebraska Fraud," *New-York Tribune*, February 20, 1854; "The People's Meeting, to Protest Against Slavery in Nebraska," *New-York Tribune*, February 17, 1854; "The Voice of the North. No Slavery Extension. The Nebraska Bill Among the Germans. Great Meeting in Washington Hall—Enthusiastic Demonstration," *New-York Tribune*, March 6, 1854; Weydemeyer resolution quoted in Foner, *History of American Labor*, Vol. 1, 283; Commons et al., *History of Labour*, Vol. 2, 619–620; Honeck, *We Are the Revolutionists*, 29–31, 43, 78–79, 141–142; Hermann Schlüter, *Lincoln, Labor, and Slavery: A Chapter from the Social History of America* (New York: Socialist Literature, 1917), 75–76. German and Irish names were, however, largely absent from the list of artisans, manufacturers, and laborers who signed the *Tribune's* earlier call for the Tabernacle meeting on February 18, which in the case of German immigrants may suggest the language barrier or the fact that Germans tended to organize in separate unions. On '48er refugees and other German immigrants in the era of the Civil War, see also Bruce Levine, *The Spirit of 1848: German Immigrants, Labor Conflict, and the Coming of the Civil War* (Champaign: University of Illinois Press, 1992).

16. "Cigar Makers' Trade Agreement Convention," in Commons et al., *A Documentary History*, Vol. VII, 344.

17. Magdol, *Antislavery Rank and File*, 131; "Memorial of democratic citizens of Greenpoint and Bushwick, N. York, demanding the repeal of the fugitive Slave law and

the restoration of the 'Missouri restriction,' July 12, 1854. Ordered to lie on the table." National Archives, Senate Records, 33A-J2, J4, 33rd Congress, 1st session); "Petition of Harrison Newhall" and "Petition of Samuel Gifford," in Massachusetts Anti-Slavery and Anti-Segregation Petitions, Senate Unpassed Legislation 1861, Widener Memorial Library, Harvard University; "Cincinnati Ohio German Workmen to Abraham Lincoln, February 1, 1861," in Abraham Lincoln Papers, Series 1: General Correspondence, 1833–1916, Library of Congress; Burritt, *A Plan of Brotherly Copartnership*, 25–26. Of the twenty-five Greenpoint and Bushwick signers whose occupations could be identified in the 1856 Brooklyn City Directory, seventeen worked as artisans or semiskilled or unskilled laborers.

18. On Sheddon (misspelled "Shedden" in the both the *Times* and the *Tribune*), see Steve Leiken, *The Practical Utopians: American Workers and the Cooperative Movement in the Gilded Age* (Detroit: Wayne State University Press, 2005) 13, 19; Mark A. Lause, *A Secret Society History of the Civil War* (Urbana: University of Illinois Press, 2011), 25; Lause, *Young America*, 131.

19. "Industrial Congress," *New York Daily Times*, June 9, 10, 12, 1854.

20. Ibid., June 12, 1854.

21. Ibid.; "National Industrial Congress–IXth Session," *New-York Tribune*, June 12, 1854. The full resolution, as passed, read, "That we recommend our fellow industrials and the European emigrants now landing upon our shores to settle upon the fertile soil of Kansas and Nebraska, and thus rescue it from the machinations of the Slaver power, as we consider the system of involuntary servitude inimical to the interests of the laboring man." An attempt by a delegate from Delaware to strike out the words after "Nebraska" failed.

22. Braidwood was a lithographer and teacher in a women's school who became the leader of Philadelphia's Working Women's Relief Association during the Civil War. On the relationship of nativism to the emerging Republican Party, see Gienapp, *The Origins of the Republican Party*, 69–102, *passim*; Laurie, *Beyond Garrison*, 275–280; Tyler Anbinder, *Nativism and Slavery: The Northern Know-Nothings and the Politics of the 1850s* (Oxford: Oxford University Press, 1992) 162–278.

23. Lause, *Young America*, 119; *New York Daily Times*, June 6, 1856. The Trenton Congress was the southernmost of the Industrial Congresses, with the exception of that held in Washington, D.C., in 1852. Of the recorded delegates in attendance, eighteen were from Philadelphia, seventeen from New Jersey, eleven from Delaware, and one from Massachusetts. The two major leaders of the opposition to antislavery resolutions were New Jersey's F. S. Mills, a Democratic editor who was later elected mayor of Trenton, and Delaware's Saxe Gotha Laws, who described himself as a "subtreasury, hard money Democrat of the Tom Benton school." S. G. Laws to Polk, August 6, 1845, in Wayne Cutler, ed., *Correspondence of James K. Polk*, Vol. X, July–December 1845 (Knoxville: UT Press, 2004), 124. On the postwar Industrial Congresses, which met between 1866 and 1875 and were organized by an entirely new generation of labor leaders, see Montgomery, *Beyond Equality*, 181; Foner, *History of the Labor Movement*, Vol. 1, 441.

24. Merritt, *Masterless Men*, 42, 57–61, 268; Zahler, *Eastern Workingmen*, 147–176; Gerald Wolff, "The Slavocracy and the Homestead Problem of 1854," *Agricultural History* 40, no. 2 (April 1966), 101–112. Although Wolff wrote to dispute the idea of a "solid South" voting against the homestead bill in 1854, his own findings lend support to the notion that Homestead was essentially a sectional issue, with important connections to the slavery issue, by 1854. In a measure of nine votes on various aspects of the bill, 39.3% of southern senators took strongly "anti" positions, while only 15.3% of northerners did so. Likewise, 69.3% of northern senators were strongly "pro," while only 17.8% of southerners were. Among the senators with the strongest pro-Homestead voting records were Charles Sumner, Benjamin Wade, Salmon Chase, and Isaac P. Walker.

25. On the parallel arguments regarding the constitutionality of slavery, see Oakes, *Freedom National*, 2–8, 15–26, 30–34; Wilentz, *No Property in Man*, 206–262.

26. Zahler, *Eastern Workingmen*, 170; James McPherson, *Battle Cry of Freedom: The Civil War Era* (Oxford: Oxford University Press, 1988), 193–194; Wolff, "The Slavocracy and the Homestead Problem," 102 05, 107–09; Andrew Johnson, "The Homestead," *Congressional Globe*, 31st Congress, 1st session, December 3, 1849–September 30, 1851, 951. Despite being a longtime supporter of Homestead measures, Johnson initially refused to vote for the bill on May 8, 1854, because, as he said, it was "tinctured . . . so strongly with abolitionism."

27. William F. Deverell, "To Loosen the Safety Valve: Eastern Workers and Western Lands," *Western Historical Quarterly* 10, no. 3 (August 1988), 269–285; Gerrit Smith, *Homes for All: Speech of Gerrit Smith, on the Homestead Bill, In Congress, February 21, 1854* (Washington, DC: Buell and Blanchard, 1854); *Speeches of Gerrit Smith in Congress* (New York: Mason Brothers, 1856); "Gerrit Smith's Vote on the Homestead Bill," *Frederick Douglass' Paper*, March 17, 1854; Stauffer, *Black Hearts of Men*, 174–175, 177–180. For Smith's defense of his actions on the Nebraska bill and his response to the *Tribune's* slander, see *Controversy between the New-York Tribune and Gerrit Smith* (New York: John A. Gray, 1855); "Gerrit Smith to His Constituents," *North Star*, August 18, 1854. For commentary on the episode by Garrisonians, see the *Liberator*, October 19, 1855.

28. Roy Marvin Robbins, "Horace Greeley: Land Reform and Unemployment, 1837–1862," *Agricultural History* 7, no. 1 (January 1933), 37; Republican Party of New York, *New York Republican State Convention; Held at Syracuse, September 18 and 19, 1856* (Syracuse, NY: 1856); *The American Presidency Project*, "Republican Party Platform of 1856," June 18, 1856, http://www.presidency.ucsb.edu/ws/?pid=29619, accessed August 23, 2016.

29. Horace Greeley to Schuyler Colfax, June 20, 1860, Greeley-Colfax Papers, NYPL.

30. Robbins, "Horace Greeley," 40. Roy Marvin Robbins also believed that Greeley "probably" wrote the party's homestead plank in 1860. Regardless, Greeley expended considerable effort at Chicago in convincing doubtful Republicans to include the measure.

31. "The Homestead Bill," *New-York Tribune*, March 2, 1859.

32. *New-York Tribune*, June 30, 1860.

33. *Brooklyn Daily Eagle*, September 7, 1860; quoted in Lause, *Free Labor*, 20. For more recent appraisals of Greeley, see Mitchell Snay, *Horace Greeley and the Politics*

of Reform in Nineteenth-Century America (New York: Rowan and Littlefield, 2011); Tuchinsky, *Horace Greeley's* New-York Tribune.

34. "The Work to Be Done," *New-York Tribune,* January 7, 1860; *Rail Splitter,* July 1, 1860.

35. Foner, *History of the American Labor Movement,* Vol. 1, 285.

36. For contemporary debates over tariff policies, see the *New-York Tribune,* March 27, 1845, March 9, 1849, October 16, 1847, March 2, 1859; Tuchinsky, *Horace Greeley's* New-York Tribune, 39, 184–185; James L. Huston, *The Panic of 1857 and the Coming of the Civil War* (Baton Rouge: Louisiana State University Press, 1999). Ariel Ron has persuasively argued that northern farmers, not urban workers, were the key demographic to be won over to protariff policies. As Ron points out, this was accomplished largely by emphasizing the symbiotic relationship between urban workers and manufactures and farmers in the northern hinterlands, who increasingly reoriented production to feed growing cities in a domestic economy that Henry Carey and other northern nationalists described as the "home market." See Ron, *Grassroots Leviathan,* 74–76, 80–81, 86–95, 103–117. On the Republicans and tariff policies, see Heather Cox Richardson, *The Greatest Nation of the Earth: Republican Economic Policies During the Civil War* (Cambridge, MA: Harvard University Press, 1997); Bensel, *Yankee Leviathan;* James L. Huston, "A Political Response to Industrialism: The Republican Embrace of Protectionist Labor Doctrines," *Journal of Amercan History* 70, no. 1 (June 1983), 50–52.

37. Tuchinsky, *Horace Greeley's New-York Tribune,* 184–186; *Pittsburgh Gazette,* November 5, 1860, quoted in Foner, *History of the American Labor Movement,* Vol. 1, 293; "Republican Party Platform of 1860: May 17, 1860," *The American Presidency Project,* http://www.presidency.ucsb.edu/ws/?pid=29620; W. M. Rease, "The Union Must, and Shall Be Preserved" [Lincoln presidential campaign broadside], (Philadelphia, 1860).

38. George Fitzhugh, *Sociology for the South, or, the Failure of Free Society* (Richmond: A. Morris, 1854), 185, 192–193; *Speech of Mr. Downs, of Louisiana, on the Compromise Resolutions of Mr. Clay. In Senate, February 18 and 19, 1850* (Washington, DC, 1850), 22; Clemens and the Muscogee *Herald* quoted in *White Slavery. The New "Democratic Doctrine"* (1856), http://www.loc.gov/resource/rbpe.09303300. The last quotations appear in a pro-Fremont broadside and therefore should be treated with caution; however, these and similar statements were circulated widely in the North in the 1850s as evidence of slaveholders' contempt for northern workingmen. I have not been able to locate a contemporary newspaper in Alabama called the "Muscogee Herald"; the author may have been referring to the *Muscogee Democrat,* based in Columbus, Georgia.

39. Fitzhugh, *Cannibals All!,* 134, 141–142, 197, 306, 327–229, 356; *Liberator,* October 7, 1864; speech of Anderson of Mississippi, Virginia Secession Convention, Fifth Day of Convention, February 18, 1861; Johnson Papers, loose letter, dated February 20, 1860, cited in Zahler, *Eastern Workingmen,* 188.

40. Henry Wilson, "Speech of Henry Wilson on the Lecompton Constitution," *Congressional Globe,* 35th Congress, 1st session, Appendix, May 20, 1858, 167–174;

Bernard Mandel, *Labor, Free and Slave: Workingmen and the Anti-Slavery Movement in the United States* (Urbana: University of Illinois Press, 2007), 162.

41. "What Is the Question," *Radical Abolitionist* (March, 1856); *Principia* I, nos. 21–36 (April 7–July 21, 1860); Jonathan A. Glickstein, "The Chattelization of Northern Whites: An Evolving Abolitionist Warning," *American Nineteenth Century History* 4, no. 1 (Spring 2003), 25–58.

42. *The Issue. White Slavery!* (Frémont & Dayton Tenth Ward Club of the City of Philadelphia, 1856); *White Slavery. The New "Democratic Doctrine"* (1856).

43. Garrison quoted in the *New York Times,* January 15, 1862; "A Democratic Workingman" [William Oland Bourne], *White Slaves* (New York: Sinclair Tousey, 1863); "The War a Rebellion of Capital Against Labor, to Enslave the Laborer," *Liberator,* October 7, 1864. Bourne's other wartime productions that use similar class language include "A Great Fraud," "Don't Unchain the Tiger," and "A Traitor's Peace!," all in William Oland Bourne Papers, Library of Congress. See also "Constitution of the Democratic Republican Workingmen's Association of the City of New York," *Iron Platform Extra—No. XXXVIII* (January 1864).

44. "An Old Democrat," *Twenty Reasons for Leaving the Democratic Party* (Frémont & Dayton Tenth Ward Club of the City of Philadelphia, 1856); *Tyranny of the Slave Power* (Frémont & Dayton Tenth Ward Club of the City of Philadelphia, 1856); *Hear What Henry Clay Said of Republican Principles* (Frémont & Dayton Tenth Ward Club of the City of Philadelphia, 1856); George M. Weston, *Southern Slavery Reduces Northern Wages* (1856).

45. Abraham Lincoln, "An Address by Abraham Lincoln Before the Wisconsin State Agricultural Society in Milwaukee, Wisconsin, September 30, 1859" (originally published in the Milwaukee *Sentinel* and Chicago *Press and Tribune,* October 1, 1859). For differing views on Lincoln's understanding of free labor and political economy, see Steven B. Smith, "Lincoln's Kantian Republic," in Buccola, *Abraham Lincoln and Liberal Democracy,* 216–238; Oliver Fraysee, *Lincoln, Land, and Labor, 1809–1860* (Urbana and Chicago: University of Illinois Press, 1994); Gabor Boritt, *Lincoln and the Economics of the American Dream* (Urbana: University of Illinois Press, 1994).

46. Lincoln, *Address Before the Wisconsin State Agricultural Society;* Foner, *Free Soil, Free Labor,* 32. Foner cites David Montgomery's estimate that 60 percent of the American labor force was employed by 1860; see Montgomery, *Beyond Equality,* 26–30. As these scholars have pointed out, this figure would have much been higher when considering only the North, and might also be corrected to include women and child workers, who had no legal right to their wages. On the agricultural revolution in the antebellum North, see Ariel Ron, *Grassroots Leviathan.*

47. Lincoln, *Address Before the Wisconsin State Agricultural Society.* On the ideological roots of this version of "free labor" in evangelical and other traditions that emphasized morality and individualism, see Glickstein in Perry and Fellman, *Antislavery Reconsidered,* 195–218.

48. On Lincoln as the "Railsplitter," see Wilentz, *The Rise of American Democracy,* 943–944, n42; Mark Plummer, "Lincoln and the Rail-Splitter Election," *Lincoln Herald* 101 (1999), 111–116. The image seems to have crystallized shortly before the 1860 Chicago convention, when Lincoln's friend John Hanks appeared with two rail planks he claimed he had made with Lincoln in 1830.

49. *Southern Slavery Reduces Northern Wages: An Address, by George M. Weston of Maine, delivered in Washington, D.C., March 25, 1856* (Washington, DC: 1856), 2–5; *Speeches of Hon. William D. Kelley. Replies of the Hon. William D. Kelley to George Northrup, Esq., in the Joint Debate in the Fourth Congressional District* (Philadelphia, 1864); "Free Labor" [from *Burritt's Bond of* Brotherhood], Philadelphia *Citizen of the World*, January 1, 1855; Seward quoted in Mandel, *Labor, Free and Slave*, 162; Evarts and Washburn quoted in Foner, *Free Soil, Free Labor*, 12, 22; Sumner quoted in Magdol, *The Antislavery Rank and File*, 118; Burritt and "We Won't Work for 10 Cents" quoted in Foner, *History of the Labor Movement*, Vol. 1, 275, 286.

50. "Speech at New Haven, Connecticut," March 6, 1860, in Roy Basler, ed., *Collected Works of Abraham Lincoln*, Vol. IV (New Brunswick, NJ: Rutgers University Press, 1953), 24–25. Although Lincoln's later reception of a strike committee from a group of machinists at the Brooklyn Navy Yard was unprecedented, he declined to give his official approval or offer to use his executive authority in support of the latter. Lincoln granted the Navy Yard committee a personal hearing in which expressed his "sympathies" with the strikers, but regretted that "he could do nothing as President," expressing his wish that "the best blood would win." *New York Daily Times*, December 5, 1863.

51. "Speech at New Haven," in Basler, ed. *Collected Works*, IV, 25; Edwin Earle Sparks, ed., *The Lincoln-Douglas Debates of 1858*, Vol. III (Springfield, IL: The Illinois State Historical Library, 1908), 375.

52. "Speech at Hartford, Connecticut," March 5, 1860, in Basler, ed., *Collected Works*, IV, 4–5; "First Debate: Ottawa, Illinois, August 21, 1858," in Basler, ed., *Collected Works*, III, 1–37. Lincoln repeated the phrase almost word for word during the Sixth Debate at Quincy, Illinois. Notably, he also implied that the right to the fruits of labor applied equally to women, referring to the bread that "her" hand earns in the earlier version of the speech. See Abraham Lincoln, "Speech at Springfield, Illinois, June 26, 1857," in Basler, ed., *Collected Works*, II, 398–410.

53. Frederick Douglass, *Narrative of the Life of Frederick Douglass, an American Slave, Written by Himself* (Boston: Anti-Slavery Office, 1845), 98, 112–116; "Garnet's Plea for the Bondsman," *Christian News*, October 17, 1850; Peter Wheeler and Charles Edwards Lester, *Chains and Freedom, or, the Life and Adventures of Peter Wheeler, a Colored Man Yet Living. A Slave in Chains, a Sailor on the Deep, and a Sinner at the Cross* (New York: E. S. Arnold & Co., 1839), 159.

54. Foner, *History of the Labor Movement*, 289–293; "Speech of Hon. Carl Schurz of Wisconsin," *Chicago Press and Tribune*, September 30, 1858, 2; Wilentz, *Rise of American Democracy*, 762.

55. "Speech at New Haven, Connecticut," March 6, 1860, in Roy Basler, ed. *Collected Works of Abraham Lincoln*, Vol. IV, 24–25.

56. *New-York Tribune*, May 29, 1856.

57. *New York Herald*, November 24, 1860. The president of the NIC that year was Joseph Evans Snodgrass, a longtime participant and opponent of slavery.

58. Lause, *Young America*, 121; "The Homestead and the Union," quoted in Zahler, *Eastern Workingmen*, 188, nn15, 16; Commerford to Johnson, December 17, 1859, quoted in Lause, *Young America*, 121; Lause, *Free Labor*, 21.

59. Lause, *Free Labor*, 22–26; Ovid Miner to William H. Seward, June 16, 1856, Seward Papers, quoted in Gienapp, *Origins of the Republican Party*, 437. After the 1856 election, an Ohio newspaper summed up the results as "The Country for Freedom—the Cities for Slavery," *Ohio State Journal*, November 7, 1856; quoted in Foner, *Free Soil*, 35, n59. As Lause points out, gatherings in the border South cities tended to express their approval of various "compromise" measures, including the Crittenden Compromise, which would have given slavery permanent sanction in the states where it already existed. But the letter of the Cincinnati German Workmen to Lincoln, cited below, casts doubt on whether such gatherings truly represented that city's workers.

60. "Speech of Hon. Carl Schurz of Wisconsin," *Chicago Press and Tribune*, September 30, 1858, 2; Wilentz, *The Rise of American Democracy*, 762; Tables 13.37, 13.38, and 13.39 in Gienapp, *Origins of the Republican Party*; Gienapp, "Who Voted for Lincoln?" in John L. Thomas, ed. *Abraham Lincoln and the American Political Tradition* (Amherst: University of Massachusetts Press, 1986), 50–96; "Cincinnati Ohio German Workmen to Abraham Lincoln, February 1, 1861," in Abraham Lincoln Papers, Series 1: General Correspondence, 1833–1916, Library of Congress. On German workers and the coming of the Civil War, see Levine, *The Spirit of 1848*, and Honeck, *We Are the Revolutionists*. See also Dale Baum and Dale T. Knoble, "Anatomy of a Political Realignment: New York Presidential Politics, 1848–1860," in *New York History* 65, no. 1 (January 1984), 60–81; Michael J. Dubin, *United States Presidential Elections, 1788–1860: The Official Results by County and State* (McFarland, NC: Jefferson and Co., 2002), 135–188.

61. *Greasy Mechanics, Attention!*, Collection of the Center for Brooklyn History, Object ID M1975.815.

Epilogue

1. Foner, *History of the Labor Movement, Vol. 1*, 298–310; Cincinnati German Workmen to Abraham Lincoln (February 1861), Library of Congress; Lause, *Free Labor*, 42–51; B. A. Gould, *Investigation in the Military and Anthropological Statistics of American Soldiers* (1869), quoted in Foner, *History of the Labor Movement*, 307.

2. Foner, *History of the Labor Movement*, 306–310; Iver Bernstein, *The New York City Draft Riots: Their Significance for American Society and Politics in the Age of the Civil War* (New York and Oxford: Oxford University Press, 1990), 99–100; Lause, *Free Labor*, 55; *New-York Herald*, November 14, 1864; Diary of Michael Shiner, https://www

.history.navy.mil/research/library/online-reading-room/title-list-alphabetically/d/diary-of-michael-shiner/1860-1865.html. James Fincher, the Machinists' and Blacksmiths' Union leader who launched the influential *Fincher's Trade Review*, complained that the organizers of the Philadelphia convention forced the compromise resolutions through without giving sufficient time to those opposed, and he severed ties with the meeting as a result. Foner, *History of the Labor Movement*, 300 and n13. Many other "workingmen's" meetings during the war were organized by Democratic politicians, and therefore must be treated with skepticism.

3. W. E. B. Du Bois first conceived of the concept of a general strike among the enslaved in *Black Reconstruction* (1935). Recently, David Roediger has argued in favor of the general strike theory in *Seizing Freedom: Slave Emancipation and Liberty for All* (London: Verso, 2014). For an account that emphasizes top-down policies but acknowledges enslaved peoples' role in their own emancipation, see Oakes, *Freedom National*.

4. Lause, *Free Labor*, 20–21, 135, 155.

5. The cost of manufactured goods rose to 125 percent above 1860 prices in 1864, while the cost of coal doubled from $5.50 a ton in 1861 to $11 by 1864. While wages may have risen as much as 43 percent between 1860 and 1865, prices rose by as much as 116 percent. Foner, *History of the Labor Movement*, 326; Foner, *Organized Labor and the Black Worker*, 15; Bernstein, *The New York City Draft Riots*, 100.

6. Foner, *History of the Labor Movement*, 328–329; Henry B. Hibbin, *Navy-Yard, Washington. History from Organization, 1799 to Present Date* (Washington: Government Printing Office, 1890), 126–127; Lincoln, "Speech at New Haven, Connecticut," March 6, 1860, in Basler, *Collected Works of Abraham Lincoln*, Vol. 4, 24–25; *New York Daily Times*, December 5, 1863; Lause, *Free Labor*, 154. See also Lincoln address to the workingmen of Manchester, England, January 19, 1863.

7. "A Democratic Workingman," [William O. Bourne] *To the Laboring Men of New York* (New York, July 18, 1863); *Don't Unchain the Tiger!* (New York, Sinclair Tousey, July 24, 1863); *Dan'l O'Connell on Democracy!* (New York, Sinclair Tousey, October 13, 1863); *An Abolition Traitor* (New York, August 29, 1863), in William Oland Bourne Papers, Library of Congress; Foner, *Organized Labor and the Black Worker*, 14–15.

8. On the occupational and ethnic makeup of the draft rioters, see Bernstein, *The New York City Draft Riots*, 23–24, 41–42, 78–124, *passim*.

9. Abraham Lincoln, "Reply to New York Workingmen" [Copy in a Secretarial Hand], March 21, 1864, in Basler, *Collected Works*, Vol. 5, 51–53; see also Lincoln's reply in full in *the Iron Platform, No. XL* (March 1864). Lincoln had earlier repeated his statement about the superiority of labor to capital in his address to Congress in December, 1861.

10. The *New York World*, quoted in *Iron Platform*, no. 40 (March 1864); Bernstein, *New York City Draft Riots*, 101–102, 111. See also the *Iron Platform*'s reply, "The President—the Workingmen—and 'the Nigger' of the 'World'" in the same issue.

11. Bernstein, *New York City Draft Riots*, 98–99. Although Bernstein claims that National Reformers John Commerford, William West, and Ira B. Davis were "intrigued" by Wood's public works projects, he offers no evidence that they supported Wood or

other Peace Democrats. By Bernstein's own account, formerly Democratic land and labor reformers like Davis and William V. Barr attempted to steer an independent course from both major parties.

12. Robbins, *Our Landed Heritage*; Howard Ottoson, *Land Use Policy and Problems in the United States* (Lincoln: University of Nebraska Press, 1963); Harold Hyman, *American Singularity: The 1787 Northwest Ordinance, the 1862 Homestead and Morrill Acts, and the 1944 G.I. Bill* (Athens: University of Georgia Press, 2008); National Archives, "The Homestead Act of 1862," https://www.archives.gov/education/lessons /homestead-act, accessed November 5, 2016.

13. National Archives, "The Homestead Act of 1862," https://www.archives.gov /education/lessons/homestead-act, accessed November 5, 2016.

14. Samuel Gridley Howe, *The Refugees from Slavery in Canada West. Report to the Freedmen's Inquiry Commission* (Boston: Wright and Potter, 1864); Robert Dale Owen, *The Wrong of Slavery, the Right of Emancipation, and the Future of the African Race in the United States* (Philadelphia: J. B. Lippincott, 1864).

15. Foner, *Reconstruction*, 68–71, 105, 245–246.

16. Ibid., 404; Petty, *Standing Their Ground*.

17. Frederick Douglass Papers, Library of Congress (Speech, Article, and Book File; Micellany, Folder 7); Janet Sharp Hermann, "Reconstruction in Microcosm: Three Men and a Gin," *Journal of Negro History* 65, no. 4 (Autumn 1980), 312–335; Hermann, *The Pursuit of a Dream* (Oxford: University Press of Mississippi, 1999); Foner, *Reconstruction*, 404. Foner cites the 1876 *Report of the Commissioner of Agriculture*, 137, for this statistic.

18. Foner, *History of the Labor Movement*, 366–367. On Steward, see David Roediger, "Ira Steward and the Anti-Slavery Origins of the Eight Hour Movement," *Labor History* 27, no. 3 (1986), 410–426; and Montgomery, *Beyond Equality*, 249–260.

19. Quoted in Montgomery, *Beyond Equality*, ix; see also Montgomery, *Worker's Control in America: Studies in the History of Work, Technology, and Labor Struggles* (Cambridge: Cambridge University Press, 1979); Gourevitch, *From Slavery to the Cooperative Commonwealth*; Leon Fink, *Workingmen's Democracy: The Knights of Labor and American Politics* (Urbana: University of Illinois Press, 1985).

20. Lause, *Young America*, 91; Ingalls, *Reminiscences*, 27–28. For the National Reformers' hostility to corporations and railroad companies in particular, see the *Working Man's Advocate*, April 13, 1844, and March 1, 1845; *Young America*, December 6, June 28, 1845; Devyr, *The Odd Book*, 4, 33, 142, 157, *passim*.

21. Richard White, *Railroaded: The Transcontinentals and the Making of Modern America* (New York: W. W. Norton, 2011); Steven Hahn, *A Nation Without Borders: The United States and Its World in an Age of Civil Wars, 1830–1910* (New York: Penguin Books, 2016), 242–243, 377–379, *passim*. In contrast to the land reformers, the "Young Americans" of the Douglas and Breckenridge wings of the Democratic Party had supported Pacific railroad construction in the 1850s and '60s. See Etal, *The Young America*, 70.

22. Foner, *Reconstruction*, 461; Montgomery, *Beyond Equality*, 4–13; Fink, *Knights of Labor*; Matthew Hild, *Greenbackers, Knights of Labor, and Populists: Farmer-Labor*

Insurgency in the Late-Nineteenth Century South (Athens: University of Georgia Press, 2007); Jackson T. Lears, *Rebirth of a Nation: The Making of Modern America, 1877–1920* (New York: Harper Collins, 2009), 133–166; Greenback-Labor platform quoted in Lause, *Young America*, 136.

23. Henry George, *Progress and Poverty: An Inquiry into the Cause of Industrial Depressions, and of Increase of Want with Increase of Wealth: The Remedy* (New York: D. Appleton, 1886).

24. Millington W. Bergeson-Lockwood, "The People Coming to Power! Wendell Phillips, Benjamin F. Butler, and the Politics of Labor Reform," in A. J. Aiséirithe and Donald Yacovone, eds., *Wendell Phillips: Social Justice and the Power of the Past* (Baton Rouge: Louisiana State University Press, 2016), 181–207.

25. William Lloyd Garrison, Jr., introduction, *Gerrit Smith on Land Monopoly [Sketch of Smith], with Introduction by Wm. Lloyd Garrison, the Younger* (Chicago: Public Publishing, 1898); Lause, *Young America*, 136. For an early example of Wendell Phillips' postwar labor activism, see *Remarks of Wendell Phillips, at the Mass Meeting of Workingmen in Faneuil Hall, Nov. 2, 1865* (Boston: Voice Publishing, 1865).

26. "Reconstruction: A Letter from William Heighton to George L. Stearns," in *The Equality of All Men before the Law, Claimed and Defended; in Speeches by Hon. William D. Kelley, Wendell Phillips, and Frederick Douglass, and Letters from Elizur Wright and Wm. Heighton* (Boston: Geo. C. Rand & Avery, 1865), 42–43.

27. Ibid.

INDEX

Figures are indicated by page numbers followed by *fig.*

ACKNOWLEDGMENTS

This book would not have been possible to write without the dedication of friends, family, and colleagues over a period of more years than I care to remember. The late David Jaffee was an early mentor who encouraged my interest in history as a returning college student and introduced me to the world of nineteenth century visual and material culture. At CUNY's American Social History Project, I found a welcoming and enouraging group of scholars who helped to confirm my decision to go to graduate school, along with a lasting mentor in the form of Josh Brown, whose kindness and humor often leavened his penetrating insights into my graduate school work. Perhaps no one has done more to shape my thinking than James Oakes, who left a deep impression on this book and without whose encouragement I would not be writing these words. David Waldstreicher of the CUNY Graduate Center and Manisha Sinha of the University of Connecticut have offered support and criticism at important times, while Matt Karp and Peter Wirzbicki of Princeton University have been generous in sharing their research and insights, among other acts of kindness.

While conducting research as a postdoctoral fellow at the American Antiquarian Society, I found abundant resources that added tremendously to this manuscript, as well as valuable feedback and friendship from Nan Wolverton, Craig Friend, David Mills, and others. Kanisorn Wongsrichanalai graciously handled the interruption caused by the COVID-19 pandemic during my tenure as an MHS-NEH fellow at the Massachusetts Historical Society; I'm indebted to him and the rest of the MHS staff for their work in enabling me to complete my research remotely. My fellow graduate students in the CUNY Early American Research Seminar (EARS) offered consistent and helpful feedback throughout the early stages of this project; I'd like to thank them, especially Madeline LaFuse, whose discovery of the 1853 antislavery lithograph that appears in the introduction provided me with the inspiration for the title of this book. And Bob Lockhart, my editor at Penn Press, has offered his expertise, insights, and endless patience throughout a process that took far longer than I anticipated and under circumstances that neither he nor I could have foreseen.

Last, I would like to thank my parents, who have encouraged my scholarly tendencies and supported me even in my more quixotic pursuits, and my partner, Kristin Fayne-Mulroy, without whose patience, support, love, and willingness to read chapter drafts the completion of this book would have been a dreary affair.

Printed and bound by CPI Group (UK) Ltd, Croydon, CR0 4YY

16/04/2025

14658413-0002